Gotthold Ephraim Lessing, Ernest Bell

Dramatic Works

Translated from the German. Edited by Ernest Bell, with a short memoir by Helen

Zimmern

Gotthold Ephraim Lessing, Ernest Bell

Dramatic Works
Translated from the German. Edited by Ernest Bell, with a short memoir by Helen Zimmern

ISBN/EAN: 9783337304348

Printed in Europe, USA, Canada, Australia, Japan

Cover: Foto ©Thomas Meinert / pixelio.de

More available books at **www.hansebooks.com**

THE DRAMATIC WORKS

OF

G. E. LESSING.

Translated from the German.

EDITED BY

ERNEST BELL, M.A.,

TRINITY COLLEGE, CAMBRIDGE.

COMEDIES.

LONDON:

GEORGE BELL AND SONS, YORK STREET,

COVENT GARDEN.

1888.

PREFACE.

Of the plays contained in this volume, the first five are here given to the English public for the first time; the other three have been translated before—the last of them several times. The translation here given of these three is based on that of the late Rev. J. J. Holroyd, the use of which has been kindly permitted by his representatives. This version, however, though it rendered the spirit of the original very successfully, did not claim to be literally accurate, and with a view to obtaining greater literalness, the pieces have been carefully compared with the original, and considerable alterations have been introduced. In the revision of 'Minna von Barnhelm' the editor has been aided by Professor Buchheim's excellent annotated edition, and would like here to express his thanks for several happy translations which he has adopted.

CONTENTS.

DAMON, OR TRUE FRIENDSHIP.

(A COMEDY IN ONE ACT.)

This play was written while Lessing was at school in Meissen, between the years 1741 and 1746.

DRAMATIS PERSONÆ.

———•———

THE WIDOW.

LEANDER,
DAMON, } *Suitors.*

ORONTE, *cousin to* DAMON.

LISETTE, *maid to the* WIDOW.

DAMON, OR TRUE FRIENDSHIP.

SCENE I.—THE WIDOW, LISETTE.

LIS. Well, it is true, our house has altered a great deal in a short time. Only a week ago it was a lively rendezvous for innumerable young gentlemen and love-sick fools. Every day some of them have dropped off. One day these stayed away, the next day those, and others the day after. God be thanked! two are still left. If they too should find their way off, our house will be deserted. Madame. . . . . Madame!

WID. Well, what is the matter?

LIS. Then I too should certainly remain no longer with you, however well off I may be. Society is the half of life.

WID. You would have been better fitted for an inn than for my service, then?

LIS. True. In an inn it is lively at any rate. If there was not so much work there, who knows what I might not have done! If one is unfortunate enough to be a servant at all, I think it is most sensible to have a place where one can have the greatest pleasure with one's work. But joking apart! What are Herr Damon and Herr Leander to you at present?

WID. What are they?

LIS. This question seems strange to you? I know well enough what they were to you before—they were your suitors!

WID. And so they are still.

B 2

LIS. So they are still? Really? Damon is then Leander's rival, and Leander Damon's. And yet Leander and Damon are the best of friends? That is a new fashion. Against that I protest with might and main. What? Rivals who do not quarrel with each other, and slander, abuse, deceive, challenge and fight each other, nice creatures they would be! No! The old way is right. Between rivals there must be enmity, or they are no rivals.

WID. It is true; I myself have been rather astonished at their behaviour. No one behaved more affectionately towards me than they did before either of them knew that they had one and the same aim. No one was more tender, no one endeavoured more to gain my favour than they. No sooner did they perceive that one was the rival of the other, than both relaxed in their zeal to please me. Each spoke in favour of the other, Damon of Leander, and Leander of Damon. Both were silent about their own affairs.

LIS. And in spite of this, you still consider both of them your suitors?

WID. Yes, I am thoroughly convinced that both love me. Both love me sincerely. Damon only appears to me too vacillating, and Leander a little too impetuous.

LIS. I should almost like to ask you something.

WID. Very well; let me hear it.

LIS. But will you answer me candidly?

WID. Shall I answer you candidly? I do not see what should make me give you a false answer. If your question does not please me I should prefer not to answer you at all.

LIS. You believe that you are loved by both, and perhaps rightly. But which of them, then, do you love?

WID. Which?

LIS. Yes.

WID. Which? The question is curious. I love them both.

LIS. Well, that is good. Will you marry them both too?

WID. You confuse matters. We were speaking at present of loving, not of marrying. All suitors that I have had have been either vain, lovesick poltroons, or low-

minded egoistic creatures. What have I not had to endure
from both sorts! Only Damon and Leander differed from
them from the very beginning. I perceived this difference
with the greatest pleasure. And I also think that I have
given them to understand plainly enough how well I
knew how to make a distinction with them. I have given
their discharge to all who were not wise enough to take it
themselves. I have only kept these two here, and I still
see them with pleasure in my house.

Lis. But what is to come of it?

Wid. I will wait and see. If I cannot become the
best-beloved of both, I can become the friend of both, I
suppose. Yes, truly, friendship appears to be now much
more charming than love. I must ascribe this to the
example of my tender lovers.

Lis. What? Friendship? Friendship more charming
than love? Dry friendship! Don't talk so philosophically,
pray. I assure you I believe only as much of it as I like.
Your heart thinks quite differently. And it would not do
it much honour either if it did agree with the lips. Just
let me try whether I understand its mute language. I
hear it; yes, yes, it speaks: "What? Are these sincere
lovers? What new kind of love is this, which the sight
of a friend can stifle. Neither of them will run the risk
of losing his friend for my sake.—Oh, the undeserving
creatures! I will hate them, yes, I will. . . . . but shall
I then be able to do so? shall I"——

Wid. Silence, silence, Lisette! You understand its
mute language very badly!

Lis. Oh, pardon me! This interruption proves to me
that I understand it very well. Well, well, how can it be
otherwise? I should be very vexed if friendship played
me such a trick. Just consider, what else but friendship
is to blame, that you are now without a suitor at all,
when you might have two of them. Ah, it would be a
shame if love were not stronger than friendship.

Wid. Alas!

Lis. Ha, ha! That I understand too. Just listen, if
I can't explain it cleverly. It says this, does it not?
"Lisette, do not force me further, to confess to you what
you know already. Would to Heaven that love were

stronger than friendship only in one of them! If you can
do anything towards making my lovers more sensitive and
less conscientious "——

WID. What wanderings are these?

LIS. Oh, I beg your pardon.—They are your own
wanderings.

WID. Suppose now I confessed to you, that I would
prefer to see them both reveal their love to me more
openly,—both strive tenderly to conquer my heart,—the
one try to take the precedence of the other,—to see even
the favours which I should bestow upon one in greater
degree estrange them a little,—to be able even to have
the pleasure of reuniting them, in order to separate them
anew,—suppose, I say, I confessed this to you, what then?

LIS. Well, certainly it would be rather more than you
were willing to confess a little while ago.

WID. But really I do not know at all what reason I
have to give account of my heart to you.

LIS. I agree with you, you have none, you do it from
mere kindness. But your kindness shall not have been in
vain, I assure you. I will do my utmost to make all
happen as you wish. But just tell me first for which
one do you think you would like best to declare yourself,
for Damon or Leander? You hesitate?—Listen, a good
idea occurs to me. You know that a year ago each em-
barked almost the whole of his fortune on a particular
ship which traffics with the East Indies. They are in
daily expectation of the return of their ships. How would
it be, if we too waited, and then declared ourselves for the
one who has been most fortunate in this transaction?

WID. I am willing. Only——

LIS. Here comes Herr Damon. Just leave me alone
with him, I will sift him.

SCENE II.—LISETTE, DAMON.

LIS. Your servant, Herr Damon! You seem to be
looking for somebody. Who is it?

DA. Leander was to meet me here. Have not you seen
him?

LIS. No! . . . . But must you go away again immediately, on this account? Stay a moment. Does the

time already seem long to you, because he cannot come immediately and prattle to you his sweet dreams of friendship? If you have only come to hear pleasing fibs, and enrapturing thoughts from your friend, stay, stay here, I will give you them as well as he. Truly, since you and Herr Leander have met here the very walls resound with the praise of friendship; I must surely have retained a little of it.

DA. These railleries are at my friend's expense. They must necessarily be offensive to me. Be silent, if you please.

LIS. Eh! The deuce might be silent under such circumstances. Just consider for yourself! You are in the house of a young, amiable widow. You love her, you seek a return of your love. But, dear me, in what a peculiar way! A friend intimidates you in your courtship. You will not offend him. Your love is much too weak to endure his groundless reproaches. You prefer to neglect your lover rather than your friend. Very well, that might pass, if only the other one was not just as whimsical a fellow.

DA. Our conduct cannot in any way appear strange to your mistress. She is aware of the affection of both of us. We both declared ourselves to her, before we knew we had declared the same thing. We endeavour to be sincere friends. Would it not therefore be unjust, if with impatient solicitation I wished to rob Leander or Leander to rob me of a heart, which may perhaps in time surrender itself to one of us from affection?

LIS. From affection? As if a woman had not equal affection for every well-favoured man. For instance, what would I care whether I got you or Herr Leander? Do not take it amiss, that for once I indulge my pride in such sweet dreams. You and Herr Leander are of healthy constitution, robust and cheerful. One cannot go wrong in the choice between two equally good things. Take the first that comes.

DA. You judge your mistress by yourself, and certainly you do not do her much honour by it. I know her too well. She has nobler ideas of love.

LIS. Ah, do not take it ill of me. Love is love. A

queen does not love better than a beggar, or a philosopher more nobly than a stupid peasant. And I and my mistress certainly would not differ a hair's breadth in the important part of love.

DA. Good morning. I have neither inclination nor time at present to refute your groundless talk. Should Herr Leander come, beg him, please, to wait a moment. I have first a little business to transact. I shall be back directly.

LIS. Bother it! Just wait another moment! You call my talk groundless? Well then, just listen, and I'll tell you something. Perhaps it will seem a little better grounded to you then.

DA. Well, I shall have to hear something extraordinary, then.

LIS. Do you know what my mistress has decided to do? She is going to wait until the two ships have come back in which you have placed your fortunes. And she will marry the one straight off who has been most successful in the business. Do you believe now, that it will be all the same to my mistress, whether she gets you or Herr Leander. Eh?

DA. What? Your mistress has decided to do that? Go and tell your tale to some one else.

LIS. Well, why does that seem so improbable to you? Is it so wicked that one rather marries a rich man than a poor one? You foolish men would sooner count your buttons, I suppose, when you cannot make up your mind. And yet I should think she has acted ten times more wisely in leaving it to fate to turn the scale and settle her feelings for her.

DA. Heavens! How unhappy I am, if you speak the truth. Could I ever have imagined, that riches had such charms for her? Do they alone make us precious? Does she not find anything in Leander or myself which could counterbalance this dazzling trifle? I could almost repent of loving a person, who so basely——

LIS. Come, come! Gently, gently! Not so much abuse. Did you expect something better? The money itself is not exactly what she desires in you. The feelings of my mistress towards you and Herr Leander

are equally balanced at present, and the money is only to
be a little addition which will give the advantage to one
scale or the other. O! grasping we are not! Do not say
that of us, mind! Although, after all, it would be no
shame for us if we were so. Why, you show her plainly
enough, by not having spoken to her again for a long time
of your love, that it would be all the same to you if she
declared herself for you or for your friend,—and Leander
has done the same. So how could she act more judiciously?

DA. Alas, that I am so enamoured of her, and that
I am so conscientious in friendship!

LIS. Would you have been better pleased if my mistress
had let you cast lots for her—the one with the most or
the fewest points to have had her for his wife? This is
a very praiseworthy custom among soldiers, when of
two culprits who are to be hanged his life is to be
granted to one, and each of them deserves it as little
as the other. Yes, yes, she ought to have followed this
fashion here too, I suppose. Oughtn't she?

DA. Your railleries are very much out of place. My
heart is. . . . . but I will go. Lisette, Lisette, how
uneasy you have made me! Good Heavens!

SCENE III.—LISETTE.

Well, he has a flea in his ear now. But what does it
profit me? I can understand him as little now as before.
If only I could have got him at least so far as to come
out with his love-declarations again. But really words
are thrown away on him;—he was on needles and pins.
Hush, here comes Leander. Let me see what can be done
with him!

SCENE IV.— LISETTE, LEANDER.

LIS. A little sooner and you would have met him.

LEA. Really? Has Damon been here already?

LIS. Yes, and he will be back again immediately. You
are to wait a little. But how cross you look to-day for
once, Herr Leander! That face does not become a suitor
at all! For shame, be lively now and nice and merry!

LEA. He who has as much cause for vexation as I——

LIS. Bah! Don't tell me that. You have a great deal on your heart to trouble you, I dare say. I can almost guess, too, what it is. Ah! love torments you! Are you tired at last of ranking friendship above it? That would only be what is right. Courage! Never mind a friend. Make my mistress another offer. I give you my word you will get her. But if you go on dallying any longer, I will not answer for anything. My mistress cannot choose. She has resigned all to blind chance,—unless one of you comes soon to take her, she means to give her heart, hand and fortune to the one who is most fortunate in the business with the East Indies.—What is the matter with you? . . . . What is the matter?

LEA. Lisette, for Heaven's sake! To the one who is most successful? Now my misery is complete.

LIS. Complete! What does that mean? Explain yourself.

LEA. Well, I will confide in you. Know then, that only last night I received news that my ship was wrecked in a storm. Cruel Fate! Was it then not enough to rob me of my fortune, must you also tear away from me the object of my so tender love?

LIS. The other abused my mistress and he abuses Fate. And both, after all, are innocent. Herr Leander, your misfortune touches me. I can well believe that it must cause one enough vexation to lose one's fortune. I have not yet gone through this painful experience, for, Heaven be thanked, I have not got a fortune. But if the vexation at losing riches is as great as the desire of gaining them, then it must be insupportable. I confess it. But to come to the other point! The object of your tender love . . . . . I presume you mean my mistress. Don't you? Listen now. . . . . this loss you have brought on yourself. But if you will obey me, Herr Leander, she may not be quite lost yet, however it may seem to be.

LEA. Speak openly, pray? I will obey you in everything which can be of use to me.

LIS. But I doubt if you will do it.

LEA. Do not doubt, I beg you.

Lis. I know your obstinacy only too well. You are too much taken up with your lofty notions of friendship. Damon, your dearest friend in the world, the most precious gift of Heaven, without which all things, all honour, all pleasure seem but despicable to you,—but vain and tasteless; Damon, your second self, whose happiness is your happiness, whose misfortune is your misfortune; Damon, the noble Damon, the——

Lea. Yes, quite so, Lisette! You will never be able to praise him sufficiently. He is the only one who will help me to bear my misfortune. I have always had the best opinion of him and the tenderest feelings towards him. I doubt not, he will now show how worthy he is of my friendship. Had he lost his fortune, mine would have been his. I should refuse for his sake the hand of the most lovable being. Damon, yes Damon . . . . . had he my heart. . . . . But I know, the true tenderness of friendship he never has been quite able to feel properly.

Lis. Yes, Herr Leander, if you wish to be happy you must forget this Damon for a time. Do not start at this proposition!

Lea. How do you mean that?

Lis. Well, I see that you demand my explanation with a tolerably composed face. Do not be afraid. I recommend no treason against your friend. Neither will he nor you yourself have cause to reproach you for anything. To be brief, go to my mistress. Make her a straightforward offer. Assure her that Damon does not love her any more. If necessary add a few fibs, which will make him more hateful to her. You will see, all will go well.

Lea. But suppose now, she persists in waiting to see who will be the most successful in this affair, nothing will help me then.

Lis. (aside) Hm! Is that the steadfast friend? Can he be talked over so easily?—(aloud) She will hardly insist upon that, Herr Leander. But suppose, even, she did, it won't do any harm to us. And I'll tell you something. I know that you and Herr Damon have several times been inclined to exchange your capitals. They are of equal value. I should think you might try to

persuade Herr Damon to do it still. He does not know
yet, I suppose, that your ship is said to have foundered.

LEA. No!

LIS. Well, that will do very well. Try to get his
capital and resign yours to him with all the profits.
You can easily do that, and you will easily be able to
hit upon a plausible pretext. Suppose you said to him:
" Dearest Damon, friendship has united us sufficiently
closely. How would it be, however, if we employed our
worldly possessions also to unite ourselves even more
firmly? Let us therefore make an exchange of the said
capitals, which we have put in the East Indian affair.
Should yours have yielded more interest than mine, I
should have to thank you for a part of my fortune. If
mine should have increased more, I shall have the pleasure
of seeing in your hands that which good luck had in
reality destined for me. And shall we not by this means
be all the more bound to assist one another with our fortunes in any case of necessity which may occur?"

LEA. Your advice is good. And also the pretext seems
plausible enough. But I fear that my friend might
entertain a suspicion of me. On this account I should
not like to make this proposal myself. Could you not
perhaps suggest this idea to your mistress? If she appeared to like it. . . . . then——

LIS. I understand you, I understand you. Rely upon
me, and make haste to go to my mistress.

LEA. Directly I have spoken with my friend. God is
my witness that my intentions throughout are honest. I
know for certain that my friend could not be sufficiently
magnanimous to fulfil the duties towards me which in
case of the loss of my fortune our friendship would
impose upon him. I will free him, therefore, from the
shame of being called an unfaithful friend by posterity.
But on my side I will show him that my words agree
entirely with my deeds. He shall have the half of my
fortune——

LIS. Considering that the whole belongs to him by
right—That is a sincere friend !

LEA. I will do everything to help him on again. Perhaps another time he may be successful. Perhaps——

Lis. Hush! hush! Herr Damon is coming back. I
will go. He might think we had had who knows what
to talk about together. I will go to my mistress. Follow
me soon.—(*Aside*) Well, that, I am sure, I should not
have expected.

Scene V.—Leander, Damon.

Lea. So I must not say anything to him about my
misfortune, which, however, is just what I asked him to
come here for. What then shall I have to say to him?
. . . . . Never mind, something will turn up.

Da. O my dearest Leander, forgive me that I have
kept you waiting.

Lea. I forgive you? How have you offended me? Do
lay aside once for all, dearest friend, this misconception
so detrimental to me, that you are able to offend me.
One friend is never angry with another. The common
herd, to whom the sweet union of souls is unknown and to
their irreparable loss will eternally remain unknown,—the
common herd, the disgrace of the human race, may quarrel
among themselves. Friendship arms a noble soul with an
insurmountable moderation. What its friend does, what
comes from its friend, is right and pleasing to it. Offences
only become offences through the evil designs of him who
offends and the sensitiveness of him who is offended.
Where, therefore, no one has evil designs and no one is
sensitive there exist no offences. And, does one friend then
foster evil designs against another? Or will one friend
then become sensitive about another? No. Therefore,
dearest Damon, even if through you the greatest disgrace
should befall me; if through you I should lose honour and
repute; if through you I should lose property and money;
if through you I should become sick, lame, blind and deaf;
if you should deprive me of father and mother; if you
even took my life; do you believe, dearest Damon, that
you would have offended me? No, however much you
might be wrong, you would none the less be right to me.
Even should the whole world condemn you, I should exculpate you, I should acquit you.

Da. I should like, Leander, to be able to answer you

with equal ardour. I will endeavour never to put your
friendship to so severe a test.

LEA. Eh, dearest friend, why so cold? Do you doubt
the sincerity of my words? Do you doubt that my
friendship would stand this test? Would to Heaven,—yes,
would to Heaven, that you would offend me, the sooner
the better, in a manner which to another would be
unpardonable. How pleased, how delighted would I be,
to practise on you the sweet revenge of magnanimous
forgiveness.

DA. And I will wish, on the contrary, that I may
never have need of this magnanimous forgiveness.

LEA. Yes, Damon, and I shall also expect the same
from you in a similar case. O, I know you too well, your
heart is noble and generous. It does not permit me to
doubt.

DA. You credit me with too much, most valued
Leander! I confess to you, full of shame, that I find
myself too weak for that. The ideas seem true and noble
to me, but their accomplishment impossible. I tremble
already in anticipation at the thought that my friendship
may perhaps some day have to bear such a severe test.
Your virtue, however, is my security. And is a friend
really constrained to use such an all too magnanimous
moderation? I know it is the duty of a friend to forgive
another, but it is also the duty of the other to give him as
little occasion for it as possible.

LEA. My friend! In forgiving, we must resemble
Heaven. Our trespasses, however great and frequent
they are, do not weary it in this its worthy employment.
Him whom one has once chosen for one's friend, one must
retain! Neither his faults nor his offences must be able
to banish him from our favour. He disgraces himself
who lets it come to this. Or is it then no disgrace to
have to confess with shame that one has been grossly
mistaken in one's choice?

DA. But, dearest Leander, tell me why you desired to
speak to me? What is the important news which you
have to disclose to me?

LEA. Do my words become tedious to you? I cannot
believe it. You know how one likes to speak of things

which are pleasant to one. And I know one also likes
equally well to hear of them. But you do not seem to be
quite in the mood for either to-day. What troubles you?
Has any misfortune befallen you? Reveal it to me!
Give me the pleasure of sharing your grief with you.
You shall then hear what I have to tell you.

DA. You are not mistaken, I am perplexed and
grieved!

LEA. And at what? O, why do you hesitate to
confide your secret to me? Do you distrust my discretion? Do you doubt that I shall help you, if it is
in my power? Or do you doubt my sympathy? Whenever I can pour out my heart to you half of my grief
vanishes immediately. Only try it! Perhaps I am so
fortunate that you also may find some relief in my confidence.

DA. It concerns you and me.

LEA. And so much the more reason to speak it out!
Or must you keep it secret? O, what one has told only to
one's friend, one has told to no one. My friend and I are
one. And if I had taken the most solemn oath, never to
breathe a word to any one of this or that, I might yet
without breaking my oath relate it to my friend. What
I confide to him, I confide to myself. And I do nothing
more than repeat it once again to myself in thought.

DA. No! No! It shall not be concealed from you!
Can you imagine what madame has resolved to do?

LEA. What?

DA. Well, just guess on what she will make the choice
between us two rest.

LEA. It was just this, my Damon,—just this that I too
had to tell you.

DA. To speak candidly, I am astounded at this base
resolution. No, Leander, rather than owe her hand to
such a shameful cause I will renounce her for ever.

LEA. And do you believe, then, that I should accept
her? We have the most disinterested intentions with
respect to her. We should love her even if she possessed
nothing whatever. And she is so self-interested. Is
despicable wealth the only thing which pleases her in us?

DA. What if we tried to foil this resolution in every

possible way? May I propose something to you? What do you think if we shared the gain and loss in this affair?

LEA. (*aside*) Hist! That is grist for my mill. The exchange would then be necessary. . . . . (*aloud*) Yes, you are right! Nothing could more easily bring her back to the right course—to choose between us for love's and merit's sake. I agree to it.

DA. O! How happy you make me again by your approval. I feared all the time, I feared you might withhold it from me in this matter. And you would have had a right to do so.

LEA. How little you give me credit for! Indeed, what right could I possibly have not to be at one with you in this? Why, all things are common between friends! What is mine is yours. And I consider that I too have a little claim upon what is yours. Away with selfishness! even though by this, fate should be so unfavourable to you that you should lose all, all. Not the half of my fortune, but the whole would be as good as yours at any time.

DA. Friend, you make me quite ashamed!

LEA. What I say, I should also do. And if I had done it, I should not, after all, have done anything more than what the duty of a friend demands.

DA. But I do not understand what hidden feeling within me makes me doubt the very truth of her resolution. Could Lisette after all——

LEA. I too have it from her. Yet we shall find that out. It is of no little importance to us both. Will you excuse me? I will go myself to our beloved and inquire.

DA. But, Leander! how will that do? Will she not be hurt by this inquisitiveness?

LEA. Do not fear, I shall know how to introduce the subject . . . . . in such a way that——

DA. Very well, I rely on your skill. Come back soon, and bring me word.

LEA. (*aside*) Well, that is a good pretext for getting away from him.

Scene VI.—Damon.

. . . . . Either I am quite unadapted for friendship or Leander has very extravagant ideas about it. . . . . I should be unhappy if the former were true. . . . . Yes . . . . . friendship . . . . . is certainly that which must primarily make life agreeable to us. . . . . So much I feel . . . . . but so much as my friend says he feels, I do not feel. . . . . Suppose he offended me . . . . he offended me in such manner . . . . . as he wished me to offend him . . . . . should I . . . . . no, I will not flatter myself . . . . . I should. . . . I should be much too weak, to forgive him. . . . . Yes, I should take it in bad part if he should pardon me on such an occasion. . . . I should even blame him . . . . . Yet. . . . . I do not think him even capable of it either . . . . . let him be what he will . . . . . but . . . . . perhaps I am mistaken. . . . . I judge him by myself . . . . . does it follow then, because I am so weak that another. . . . . But certainly such a perfect friendship is not for this world. . . . . I wonder whether Leander really thinks as he speaks. . . . . . Stop. . . . . I will . . . . . yes, suppose I told him, that I had received news that my vessel was wrecked. Then I shall see whether his generosity . . . . . it would be rather a joke, if I saw him perplexed. . . . . But no . . . . . that was a mean thought. . . . . To put one's friend to a test, is to wish to lose one's friend. . . . . No . . . . . but suppose the widow held to her foolish resolution. . . . . Suppose Leander became happy through her . . . . . shall I be able to remain his friend? . . . . . I tremble . . . . . yes I feel my weakness. . . . . I should be angry with him. . . . . I should grow envious . . . . . ah, I am truly ashamed of myself.——

Scene VII.—Oronte, Damon.

Oro. Well, there you are! D'ye see? Cousin, I have had to look for you in ten different houses! D'ye see? I should have expected to find you anywhere sooner than at the young widow's.

Da. What the deuce brings you here, cousin?

c

ORO. Well? Can't you tell what I want? D'ye see? Make yourself ready to hear some news which will half kill you. D'ye see? And if you still have a little reason left, d'ye see, will drive you mad.

DA. You frighten me! What is it then?

ORO. Did I not tell you, d'ye see, that you would have bad luck with your capital? D'ye see? See there, read that. . . . . Your ship is wrecked. . . . . There, just read that, d'ye see . . . . . you will find all particulars, d'ye see?

DA. Really!

ORO. Well, didn't I tell you before, d'ye see? But you young fellows never let yourselves be told, d'ye see? You want to know everything, everything best. All right, d'ye see, all right!

DA. I should not have expected this misfortune——

ORO. Is that all one can say, d'ye see, when one loses one's fortune? O carelessness! O iniquitous careless-ness! D'ye see? Up to twelve thousand thalers, d'ye see, twelve thousand thalers! Well, cousin, say what you will do now! D'ye see? You are forsaken, forsaken by the whole world, and rightly, d'ye see? Can you deny that I told you beforehand? Can you deny it? D'ye see? How many times have I given you the golden rule? What gets into the water is as good as half lost, d'ye see?

DA. Ah! let the money go where it likes—if only——

ORO. Ah, never mind the money. Sensible talk that! D'ye see? Damon, Damon, a man who can think like that, is not worthy to be my cousin. D'ye see? Ah, never mind the money. No, Heaven be thanked, d'ye see? I never was so foolish and godforsaken in my youth. Do you think, d'ye see, that the young widow will marry you now? D'ye see? She would have to be a stupid! D'ye see?

DA. Yes, cousin, this is my fear. And this is also the only thing which makes my misfortune painful to me.

ORO. The fool! D'ye see? As if it were not painful enough without it! D'ye see? Yet, cousin, that you may see, d'ye see, how well disposed I am towards you, d'ye see,

I will advise you under the circumstances: Announce your bankruptcy.

Da. What, such a mean——

Oro. What, what, mean? D'ye see? You call it mean, d'ye see, to be a bankrupt? The deuce, d'ye see? Have I not been bankrupt five times? And have I been mean? D'ye see? Haven't I got all my money from the bankruptcy? D'ye see? My wife caused my first failure, d'ye see? She was a proud, extravagant fool! May Heaven bless her, d'ye see? But may Heaven also reward her, for no doubt she is there, d'ye see, as she always liked to be where there were gay and grand doings, d'ye see—may Heaven reward her, I say, d'ye see, that she has helped me to such a short road to wealth. D'ye see? Do you think, cousin, I should have stopped with five failures, if I had not been expressly forbidden, d'ye see, to begin business again? D'ye see?

Da. No, cousin, I cannot flatter you at all. The wealth so basely acquired brings you little honour.

Oro. Ah, ah! honour! Honour! D'ye see? Honour is the question! Many a one, d'ye see, must starve in spite of all his honour. Ah, honour! What a fanciful fellow you are! D'ye see? I suppose it will be all the same to my heirs, d'ye see, whether I had my money with honour or without honour. D'ye see? They will be grateful to me, even if I had stolen it. D'ye see?

Da. No, cousin, if your heirs are sensible, they will employ their inheritance after your death to restore their fortunes to those who have been rendered unhappy by your failures.

Oro. What, what? D'ye see? My heirs are to do that! Well, if I thought that, certainly, d'ye see, certainly, I would sooner have everything I possess put in my grave with me. Shall I have toiled and moiled for nothing? Five times I have had to swear. Should I have sworn five times for nothing? D'ye see? Well, listen, cousin, as I see that you would act so contrary to right and duty—d'ye see?—I will just omit you in my will. D'ye see? Then you may see, after all, what one does when one has nothing. D'ye see?

Da. Heaven will then provide for me.

c 2

ORO. Who, who? D'ye see? Who will provide for
you? Heaven? Yes, comfort yourself, yes; Heaven will
provide for you as for the sparrows in winter. Heaven
wants us, d'ye see, just to look after ourselves. For this
reason it has given us wit and intelligence. D'ye see?

DA. Yes, and wickedness and avarice also to many a
one, in case wit and intelligence should not be sufficient.

ORO. Cousin, is that meant for me? D'ye see? Don't
you be so impertinent! But I know what you are
reckoning on now. D'ye see? You think now you will
make a good match. But, I will snatch the lamb from
the wolf yet! D'ye see? Leander has now the right to
it. His ship has arrived safely, although they had written
him at first, d'ye see, that it had been lost. It is, however, nothing but a mistake, d'ye see? Yours, yours is
gone to the deuce, d'ye see?

DA. What? They had written that to Leander? And
he said nothing to me!

ORO. Must one stick everything under your nose then?
D'ye see? Well, well, you will find out, what harm
your misfortune will do you in spite of your honour and
Heaven. I am going myself to the widow now. She
shall hear everything. D'ye see? Good bye. D'ye see?

SCENE VIII.—DAMON.

Vexatious news! . . . . . I lose my fortune. . . . . that
might pass. . . . . Who knows had Leander been unlucky,
whether I might have been sufficiently generous to help
him. . . . . What a disgrace for me if I had proved false to
him! . . . . . Heaven has wished to guard me against
that. . . . . I am fortunate in all my misfortune. . . . .
but I lose the amiable widow at the same time. . . . . she
will give herself now to Leander without any scruple
. . . . . to Leander. . . . . but then Leander is my friend
. . . . . love. . . . . that confounded love. . . . . does
not my friend deserve her just as much as I do? Why
should I care much for a woman, whose heart, if even I
had got it, I should only have got for the sake of my
money? And yet. . . . . she is amiable. . . . how I have
to struggle with myself! . . . . . But Leander. . . . . could

it be true that he received this false news? . . . . . and
could he have withheld it from me? . . . . . how could he
have accepted the proposal which I made him? . . . . .
most strange thoughts arise in me. . . . . but away with
them. . . . . they disgrace my friend.——

SCENE IX.—LISETTE, DAMON.

LIS.   So lonely? And so sorrowful?

DA.   Alas, Lisette, to lighten my grief, I must tell it to
the first person I meet, whoever it is. I have been unfortunate. My ship has been lost in a storm. I have the
most certain information. Heavens! and at the same time
I lose all hope of your mistress——

LIS.   What? Wasn't Leander's misfortune enough?

DA.   How? Leander's? His ship has arrived safely,
you know. What other misfortune has happened to him?

LIS.   Yes, his ship has come in as nicely as yours. He
told me so himself just now.

DA.   Told you so himself?—My suspicion is, then, after
all, not without grounds. . . . . In spite of it, Lisette, you
can believe me, that that was merely an error about his
ship. . . . . but could my friend have committed a false
act towards me, I wonder?

LIS.   False? How false? Heaven forbid! Leander is
the truest friend in the world. Ha! ha! ha!

DA.   Why do you laugh?

LIS.   Yes, that is certain. You can rely on his fidelity
now. Ha! ha! ha! He will stand by you honestly.
Ha, ha, ha!

DA.   I certainly hope so too.

LIS.   And I too. Ha, ha, ha! I know his good intentions. Ha, ha, ha!

SCENE X.—ORONTE, THE WIDOW, LEANDER, DAMON, LISETTE.

WID.   Dearest Damon, I have heard the sad tidings
from your cousin. I assure you your misfortune could
not have touched me more, if it had happened to myself.

LEA.   My dearest friend, fortune has been adverse to you.
I know your mind is too composed to be troubled greatly

by this transitory loss. I hope also that you will be easily
reconciled to fortune. It may restore to you more richly at
some future time that of what it has deprived you now.

Oro. Yes, cousin, d'ye see? Some future time, some
future time. Ha! ha! ha!

Lea. You, Madam, have had the kindness to declare
yourself for the most fortunate of us two. Heaven willed
that I should be the one. But I shall only consider
myself in reality to be such, when through the precious
gift of your heart——

Wid. And can you repeat this offer, Leander, in the
presence of your friend?

Da. Just Heaven! What do I hear?

Lea. O Madam, I know my friend too well. He will
not attempt to stand in the way of your happiness. He
cannot offer you anything but his heart. I can accompany
mine with a chest of gold.

Da. Leander, you will. . . . . Anger and astonishment
deprive me of words.

Oro. Listen, cousin, I will just tell you something,
d'ye see? You cannot marry the pretty widow now. That
is pretty certain, d'ye see? She won't be of much use to
Leander either. D'ye see? She pleases me well enough.
D'ye see? I should not mind having her. I think you
had better propose me to her, d'ye see? I am too timid
for it. D'ye see? See to this. Do all that is in your
power, and I promise I will not forget you in my will. D'ye
see? I can bring her two chests of gold, d'ye see?

Lea. I implore you, Madam, speak, that my friend may
know what he has to hope.

Oro. Madam, do not speak too quickly! D'ye see? My
cousin knows a nice bridegroom for you, d'ye see, who
might well suit you. You can get two chests of gold
with him. D'ye see? Cousin, cousin, tell her, do!

Wid. That will be unnecessary. My resolution is
already taken. It is true, Leander, that I have said, I
would choose the most fortunate of you. I will keep my
word. You, dearest Damon, are the most fortunate!

Da. I?

Lea. Damon?

Oro. What? what do you say? My cousin? Dear me,

why? It is his ship that has been lost, madam! D'ye
see? Leander has one chest of gold, d'ye see? And I
have two, d'ye see? Consequently, consequently you must
mean me.

WID.   Yes, yes, Damon, you have been the most fortunate in this affair. You have been fortunate in finding
an opportunity to show your noble mind in such an ex-
ceptional manner. But your greatest good fortune is, that
you have now received light to perceive the falseness of
your friend, whose pompous gibberish has dazed you
hitherto. Leander, consider your conduct. You had received the tidings that your ship was lost. In your
anxiety you sought relief from me. You disregarded your
friend in a shameful manner. My resolution to declare
myself for the most fortunate was only disagreeable to
you in as far as you feared that you would not be the one.
You tried to persuade me that Damon loved me no longer.
And, lastly, think of the exchange to which I was to tempt
Damon at a time when you thought that his affairs stood
better than yours. Consider all this, and be ashamed to
have deceived a friend who esteemed you above everything. Go! Enjoy your wealth, which could really have
fallen to no unworthier man.

DA.   Leander, am I to believe it? You wished to
deceive me?

LEA.   Damon. . . . . I have wronged you. Farewell!

DA.   Leander, dearest Leander! where are you going?
Stay!

LEA.   Let me go, I beg you, I must flee from your
presence. I die with shame. It is impossible,—you cannot forgive me.

DA.   I not forgive you? Leander, would that my forgiveness were anything to you! Yes, yes! All is forgiven
you already. Remain here, my friend! You have been
rash. But the man, not the friend, has committed this
rashness. Madam, you are angry with Leander. I refuse
all, if with me you do not forget everything. If you
separate us, I shall necessarily be the most unhappy. I
know how difficult it is to find a friend. And if for the
first offence one will forsake him, one will seek a lifetime
for one in vain.

LEA. Damon. . . . . judge from these tears whether I am moved!

WID. Well, Leander! Damon forgives you. And I myself do not know whether I am more moved by his generosity or your repentance. Let us also begin our friendship anew. O Damon, how tender will your love be, since your friendship is so tender!

ORO. So my wooing was no good, after all!

DA. Confess at least, dear Leander, that it is a little more difficult to practise the duties of friendship, than to rhapsodise about it.

LEA. Yes, Damon, I have often spoken of friendship, but only to-day have I learned from you what it is.

WID. Damon! Damon! I fear, I fear, I shall become jealous. Not, indeed, on account of a woman, but of Leander!

THE YOUNG SCHOLAR.

(A COMEDY IN THREE ACTS.)

This play was sketched and partly written while Lessing was at school at Meissen, and completed at the University of Leipzig in 1747. It was represented for the first time at Leipzig under the direction of Frau Neuber, in January 1748.

DRAMATIS PERSONÆ.

CHRYSANDER, *an old merchant.*

DAMIS, *the young scholar, son of* CHRYSANDER.

VALER, *suitor to* JULIANE.

JULIANE, *adopted daughter of* CHRYSANDER.

ANTON, *servant to* DAMIS.

LISETTE, *servant girl.*

The scene is in DAMIS' *study.*

THE YOUNG SCHOLAR.

ACT I.

Scene I.—Damis (*at a table covered with books*), Anton.

Da. Then the post has not yet come in?

An. No.

Da. No? Did you ask for the right one? The post from Berlin——

An. Of course; the post from Berlin; it has not arrived yet. If it doesn't come in soon, I shall shortly have walked my legs off. You go on just as if it would bring you—who knows what? Now I'll wager that if it does come at all, it will bring some new rubbishing volume, or a newspaper, or else a trashy pamphlet.

Da. No, my good Anton; this time it will be something more than that. Ah! if you knew what——

An. Do I want to know it then? Much good would it do me, except to give me one more laugh at you, and is that anything unusual?—Have you anywhere else to send me? If not, I have a little business at the town cellar; may be your errand lies the same way! Eh?

Da. (*angry*). No, you scamp.

An. See there; he has read everything but the 'Book of Manners.' But think a moment. No errand to the bookseller's?

Da. No, you scamp.

An. I hear that "scamp" so often, that I shall end by believing myself that it is my own Christian name. To the bookbinder's, perhaps?

DA. Hold your tongue or——

AN. Or to the printer's? I know my way to these three, Heaven be praised, like the dyer's horse round the cylinder.

DA. Don't you observe, knave, that I am reading?—Do you mean to disturb me any longer?

AN. (*aside*). Hullo! He is really getting angry. Steady, Anton. . . . . But do just tell me what sort of book that is you are reading. My stars! What stuff it is. You understand it? Can any man read such scratchings, such fearful zigzags? If that isn't Faust's hell-charm, at the very least . . . . . oh dear! Everybody knows how it goes with people who will learn everything. . . . . The evil spirit leads them astray at last, and they learn witchcraft too.

DA. (*looks good-humoured again*). Why good Anton! This is a book written in the Hebrew tongue, by Ben Maimon Jadchasacka.

AN. I daresay! who is going to believe that? I know what Hebrew is, at any rate. Isn't it the same thing as the original language, the scriptural speech, the holy word? Our parson uttered that more than once from the pulpit, when I was still at school. But, goodness, he had no books like that. I have peeped into all his books; I once had to help him to shift his quarters from one house to another.

DA. Ha, ha, ha! That's quite likely. It is wonderful enough if a country parson knows as much as the name. In fact, between you and me, my dear Anton, clergymen in general are poor heroes in the field of learning.

AN. Come, come, that cannot apply to all of them. At any rate the M.A. in my native village is among the exceptions. Surely! The schoolmaster himself has told me more than once that the parson is a very learned man; and I must believe what the schoolmaster says; for as the parson has often told me, he is no bad schoolmaster; he knows a word or two of Latin, and can give his opinion on it.

DA. That's capital. So the schoolmaster praises the parson, and the parson, not wishing to be ungrateful, praises the schoolmaster. If my father were here, he

would of course say, *manus manum lavat.* Have not you
noticed his silly habit of lugging in a scrap of Latin
at every opportunity? The old idiot thinks that as he
has so learned a son, he too must show that he once went
through the schools.

AN. Well, I always thought it must be something
silly; for he often mutters something in the midst of his
talk, of which I can't understand a word.

DA. Don't conclude from that, though, that everything
you don't understand is silly; else what a lot of silly
trash I should know. But, oh, sweet learning, how much
does a mortal who possesses you owe to you! And how
lamentable is it, that only the fewest know you in your
completeness! The theologian believes he possesses you
through a medley of scriptural sentences, frightful narratives, and misapplied figures of speech. Those learned
in the law imagine you are theirs, by reason of their
unhappy skill in perverting the useless laws of countries
that have ceased to exist, to the prejudice of justice and
reason, and in expressing the most frightful decisions in
a still more frightful language. The physician believes
that he has really mastered you when by means of a
legion of barbárous words he can make those who are in
health ill, and those who are in sickness worse. But, oh
deluded fools, truth will no longer leave you in these
errors which reflect disgrace on her. Occasions arise
when you yourselves recognise how defective your knowledge is; and then, full of mad arrogance, you measure
all human knowledge by your own, and even cry aloud,
in a tone which seems one of pity for all mortals, "Our
knowledge is fragmentary." No, believe me, my dear
Anton, man is certainly capable of a knowledge of all
things. To deny this is to make a confession of one's
own laziness or of one's mental mediocrity. If I reflect
how much I know for my few years, I am still more convinced of this truth. Latin, Greek, Hebrew, French,
Italian, English . . . . . that makes six languages, of all
of which I am a master; and I am only twenty years old.

AN. Soft! You have forgotten one—German.

DA. True, my dear Anton. Then that makes seven
languages, and I am only twenty years old.

AN. Hem! You are making fun either of me or of
yourself. What? You are not going to reckon your
knowledge of German as learning? I didn't mean what
I said seriously.

DA. And so you think that you yourself know German.

AN. I not know German? It would be the deuce's
own joke, if I spoke the language of the Calmucks without
knowing it.

DA. There is knowledge and knowledge. You know
German; that is, you know how to express your thoughts
by sounds which a German can understand, that is, which
arouse in him the thoughts which you have in your mind.
But you do not know German; that is, you do not know
which words of this language are vulgar or low, which
are coarse and which graceful, which express nothing and
which something, which are obsolete and which in actual
use; you don't know its rules; you have no scholarly
knowledge of it.

AN. What is there that a learned man can't teach us!
If it only depended on your "that is," I do believe that
you would go so far as to dispute my being able to eat.

DA. Eat? Now in very truth, if I choose to be accurate, you can't do that either.

AN. I can't eat, can't I? Nor drink, I suppose?

DA. You can eat; that is, you can cut up your food,
put it in your mouth, chew it, swallow it, and so forth.
You cannot eat; that is, you do not know the mechanical
laws in accordance with which the process of eating goes
on; you do not know what is the function of each muscle
in this operation. You know not whether the digastricus
or the masseter, whether the internal or the external
pterygoideus, whether the zygomaticus or the platysma-
myodes, whether. . . . .

AN. Oh dear! Whether, whether! The only "whether"
I pay attention to, is whether my stomach gets any food,
and whether it agrees with me. But to return to the
languages; would you think, now, that I understand one
which you don't?

DA. You understand a language which I don't?

AN. Yes, think a bit.

DA. Perhaps you know Coptic?

An. Coptic? No, that I don't.

Da. Chinese? Malabar? Though I do not know how you should.

An. How you beat about the bush. Did not you see my cousin? He visited me a fortnight ago. He spoke nothing but this language.

Da. The Rabbi who came to me a short while ago was surely not your cousin?

An. I am not exactly a Jew, am I? My cousin is a Wend; I know Wendish, and you don't.

Da. (*reflectively*). He is right. That my servant should understand a language, which I cannot understand! And that language too one which is not a mere dialect. As I remember, it must be closely allied to Hebrew. Who knows how many roots which are lost in the one I may discover in the other! The thing begins to run in my mind.

An. There, now! But do you know what? Double my wages and you shall soon understand as much of it as I do myself. We will be industrious and talk Wendish together, and . . . . . in short, think it over. I am forgetting my errand to the town-cellar altogether, over this confounded palaver. I will be back and at your service again soon.

Da. Stay here now; stay here.

An. But here's your father coming. Don't you hear? We could not talk longer, anyhow. (*Exit.*)

Da. I wish my father would leave me undisturbed. Does he think I am such an idler as himself?

SCENE II.—DAMIS, CHRYSANDER.

Chrys. Always over those confounded books! My son, one may have too much of a good thing. Amusement is as necessary as work.

Da. My father, study is amusement enough for me. He who seeks for other pleasures than knowledge, cannot have tasted its true sweetness.

Chrys. Don't say that! I also studied in my youth. I penetrated to the very marrow of learning. But as for being always engaged over my books—by no means. I

went out, I played, I went into society, I made friends
with the girls. What the father did in his youth, the
son can also do, and ought to do. *A bove majori discat
arare minor,* as we Latin scholars say. Especially let
me recommend the girls to you, *de meliori,* as we Latin
scholars say. Those fellows are fools who warn a young
man off from the girls as if they were worse than scorpions;
who bid him to avoid them, as we Latin scholars say,
cautius sanguine viperino——

DA. *Cautius sanguine viperino?* Ay, that's Latin; but
how runs the whole passage?

> Cautius timet flavum Tiberim tangere? cur olivum
>   Sanguine viperino
> Cautius vitat? . . . . .

Oh, I understand quite well, father. You have not gone
to the fountain-head! If you had you would have known
that, in this very Ode, Horace describes love as a very
injurious passion, and woman as——

CHRYS. Horace? Horace? Horace was an Italian, and
meant Italian women. Yes! I too warn you against
those girls of Italy. They are dangerous. I have a good
friend who in his youth. . . . . But no, one must not
scandalize people. . . . . German girls, on the other hand,
German girls! It is quite another thing to have to do
with them. I should not be the man I am if the society
of women had not given me a thorough polish. I should
think one could see that in me. You have read enough
in dead books, dip for once into a living one.

DA. I am astonished.

CHRYS. Ah, you will be yet more astonished when you
see a little deeper. Woman, you must know, is a new
world for a young man, where he finds so much to stare
and wonder at——

DA. Yet listen to me! I am astonished, I repeat, to
hear you talk in a way which by no means expresses the
same precepts which you gave me when I went to the
high school.

CHRYS. *Quæ, qualis, quanta!* Now, and then! *Tempora
mutantur,* as we Latin scholars say.

DA. *Tempora mutantur!* Do pray lay aside such vulgar

prejudices. The times do not alter: for let us just consider; what is time?——

Chrys. Hold your tongue! Time is a thing that I am not going to let you waste with your useless chatter. The precepts I gave you at that time were suited to the measure of experience and intelligence you had then. But now I trust you have so much of both that you will not make a business of your pleasure. On these grounds, then, I advise you——

Da. Your words have a certain semblance of truth; but I go deeper. You shall see directly, the *status controversiæ*——

Chrys. Oh, the State of Controversia may lie in Barbara or in Celarent for aught I care. I didn't come here to dispute with you, but——

Da. But to learn the terms used in the art of disputation! Good. Then you must know that neither Barbara nor Celarent have——

Chrys. I shall go mad! Be off with your pack of nonsense, Mr. Pedant, or——

Da. Nonsense! These odd terms are, it is true, relics of the scholastic philosophy; but nevertheless such relics——

Chrys. Over which I shall lose all patience, if you don't listen to me at once. I come to you to discuss the most serious matter in the world. . . . . for what is more serious than marriage? . . . . and you——

Da. Marriage? Speak of marriage to me? To me?

Chrys. Ha, ha! Does that make you attentive? Well, then, *ausculta et perpende!*

Da. *Ausculta et perpende? Ausculta et perpende?* A happy idea——

Chrys. Oh, I have ideas——

Da. Which I have here got hold of.

Chrys. You?

Da. Yes; I. Do you know where this *ausculta et perpende* comes from? I have just lighted on the discovery that it is from Homer. Ah! What is there I can't find in my Homer?

Chrys. You and your Homer are a pair of fools.

Da. I and Homer? Homer and I? We two? Ha,

ha, ha. By all means, father. Thank you, thank you.
I and Homer; Homer and I. . . . . But listen : Whenever
Homer. . . . . he was in truth no fool—as little of that
as I myself. . . . . whenever, I say, he makes his heroes
rouse their men to valour, or begin a discussion in a
council of war, the commencement of their speech is,
"Listen to what I utter and think thereon!" For
instance, in the Odyssey

Κέκλυτε δὴ νῦν μὲν, Ἰθακήσιοι, ὃ τί κεν εἴπω

And then there often follows

Ὣς ἔφαθ.' οἱ δ' ἄρα τοῦ μάλα μὲν κλύον, ἠδ' ἐπίθοντο.

That is: Thus spake he, and they obeyed the words
which they had heard.

Chrys. Oh! they obeyed him, did they? Well, there
is some sense in that. Perhaps Homer is no fool after all.
Look to it that I may be able to make a recantation
concerning you too. So now again to business : I am
aware, my son——

Da. Patience for one instant, father. I am just going
to sit down and make a note of this remark.

Chrys. Make a note? What is there to make a note
of in this? To whom does it matter whether this scrap
is out of Homer or out of a hymn-book.

Da. It matters to the learned world; my honour and
Homer's is concerned in it! For fifty such remarks are
the making of a philologist. And this one is new, I must
tell you, quite new.

Chrys. Well then, write it down another time.

Da. But suppose I forget it? I should be inconsolable.
Please have the goodness at least to remind me of it
again.

Chrys. Well, well, I will do so; only do now listen to
me. I am, my son, acquainted with a most amiable girl;
and I am aware that you too know her. Should you feel
desirous——

Da. I acquainted with a girl, an amiable girl? Oh,
father! If any one heard that, what would they think of
my scholarship? . . . I know an amiable girl?

Chrys. Now, upon my word, I don't think any innkeeper would be as alarmed when charged with knowing such and such a scamp, as you are because you are said to be acquainted with a girl. Is that, then, a reproach?

Da. At any rate, it is no honour, and least of all for a scholar. Every one acquires by degrees the habits of those with whom he associates. Every woman is frivolous, proud, loquacious, quarrelsome and childish all her life long, let her grow as old as she may. Hardly a single woman knows that she has a soul about which she ought to be infinitely more concerned than about her body. To dress, undress, and dress themselves anew, to sit before a mirror, admire their own charms, and devise affected airs; to remain idle at the window with inquisitive eyes, read senseless novels, and, at best, take a needle in hand to pass away the time. That is their employment; that is their life. And do you think that a student could know anything more of such a silly race of creatures than their outward form, without injury to his reputation?

Chrys. Good Heavens, man! Your mother will turn in her grave. Just remember she was once a girl. Reflect that things cannot be otherwise than nature has made them! Besides, as we Latin scholars often say, *nulla regula sine exceptione.* And the girl of whom I am thinking, and whom you know, is certainly an exception.

Da. No, no, I will swear it. Our cousins excepted, and Juliane. . . . .

Chrys. And Juliane? *Bene!*——

Da. And her maid excepted, I don't know a single bit of womankind. Yes, may Heaven punish me if I ever allow the ideas of becoming acquainted with any more to enter my head!

Chrys. Well, well! As you please. Enough, you know Juliane.

Da. More's the pity.

Chrys. And it is just Juliane concerning whom I want to know your thoughts.

Da. Juliane? What I think of Juliane? O father, if you inquired what I thought about Erinna, Corinna, Telesilla, or Praxilla——

Chrys. Good gracious! A moment ago he swore he

D 2

didn't know a single girl, and now mentions half-a-dozen wenches *——

DA. What, father?

CHRYS. Yes, my son! You do not recognise that termination I suppose? *Netrix, Lotrix, Meretrix.* . . . .

DA. Good Heavens! To allude to famous Greek poetesses by such a term.

CHRYS. Aye, aye. Poetesses, quite so quite so. *Lotrix, Meretrix, Poetrix*——

DA. *Poetrix?* Oh, my poor ears! You must say, *poetria,* or *poetris.*

CHRYS. *Is* or *Ix,* as you please, Mr. Lexicon.

SCENE III.—CHRYSANDER, DAMIS, LISETTE.

LIS. Quick, Mr. Chrysander, down to the parlour. Some one wants to speak to you.

CHRYS. Now who can the fool be who must needs come to disturb me at this very moment. Who is it?

LIS. How should I know every fool?

CHRYS. What's that? You have an unlucky tongue, Lisette, to call an honest gentleman a fool. For he surely is an honest gentleman. How else should he want me?

LIS. Come, come, you will surely pardon my tongue the fault that yours committed.

CHRYS. Which mine committed?

LIS. Oh, do go. The honest gentleman is waiting.

CHRYS. Let him wait. I didn't tell the fool to come. I shall return directly, my son. (*Exit.*)

LIS. (*aside*). I must see whether I can make anything out of my young mistress's odd fancy.

SCENE IV.—LISETTE, DAMIS.

DA. Now, then! Is not Lisette going as well?

LIS. Your most obedient servant. If you give orders I shall obey them. But at least tell me first how, in Heaven's name, you can exist in such continual solitude?

---

* There are two plural forms of the word Mensch, namely, Menschen and Menscher. The latter, which is the word in this passage, is used only of a woman of doubtful reputation.—ED.

What do you do all day in your study? Don't your moments turn to hours?

DA. Oh! Of what use are such questions? Off with you! Off!

LIS. Surely you can't be at your books the whole time. Books! such dead companions! No; I am for the living, and Mamselle Juliane's taste is the same. Of course we read now and then; about a knight errant, or a Banise,* or something good of that sort. But we never stand it for more than an hour at a time. To continue at it for whole days, as you do—Heaven help us! We should be dead by the third day. And then, what's worst of all, not to speak a word the whole time; that would be a purgatory to us. It cannot be a superiority belonging to the whole of your sex, for I know men-folk who are just as fickle as we are, or even more so. It can only be a few mighty souls who possess these peculiar gifts.

DA. Lisette does not speak altogether foolishly. It is a pity that so good a mother-wit should not be improved by learning.

LIS. You make me blush. I could almost pay you for that, and recount to you the succession of panegyrics which were made on you by the people at the garden-party yesterday. But I won't offend your modesty. I know scholars set only too much store by this virtue.

DA. Panegyrics on me?

LIS. Yes, yes, on you.

DA. Pray do not trouble yourself about me, my dear Lisette   I will treat the praise as belonging to another, and thus my modesty will be at peace. Come, tell me about it. I only want to hear it on account of your lively and artless way of expressing yourself.

LIS. Oh my way is surely none of the best. I had no teacher such as you. But I will do your bidding. You know, I suppose, who the gentlemen were who were entertained in the garden yesterday by your father.

DA. No, that I don't. As I had no desire to be present

---

* Princess Banise was the heroine of a famous novel written at the end of the eighteenth century, entitled, *Asiatische Banise oder blutiges, jedoch muthiges Pegu.*—ED.

at the party, I did not trouble myself at all about it. It is to be hoped they were themselves worthy of praise, in order that one may have some ground for being proud of their praise.

Lis. They are tolerably worthy people. But how would it affect you if they were not? You mean, you know, from modesty, to treat the praise of yourself as applying to somebody else. And does the truth depend on the lips which utter it? Listen now——

Da. Heavens! I hear my father returning. For goodness' sake, dear Lisette, don't let him see how long you have stayed with me. Go quickly for a moment into the cabinet there.

SCENE V.—DAMIS, CHRYSANDER.

Chrys. That confounded Valer! He couldn't have come at a more inopportune time. Why the devil should he come back from Berlin just to-day? And why should he at once announce himself to me? Ah! in order. . . . . No, Herr Valer, you are too late for that. Now, my son . . . . . (DAMIS *stands abstracted as if in deep thought*). Do you hear, my son?

Da. I hear: I hear everything.

Chrys. Briefly, you comprehend, I suppose, what I meant just now. To a wise man three words are enough. *Sapienti sat*, we Latin scholars say. Answer, if you please.

Da. (*still as if in thought*). What am I to answer?

Chrys. What is there to answer? I'll tell you. Answer that you have understood me; that you are pleased with my offer; that you like Juliane; that you will obey me in all things. . . . . Now, will you answer this?

Da. I will see at once. (*In feigned absence of mind he takes up a book.*)

Chrys. What can the book contain on these points? . . . . . Answer from your heart and not from a book . . . . . *Ex libro doctus quilibet esse potest*, as we Latin scholars say.

Da. (*as if reading in the book*). Perfectly right. But what further?

Chrys. The rest follows like Greek. You say "yes,"

she says " yes." Then comes betrothal, and soon after,
marriage; and then. . . . . you'll soon see what then.

DA. But suppose this supposition——(*Still as if reading.*)

CHRYS. Oh, I never suppose anything which is in the
least degree doubtful. Juliane is a ward; I am her
guardian; I am your father; what can suit me better
than to make you two happy? Her father was my friend,
and a good fellow, though a fool. He might have made a
fair bankruptcy; his creditors would have been brought
to accept an agreement to take a third of their money,
and he was simple enough to pay all, down to the last
farthing. But what am I thinking of? You knew him,
didn't you?

DA. Not personally. But the circumstances of his life
are perfectly familiar to me. I have read it in some biography or other.

CHRYS. Read it? Read it in print?

DA. Yes, yes. Read it. He was born about the middle
of last century, and died about twenty years ago, as
Superintendent-general* in Pomerania. Oriental languages
were his strong point. But all his books are not equally
good. This is one of the best. The man is said to have
had a singular habit of——

CHRYS. Who are you talking of?

DA. Didn't you ask me whether I had known the author
of this book.

CHRYS. I think you are dreaming; or else there is
something gone wrong with your brains. I asked you
whether you had known Juliane's father.

DA. Pardon me, if I answered a little absently. I was
thinking why the Rabbis call the Schurek M'lo " Pum."

CHRYS. Oh, damn your Schurek! Now, just attend
to what your father is saying to you . . . . (*takes the book
out of his hand*). You did not know him, then? Now
I come to think of it, it is hardly possible you should
have known him. Juliane was still very young when he
died. Immediately on his death I took her into my house,
and—thank Heaven!—she has received much kindness
here. She is fair and virtuous. To whom should I give

---

* A high office in the Lutheran Church.

her in preference to you? What do you think? Answer. You stand there as if you were asleep.

DA. Yes, father. There is only one point to consider ——

CHRYS. You are right; there certainly is one to consider; namely, whether you feel yourself competent to accept a public post, because, though——

DA. What? competent? . . . . You doubt my ability then? How unlucky that I can't at once give you most unquestionable proof of it. However, it must come this evening; believe me, this very evening. That confounded post! I can't imagine where it is loitering.

CHRYS. Calm yourself, my son. The question is not put through any mistrust of you, but merely because I believe that it does not do for a man to marry before he has an appointment; just as there is no need, to my mind, for a man to take a post until he knows where to provide himself with a wife.

DA. Oh! confound marriage! Confound the wife! Will you excuse my leaving you alone? I must send that fellow to the post at once. Anton! Anton! It is quite impossible to do anything with the rascal; I must just go myself.

Scene VI.—Anton, Chrysander.

AN. Did not Herr Damis call me? Where is he? What am I to do?

CHRYS. I don't know what he has in his head. He calls you—means to send you to the post—bethinks himself that it is impossible to do anything with a rascal like you, and goes himself. Now tell me, do you want to remain an ass all your life?

AN. Gently, Herr Chrysander! I have no part in your son's folly. I have been obliged to go to the post for him more than a dozen times to-day. He expects letters from Berlin. Is it my fault that they don't come?

CHRYS. By all that's wonderful! But you have been with him some time now; you ought to know his character and way of thinking a little, eh?

AN. Ha, ha! That depends on what we scholars call knowledge of character! In that art I am a master, upon my honour! I only have to speak a word with a man, I only have to look at him, and, presto! I know the whole man! I know at once whether he is reasonable or capricious, liberal or niggardly——

CHRYS. I do believe you are pointing to me!

AN. Oh, never mind about my hands! . . . . Whether he's——

CHRYS. You shall show your skill at once. I have proposed a marriage to my son; now, just say, if you know him, what he will do.

AN. Your son? Herr Damis? Excuse me, with him my art, otherwise so successful, goes begging.

CHRYS. Go you with it, you rascal, and don't boast.

AN. It is quite impossible to know the humour of a young scholar, or to draw any inference from it. And thát which is impossible, Herr Chrysander . . . . is impossible.

CHRYS. And how so?

AN. Because he has none.

CHRYS. None?

AN. No, not none, but a fresh one every moment. The books and examples he meets with are the winds by which the weathercock of his thoughts is ruled. To keep to the question of marriage, since that is at present before us, I fancy that. . . . . In the first place you must know that Herr Damis has never concealed anything from me. I have always been his confidant, and have always been the man whom he preferred to have to do with. We have held discussions together at the university, for whole days, whole nights. And I fancy he must find something in me, some quality, which he finds in no one else——

CHRYS. I'll tell you what quality it is—your stupidity! It pleases him when he sees that he knows more than you. If you are a rascal, and do not contradict him, and praise him to his face, and admire him——

AN. Come, confound it! There you are betraying the whole of my policy! How cunning an old merchant is.

CHRYS. But we mustn't forget our principal object. About marriage——

AN. Why, on that matter he has the deuce's own

whims in his head. For instance; I remember a time
when he wouldn't have married at all.

CHRYS. Not at all? Then I must marry again. You
don't think I will let my name die out? The scoundrel.
But why?

AN. For this reason ; because there have been learned
men who held celibacy was most fitting for a scholar.
God knows whether these gentlemen were too spiritual or
too fleshly in their disposition! In his capacity of old
bachelor that is to be, he had already provided himself
with various ingenious excuses.

CHRYS. Excuses! Can such a profligate, who holds
this sacred sacrament—for I must say in passing, I am
by no means pleased with our theologians who will not
allow marriage to be a sacrament—he, I say, who
despises this holy sacrament, can he venture to excuse his
godlessness? But I believe you are fooling me, fellow; for
only a moment ago he seemed to approve of my proposal.

AN. The devil must have had a finger in it then. How
did he behave? Tell me, did he stand there as if he had
been stunned? Did he look fixedly on the ground? Did
he put his hand to his head? Did he reach towards a
book, as if he would read it? Did he let you go on talking without interruption?

CHRYS. You have hit it! You depict him as if you
had seen him.

AN. Oh, then there is little hope! When he goes on
in that way he means you to consider him abstracted. I
know his ways. He hears all you say to him, but you
are to believe that through the intensity of his reflection
he has not heard it. He sometimes answers too, but
when you place his reply before him again he will never
admit that it was given in answer to that which you
wanted to know from him.

CHRYS. Now, whoever after that won't admit that too
much learning confuses the brain deserves to be learned
himself. Heaven be praised that I knew how to hit the
happy mean in my youth! *Omne nimium vertitur in vitulum,*
as we Latin scholars jocosely say. But may God be
gracious to the scamp if he remains obstinate in his resolution! If he affirms that it is not necessary to marry

and beget children, doesn't he give me to understand that
I need not have begotten him? The thankless son!

An.   True; there can be no greater ingratitude under the
sun than when a son will not show recognition of the pains
his father must have taken to bring him into the world.

Chrys.   No. Certainly the holy estate of matrimony
shall find its defender in me.

An.   Your intention is good; but many such defenders
as you would reduce the custom returns on eatables con-
siderably.

Chrys.   How so?

An.   Think. Three wives and scarcely a son by the
third.

Chrys.   Scarcely! What do you mean with your
" scarcely," you scoundrel.

An.   Whew; you understand something worse than I
meant by that.

Chrys.   But between ourselves, Anton; if the women
of twenty years back had been like the women of the
present time, I should give way to strange thoughts. He
is far too little like me! Yet the women of twenty years
ago were not so daring as now, not so faithless as in these
days, nor yet so——

An.   Are you sure of that? In truth, then, they did
great wrong to my mother, from whom her husband,
who declined to be my father, was separated three and
thirty years ago. But that's a matter I don't like to think
of. The whims of your son are more amusing.

Chrys.   Say, more vexatious. But tell me what were
his excuses?

An.   His excuses were fancies which did not grow in
his own brain. He said, for instance, that as long as he
was under forty, when any one asked why he didn't marry
he should answer that he was too young; but when he
was over forty he would reply he was too old. I don't
know the name of the sage who is supposed to have said
the same thing. Another pretext was this: he wouldn't
marry because he was think_ing every day of turning
monk, and didn't turn monk because every day he was
thinking of marrying.

Chrys.   What! He'll turn monk, too, will he? There

one may see what a bad character, with no reverence for the holy state of matrimony, may come to. I never thought to find this in my own son.

AN. Don't be alarmed. In your son everything is merely transitory. He had read the notion in the biography of a sage ; he took a fancy to it, and at once resolved to produce it as his own when occasion offered. But the whim was soon expelled by another, just as—just as . . . . . What a pity I can't hit on anything like it! In short, out it went. Now he would marry, and marry a perfect devil of a wife.

CHRYS. If only more fools would adopt this fancy, that good fellows might remain free from bad wives.

AN. Yes, thought he, it would sound well if it were said of him that the famous Damis is among the number of the learned whom Heaven has plagued with bad wives, but still the learned world cannot complain of him for being in the least prevented, by his domestic crosses, from supplying them with countless learned writings.

CHRYS. Writings! Yes, which cost me huge sums. What bills I have had to pay for him at the printer's! The rascal!

AN. Patience! He has only just begun to write. Things will be better soon.

CHRYS. Better? Perhaps people will count him among those who have written his father out of house and home.

AN. Why not? If it brings him honour——

CHRYS. Honour be damned.

AN. For that a young scholar will do everything. If after his death it should be said that the famous Damis was among the sages who went to the deuce! What's the odds? It is enough that he is called learned and famous.

CHRYS. Fellow, you alarm me. But you who are much older than he is, can't you give him good advice now and then ?

AN. Oh! Herr Chrysander, you know very well that I receive no salary as tutor. And then my stupidity——

CHRYS. Which you assume in order to make him still more stupid.

AN. (aside). Ah, he knows me. (aloud) But do you suppose

he was in earnest about the ill-tempered wife? Not in the least. An hour afterwards he was going to choose a learned woman.

CHRYS. Well, that would, at any rate, be sensible at last.

AN. Sensible? In my humble opinion it was the very stupidest idea he could have adopted. A learned wife! Just think. A wife resembling your son. An honest fellow would be seized by fear and horror at such an idea. Heavens! before I allowed a learned woman to be tied on to me——

CHRYS. Fool, fool! They go off like anything amongst better people than you. If there were more of them, who knows whether I might not choose one for myself?

AN. Do you know Carlin?

CHRYS. Carlin? No.

AN. My former comrade; my good friend? You don't know him?

CHRYS. No.

AN. He wore a light grey coat with red facings, and red and blue shoulder-knots on his Sunday uniform. You must have seen him with me. He had rather a long nose. It was a family mark. For he would fain show from history that his great-great-grandfather, who was present at a certain tournament as a groom, had one just as long. His one defect was that his legs were a little crooked. Do you remember him now?

CHRYS. How should I know all the rabble that you know? But what about him?

AN. You really don't know him? Ah! then you know one great soul the less. I will enable you to make his acquaintance; I am well esteemed by him.

CHRYS. I believe you are sometimes as mad as my son. However do you come on this nonsense?

AN. Well, this Carlin, I was going to say—Oh, it is vexatious that you do not know him—this Carlin, I say, once served a gentleman who had a learned wife. The confounded scamp! He was good-looking, and so, as desire is not ruled by regard to rank . . . . . In short, he must have got to know her better. Where otherwise should he have got so much sense? At last her husband too observed that our friend was learning from the lady; he got his dismissal before he expected it. Poor lady!

CHRYS. Silence. I won't listen either to your whims or to my son's any more.

AN. Listen to one more—his pet whim; he wanted to marry more than one wife.

CHRYS. But one after the other.

AN. No, at least half-a-dozen at a time. The Bible, authority, and custom notwithstanding. He was just reading a book then——

CHRYS. Ah, those infernal books! I'll hear no more; and there's an end of it. He won't want to take more than one, provided only he takes the one whom I mean for him. And what do you think, Anton?—*quid putas?*—as we say. Will he do it?

AN. Perhaps, and perhaps not. If I knew what book he had read last, and could read it myself, and if——

CHRYS. I see I shall be obliged to use your help. You are a swindler, it's true, but I am aware that one may do more nowadays with cheats than with honest people.

AN. Ay, Herr Chrysander, what do you take me for?

CHRYS. No compliments, Herr Anton. I promise you a reward suitable to your service, if you can persuade my son to marry Juliane, *quovis modo*, as we Latin scholars say, by telling truths or lies, by honest practices or crooked ways, *vel sic vel aliter*, as we Latin scholars say.

AN. Whom? Juliane?

CHRYS. Juliane; *illam ipsam*.

AN. Our Juliane? Your ward, your foster-daughter?

CHRYS. Do you know of any other?

AN. This is impossible, or what I have heard of her cannot be true.

CHRYS. Heard! You have heard something about her then. Surely nothing bad?

AN. Certainly nothing good.

CHRYS. Well! I held the girl in high esteem. Surely no youngster has . . . . . Eh?

AN. If it were no more than that . . . . fashion excuses such slight-mistakes as that. But it is something much worse for a good maiden who does not want to be a maiden any longer.

CHRYS. Something worse? I don't understand you.

AN. And yet you are a business man.

CHRYS. Worse? I always thought that reserve and good principles were the chief——

AN. No longer, no longer; they were so twenty years ago, as you so wisely remembered just now.

CHRYS. Explain yourself more clearly; I have no desire to guess at your silly thoughts.

AN. Nothing is easier, however. In a word, she is said to have no money. People say that out of consideration for her father, who was a good friend of yours, you adopted Juliane from her ninth year, and brought her up out of charity.

CHRYS. In saying that people told you no lie; but all the same, no other but my son shall have her, provided only that he . . . . look here, Anton, I must make the whole riddle plain to you. It lies only with me to make Juliane rich in a short time.

AN. Yes, with your own money, and you might make me rich in the same manner; will you be so good?

CHRYS. No, not with my own money. Can you hold your tongue?

AN. Try it.

CHRYS. Listen then. This is how it stands with Juliane's property. Her father lost all his money, through a lawsuit which at last he had to abandon, a short time before his death. Now, a certain document has fallen into my hands for which he long sought in vain, and which puts the whole business in another light. It is only necessary for me to give enough money to recommence the lawsuit. The document itself I have already sent to my lawyer at Dresden.

AN. Heaven be praised that you are a business man again. Just now I hardly knew what to make of you. But have you Juliane's consent already?

CHRYS. Oh, the good child will, as she says, obey me in all things. Until now Valer reckoned upon winning her. A little while ago, he even opened his heart to me. Before I found the document——

AN. Of course, Juliane was not of so much importance to us then; so you gave him encouragement?

CHRYS. Certainly. He has come back from Berlin to-day, and has been to call on me already. I fear, I fear . . . . . But if only my son will . . . . and he, Anton, you know . . . . A fool may be caught on many sides, and a man like you can catch on many sides. You shall see that I am grateful.

AN. And you shall see that I am entirely at your service, especially if gratitude first rouses me, and——

SCENE VII.—ANTON, CHRYSANDER, JULIANE.

JU. Come, Herr Chrysander, do come down at once. Herr Valer is there to wait upon you.

CHRYS. You seem very happy about it, young miss.

AN. (whispers to Chrysander). Ah! Valer has caught the bird already.

CHRYS. That would be rather serious.

(*Exeunt* ANTON *and* CHRYSANDER).

SCENE VIII.—JULIANE, LISETTE.

LIS. (peeps out of the cabinet). Hist, hist!

JU. Well, for whom is that meant? Lisette, is that you? What are you doing here?

LIS. Yes, you will never believe that I and Damis have gone so far that he has to conceal me. I can twist him round my finger already. One more interview like the last, and I have bagged him.

JU. And so, although in joke, I had a very good idea after all. Would to Heaven that the union which his father——

LIS. His father! the rascal, the miser! I have just learnt what he is.

JU. What names you call him! His goodness is only too great. In order to make his good actions complete he offers me his son's hand, and with it all his property. But how unhappy am I in this. Gratitude and love, love for Valer, and gratitude——

LIS. A minute ago I was under just the same delusion. But, believe me, I have it now from his own lips; not from friendship for you, but from friendship to your property he wishes to bring about this union.

Ju. My property? You are mad. What have I that I did not get from him?

Lis. Come, come. This is not the place for talking. I will tell you all that I have heard another time.

ACT II.

Scene I.—Lisette, Valer, Juliane.

Lis. (*within*). Come in here; Damis has gone out. You can have a word with one another in private here.

Ju. Yes, Valer; my resolution is taken. I owe him too much; by his kindness he has obtained the greatest right over me. Cost what it may, I must consent to this marriage, since Chrysander desires it. Or shall I sacrifice gratitude to love? You are yourself virtuous, Valer, and in your society I have learnt to think more nobly. To show myself worthy of you I must do my duty even at the loss of my happiness.

Lis. A marvellous moral, truly!

Va. Then what becomes of your promise, your vow, and your constancy? Is it right to act contrary to a duty which really unites us, in order to fulfil an imaginary one?

Ju. Oh! Valer, you know better what belongs to such promises. Do not abuse my weakness. My father's approbation was not given to that promise.

Va. What father?

Ju. The one to whom I am bound to give that title on account of his kindness. Do you consider it no benefit to be rescued from poverty and all its attendant miseries? Ah! Valer, I should not now possess your heart had not Chrysander's care caused me to be brought up in virtue and honour.

Va. Benefits cease to be benefits if one seeks to be repaid for them. And what else is Chrysander doing than this, my over-conscientious Juliane, seeing that he only wants to marry you to his son because he sees his way to recovering for himself the greater part of your patrimony?

Ju. Do not rely on such a strange report as this. Who knows what Lisette has heard?

Lis. Nothing but what fits in perfectly with the rest of his conduct. A man who has already trumpeted his good deeds abroad, who can count them on his fingers to any one, looks for something more than the mere reward of Heaven. And are these, then, the first tears you have shed through vexation at being dependent on such a selfishly liberal man?

Va. Lisette is right! . . . . But, alas, I feel it. Juliane no longer loves me.

Ju. She loves you no longer? This suspicion only was wanting to make her grief complete. If you knew how much it cost her to remain deaf to the promptings of love · if you knew, Valer. . . . . oh, how mistrustful men are!

Va. Do not misinterpret the fear of a lover whose whole happiness is at stake. So you do love me still, and yet you will give yourself to another?

Ju. Will? Could you torture me more cruelly?—"I will?" say, rather, " I must."

Va. You must! Never yet has a heart but the one that wished it been compelled to allege necessity as its excuse——

Ju. Your reproaches are so bitter, so bitter, that for vexation I shall leave you.

Va. Stay, Juliane, and say at least what I am to do in this matter.

Ju. As I do, submit to fate.

Va. Ah, leave innocent fate out of the question.

Ju. Innocent? You mean it is I that am to blame? Detain me no longer.

Lis. If I don't soon interfere, they will be quarrelling through sheer love. . . . . What you are to do, Herr Valer? A mighty question! Why, move Heaven and earth so that this good young lady "need not"! Bring the father to other thoughts; and get the son over to your side. . . . . The son is easy enough to manage; leave him to me. Poor dear Damis. I am without doubt the first girl to flatter him, and I hope therefore to be the first to be flattered by him. In good sooth, he is so vain, and I am so skilful that I would soon flatter him even

into making me his wife were it not for his confounded
father! See now, Herr Valer, this is mistress Juliane's
idea! Now do you invent some snare for the father.

Ju. What's that you say, Lisette? *My* idea? Oh
Valer, don't believe such nonsense! Did I tell you to do
anything more than to give him a bad opinion of me?

Lis. Exactly so, a bad opinion of you, and if possible
a proportionally better one of·myself.

Ju. There is no bearing with you——

Va. But, dearest Juliane, say, at all events——

Ju. Say what? Perhaps that I will rush into your
arms, even though I should sin against all virtue in so
doing! That I will strive to become yours with an eager-
ness, with a zeal, which must some day necessarily make
me contemptible in your eyes? No, Valer——

Lis. Don't you hear, that she would rather leave us
free to act! She is like the lovely Aspasia—or whatever the princess's name was in that thick novel. Two
knights laid claim to her. "Fight with one another"
said the lovely Aspasia; "he who overcomes the other
shall have me." Nevertheless she favoured the knight in
the blue armour more than the other——

Ju. Oh, the silly girl—bother her blue knight!
(*Breaks away and runs off.*)

SCENE II.—Lisette, Valer.

Lis. Ha, ha, ha!

Va. It is no joke to me, Lisette.

Lis. Not? Ha, ha, ha!

Va. I believe you are laughing at me.

Lis. Oh, laugh with me, then, or I shall have to laugh
again because you won't. Ha ha, ha!

Va. I am in despair! In the uncertainty whether
she loves me——

Lis. Uncertainty? Are all men so hard to convince? Do they all become such anxious doubters as
soon as love warms them a little? Have done with
those whims of yours, or I shall laugh again. Set your
wits rather to work to plan something that old Chrysander——

VA. Chrysander does not trust me, and cannot trust me. He knows my feeling for Juliane. All my persuasion would be in vain. He would soon discover the interested motives which are its source. And if I were to make an actual offer of marriage what good would that do? He is outspoken enough to tell me to my face that I must waive my claim in favour of his son, who has the greatest right to Juliane, on account of his father's kindness to her. . . . . What, then, am I to do?

LIS. O those wonderful people, who want everywhere to go only along the level road. Listen what I have thought of. The document, or whatever the thingummy-bob is called, is the only reason for Chrysander's liking for this match, and he has sent it to his lawyer. How if we were to write a letter purporting to come from this advocate, in which. . . . . in which——

VA. In which he expressed his doubts as to the legality of the document you mean? The idea is not so bad. But suppose the lawyer happens to write just the opposite to him, then our deception will be discovered.

LIS. What an objection! Of course you must tune him up. It has always been usual for a lover to make some sacrifice.

VA. But suppose now the lawyer is an honest man.

LIS. You really go on as if you had only been in the world a month. As the present is, so is the lawyer. If nothing at all comes, the most contemptible swindler is the most honest of men. If something comes, but of no great value, his conscience still maintains its balance pretty well. Temptations may then arise, I dare say, but a very little consideration overthrows them! But only let really considerable advantages be offered, and straightway the most honest lawyer is no longer the most honest. He puts his honesty along with the gold pieces into his coffer where the former begins to rust before the latter. I know these gentlemen.

VA. Your judgment is too sweeping. All persons of the same profession have not the same sentiments. I know various honourable old attorneys——

LIS. What do you want with your old fellows. It is just as if you said that the great round cuffs, little pointed

buttons, the frightful ruffs big enough to make sails of,
the broad square-toed shoes, the deep pockets, in short
the whole get-up in which your fathers may have appeared on gala days, were still the fashion, because sometimes here and there one sees a few bent, tottering, old
fellows creeping along the streets in that style of dress.
Let them and your ancient old honest lawyers die in
peace. Fashion and honesty are going the same road.

Va. One hears directly where the girl is most eloquent.

Lis. You mean, I suppose, where there is slander afloat?
No, truly, I have not chattered so much for the sake of
slander merely. My chief object was to make you see
how much gold can do everywhere, and what an excellent
game a suitor has in his hand, if he is liberal towards all
—towards the lady, the lawyer and your humble servant.
(*Makes a curtsey.*)

Va. Rely on my gratitude. I promise you a very
considerable dowry, if all goes well——

Lis. Ah! How nice! A dowry! You hope, I suppose, that I shall be left an old maid?

Va. If you are afraid of that, I'll promise you the
husband as well. But come, Juliane will be expecting
us, doubtless. We will consider our business further in
concert.

Lis. Go on before; I must wait here a little for my
young sage——

Va. Perhaps he is already below with his father.

Lis. We must have our conversation alone. Go. You
haven't spoken to him yet, of course?

Va. What wouldn't I give if I could dispense with
that altogether. As far as he is concerned I would avoid
this house more than bedlam, were it not that a more
agreeable object——

Lis. Well, go, then, and don't keep this more agreable
object waiting for you any longer.

Scene III.—Anton, Lisette.

An. Hullo! What is she doing in my master's study?
Valer went out just now, Juliane a little while before,

and you are still there. I do believe you hold your meetings here, Lisette; I shall let my master know this. I will have my revenge—for yesterday, do you remember?

LIS. I verily believe you are scolding! What about yesterday?

AN. A box on the ear is soon forgotten by the giver, but he whose teeth have chattered from it thinks of it a good while. Just take care, just take care.

LIS. What right have you, then, to kiss me?

AN. The deuce! How common boxes on the ear would be if every one who wanted to kiss you got one? Well, my master shall give you a fine——

LIS. Your master! He won't do much to me.

AN. Won't he? How often has he not said that so holy a place as a study must not be profaned by such unsanctified creatures as you? That the god of learning. . . . . stay, what does he call him—Apollo—can't endure a woman. The very smell of them is disagreeable to him. He flies before them like the kite before the doves. . . . . And do you think my master would permit you to chase his beloved god out of the room?

LIS. Why, you fool, I believe you think that the good god will have nothing to do with any but you men? Hold your tongue, or——

AN. Yes, another like yesterday's, perhaps.

LIS. A better one than that. The simpleton deserved more than one yesterday. He comes to me when it is dark; he wants to kiss me, I drive him off; he comes again, I hit him on the mouth; it hurts him, he leaves off; he scolds me and goes . . . . I could give you another, when I think of it.

AN. And so I ought to have waited to see how often you would have repeated your caresses?

LIS. Granting some more would have followed, they would have become weaker and weaker; very likely the last ones would have altogether . . . . but such a stupid donkey deserves nothing.

AN. What's that? Do you mean that really, Lisette? I could almost forget the box on the ears, and be reconciled to you again.

LIS. As you please about that. Of what importance

is your good-will to me now?   I am on the track of quite
other game now.

AN.   Other game!   Alas, Lisette!   That is a box on the
ears that I shall not forget so soon !   Other game?   I
should have thought you would have been content with
one who ran into your net of his own accord.

LIS.   And that is just why he is of no value. . . . . But
tell me, where is your master ?

AN.   Thank your stars that he stays away so long, and
be off.   If he catches you, you are in danger of being
whipped out.

LIS.   That's my affair.   But where is he ?   Hasn't he
come back from the post yet?

AN.   How do you know that he has gone to the
post.

LIS.   Enough, I do know it.   He wanted at first to send
you.   How came it that he went himself?   Ha, ha !   " It
is quite impossible to do anything with the rascal."   In
truth, that piece of praise makes me quite in love with you.

AN.   Who the dickens can have told you that?

LIS.   Oh, nobody ; only tell me—has he come back?

AN.   A long time ; he is downstairs with his father.

LIS.   And what are they doing together ?

AN.   Doing?   Quarrelling.

LIS.   The son, of course, is trying to convince the father
of his cleverness.

AN.   Something of the sort, no doubt.   Damis is quite
beside himself.   He won't let the old man put in a single
word, he counts up to him a thousand books he has seen,
a thousand he has read, a few more thousands he means
to write, and a hundred booklets which he has already
written.   First he names a dozen professors who, not without cause, had given him a written certificate of merit
with their seals set to it ; then a dozen penny-a-liners,
who make excellent trumpets for a young sage, if one puts
silver mouthpieces on them ; then a dozen journalists, who
have humbly begged him to become their colleague.   His
father looks quite bewildered.   He fears for his son's
health, he keeps saying, "My son, don't excite yourself
so ; "   " Spare your lungs ;" " Just so ;" " I believe you ;"
" Be contented ;" " It wasn't meant in that way."

Lis. And Damis?

An. Damis keeps on. At last his father makes a final
exertion. He outshouts him by sheer force, and pacifies
him with such a mass of praise, as no one in the world
ever has deserved, does deserve, or will deserve. Then
the son becomes reasonable once more, and now. . . . .
they pass to another subject, another matter, to——

Lis. To what, then?

An. Thank goodness, I can hold my tongue!

Lis. You won't tell it me?

An. Never. I am, it is true, an indifferent sort of
fellow in other things, but when it is a question of
silence——

Lis. Is that what you are like?

An. I thought you would have been pleased that I
could hold my tongue; especially about marriage affairs,
and what belongs to them——

Lis. Is that all you know? I knew that long ago.

An. How well she tries to take me in! So there was
no need to tell you that?

Lis. Oh dear, no! But I know what I'll do to revenge
myself for your rascally distrust of me. You shall not
dare to keep a secret from a girl of my profession again.
Do you remember in what terms you spoke of your master
a short while ago?

An. Remember! Can a man who is up to his ears
in work, and has so much to say all day long as I have,
remember every trifle?

Lis. I should think that slandering your master was
rather more than a trifle.

An. What! Slandering?

Lis. Ha, ha! You, sir, who are up to your ears in
work, do you bethink yourself now. What was it you
said about him to his father just now?

An. Either the girl has the devil in her, or that confounded old fellow must have blabbed. But come, Lisette,
do you really know what I said? What was it, then?
Just let me hear?

Lis. You will hear it all when I tell your master.

An. Oh, dear, I do believe you are in earnest. You
surely don't want to ruin my credit with my master? If

you really know anything, don't be a fool! . . . . . You
women never understand a joke. I have forgiven you
a box on the ears and you are going to take revenge for a
little bit of fun. I'll tell you everything, you know.

Lis. Tell me, then.

An. But you won't tell anything?

Lis. The more you tell, the less I'll tell.

An. What else should it be but that the father again
proposed the marriage with Juliane to his son? Damis
appeared to be listening, and. . . . . I can't tell you any
more.

Lis. No more? Very well, then, your master shall hear
everything.

An. For Heaven's sake, Lisette! . . . . . I will confess——

Lis. Confess, then.

An. I can only confess that I really did not hear anything more. I was sent away at the moment. You know
well enough that when one is not on the spot one can't
hear much ——

Lis. That's clear. But what do you think,—will
Damis make up his mind to it?

An. If he has not done so yet I shall do my
utmost to make him. I am to be paid for my trouble,
Lisette, and when I am paid, you know, then you
also——

Lis. Yes, yes, I promise you; you shall be well paid!
Just dare to do it.

An. What?

Lis. Just have the audacity——

An. What?

Lis. You blockhead! My young lady doesn't want
your Damis-——

An. What does that matter?

Lis. It follows that it is my will, too, that he should
not get her.

An. It follows that, if my master wishes to have her,
it must be my will that he shall get her.

Lis. Listen! You want to be my husband, and have
a will of your own?. Don't imagine that, my boy. Your
will must be mine, or——

AN. Hush! the deuce! He is coming! do you hear? He is coming! Now look for the hole the carpenter has left. At any rate, hide yourself; hide, or he will do for both of us. ·

LIS. (*aside*). Stop, I will take in both of them. Where shall I go? Where? Into the cabinet?

AN. Yes, yes! in with you! Perhaps he'll go again soon. . . . . And I will sit down here quickly. (*Seats himself at the table, takes up a book, and pretends not to see* DAMIS.)

SCENE IV.—ANTON, DAMIS.

AN. (*as if to himself*). Yes, these learned men, how happy they are! What an ass my father was not to have put me to that profession. By Jove! How delightful it must be to know everything in the world, as my master does. My stars! Fancy understanding all those books! If one merely sits among them, whether one reads them or not, one becomes at once quite another being. I feel it, I really do feel it, intellect is being exhaled over me from them. Certainly he is right; without learning man is nothing more than a brute. Stupid brute that I am. (*Aside*). I wonder how long he'll let me abuse myself. (*Aloud*). We are truly absurdly matched, I and my master. He yields to none in learning, I to none in ignorance. I will begin reading this very day. If I live to be eighty I may become a fine fellow yet. Only begin briskly. Here are books enough. I shall pick out the smallest, for one must not overdo it at first. Ah! Here I light on the loveliest of little books. Such a book will surely let itself be read and enjoyed. Begin at once, Anton. I suppose it does not matter which end you begin at. In truth, it would be a shame for my master, who is so marvellously, so fearfully, so horribly learned, were he to have such an ignorant servant any longer.

DA. (*coming close up to him*). Yes, certainly, it would be a shame for him.

AN. Heaven help us! my master.

DA. Don't be frightened. I have heard all.

AN. You have heard all? . . . . I beg a thousand pardons, if I have said anything wrong. I was so capti-

vated, so captivated by the beauty of learning—forgive
me my stupid prank—that I wanted to become learned
myself.

DA.   Don't blame yourself for the wisest idea you ever
had in your life.

AN.   Twenty years ago it might have been wise
enough.

DA.   Trust me, you are not yet too old to learn.
We can already give several examples in our republic of
men who in like manner did not throw themselves into
the arms of the Muses earlier.

AN.   Not into their arms only! I will throw myself
into their laps. But in what town do these people dwell?

DA.   In what town?

AN.   Yes. I must go thither to make their acquaintance.
They must tell me how to set about it.

DA.   What do you mean by a town?

AN.   Do you fancy I don't know what a republic is?
Saxony, for instance. And a republic contains more than
one town? Doesn't it?

DA.   What an idiot! I speak of the republic of the
learned. What is Saxony, or Germany, or Europe, to us
learned men? A sage like me belongs to the whole world;
he is a cosmopolitan; he is a sun which must give light
to the whole earth.

AN.   But surely the republic of the learned must be
somewhere.

DA.   Be somewhere, you stupid fellow? The republic
of the learned is everywhere.

AN.   Everywhere? Then it is in the same place as the
republic of fools. For I have been told that that too is
everywhere.

DA.   It is indeed true that fools and wise men, the
learned and the ignorant, are everywhere intermingled,
and that too in such a way that the latter always compose
the majority. You can see that in our own household.
By what a number of fools and ignorant persons do you
find me surrounded here. Some of them know nothing,
and know that they know nothing. You are among these.
But they would like greatly to learn something, and on
this account they are the most bearable of all. There are

others who know nothing and wish to know nothing;
they think that they are happy in their ignorance ; they
shrink from the light of learning.

AN. What a race of owls !

DA. There are others again who know nothing, and
yet believe they know something. They have learnt
nothing, absolutely nothing, and yet they want to appear
as if they had learnt something. These are the most
intolerable of all fools, and, to confess the truth, my father
is one of them.

AN. You surely are not going to make out that your
father—bethink yourself,—your father, is an arch-fool ?

DA. Learn to discriminate. I do not abuse my
father in so far as he is my father, but in so far as I may
regard him as one who wishes to usurp the credit of being
learned without deserving it. In that respect he deserves
my displeasure. I have often given him to understand
how he irritates me when, as an old merchant, as a man
who can know nothing except good and bad wares, about
true and false money, and at the best only knows how to
give away the one for the other—when he, I say, makes
such a show with his school-boy scraps, of which I of
course still remember something. In this regard he is a
fool, be he my father or no.

AN. What a pity, what an eternal pity that I did not
know about "in so far" and "in that regard" when I was
a youngster. My father should certainly not have thrashed
me so often for nothing. He should have received as good
as he gave, not in so far as he was my father, but in so
far as he was one who struck me first. Hurrah for
learning !

DA. Stop. I bethink me of a principle of natural law,
which will support this idea excellently. I must just look
it out in Hobbes. Patience! I will make a capital work
out of this, you will see.

AN. In order to prove that one may strike one's
father back ?

DA. By all means, *certo respectu*. But one must take
care that when one strikes him, one intends to strike,
not one's father, but the aggressor ; for otherwise——

AN. Aggressor? What sort of thing is that ?

Da.   So he is termed who gives the first blow.

An.   Ha, ha! Now I understand.   For instance, if, sir, one of those little fits of learned madness were to come over you again, which make themselves felt on my back by a good cudgelling, you would be . . . . . what is it? . . . . . the aggressor; and I should be entitled to get hold of the aggressor, and——

Da.   You are mad, fellow.

An.   Don't be alarmed; I think I should know how to regulate my thoughts so as to put the master aside for the time.

Da.   Well, in truth, that would be a remarkable example of what fatal errors a man may fall into if he does not know on what principle one truth or another is to be decided.   The thrashings which a servant gets from his master do not come under the natural law, but the civil law.   When a servant hires himself out, he hires his back out at the same time.   Observe this principle.

An.   That is civil law, is it?   What a vile law.   But now I see.   That confounded learning can just as well help one to blows as protect one from them.   What wouldn't I give if I could comprehend all its subtleties as easily as you. . . . . Oh, Herr Damis, take pity on my stupidity.

Da.   Well, if you really mean it, set to work.   I am pleased to have made a proselyte to learning by my example.   I will give you ample support by my advice and instruction.   If you make anything of it I promise to introduce you to the learned world myself, and make you known to it by a special work.   Perhaps I may take the opportunity to write something *De eruditis sero ad literas admissis* or *De opsimathia* or even *De studio senili*, and so you will become famous at once.   But just let me see if there is much to expect from this thirst for knowledge of yours?   What book had you in your hand just now?

An.   It was a very little one——

Da.   Which?

An.   It was delightfully bound, with gilt back and edges.   Wherever did I put it?   There, there.

Da.   That one?   That?

An.   Yes, that!

Da.   That?

AN.   Have I done wrong? As it was so nice and small——

DA.   I could not myself have suggested a better one for you.

AN.   I thought it must be a good book. Would it otherwise have such a good dress?

DA.   It is a book that has no equal. I wrote it myself. Do you see? . . . . . *Auctore Damide.*

AN.   You wrote it? Well, I have always heard that people keep their own children better dressed than their step-children. That shows paternal love.

DA.   In this book I have, so to speak, surpassed myself. As often as I read it, I learn something new from it.

AN.   From your own book?

DA.   Are you surprised at that? . . . . The deuce! I just remember—good Heavens!—the poor girl! She can't still be hidden in the cabinet? (*Goes towards it.*)

AN.   In Heaven's name, where are you going?

DA.   What now? To the cabinet. Have you seen Lisette?

AN.   Now I am lost! No, Herr Damis, no; as I live she is not in there.

DA.   You saw her go out then. Has she been gone long?

AN.   I haven't seen her go in, on my honour. She is not there; only believe me she is not there——

SCENE V.—LISETTE, DAMIS, ANTON.

LIS.   Assuredly she is still in.

AN.   Oh, the wretch!

DA.   Have you remained here all this time? Poor Lisette! I didn't at all want you to do that. As soon as my father was out of the room you might have come out again.

LIS.   But I didn't know whether I should be doing right, so I preferred to wait until he who had hidden me bid me come out again.

AN.   The devil! what hiding are they talking about? (*Asid. to* LISETTE). So, my sly little kitten! Has my master himself hidden you once before? Now I know how to interpret that box on the ears yesterday. You false one!

Lis. Be quiet; don't say a word about my having been with you just now, or . . . . . you know what——

Da. What are you two chattering about together there? May not I hear it?

Lis. Nothing. I merely told him to go downstairs, so that he could tell my young lady, if she asks for me, that I am gone out. Juliane is suspicious; but I suppose she would seek me here if she wanted me.

Da. That's sensible. Off with you, Anton.

An. Do you wish it really, Lisette?

Lis. Certainly, go, leave us alone.

Da. Will you go at once?

An. But just consider for yourself, Herr Damis; when her chattering becomes wearisome to you, which will be very soon, who is to help you to drive her out of the room, if I am not by?

Lis. Just wait and I'll give your slanderous mouth——

Da. Don't be uneasy. When she becomes troublesome to me I doubt not she will have the sense to go of her own accord.

An. But just consider; a woman in your study! What will your god say to you? He does not like the vermin, you know.

Lis. Shall I have to turn you out of the room?

An. That would be delightful. The confounded girls. They can flatter themselves into favour with old Harry himself. (*Exit.*)

Scene VI.—Lisette, Damis.

Da. And where were we when we left off?

Lis. ·Where were we? On the subject of which I always hear and speak with the greatest pleasure—your praise. If only it were not such a delicate matter to praise a man to his face! . . . . I can't possibly put you to the torture.

Da. But I assure you, Lisette, again, I am indifferent to the praise. I should merely like to hear, in what

different ways different people have viewed the same
subject.

Lis. Each one praised in you that particular quality
which he thought was deserving of commendation in himself. For instance, the fat little man, with the serious
air who laughs so rarely, but who when he does once
begin, overturns the whole table with the shaking of his
stomach——

Da. Who is that, pray? I cannot guess from your description. Descriptions are ticklish things. It is no easy
matter to make them so that one may recognise the thing
described at the first glance. But nothing amuses me
more than the frequency with which I meet with descriptions instead of definitions in the works of this and that
great philosopher—of men, positively, who have given
their names to whole sects. That happens because these
good gentlemen have more imagination than judgment. In
defining, the intellect must probe into the interior of
things; but in describing, one must only regard the
external characteristics, the——

Lis. We are departing from our subject, Herr Damis.
Your praise.

Da. Certainly; go on, Lisette. Of whom was it that
you were just going to speak?

Lis. Eh? Don't you know the little man, then? He
is always puffing out his cheeks——

Da. Perhaps she means the old Councillor?

Lis. Right, but his name——

Da. What does it matter?

Lis. "Yes, Herr Chrysander," said the Councillor whose
name doesn't matter, "your son may one day become one
of the best councillors in the world, if he will only apply
himself to it. The office requires an alert mind, which he
has; nimble tongue, which he has; a deep insight into
politics, which he has; a power of putting the thoughts
neatly on paper, which he has; a subtle attentiveness to
the slightest movements of turbulent citizens, which he
has; and if he has them not—practice, practice! I remember how it was with me at first. Of course one
cannot bring the ability for so hard an office with one
into the world——

Da. The fool! It is indeed true that I possess all these abilities, but with the half of them I might become an Alderman, and not a mere——

Scene VII.—Anton, Lisette, Damis.

Da. Now then, what are you back here for? .

An. Mistress Juliane knows now that Lisette has gone out. Don't be afraid; she won't disturb us.

Da. Who told you to come back here?

An. Could I leave my master alone, do you think? And besides such a qualm came over me all at once, such an anxiety; my ears began to tingle, especially the left one. . . . . Lisette, Lisette!

Lis. What do you want?

An. (*aside to Lisette*). What have you two been about alone? I bet it was something about me.

Lis. Be off;—I don't know what the fool wants.

Da. Go, Anton; it is high time; you must go to the post again. I don't know at all why it is so late. . . . . Will you go at once?

An. Come with me, Lisette.

Da. Why should Lisette go with you?

An. And why should she be with you?

Da. You ignoramus!

An. Yes, truly it is my misfortune that I am ignorant. (*Aside to Lisette*). Speak rather loud, at any rate, so that I can hear what passes between you—I shall listen. (*Exit.*)

Scene VIII.—Lisette, Damis.

Lis. Let us speak rather low. You know we are not secure from listeners.

Da. Good. Go on, then, softly.

Lis. You know Herr Chrysander's confessor, do you not?

Da. Confessor? Do you expect me to know all such literary botchers.

Lis. He, at any rate, seemed to know you very well. " Herr Damis might certainly become," said he, interrupting the fat Councillor, " a good preacher, too. I believe

that I have observed in him in a high degree, all the
requisite qualifications; a fine physique, a strong clear
voice, a good memory, a refined style of delivery, a becoming confidence, a ripe intellect which can hold boldly to
its own opinion. I am only afraid about one point. I
fear, I fear, that he too is a little infected by freethinking
ideas." . . . . "Eh? Freethinking?" shouted the doctor,
who was already half tipsy. "The freethinkers are right
good fellows! Will he be unable to cure anybody on this
account. If I had my way, he should become a doctor.
He knows Greek, and Greek is half the art of medicine,"
(*gradually raising her voice again*). "In truth, one cannot
give oneself the courage needful for that. Yet it comes
by itself if one has only practised a little." "Ah!" inter-
rupted an old merchant, "it is with you medical gentlemen, I suppose, as with the executioners: the first time
they behead a man they shudder and quake; but the
oftener they repeat their experiment the brisker it goes."
At this remark, they laughed a whole quarter of an hour,
—on and on,—they even forgot their drinking over it.

SCENE IX.—LISETTE, DAMIS, ANTON.

AN.   The post, sir, will not come in before nine o'clock
to-day. I have inquired. You can rely on that.

DA.   Must you disturb us again already, idiot?

AN.   I shall be very glad if I have disturbed you just
in time.

DA.   What do you mean by "in time?"

AN.   I will make my meaning clearer to Lisette. May
I speak a word in her ear?

LIS.   What have you to say in my ear?

AN.   Only one word (*speaking low*). Do you think I
haven't listened? Didn't you say you "had not courage
enough for that? but if only you had practised a
little?" . . . . . Oh! I heard it all. To cut the matter
short, our ways lie in different directions. You shameless,
horrid——

LIS.   Speak out, do, what you mean.

DA   Get out of my sight again at once! And don't
appear in my presence again, until I call you, or until

you bring me letters from Berlin. . . . . I can hardly bear this waiting. . . . . Such is the result of excessive joy. I ought by rights to call it hope, since joy belongs to the present, hope to the future. But in this case the future is already as certain as the present. I use the language of the prophets who, however, can hardly have been so certain of their matters as I. The whole Academy must be blind, if. . . . . What! are you standing there still? Will you be off?

Scene X.—Lisette, Damis.

Lis. There you see. That is how these people praised you.

Da. Oh! If they can't praise better than that, they might as well leave it alone altogether. I don't wish to boast, but for this much I surely can give myself credit without arrogance. I shall leave my bride the choice whether she prefers having a Doctor of Divinity, of Law, or of Medicine, as her husband. I have graduated in all three faculties, in all I have——

Lis. You speak of a bride? Are you, then, really going to marry?

Da. Has she, too, heard of it already, Lisette?

Lis. Does a marriage come about in any house whatever, without the likes of us? But I could never have imagined that you would decide on Juliane—on Juliane!

Da. I do this chiefly to please my father, who urges me in this matter in the most unusual way. I am quite aware that Juliane is not worthy of me. But shall I offend my father about such a trifle as marriage? And besides, I have a fancy, which he will indulge me in.

Lis. Yes, in truth, Juliane is not worthy of you; and if only every one knew my mistress as well as I do——

Scene XI.—Anton, Damis, Lisette.

An. (aside). I cannot leave these people alone in this way. . . . . Herr Valer asks whether you are in your room? Are you still there, Herr Damis?

Da. Just tell me, you ignorant lout, have you made it your special object to-day to annoy me?

F 2

LIS. Let him stay there, Herr Damis. He will not keep away, you'll see.

AN. Yes, now I shall stay; now, perhaps, when what I must not hear or see is already over.

DA. What is over?

AN. You know very well.

LIS. (*speaking low*). Help me, now, Anton, to make Juliane as black as we can in your master's estimation. Will you?

AN. Yes, very likely; by way of gratitude, perhaps——

LIS. Hold your tongue, then, at any rate. . . . . Of necessity, Herr Damis, you will get on ill with Juliane. I feel pity for you beforehand. The whole world does not contain a worse girl——

AN. Don't believe it, Herr Damis; Juliane is a right good child. You could not get on better with any one in the world. I wish you happiness beforehand.

LIS. Really? You must be very kindly disposed towards your master, when you want to prate such an intolerable nuisance round his neck.

AN. And you must be a good deal more kindly disposed towards your young mistress, when you grudge her so good a husband as Herr Damis will prove.

LIS. A good husband! Of a truth, a good husband is all she desires. A man who will permit everything——

AN. Ho, ho! Everything? Do you hear, Herr Damis, for what Lisette takes you? On this account you would like to be his wife yourself, I suppose? Everything, eh? That everything includes, I suppose. . . . . you understand me, of course?

DA. But in earnest, Lisette. Do you really believe your young lady will make a thoroughly bad wife? Has she truly many bad qualities?

LIS. Many? She has all that any one can have, not excepting those which contradict one another.

DA. Will you not give me a list of them?

LIS. What shall I begin with? She is silly.

DA. A trifle.

AN. And I say—a lie.

LIS. She is quarrelsome.

Da.   A trifle.

An.   And I say—a lie.

Lis.   She is vain.

Da.   A trifle.

An.   A lie ! say I.

Lis.   She is no housewife.

Da.   A trifle.

An.   A lie !

Lis.   By extravagant show, by constant pleasure parties, and feasts, she will ruin you.

Da.   A trifle.

An.   A lie.

Lis.   She will hang the anxiety of a host of children on your neck for you.

Da.   A trifle.

An.   The best wives are the first to do that.

Lis.   But children that are not your own.

Da.   A trifle.

An.   And a trifle, too, that is fashionable !

Lis.   A trifle? What do you mean, Herr Damis ?

Da.   I mean that Juliane cannot be bad enough. Is she silly? I am so much the more sensible. Is she quarrelsome? I am so much the calmer. Is she vain? I am so much the more philosophically minded. Is she lavish? She will cease when she has nothing more. Is she prolific? Then she will see what she can do when she tries to get the better of me. Let each immortalise itself as it can ; women through children, men through books.

An.   But don't you see that Lisette must have an object in slandering Juliane in this way.

Da.   Ah! Truly, I do perceive it. She does not grudge me to her, and therefore describes her completely in accordance with my taste. She has no doubt concluded that I will only marry her mistress because she is the most unbearable of girls.

Lis.   Only for that? Only for that? I have concluded that? I must have supposed you weak in the head, then. Just consider——

Da.   You go too far, Lisette ! Do not you give me credit for thinking at all? What I have said is the result of only too severe thought. Yes, it is settled. I mean to increase the number of the apparently unhappy learned, who have married bad wives. This resolution is not of to-day.

AN. Well, really! What is there the devil can't do? Whoever would have let himself dream of it, and now it is to become true. I must laugh; Lisette wanted to draw him out of the marriage and only urged him the more to it, and I wanted to urge him to it, and should soon have dissuaded him from it.

DA. One must marry some time or other. I cannot calculate on a thoroughly good wife; so I choose a thoroughly bad one. A wife of the ordinary kind, who is neither cold nor warm, neither very good nor very bad, is of no use to a learned man, of no use whatever. Who will concern himself about her after his death? And yet he deserves that his whole house shall be immortal with himself. If I can't have a wife who will one day find a place in a treatise *De bonis eruditorum uxoribus*, I will at least, have one with whose name an industrious man may enlarge his collection *De malis eruditorum uxoribus.* Yes, yes; besides I owe it to my father as his only son to take the most careful consideration for the maintenance of his name.

LIS. I can hardly get over my amazement. . . . . I have considered you, Herr Damis, such a great soul——

DA. And not wrongly. In this very matter I consider that I give the strongest proof of it.

LIS. I could almost burst! . . . . Yes, yes, the strongest proof that no one is so hard to catch as a young scholar. Not so much on account of his insight and shrewdness, as of his folly.

DA. What impertinence! A young scholar? a young scholar?

LIS. I will spare you the rebukes. Valer shall at once have intelligence of all. Your servant. (*Exit*).

SCENE XII.—ANTON, DAMIS.

AN. There, you see! She runs off now, as you won't dance to her piping.

DA. *Mulier, non homo !* I shall soon accept this paradox as truth. By what does one show that one is a human being? By reason. By what does one show that one has reason? When one knows how to value properly learning and the learned. A woman can never do this, and therefore she has no reason, and therefore is not a human being. Yes, indeed, yes. In this paradox lies more truth than in twenty manuals.

AN. What was I saying? Did not I tell you that Herr Valer has been asking for you? Won't you go and speak to him?

DA. Valer? I will wait for him. The time when he stood high in my estimation is past. He has laid his books aside for some years. He has had the notion put into his head that one must give oneself the last finish by social intercourse and knowledge of the world, to render useful service to the state. What more can I do than pity him? And yet I shall at last have to feel ashamed of him too. I shall have to feel ashamed of having ever held him worthy of my friendship. Oh, how fastidious one ought to be in one's friendships. Yet what has it availed me that I have been so in the highest degree? In vain have I avoided all acquaintance with mediocre persons, in vain have I striven to associate only with genius, only with original minds; notwithstanding this Valer deceived me under the mask of such a one. Oh Valer, Valer!

AN. Let it be loud enough, if he is to hear it.

DA. I could have burst with rage at his cold compliments. Of what did he speak with me? Of worthless trifles. And yet he came from Berlin, and might have been the first to inform me of the most pleasing of all news. Oh, Valer, Valer!

AN. Hush! He is coming, really. You see he does not let himself be called three times.

SCENE XIII.—DAMIS, VALER, ANTON.

VA. Pardon me, dearest friend, for disturbing you in your studious tranquillity——

AN. He had better say "idleness" at once.

DA. Disturbing? Do I imagine you would come to disturb me! No, Valer, I know you too well; you come to bring me the most pleasing news, which is worthy of

the attention of a scholar who is expecting his reward
. . . . . A chair, Anton ! . . . . . Sit down.

VA. You are mistaken, my dear friend. I come to
complain of your father's fickleness. I come to ask an
explanation from you, on which my whole happiness will
depend.

DA. Oh ! I could see at once from your manner that my
father's presence prevented you just now from speaking
to me more confidentially, and expressing your joy to me at
the honour which the just decision of the Academy——

VA. No, my all too learned friend ; let us speak for a
moment of something less indifferent.

DA. Something less indifferent ? Is my honour then
a matter of indifference to you ? False friend !

VA. That title will befit you if you divert me longer
from that which, for a tender heart, is all important.
Is it true that you wish to marry Juliane, and that
your father means to bind this too fond girl by bonds of
gratitude, to act less freely in her choice? Have I ever
made a secret with you of my love for Juliane? Have
you not always promised me to assist my love.

DA. You are getting warm, Valer, and forget that
the cause is a woman. Put this trifle out of your
thoughts . . . . . You must have been in Berlin when
the Academy adjudged the prize for this year. The
subject was "The Monads." Have not you chanced to
hear that the motto——

VA. How cruel you are, Damis ! Answer me, do.

DA. And you won't answer me? Think. Has not
the prize been assigned to the motto *Unum est necessarium ?*
I flatter myself at least——

VA. I shall soon flatter myself about nothing at all
when I see you so evasive. I shall soon have to believe,
too, that the report which I took for a joke of Lisette's is
true. You consider Juliane unworthy of you, you hold
her to be the shame of her sex, and for this very reason
you are going to marry her. What a monstrous idea !

DA. Ha, ha, ha !

VA. Yes, laugh on, Damis, laugh on. I am a fool for
being able to believe such folly of you for a moment.
Either you have made fun of Lisette, or she has made fun

of me. No! such a resolution could only enter a disordered brain! To hold it in abhorrence one needs only to think reasonably—far from nobly—as we know you are wont to think. But solve for me, I implore you, this torturing enigma.

Da. You will soon succeed, Valer, in drawing my attention to your gossip. So you really desire that I should subordinate my fame to your silly fancy? My fame! But in truth, I will rather believe you are joking. You wish to try if I, too, am unstable in my resolutions.

Va. I joking? Cursed be the joke which enters my mind!

Da. I shall be the better pleased if you will talk seriously. What I say to you is, the paper with the motto *Unum est necessarium*——

Scene XIV.—Chrysander, Damis, Valer, Anton.

Chrys. (*with a newspaper in his hand*). Well, is it not so, Herr Valer? my son is not to be dissuaded from the marriage. Don't you see that it is not so much I as he who is bent on this marriage?

Da. I! I am bent on the marriage?

Chrys. Hist! hist!

Da. What does "Hist! hist!" mean? My honour suffers in this. Might not people think that I cared, who knows how much, for a wife?

Chrys. Hist, hist!

Va. Oh, pray don't stand upon ceremony. I see it well enough! You are both against me. What ill-fortune it is which brought me into this house. I meet an amiable being, I please her, and yet I must after many hopes, in the end lose all hope. Damis, if I ever had any right to your friendship——

Da. But isn't it so, Valer? For one thing one must be angry with the Berlin Academy. Just think, in future the subjects for the prize essays will be made known two years previously. Why two years? Wasn't one enough? Does it take the Germans for such dawdlers? Since its revival, I have sent in my treatise every year, but, without boasting, I have never worked at any more than a week.

CHRYS. But do you know, you good people, what has occurred in the Netherlands? I have the very latest newspaper here. They have come to blows pretty smartly. But I really am quite angry with the allies. Haven't they made a strange business of it again?

AN. Now, there they are, all three talking about different things. The one talks of love, another of his treatises, and the third of war. If I, too, am to talk about anything special, it shall be about supper. To fast from mid-day till six o'clock in the afternoon is no joke.

VA. Unhappy love.

DA. That ill-advised Academy.

CHRYS. Those stupid allies.

AN. The fourth voice is still wanting;—those dawdling meat-jacks.

SCENE XV.—LISETTE, DAMIS, VALER, CHRYSANDER, ANTON.

LIS. Well, Herr Chrysander, I thought you were gone to call the gentlemen to supper, but I see you want to be called yourself. Supper is already on the table.

AN. It was high time. Heaven be praised!

CHRYS. Quite true, quite true, I had almost forgotten it altogether. The newsman stopped me on the stairs. Come, Herr Valer; we will consider the present state of the country together over a glass of something. Put Juliane out of your head. And you, my son, may chat with your bride. You will have a capital wife; not such a Xantippe as——

DA. Xantippe? How do you mean? Are you, too, still under the popular delusion that Xantippe was a bad wife?

CHRYS. Do you mean to consider her a good one, then? You surely are not going to defend Xantippe? Pshaw! That is an A, B, C blunder. I believe the more you learned ones learn the more you forget.

DA. I maintain, however, that you cannot produce a single valid piece of evidence for your view. That is the first thing which makes the whole matter suspicious, and for the rest——

LIS. This everlasting palaver.

CHRYS. Lisette is right. My son, *contra principia
negantem non est disputandum.* Come, come!

　　　　　　　　(*Exeunt* CHRYSANDER, DAMIS *and* ANTON.)

VA. Now all is over with me, Lisette. What am I to
do?

LIS. I know of nothing; unless the letter——

VA. This deceit would be too bad, and Juliane will
not agree to it.

LIS. Eh, deceit? If deceit is useful, it is admissible.
I see clearly I shall have to do it myself. Come away,
now, and take courage again. (*Exeunt.*)

ACT III.

SCENE I.—LISETTE, ANTON.

LIS. Wait, Anton, will you?

AN. Leave me alone. I do not want to have anything
to do with you.

LIS. Shan't we make it up again, then? Will not you
do what I asked you?

AN. I am to do something to please you?

LIS. Anton, dear Anton, darling Anton, do do it. How
easily you can give the old man the letter and tell him
the postman has brought it.

AN. Go, you serpent! (*Aside*) How she can wheedle
now! (*Aloud*) Don't stop me; I must fetch my master a
book. Let me go.

LIS. Fetch your master a book? What does he want
with a book at table?

AN. He finds the time long; and if he does not want
to be idle, he must make himself something to do, I
suppose.

LIS. He finds the time long? At table? Now if it
was in church. Don't they talk at all, then?

AN. Not a word. I am a rogue if a funeral meal could
go off as quietly.

LIS. At any rate, the old man will talk.

AN. He talks without talking. He eats and speaks at

once; and I believe he would give, who knows what, if
he could drink too as well, all three of them at once. The
newspaper lies by his plate, one eye is on this and the
other on that. He chews with one jaw and speaks with
the other. So of course it cannot be otherwise than that
his words should stick on what he is chewing, so that
with much difficulty one just hears him mutter.

Lis. But what are the rest doing?

An. The rest? Valer and Juliane look half-dead.
They don't eat and don't speak; they look at each other;
they sigh; they drop their eyes; they glance first at the
father, then at the son; they turn white; they turn red.
Both rage and despair glance from the eyes of both; but,
hurrah! quite right! Don't you see it can't go as you
want? My master will have Juliane, and if——

Lis. Yes, your master! But what is he doing?

An. Nothing but silly tricks. He scratches on his plate
with his fork; hangs his head; moves his mouth, as if he
were talking to himself, wabbles his chair about, then upsets
a wine glass, lets it lie, does not seem to notice anything
until the wine is going to run on to his clothes; he
flies into a passion and even says that I spilt it. But
enough chattering; he will swear at me if I don't fetch
him the book soon. I must look for it. It is on the table
at the right hand side, he says. Yes, on the right hand;
but which right hand does he mean? If I come so, this
is the right hand; if so, this; if I come this way, it is
this; and it is this, if I come like this (*approaching all four
sides of the table*). Tell me now, Lisette, which is the right
right hand?

Lis. I know that as little as you. Bother the book;
let him bring it himself. But, Anton, we are forgetting
the most important thing, the letter——

An. What, your letter again? Think. Am I to deceive
my master on your account?

Lis. But it shall be no loss to you.

An. Really? Isn't it my loss if I have to give up
what Chrysander has promised me?

Lis. But Valer promised you that you shall lose nothing.

An. Where does he promise me that, please?

Lis. Strange fellow! I promise it you in his name.

An. And even if you keep your word in his name, a lot I shall get ! No, no. A sparrow in the hand is better than a dove on the roof.

Lis. But if you are sure of catching the dove, it will be better than the sparrow, I suppose.

An. Sure of catching! As if everything let itself be caught. If I want to seize the dove, I must let the sparrow fly out of my hand. Eh?

Lis. Let it fly, then.

An. Good. And now suppose the dove, too, makes off. No, no, young woman, Anton is not so stupid as that.

Lis. What a childish fuss you do make! Think how fortunate you may be.

An. How, then? Let me hear.

Lis. Valer has promised to give me a dowry. What are a thousand thalers to such a capitalist?

An. Is that what you reckon on?

Lis. I take it at the lowest. He wouldn't let you go away empty-handed either, if you were helpful to me. Then I should have money, and you too would have money; couldn't we become a most charming couple?

An. We? A couple? Ah ! if my master hadn't hidden you.

Lis. Are not you downright silly? Why, I have told you all that passed between us. Your master, that dear book-worm !

An. Yes, those book-worms, too, are cursed animals. It is quite true a girl like you with a thousand thalers is worth at least a thousand thalers; but still that cabinet, that cabinet——

Lis. Do stop, Anton, and don't let one beg you so long.

An. But why won't you give the old man the letter yourself?

Lis. I have told you the reasons for that; Chrysander could so easily suspect——

An. Yes, yes, you little monkey, I see it well enough; you want to have the chestnuts out of the ashes, and you use a cat's paw for them.

Lis. Very well, my dear puss, do it, then.

An. How she does get over one! Dear puss! Well, give it here—the letter, give it me.

Lis. There, my incomparable Anton.

An. But it is all right about the dowry, I suppose?——

Lis. Rely on it——

An. And about my reward besides?

Lis. That it is.

An. Very well, the letter will be delivered.

Lis. But as soon as possible.

An. At once, if you like. Come! . . . . . My stars. who is coming? The deuce! It is Damis.

SCENE II.—DAMIS, ANTON, LISETTE.

Da. Where is that rascal dawdling with the book?

An. I was just going to, I was. . . . . Lisette and . . . . . in short, Herr Damis, I can't find it.

Da. Not find it! Why, I told you on which side it was?

An. On the right hand, you certainly did say; but not on which right hand. And that is what I was just coming to ask you.

Da. You blockhead, can't you guess that I speak of the side where I sit?

An. That is true, too, Lisette; and we have been cracking our brains over this! Herr Damis is really cleverer than we are (*makes a long nose behind Damis's back*). Now I shall find it, I suppose. Bound in white with red edges, is it not? Go, please, I will bring it at once.

Da. Yes, it is time now, when we have already risen from table.

An. Already? The deuce, I have not had enough yet. Have you all got up.

Da. My father will still be there, learning the newspaper by heart, that he may play the politician at his club to-morrow. Go at once if you think you can be filled with his political scraps. But what does Lisette want here?

Lis. Am I not as bearable now as I was before?

Da. No, assuredly not. I thought before that Lisette had at least so much sense that her chatter could be bearable for a quarter of an hour; but I was mistaken. She is as stupid as the rest of the household.

Lis. I have the honour to give thanks in the name of all the others.

An. The deuce! Why, that is quite a different tone. Heaven grant they may have a good quarrel. But I should not care to listen. . . . . Lisette, I'll go at once.

Lis. (*aside to him*). Don't forget the letter; be quick about it.

Da. So. Have you to ask Lisette for permission? I order you; stay where you are. I should like to know where you had to go.

An. To the post, Herr Damis, to the post.

Da. Ah! that's true; go then, go.

Scene III.—Damis, Lisette.

Da. Lisette can also take herself off at once. Is my room never to be empty to-day? First that man is here, then this; then this woman, then that. Am I not to be alone a moment? (*seats himself at the table*). The Muses demand solitude, and nothing chases them away sooner than a tumult. I have so much, and such important business, that I don't know where to begin first, and yet people disturb me. The greater part of the afternoon has been spent on such a worthless matter as marriage. Is my evening, too, to be snatched away through this eternal running in and out? I believe that in no household can idleness reign as in this.

Lis. And particularly in this room.

Da. In this room? Uneducated, ignorant girl.

Lis. Is that reproach or praise?

Da. What a low-minded being! To think of deeming ignorance and stupidity no reproach! No reproach? I should just like to know what conceptions of shame and honour such a deranged babbler has. Perhaps we shall hear that with her learning is a reproach.

Lis. Certainly, if it is always of the same stamp as in you.

Da. No, that it is not; very few have carried it so far——

Lis. That one cannot decide whether they are foolish or learned?

Da. I could go out of my mind——

Lis. Do it, and get into a wiser one.

Da. How long shall I yet be exposed to the abuse of this most worthless creature?. . . . . Thousands would count themselves happy if they had only the tenth part of my deserts. I am only twenty years of age, and how many should I find who, with almost three times these years, are yet. . . . . But I speak in vain. What honour can it bring me to convince an idiotic creature of my ability. I understand seven languages perfectly, and am only twenty years old. On the whole compass of history, and all branches of knowledge allied to it, I am without equal——

Lis. And you are only twenty years old.

Da. How strong I am in philosophy is proved by the high degree which I attained even three years ago. The world will recognise it yet more unmistakeably in my treatise on Monads. . . . . Ah! that confounded post.

Lis. And you are only twenty years old.

Da My satirical panegyric on "The Nymph of Posterity," can give an everlasting proof of my more than Demosthenic eloquence.

Lis. And you are only twenty years old.

Da. In poetry too, I may fairly reach out my hand towards the most imperishable laurels. In comparison with me, Milton shrinks to nothing, and Haller beside me is a mere babbler. My friends to whom hitherto I have often read over my attempts, as I am pleased to call them, will now hear no more of them, and always assure me most sincerely that they are already sufficiently convinced of my more than godlike poetical vein.

Lis. And you are only twenty years old.

Da. In short, I am a philologist, an historian, a philosopher, an orator, a poet——

Lis. And you are only twenty years old! A beardless philosopher, and an orator who is not yet of age; beautiful rarities.

Da. Be off! Out of my room this instant.

Lis. This instant? I should like so much to bring in that nice sentence once more—and you are only twen' . . .

years old. Have you nothing more to say in your own
praise? Oh, something more! Won't you? Then I'll do
it myself. Listen well, Herr Damis: you are not yet wise,
and you are already twenty years old!

Da. What? How? (*Gets up angrily*).

Lis. Good-bye, good-bye!

Da. Good Heavens! What one has to endure from
these uneducated brutes! Is it possible that an ignorant
female——

Scene IV.—Chrysander, Anton, Damis.

Chrys. This is an accursed letter, Anton. Eh, eh! My
son, my son, *post cœnam stabis, vel passus mille meabis.* You
surely are not going to sit down again so soon?

Da. Others, who have nothing to do, may trouble
themselves about such barbarous rules of health. Important business——

Chrys. What have *you* got to say about important
business?

Da. I? Why not, father? Most of the books which you
see here on the table are waiting, some for my notes, some
for my translation, some for my refutation, some for my
defence, and some also for my mere opinion.

Chrys. Let them wait. Now——

Da. Now I really can't do everything at once. If I
could only get the most important of them settled. You
have no idea, what investigation and brain-racking a
certain inquiry here costs me. A single trifle is still
wanting to enable me to prove that Cleopatra applied
the snakes to her arm and not to her breast——

Chrys. Snakes don't do much good anywhere. One
almost crept into my bosom, too, a short time ago; but
there is still time. Listen a moment, my son; I have here
received a letter which——

Da. How? A letter? A letter? My dear Anton, a
letter. My dearest father, a letter? From Berlin? Don't
keep me in suspense any longer. Where is it? Now you
will cease to doubt, will you not, of my ability? How
happy I am! Anton, do you, too, know already what it
contains?

Chrys. What means this extravagance? The letter is

not from Berlin; it is from my lawyer in Dresden, and from what he writes your marriage with Juliane can come to nothing.

DA. Worthless fellow! So you haven't been to the post yet?

AN. Why I have told you that before nine o'clock there is nothing for me to go to the post for.

DA. Ah! *Verberabilissime, non fur, sed trifur !* Heavens, that through anger, I should have to use even the abusive language of Plautus. Will a fruitless run kill you, then?

AN. Are you abusing me? As I have not understood it, let it pass.

CHRYS. But just tell me, Damis; you still have a little feeling of repugnance to Juliane, haven't you? If that is so I will not force you. You must know I am not one of those fathers——

DA. Is marriage again on the carpet so soon? If only you would not trouble yourself about my repugnance. Enough, I marry her——

CHRYS. That means, you are going to force yourself to do so on my account. I will not have that at all. If you are my son, you are still a man; and every man is born free; he must be able to do as he pleases; and . . . . . in short, I give you your word back again.

DA. Back again? And a few hours ago I could not make up my mind fast enough for you. How am I to understand that?

CHRYS. You are to understand it in this way, that I have considered it, and that since Juliane does not please you she does not suit me either; that I have learned what her real circumstances are from this letter, and that . . . . . You see of course that I have only just received the letter. Indeed, I don't really know what I am to think of it? It is not my lawyer's own handwriting, certainly. (DAMIS *seats himself at the table again.*)

AN. Not? Oh, the good people must know how to write more than one hand.

CHRYS. It is almost too soon, as well. It is scarcely eight days since I wrote to him. Can he have inquired into the matter already, in so short a time? From whom did you get the letter, Anton?

An. From Lisette.

Chrys. And Lisette?

An. From the postman, no doubt.

Chrys. But why doesn't the fellow bring the letters to me himself?

An. They could not alter themselves in the hands they pass through, could they?

Chrys. One doesn't know. . . . . The reasons, however, which he brings forward are worth listening to. So I must take the safest road, I suppose; and to you, my son . . . . but I do believe you have seated yourself at the table again, and are studying.

Da. Good Heavens! I have work to do; I have a great deal of work to do.

Chrys. Well, then, in a word, in order not to waste your time, the marriage with Juliane was nothing but an idea which you may forget again. When I come to consider it rightly, Valer has indeed the best right to her.

Da. You deceive yourself if you think that I shall withdraw from it now. I have carefully considered everything, and I must tell you in quite plain words that a bad wife shall aid me to make my fame immortal, or rather that I will make a bad wife, who would not be thought of if she had not married a learned man, immortal together with myself. The character of such a wedded fiend will throw a certain light on mine——

Chrys. Well, well, take a bad wife, then; but take one with money, for with such a one the wickedness is still bearable. My first wife, of pious memory, was one of that sort. For the twenty thousand thalers, which I got with her, I would have married the foul fiend's sister. You must not misunderstand me, I don't mean it literally. But if your wife is to be a bad one, what do you want with Juliane? Listen; I know an old widow, who has quarrelled four husbands into the grave. She has plenty to live on; I should think she would suit you, take her! I made your mouth water, I must therefore put something into it. If you must have a Xantippe you can find no better one.

Da. Bother Xantippe! I have told you more than once that Xantippe was not a bad wife. Have you forgotten the grounds of my evidence again already?

CHRYS. Eh? What? My evidence is the A B C book. He who could write a book, that has become so popular, must have understood the matter better than you. And, in short, it is of importance to me for Xantippe to be a bad wife. I could not be at peace with myself if I had praised my first wife so often. So be silent with your foolery; I don't care to be taught by you.

DA. Those are the thanks we get when we try to help people out of their errors.

CHRYS. Since when, then, has the egg been wiser than the hen, eh? Herr Doctor, do not forget that I am the father, and that it depends on the father when the son shall marry. I will not have Juliane thought of any more.

DA. And why not?

CHRYS. Shall I encumber my only son with a penniless girl? You are not worth the trouble I take about you. You know, of course, that she has no property?

DA. Had she more before, when I was to marry her, than now!

CHRYS. You don't understand it. I knew what I was doing before; but I also know what I am doing now.

DA. If she has no money it is so much the better. People won't be able to accuse me then of having taken a bad wife for the sake of her money. They will have to admit that I had no other object than that of exercising myself in the virtues which are required for enduring such a wife.

CHRYS. Such a wife! Who has told you that Juliane will be a bad wife?

DA. If I were not convinced of it *a priori*, as we scholars are wont to say, I might have concluded it from the fact that you are in doubt about it.

CHRYS. That's nice impertinence, my son! nice impertinence! I have brought up Juliane; she has enjoyed much kindness at my hands. I have instructed her in all that is good. He who speaks evil of her speaks evil of me likewise. What? *I* not know how to bring up a girl? *I* have not brought up a girl who has grown up under my care that she will make a good, honest wife! It is true I have not been able to make her rich; I myself am still

in need of this blessing. But that I have not made her
virtuous, and sensible, only one who is as stupid as you,
my son, can say of me. Don't take it ill that I speak out.
You are such a dried fool, such a stockfish . . . . . don't
take it ill of me, my son . . . . . such an overworked
smoked herring . . . . . but don't take it ill of me——

DA. (*aside*). I shall believe directly that his first
business was in the salt-fish line. . . . . (*aloud*). Very
well, father; I will say nothing of Juliane's virtue.
Virtue is often a species of stupidity. But as for her good
sense, you must allow me still to have doubts on that head.
I have been back here again now for a considerable time,
I have also taken the trouble sometimes to speak a word or
two to her. But has she ever once turned her thoughts to
my learning, do you think? I don't care to be praised; I
am not so vain; but one must let people have their due——

SCENE V.—CHRYSANDER, DAMIS, VALER.

CHRYS. Good, Herr Valer, good! You come just in the
nick of time.

DA. What does this intolerable man want here again?

VA. I come to take leave of you both——

CHRYS. Take leave? So early? Why then?

VA. I don't believe you ask that in earnest.

CHRYS. God knows, Herr Valer, I am in most earnest
earnest. I certainly won't let you go.

VA. In order to torture me more cruelly still? You
know how dear to me the being whom you take from me
to-day has always been. But the misfortune would be
small if it fell on me alone. Are you going to unite
this beloved being to one who hates her as much as I
adore her? My whole soul is full of despair, and from
this time forth I shall neither here, nor anywhere else in
the world, become tranquil again. I go to——

CHRYS. Don't go, Herr Valer, don't go! The evil may
perhaps be remedied yet!

VA. Remedied? You insult me if you believe that I
can ever recover this blow. It would be a mortal one to
a less tender heart than mine.

DA. What twaddle! (*Seats himself at the table.*)

VA. How fortunate you are, Damis. Learn at any rate, to recognise your good-fortune; it is the least thanks that you owe to Heaven. Juliane will be yours——

CHRYS. Eh? Who says so? She shall be yours soon enough, Herr Valer; only have patience!

VA. Cease your cold scoffing——

CHRYS. Scoffing? You must know me but little. What I say, I say. I have considered the matter again; I see that Juliane does not suit my son, and he suits Juliane still less. You love her; you have been suing me for her a long time; first come, first served. I have just spoken about it to my son. . . . . You know him——

VA. Heavens, what do I hear! Is it possible? What a happy change! Allow me to embrace you a thousand times. Then I am to be happy after all? Oh, Chrysander! Oh, Damis!

CHRYS. Talk to him, and bring him to reason. I will go to Juliane and inform her of my altered resolution. She won't take it ill of me, will she?

VA. Take it ill? You will give her life again, as you have given it me.

CHRYS. Eh? Can I? (*Exit.*)

SCENE VI.—DAMIS, VALER, ANTON.

VA. And in what terms shall I address you, dearest friend? The renewal of your father's promise would justify me in passing you over altogether. I have won, as soon as ever Chrysander ceases to use pressure on Juliane. But how agreeable it will be to me if I can thank you in part for my possession of her.

DA. Anton!

AN. (*comes forward*). What about him? Has the post come into your head again?

DA. Go at once! It must certainly have come in.

AN. But I tell you, it can't come before ten o'clock in such bad weather.

DA. Do you add on another hour? Go, without further words! And if you come back with nothing, take care for yourself.

AN. If I don't sleep sound to-night, I shall never

believe again as long as I live that weariness can help to make me do so. (*Exit.*)

Scene VII.—Damis, Valer.

Va. Well! instead of answering, you speak with your servant!

Da. Pardon me, Valer; you spoke to me, did you? My mind is full; it is impossible for me to hear everything.

Va. So you want to dissemble with me, too? I remember the time very well when I was under the same strange delusion, and thought it showed one's learning to be as abstracted as possible and attend to nothing but one's book. But, believe me, he must be very simple whom you expect to deceive with this humbug.

Da. And you must be still simpler if you believe any other head is as empty of ideas as your own. And does your twaddle deserve that I should listen to it? You have won, as soon as Chrysander ceases to use pressure on Juliane; you are justified you know in passing me over.

Va. That must be a curious sort of abstraction, I think, in which a man hears what another says so exactly that he can repeat it word for word.

Da. Your jesting is very sorry (*looks again at his book.*)

Va. But still to be felt!. . . . . What a torture it is to have to do with a man like you? There are few such——

Da. That I believe myself.

Va. But there would be more if——

Da. Quite so; if true learning were not so hard to attain, if the natural capacity for it were commoner, and untiring industry not such a toilsome thing——

Va. Ha, ha, ha!

Da. The laugh of a real idiot!

Va. You speak of your learning, and I, pardon me, was going to speak of your folly. In this I meant there would be more like you if this same folly did not become a burden to its slaves.

DA.   Do you deserve that I should answer you? (*Looks at the book again.*)

VA.   And do you deserve that I should still be friend enough to speak to you without dissimulation. Believe me, when you have more sense you will repent of your follies——

DA.   When I have more sense? (*Scornfully.*)

VA.   Are you indignant at that? This is strange! With your years your body cannot yet be full-grown, and you think, nevertheless, that your mind has already attained its highest possible perfection? I should consider him my enemy who would deny me the privilege of increasing my intelligence day by day.

DA.   You?

VA.   You become so scornful, my rival. . . . . but there she is herself! (*runs towards her*) Oh, Juliane——

SCENE VIII.—JULIANE, DAMIS, VALER.

JU.   Oh, Valer! What a happy change!

DA.   (*turning in his chair.*) I have doubtless, Mademoiselle, to thank an error for the honour of seeing you here. You perhaps think that you are entering your own chamber.

JU.   That error would be unpardonable! No, sir, it happens by order of your father that I set foot on this sacred spot. I come to retract a bargain with you, and to beg your Muse's pardon for having almost run the risk of alienating so amiable a soul from her.

VA.   How delighted I am, lovely Juliane, to see you in your playful mood again.

DA.   If I rightly understand a girl's rubbish you come to annul a *pactum*, which has nevertheless all the *requisita* which are demanded for an irrevocable *pactum*.

JU.   And if I may understand the gibberish of a young scholar you have hit the mark.

DA.   My father is an idiot. Is it in his or your power alone, Mademoiselle, to annul an agreement which remains firm on my side? . . . . . We shall see. Now might I beg of you to leave me in quiet. (*Turns to the table again.*)

Va. What behaviour! Did any man ever behave so to a girl to whose possession he lays claim?

Da. And has any one ever been so troublesome to a busy scholar? To get quit of this vexatious company I must myself leave my four walls. (*Exit.*)

Scene IX.—Valer, Juliane.

Ju. And we do not laugh at him?

Va. No, Juliane; may a better joy fill our hearts now; and besides there is a sort of cruelty in making ourselves merry over so pitiable a fool. How shall I describe to you the emotions of my heart, now, when all its happiness has been given back to it? I implore you, Juliane, if you love me, leave this dangerous house this very day with me. Do not any longer expose yourself to the vehemence of a changeable old man, the ravings of a young pedant, and the weakness of your own too gentle disposition. You have been taken from me and given back in one day; let it be the first and last which shall play with us so cruelly.

Ju. Be calm, Valer. Let us not do anything which might draw down reproaches on us from Chrysander. You see he is in the right way; and I love him as much as I despise Damis. I should ill repay his kindness by mistrustfully suddenly withdrawing myself from his care.

Va. You still speak of kindness always? I shall not feel at peace until I have freed you from these dangerous bonds. Permit me to annihilate them entirely, and as for the selfish old man——

Ju. Do not call him that, Valer; he is not so; and his change of mind already shows that Lisette was wrongly informed, or has deceived us. Indeed, I don't know to whom I ought to ascribe this change. . . . . (*Reflecting.*)

Va. Why so thoughtful all at once? The cause which moved him may be what it will. I know, at any rate, that it is a dispensation of Providence.

Ju. Of Providence, or else of Lisette! It now suddenly occurs to me what she said about a letter. Could Lisette's excessive zeal——

VA. What imagination, dearest Juliane! Why, she knows that your good principles will not consent to this petty deceit.

JU. Nevertheless, the more I think of it——

VA. Even if it were so, would you on this account——

JU. Even if it were so? How?

SCENE X.—LISETTE, VALER, JULIANE.

JU. You come as if called, Lisette.

LIS. Well? Don't my affairs go on excellently? Won't you come down with me and listen how Damis and Chrysander are quarrelling? "You shall not have her;" "I must have her;" "I am your father;" "You have promised her to me;" "I have changed my mind;" "I have not, so it must go on;" "That is impossible;" "Impossible or not. . . . . in short, I won't withdraw; I will prove to you from books that you must keep your word with me;" "You and your books may go to the deuce." Why do I repeat so much of their silly talk? The father is right; he manages cleverly; but he certainly wouldn't manage so cleverly if I had not been so clever first.

JU. How do you mean that, Lisette?

LIS. I don't like praising myself. Briefly, my dear mistress, I am your guardian angel!

JU. You? And how, then?

LIS. By paying a deceiver in his own coin. The horrid old——

JU. And so you have deceived Chrysander?

LIS. Don't say that. One does not deceive a deceiver, one only gets the better of him. I have got the better of him.

VA. How?

LIS. It is bad enough that you have forgotten it again already. I should imagine that to be grateful people would require a better memory.

JU. You have, then, actually palmed off the false letter on him, I suppose?

LIS. Heaven forbid! I have merely sought to change his mind by a forged letter, and I have succeeded in it.

JU. You have done that? And I owe my happiness

to a deceiver? Let the result be what it will, Chry
sander shall hear of it at once.

Lis. What does that mean? Are these the thanks 1
get?

Va. Consider, Juliane! Stay.

Ju. Impossible, Valer; let me go. (*Exit* Julianz.)

Scene XI.—Valer, Lisette.

Va. Heavens! Now all is over again.

Lis. Well, she may have her way! I could spit poison
and gall, I feel so wild! To call me a deceiver in return
for my good-will! I hoped she would fall on my neck
for joy. . . . . How the old man will storm at me! He
will drive me and you out of the house. What do you
propose to do now?

Va. Ah! What am I to do now, Lisette?

Lis. I think you answer me with my own question!
That is easy. I have come to the end of my good advice.
I'm likely to meddle in such a business again soon!

Va. But at what an unlucky moment, too, you came,
Lisette. I had told you that Juliane would not consent
to this trick. Couldn't you have held your tongue a while
longer?

Lis. Could I imagine that she would be so extra-
ordinarily obstinate? You can easily fancy how it is with
people of my sort: if you had given me ever so much,
I could not have concealed from her any longer that
she owed her happiness to me: Joy is talkative, and
. . . . . Oh, I should like——

Scene XII.—Anton, Valer, Lisette.

An. (*with letters in his hand*). Ha, ha! You are holding
a meeting again! If my master knew what wicked
plots were being laid against him in his own room, he
would, Lisette. . . . . But how queerly you are standing there together! Herr Valer looks troubled; you are
fiery, as fiery as a turkey-cock. Have you been fighting, or otherwise taking exercise? Eh, eh? Lisette,
listen. . . . . (*in a low voice to* Lisette). You surely

haven't fallen out with him about the dowry? He hasn't
withdrawn his promise, has he? That would be a cursed
trick. (*Aloud*). No, no, Herr Valer, what a man promises
that he must keep to. She has served you well, and so
have I. The deuce! Do you suppose, then, people of
honourable mind will feel no qualms of conscience, when
they have deceived their masters for nothing at all? I
am not going to let myself be humbugged, and my claim
at any rate. . . . . Devil take me! I'll employ a lawyer,
a regular bulldog of a lawyer, who you may be sure shall
give you so much to do——

LIS. Oh! be quiet, fool.

VA. What do you mean? Whom are you speaking
to?

AN. My stars! I am speaking to our debtor. You
might understand that by my tone I should think.

VA. And who then is your debtor?

AN. Does it come now to this, that you want to deny
the debt? Listen; my lawyer will put you on your
oath——

VA. Lisette, do you know what he means?

LIS. The madman! I wanted him just now to deliver
the letter, and promised him a reward from you, if the
matter turned out well.

VA. Nothing more?

AN. I should have thought that was enough, though.
And how does it stand with Lisette's dowry? I must take
as much care about her property as about mine, since it is
going to be mine, you know.

VA. Don't be uneasy. If I attain my happiness I
certainly won't forget yours.

AN. But suppose you don't? A promise is still a
promise.

VA. Even in that case I will not leave your zeal unrewarded.

AN. Oh, that is fine talk, fine talk.

LIS. Just be quiet, do.

AN. What a fool you are; I am speaking for you, too.

LIS. But it is quite unnecessary.

AN. Unnecessary? Haven't you been quarrelling?

LIS. Well, why not?

An. Hasn't he withdrawn his promise?

Lis. No.

An. Oh then, pardon me, Herr Valer. Anger can easily seize an honest man. I am a little hasty, especially in money matters. Don't be afraid of the lawyer.

Va. Can I linger here any longer in such torturing uncertainty? I must speak to her; perhaps she hasn't done it yet.

Lis. But if she has done it, don't you go too near the old man.

Va. I have known nothing of the whole affair.

Lis. So much the worse, then, for me. Go along.

Scene XIII.—Anton, Lisette.

An. So much the worse for you? What, then, is so much the worse for you? Why mustn't he go near the old man? What are you up to, again.

Lis. That confounded letter.

An. What letter.

Lis. The one I gave you just now.

An. What about it?

Lis. It is all in vain; my trouble is for nothing.

An. How so? As I live I have delivered it properly. Don't talk any nonsense and shift the blame on to me.

Lis. It was delivered right enough; and it has already had its effect, too. But Juliane has herself upset the calculation. She insists on letting the old man know that the letter was forged, and has probably done it already.

An. What the deuce! She herself? We shall fare nicely. You see, the sparrow and the dove are gone now. And the worst of all is that, while I was going to catch the dove, I have tumbled into the mud. Or, to speak to you plainly, and without metaphor, I have lost the promised reward from the old man, and the imagined one from Valer escapes me too, and all the profit I shall make out of this business is a "To the devil with you," accompanied by a gracious poke in the ribs. . . . . Will you still take me after that, Miss Lisette? Oh, you must. I'll teach you to make people unfortunate——

Lis. I shall be better off, of course? We take our road

together, and when we are once united, you will have to
see how you will maintain me.

AN.   Maintain you? In these hard times? If I could
only go round with you, like the man with the big beast
that has a horn on its nose.

LIS.   Don't distress yourself, I'll soon turn you into a
beast with a horn. It will amount to the same thing, I
suppose, whether you go round with me, or I with you.

AN.   Well, certainly, with you one knows, at any rate,
where one is. . . . . But, not to mix things up, where is
my master? Here at last are his confounded letters.

LIS.   Do you see him?

AN.   No; but if I don't mistake, I hear him now.

LIS.   Just let him come; I will make him mad yet, to
finish up with.

SCENE XIV.—ANTON, LISETTE, DAMIS (*advances in deep
thought;* LISETTE *slips behind him and imitates his gestures*).

AN.   Stay! I will keep him on the hook a little longer,
and not give him the letters at once. (*Hides them.*) Why
so lost in thought, Herr Damis? What have you on your
mind again?

DA.   Hold your tongue.

AN.   That's a short answer! But shall not a servant
be anxious about his master? It would be quite reasonable too for me also to know what you were thinking of. Even a blind hen sometimes finds a grain, and
perhaps I might——

DA.   Silence!

AN.   That's a still shorter answer. If it gradually
decreases in this way, I shall see presently what is left.
What are you reckoning on your fingers? What has your
poor nail done to you that you bite it so? (*Sees* LISETTE.)
And, the deuce! what sort of ape is that? Are you mad?

LIS.   Hold your tongue.

AN.   For Heaven's sake go! If my master wakes out
of his sleep and sees you——

LIS.   Silence!

AN.   Are you making fun of me or of my master? Just
look behind you, Herr Damis.

DA.   (*walks up and down a few times in deep thought,*

Lisette *in the same fashion behind him; and when he turns she slips round quickly, so that he does not see her).*

" The flame of my marriage-torch
  Shall now by myself be sung."

An. Ho, ho! you are making verses? Come, Lisette, we must leave him alone now. On occasions like this he has already kicked me out of the room, more than once. Come; he is sure to call us back again, himself, as soon as he is done, and perhaps the whole house as well.

Lis. (*While* Damis *turns, she remains motionless in front of him, and assumes his tone.*)

" The flame of my marriage-torch
  Shall now by myself be sung."

(Damis *pretends not to see her, and runs against her.*)

Da. What's that?

Lis. What's that? (*Both as if they were coming to themselves*).

Da. Ignorant, low-minded fellow! Haven't I told you often enough to let no one into my room, or at the most only my father. What does she want here?

Lis. Ignorant, low-minded fellow! Haven't you told me often enough that I must leave the room? But can't you imagine that she who has been allowed to be in the cabinet, will also have permission to be in the room? Ignorant, low-minded fellow!

An. Which am I to answer now?

Da. Turn her out of the room at once.

An. Turn her out? By force?

Da. If she won't go quietly——

An. Lisette, go quietly——

Lis. As soon as it suits me.

Da. Turn her out, I say.

An. Come, Lisette, give me your hand; I will lead you out with all ceremony.

Lis. You bear! Who would presume to lead a girl with uncovered hands?

An. Oh, I know how to behave, too! In the absence of a glove . . . . . (*takes the lappet of his waistcoat*). May I have the honour——

DA. I see clearly I shall myself have to——(*rushes at her*).

LIS. Ha, ha, ha! I only wanted to make you do it! Good-bye. (*Exit.*)

SCENE XV.—ANTON, DAMIS.

DA. Now all my thoughts are scattered again! The fire is gone out. The imaginative power is dispersed. The god who must inspire us has deserted me. . . . . The cursed creature! What vexation she has caused me to-day. How scoffingly she has behaved to me. Heavens! To mimic me so ridiculously in my reverie.

AN. But you didn't see it, you know.

DA. I didn't see it?

AN. Did you? Is it possible? And you only pretended that?

DA. Silence, idiot! I'll see if I can bring myself again into the ecstasy.

AN. You had better not do so; the verses over which one looks so black, cannot possibly turn out well. But mayn't one know what it is going to be? An evening song, or a morning song?

DA. Blockhead!

AN. A penitential song.

DA. Ninny!

AN. A feasting song! Not that, either! . . . . You surely are not going to make a dirge? As I am an honest man, if I were ever so great a poet, I would leave them unmade. Dying is the most absurd trick that a man can play himself. It doesn't deserve a verse, let alone a song.

DA. I must have pity on your ignorance. You know no other sort of poems than those you have met with in your hymn-book.

AN. There are others, then, I suppose? Let me hear what you compose.

DA. I am composing . . . . . an *Epithalamium*.

AN. An *Epithalamium*. My stars! That's a difficult thing! And can you really manage that? Art is wanted for that. . . . . But, Herr Damis, in confidence, what is an *Epith—pitha—thlamium?*

DA. How can you say that it is difficult, if you don't know yet what it is?

AN. Eh? Why, the word is quite hard enough. Just tell me what it is under some other name.

DA. An *Epithalamium* is a *Thalassio*.

AN. Oh, ah! Now I understand. An *Epithalamium* is a . . . . . what do you call it?

DA. *Thalassio*.

AN. A *Thalassio*; and you can make that? You will want a good deal of time for that, at any rate. But, I say, if any one asks me now what a *Thalassio* is, what am I to answer?

DA. Then you don't know what a *Thalassio* is, either?

AN. I for my part know well enough. A *Thalassio* is an . . . . . what do you call the other word?

DA. *Epithalamium*.

AN. Is an *Epithalamium*. And an *Epithalamium* is a *Thalassio*? Haven't I remembered it correctly, eh? But then that might not be clear to other people, who don't understand either word.

DA. Well, then, tell them a *Thalassio* is a *Hymenæus*.

AN. The deuce! That is giving people trouble. An *Epithalamium* is a *Thalassio*, and a *Thalassio* is a *Hymenæus*. And so, the other way, a Hym—hym. . . . . The deuce may remember the names.

DA. Right, right. I see, though, that you are beginning to attain a conception of things.

AN. I a conception of this? As I am an honest man, you are mistaken. A goblin must have whispered it to me if I know what those outlandish words mean. Tell me their English names; or havn't they any?

DA. They have one, truly, but it is far removed from the grace and expressiveness of the Greek or Latin. Just say yourself whether a "Marriage poem" does not sound much poorer than an *Epithalamium*, a *Hymenæus*, a *Thalassio*.

AN. Not to me; certainly not to me. For I understand one and not the other. So you have been desiring to compose a marriage poem. Why didn't you say that at once? . . . . Oh! I have an acquaintance with marriage poems which is astonishing. I must just tell you how I

came by it. My lately deceased father had a cousin. . . . . .
and so, in some degree, he was my cousin too——

DA. What rubbish is coming?

AN. You won't wait for it? Well. It is your loss.
So to proceed; you were going to compose verses on a
marriage? But on what marriage?

DA. What a question! On my own.

AN. So you are still going to marry Juliane. The old
man won't have it, you know!

DA. Oh! He!

AN. Quite true. Why should a son trouble himself
about his father? But tell me, is it becoming for one to
compose verses on one's own marriage?

DA. It certainly is not usual; but so much the better.
Minds like mine love the peculiar.

AN. (*aside*). Hist! I'll play him a trick now. . . .
(*Aloud.*) I say, Herr Damis, I would myself gladly see you
marry Juliane.

DA. Why so?

AN. I don't know whether I dare make so bold as to
tell you. I have. . . . . I have myself——

DA. Out with it.

AN. I have myself tried to make verses on your
marriage, and therefore I should not like that my trouble
should be lost.

DA. They must be something splendid!

AN. Certainly! For that is my failing; I either do
something excellent or else nothing at all.

DA. Give it me. Perhaps I may improve your rhymes,
so that they may do honour to both of us.

AN. Listen; I will read them over to you. (*Feels for
a scrap of paper in his pocket.*) I must tell you, I have not
quite finished it yet. But the beginning, out of which one
can always make the end, runs thus. . . . . Push the
light a little nearer to me. . . . .

> *Thou, oh noble skill,*
> *For our proposèd end,*
> *Effective means.* . . . .

DA. Stop! You are a miserable bungler. Ha, ha!
That "Thou oh" is quite useless. "Noble skill" says

no less, and "Thou, oh noble skill" no more. *Deleatur
ergo*, "Thou, oh." But that there should not be two
syllables wanting, strengthen the epithet noble, after
the manner of the Greeks, and say "super-noble." I am
quite aware that "super-noble" is a new word; but I
know too that it is new words which most chiefly distinguish poetry from prose. Remember these little dodges.
You must by all means strive to say something unheard
of, something that has not yet been said. Do you understand me, you stupid devil?

AN.   I will hope so.

DA.   Then your first verse is, *Super-noble skill*, and so on.
Now read further.

AN.   *For our proposèd end*
             Effective means to send,
             And, when the hour doth will,
             With thy own strength to strive,
             Shalt, till this planet's ball
             To its first Cha—Cha—Chaos fall,
             Like to a poplar thrive.

But, Herr Damis, can't you tell me what it was I thought
of here? Confound it! That is fine; I don't understand
it myself any more, "To its first Cha—Chaos. I
should never have thought I had the word in my mouth,
it sounds so dreadful to me.

DA.   Show it——

AN.   Wait, wait! I will read it over to you once more.

DA.   No, no; hand me the paper.

AN.   You can't possibly read it. I have written much
too badly; not a letter stands upright. They are all
jumping on one another's backs.

DA.   Give it me!

AN.   (*gives him the paper trembling*). The deuce! It is
his own writing.

DA.   (*looks at it for a time*). What does this mean?
(*Jumps up angrily.*) Cursed traitor, whence did you get
this leaf?

AN.   Not so angry; not so angry!

DA.   Whence did you get it?

AN.   Are you going to throttle me?

DA.   Whence did you get that leaf, I ask?

                                        H 2

AN. Let me go first.

DA. Confess.

AN. From. . . . . from your. . . . . waistcoat-pocket.

DA. Untaught brute! Is that your honesty? That is a theft, a *plagium*.

AN. The deuce! To make a thief of me for such a trifle!

DA. Trifle? What! Call the commencement of a didactic philosophical poem a trifle?

AN. You said yourself it was good for nothing.

DA. Yes, in so far as it was intended for a marriage-cantata, and in so far as you were composer of it. At once produce the other manuscripts which you have stolen from me of late. Am I to see my work in the hands of strangers? Am I to permit a hideous jackdaw to adorn himself with my beauteous peacock plumes? Out with them quickly, or I shall adopt other measures.

AN. What do you want? I haven't got a single letter more of yours.

DA. Turn all your pockets inside out at once.

AN. I dare say! If I turn them inside out, everything I have got in them will fall out.

DA. Do it, and don't enrage me.

AN. I am a scoundrel if you find so much as a scrap of paper on me. But still that you may have your will, here is one; here is another. . . . . what do you see? There is the third; that too is empty. Now for the fourth. . . . . (*When he turns it out, the letters fall out.*)
. . . . The deuce! those damned letters! I had quite forgotten them . . . . . (*Stoops to pick them up again quickly.*)

DA. Give it me, give it me! What fell there? It is something else of mine I expect.

AN. As true as I live it is nothing of yours. It might rather be something addressed to you.

DA. Don't delay me; I have other things to do.

AN. Don't delay me. You surely know that I must be going to the post again directly. I know there are letters there.

DA. Go then, go! But show me first what you picked up so quickly. I insist. I must see it.

An. The deuce! If that's so, I need not go to the post.

Da. How so?

An. Well, well! There they are. I shall be off at once. (*Gives him the letter and is running off.*)

Da. (*looking at it*). Ha! Anton, Anton! This is just the very letter from Berlin I am expecting. I know it by the address.

An. It may well be that it is it. But, Herr Damis, don't be. . . . . be angry. I had quite forgotten it, on my soul.

Da. What had you forgotten?

An. That I have been carrying the letter in my pocket for almost half-an-hour already. That confounded chattering!

Da. Since it is here now, I will forgive you that stupid blunder. . . . . But, my dearest Anton, what unparalleled, what priceless news must this contain! How pleased my father will be! What honour, what praise! Oh, Anton! I will read it at once to you. . . . . (*Breaks it open quickly.*)

An. Gently, you are tearing it up. There now. Didn't I say so?

Da. No harm is done. We can still read it. First of all I must tell you what it is about. You know, or rather you do not know, that the Prussian Academy offered a prize for the best dissertation on the theory of Monads. It occurred to me quite late to take this prize out of the mouths of our philosophers. So I set about it at once, and wrote a treatise, which must have arrived just in the nick of time. . . . . A treatise, Anton. . . . . I don't know myself where I got it from, it is so learned. It is now a week since the Academy made known their judgment on the writings sent in, which must necessarily have gone in my favour. I, I and no other, must have the prize. I have solemnly engaged one of my friends on the spot to give me news of it at once. Here it is; now listen :

" My dear Damis,

" How well you know how to get an answer from your friend. You threaten me with the loss of your affec-

tion if you do not hear from me the first intelligence as to
whether you, or another, has carried off the Academy's
prize. I must therefore with all speed report to you that
you have not (*stammering*). . . . . obtained it, and also
(*more and more timidly*). . . . . could not . . . . . have
obtained it."
What? I have not obtained it? And who has, then?
And why not?
"But allow me to speak to you as your friend."
Speak, traitor.
"It was impossible for me to do you the ill service of
giving in your treatise.". . . . .
So you have not sent it in, false man! Heavens!
What a blow! . . . . . And so your negligence, unworthy
friend, is to deprive me of the reward I merit?. . . . .
How will he excuse himself, the worthless fellow?
"If I am to confess the truth, you appear to have done
something quite different from what the Academy required. They did not wish you to discuss what the word
monad signifies grammatically; who used it first; what it
means in Xenocrates; whether the Monads of Pythagoras
were the Atoms of Moschus, &c. How do these critical
trivialities concern them, especially when the main subject
was lost sight of among them? How easily might somebody have guessed your name, and then you might have
been exposed to jests such as I found on you only a few
days ago in a learned journal. . . . ."
What do I read? Can I believe my eyes? Oh, cursed
paper. Cursed hand that wrote thee! (*Throws the letter
on the ground and tramples on it.*)
AN. The poor letter! But one must read to the
end. (*Takes it up.*) Perhaps the best is still to come,
Herr Damis. Where were you? Here it is; listen now.
"In a learned journal. . . . . They call you a youthful
scholaraster who would like to shine everywhere, and
whose passion for scribbling——"

DA. (*snatches the letter out of his hand*). The damned
correspondent! This is the reward the letter deserves!
(*tears it.*) You tear my heart, and I tear your shameless
news. Would to God I could do the same with your

entrails! But. . . . . (*to* ANTON.) You worthless ignorant brute! It is all your fault!

AN. Mine, Herr Damis?

DA. Yes, yours. How long did you keep that letter
in your pocket?

AN. Sir, my pocket can neither read nor write; if you
should think that it can have altered it——

DA. Silence! . . . . Can I survive such abuse?. . . . .
Oh, ye stupid Germans. Yes, truly, it needs another
genius to value properly such works as mine. You
will ever remain in the darkness of your barbarism, and
be a laughing-stock to your intelligent neighbours. But
I will be revenged on you, and from this time forth will
cease to be called a German. I will leave my thankless
fatherland. Father, relations and friends are all, all
unworthy that I should recognise them any longer, since
they are Germans; since they are of the people who
casts its greatest spirits with violence from itself!
I am sure that France and England will recognise my
desert——

AN. Herr Damis, Herr Damis, you are beginning to
rave. I am not safe with you; I shall have to call some
one.

DA. They will feel in good time, those stupid Germans,
what they have lost in me! To-morrow I will make
arrangements to leave this unhappy country——

SCENE XVI.—CHRYSANDER, DAMIS, ANTON.

AN. God be thanked that some one has come.

CHRYS. That confounded girl Lisette! And (*to* ANTON)
you, you rascal! You too shall have your postman's pay.
To deceive me so! Very good! . . . . My son, I have
reflected; you are right; I cannot now take Juliane from
you again. You shall have her.

DA. Juliane again already? Now, when I have quite
other matters to decide. Do stop talking of it. I don't
want to have her.

CHRYS. It would be wrong of me to desire to oppose
you any longer. I leave every one his freedom. And I
see clearly that Juliane pleases you.

DA. Me? A stupid German woman?

CHRYS. She is a pretty, virtuous, upright girl; she will bring you a thousand joys.

DA. You may praise her or abuse her; it is all the same to me. I know how to act in accordance with your will, and that is, not to think of her.

CHRYS. No, no. You shall not be able to complain of my severity.

DA. And you still less of my disobedience.

CHRYS. I will show you that you have a good father, who regulates his acts more in accordance with your will than his own.

DA. And I will show you that you have a son who renders you in all things due submissiveness.

CHRYS. Yes, yes. Take Juliane. I give you my blessing.

DA. No, no. I will not thus provoke you.

CHRYS. What does this opposition mean? You provoke me by that.

DA. I cannot believe that you have already changed your mind for the third time in earnest?

CHRYS. And why not?

DA. Oh, let it be as it may. I too have changed, and am firmly resolved not to marry at all. I must travel, and the sooner I set about it the better.

CHRYS. What? You will rush off into the world without my leave?

AN. This is a joke. The third man is still wanting, and I will fetch him at once. Damis won't have Juliane; perhaps Valer will catch her. (*Exit.*)

SCENE XVII.—CHRYSANDER, DAMIS.

DA. Yes, yes, In twice four-and-twenty hours I must already be on my way.

CHRYS. Whatever has come into your head?

DA. I have for some time been tired of staying in Germany, in this northern abode of rudeness and stupidity, where all the elements hinder one from being wise; where a mind like mine is born hardly once in a hundred years.

CHRYS. Have you forgotten that Germany is your fatherland?

DA. What is fatherland to me?

CHRYS. You reprobate; better say at once, what is your father to you. But I will show you: you must take Juliane; you have given her your word, and she has given hers to you.

DA. She has withdrawn hers, as I do mine now; therefore——

CHRYS. Therefore, therefore! To speak briefly of the matter: do you realise that I am able to disinherit you if you don't obey me?

DA. Do what you please. Only, if I may beg a favour, leave me alone now. Before I start, I must finish two papers which, out of pity, I will leave behind to my countrymen. I beg of you again to leave me.

CHRYS. Wouldn't you prefer to turn me out?

SCENE XVIII.—VALER, ANTON, CHRYSANDER, DAMIS.

VA. How? Damis? Is it true that you have come to yourself once more? . . . . . That you renounce Juliane?

CHRYS. Oh, Herr Valer, you could not come at a more unlucky time for me. You strengthen him nicely in his obstinacy. You deserved, didn't you, that I should accommodate myself to your wishes? To try to deceive me in such an impious way! My son, don't oppose me any longer, or——

DA. Your threats are useless. I must show myself to foreign lands, which have as much right to me as my fatherland. And you don't want me to drag a wife about with me, do you?

VA. Damis is right to insist on travelling. Nothing can be more beneficial to him in his circumstances. Let him have his way, and let me have Juliane, whom you have so solemnly promised to me.

CHRYS. Promised? One need not keep one's word with liars.

VA. I have already assured you on my oath, that Lisette alone attempted this deceit; without her we should have known nothing whatever of the document . . . .

How fortunate it would have been had it never come to
light! It is the most cruel fortune that Juliane could
have met with. How gladly would she sacrifice it, if she
could thus obtain freedom for her heart!

CHRYS. Sacrifice? Consider, Herr Valer, what that
means. We merchants like to take a man at his word.

VA. Oh, pray, do so here. Juliane resigns the document to you with joy. Begin the suit if you like; the
gain from it shall be entirely yours. Juliane considers
this the smallest token of her gratitude. She thinks
herself indebted to you for much more.

CHRYS. Come, come, she has always seemed full of
gratitude towards me. . . . . But what Valer, will you,
as her future husband, say to this gratitude?

VA. Think better of me. I loved Juliane when she
had no hopes of anything. I love her still, without the
slightest selfish object in view. And, besides what sort
of present, does one make an honest man, when one
presents him with a long lawsuit?

CHRYS. Valer, are you in earnest?

VA. Claim even more than the document; half my
fortune is yours.

CHRYS. God forbid that I should wish to have a farthing
of your fortune. You mustn't think me so selfish. We are
good friends, and the old agreement still holds. Juliane
is yours. And if the document is to be mine, she is all
the more yours.

VA. Come, Herr Chrysander, confirm this to her yourself. How pleased she will be to be able to make us both
happy.

CHRYS. If that is the case, Damis, as far as I am concerned, you can start this very night. I shall thank God
when I have got such a fool out of the house again.

DA. Go, if you please, and leave me alone.

VA. And have I, after all, to thank you, Damis, for my
happiness? I do so with the sincerest affection, although
I know that I am not the cause of your change of mind.

DA. But the true cause? . . . . . (*to* ANTON). Cursed
fellow, couldn't you hold your tongue. . . . . Please go,
Valer. (*While* CHRYSANDER *and* VALER *are preparing to
go,* ANTON *stops* VALER.)

An. (*in a low voice*). Not so fast! How stands it with Lisette's dowry, Herr Valer? and with——

Va. Don't be uneasy; I will keep my word better than I promised.

An. Hurrah! Now the dove is caught.

Scene XIX.—Damis (*at the table*), Anton.

An. One word more, Herr Damis, I have to say to you.

Da. Well?

An. You are going to travel——

Da. Come to the point! This is already more than one word.

An. Well, then; my discharge.

Da. Your discharge? You suppose, perhaps, that I should take an ignorant ass like you with me?

An. You won't? And I have my discharge then? God be thanked! Now receive yours, also, which shall consist in a little advice. I have witnessed your follies for more than three years now, and I have done foolishly enough myself during the time, since I know that a servant, be his master ever so foolish——

Da. Shameless idiot! Will you get out of my sight!

An. Well, well! He who won't be advised can't be helped either. Remain Herr Damis the Scholar for the rest of your life. (*Exit.*)

Da. Go, I say, or. . . . . (*Throws the book after him, and the curtain falls.*)

THE END.

THE OLD MAID.

(A COMEDY IN THREE ACTS.)

Non tu nunc hominum mores vides?
Dum dos fit, nullum vitium vitio vertitur.—*Plautus.*

"The Old Maid" was written at Leipzig during the years 1746—1748

DRAMATIS PERSONÆ.

———•———

FRÄULEIN OHLDINN.

LELIO, *her cousin.*

LISETTE, *maid to* FRÄULEIN OHLDINN.

HERR ORONT.

FRAU ORONT.

HERR VON STAMP, *a captain.*

PETER, *a cake seller.*

CLITANDER, *a friend of* LELIO.

KRÄUSEL, *a poet.*

A TAILOR.

HERR REHFUSS.

————————————————

The scene is in a parlour.

THE OLD MAID.

ACT I.

SCENE I.—FRÄULEIN OHLDINN, HERR ORONT, FRAU ORONT

HERR OR. Ah! What whims! One never grows too old for that. And how old are you, then? How long is it since I saw you carried in the nurse's arms? If it were fifty, one, two . . . . . well, say some fifty years——

FR. OHL. Why not eighty at once? If you take me to be as old as that why do you talk to me so much about marriage?

HERR OR. Oh, come now! You are not too old! Not at all too old. Four-and-fifty is just the right age for a marriageable girl. If the young things marry so young, it will follow that the children too——

FR. OHL. What nonsense about your four-and-fifty years——

FRAU OR. (*to* HERR OR). Quite true. You are mistaken, my dear. You even cannot be as old as that yet.

HERR OR. I should be glad if that were so. I and the century go along together. Have you anything to complain of in my age? Am I not still——

FRAU OR. Well, well. Then you can't have known her as a child.

HERR OR. Oh! bother the child——

FR. OHL. If you won't believe me. my baptismal certificate can prove that I shall only be fifty next Easter.

HERR OR. What? You only just fifty? I thought you were who knows how old. Ah! Then your time is not past yet. Sarah was ninety years old. And to judge from your face, I should certainly not have taken you for younger than——

FR. OHL. What? My face . . . . . my face . . . . . whoever does not like it——

HERR OR. Who says that? Your face has its lovers still. Otherwise, would Captain von Stamp——

FR. OHL. What? A *von?* Is he actually of noble birth?

HERR OR. Certainly; indeed he is of one of the noblest families. He is in great favour with the king, who has graciously given him his discharge, since he had the misfortune to be incapacitated for further service during the last campaign.

FR. OHL. Incapacitated? No. I recollect now. I won't have him. Turn your attention to another. I can only pity him.

HERR OR. But he will have no one but you. And do you desire to have a husband who is always on a campaign, and who can be with you for hardly two nights in the year? Discharged officers are the best husbands; if they can no longer show their courage against the enemy, they are so much the more manly in their behaviour towards their . . . . . but I am going too far. You cannot understand——

FR. OHL. Oh, just fancy——

HERR OR. Ah! You do understand, then? I think——

FR. OHL. I think you only want to make fun of me.

HERR OR. Or else you of me. If I say you understand that won't suit you. If I say you don't understand that won't suit you either. I see well enough that your head is just as full of caprice as it is of years. Will you, or will you not?

FR. OHL. Lord preserve us! Must one get in a passion immediately? Calm him, Frau Oront, do.

FRAU OR. You must treat her with a little more mildness, my dear husband. You surely must know from my case how a woman feels when one says things of this kind to her for the first time.

FR. OHL. O! the first time . . . . . the first time. If I had wanted to marry——

HERR OR. Then you don't want?

Fr. Ohl. Good gracious! You are really too violent.
. . . . Can one make up one's mind on such important
matters on the spot?

Herr Or. Yes, yes. One can and must. In the very
first transport. If the confounded deliberation comes in,
all is over at once. Thank God, deliberation is no fault of
mine. Shall your handsome fortune go to smiling heirs?
It will last long in the hands of your spendthrift cousin.
Get children of your own, and you know to whom you are
leaving it. Through marriage you come into a high
aristocratic family, you know not how. And do you want
to go to your grave, then, without having tasted the divine
delights of matrimony?

Fr. Ohl. Come now, my consolation would be that I
had not been forced to endure its discomforts too.

Frau Or. Oh! They are tolerable through the enjoy-
ment it brings us. And if a pair like my dear husband
and myself meet, there is little to say about them. Is it
not so, my dearest darling? We——

Herr Or. Yes, it is true, my little treasure; we have
made life so sweet for one another, so agreeable . . . . . we
are a pattern of a happy marriage to our neighbours.

Frau Or. We have been always one body and one
soul——

Herr Or. We know nothing of strife or quarrelling.
The wish of one has always been the will of the other
. . . . Yes, my angelic little wife.

Frau Or. That's true, my darling little husband.

Fr. Ohl. Really such a pair quite make one's mouth
water.

Herr Or. And that now for nearly six and twenty
years.

Frau Or. So united, as loving as turtle doves——

Herr Or. For six and twenty years.

Frau Or. You are mistaken, my dear; only four-and-
twenty.

Herr Or. Eh? What? Reckon it up.

Frau Or. Very well; four-and-twenty and no more.

Herr Or. Why not? From the year of Our Lord
1724. I am positive about it; I have written it on my
cupboard door.

FRAU OR. Cupboard—cupboard. . . . . an excellent piece
of cupboard love. I see clearly that your one pleasure is
to contradict me.

HERR OR. Gently! You put down your own foolish
disposition to me. Love of contradiction is your particular
fault, and not your only one, to my sorrow.

FRAU. OR. My fault? The senseless man!

HERR OR. I senseless? Senseless? What prevents
me——

FRAU OR. Do not on any account marry, my dear
madam. That is what all men are like; and the best of
them is not worth a toss.

HERR OR. What? Not worth a toss? Woman, I shall
strike you. Not worth a toss?

FRAU OR. Yes, yes. He is worth a toss.

HERR OR. It's lucky for you that you retract? From
1724 to 1748 not more than four and twenty years?
Are you mad?

FRAU OR. Or are you? Just count. 24 to 34 is ten years,
34 to 44 makes twenty, 45, 46, 47, 48 are four years,
which makes four and twenty years.

HERR OR. You impious woman! You only want to
contradict. Just let me count: 24 to 34 are ten, 34 to
44 make twenty; 45, 46, 47, 48, are, are. . . . . stop, I
have made a miscalculation: 24 to 34, ten years, 34 to 44
is also ten years, making twenty years: 45, 46, 47, 48
. . . . . curse it! Now, Mistress Ohldinn, make up your
mind at once. What will you do? That only I may get
rid of this confounded stickler!

FRAU OR. You will work your own unhappiness if you
obey him. For God's sake say no.

FR. OHL. Ah, my dear Frau Oront, one can see your
animus against your husband only too clearly.

HERR OR. You bad woman! So you want to bring my
reward to nothing; Speak, Mistress Ohldinn, speak.

FR. OHL. Well then. . . . . yes. . . . . if——

HERR OR. Ugh! What "if"? You can accept all the
conditions joyfully. So I have your word, and my end is
attained. Good. Another fifty reichsthalers won.

SCENE II.—FRÄULEIN OHLDINN, FRAU ORONT.

FR. OHL. There he goes, and a half answer——

FRAU OR. You were caught! Such an unreasonable man; give him an inch and he'll take an ell!

FR. OHL. Well, well,. . . . . As God wills.

FRAU OR. God forbid! You won't do that, surely. I will run after the scamp, I'll run after him.

FR. OHL. Don't take it ill of me. But you seek every opportunity of quarrelling with your husband. That is not at all nice conduct.

FRAU OR. Ah! I see your head is turned too. You imagine all kinds of sugar-plums with a husband. Misfortune has for a long time spared you——

FR. OHL. Oh, tut, tut! People bring their unhappiness on themselves. The husband is master——

FRAU OR. And you seem to be sorely in need of one. Good-bye. Do as you like.

SCENE III.—FRÄULEIN OHLDINN. *Afterwards* LISETTE.

FR. OHL. The envious creature! So Heaven will deliver me also some day. I quite tremble for joy. Oh, how hard that yes was. Thank God it is said.

LIS. What sort of visit have you had again? Herr Oront wanted to borrow money, eh?

FR. OHL. The silly thinks that there is nothing to be found with me but that miserable money.

LIS. Eh? He surely didn't bring you a lover? Though nowadays too lovers have turned into a kind of money-borrowers. That is. . . . . but you are beyond such matters. And besides, marriage is a very hell——

FR. OHL. God forbid! Are you thinking what you say, Lisette?

LIS. Only what you have said times without number. Alas, that no one will carry me off to hell! I should never have had patience so long as you. And if you don't take steps soon it will be too late.

FR. OHL. Too late, you silly creature? How old am I, then?

LIS. That is not a calculation for me. I can't count up to fifty.

I 2

FR. OHL. Your stupid mockery alone might make me do something which would be disagreeable to you and my cousin.

LIS. Gently, then! Gently! I might end by making you desperate——

FR. OHL. In short, I *am* going to marry. Captain von Stamp has just proposed to me through Herr Oront. I have given him my acceptation, and I hope the matter will be settled this very day.

LIS. What an incomparable dream! It must have made you very happy last night. How do you lie when you want to have such dreams? On your back? Or on your stomach? Or——

FR. OHL. Joking apart! What I have said is true. And I am going this very minute to put my bills and documents in order.

LIS. In that you do quite right. For they are of more importance, I suppose, in the marriage than you——

FR. OHL. Silence! You insolent thing!

SCENE IV.—LISETTE, *afterwards* LELIO.

LIS. Oh! What delightful news for her cousin! I wonder whether he is in his room? Herr Lelio! Herr Lelio! Husband-hunting is an essential complaint of women, be they as young or as old as they may. Ah! In fact, I find I am not quite healthy myself. Herr Lelio!

LE. What is it? Well, Mademoiselle Lisette! I should have thought, little fool, you might have taken the trouble to come to me in my room.

LIS. Your humble servant! That would be venturing too far into the enemy's camp. This is neutral territory. Here I can defy your assaults.

LE. Ah! He who will only venture the attack will carry you at all points.

LIS. What a pity no one hears you, or I should thank you for your kind recommendation. But to business. I have a most extraordinary piece of new news to tell you.

LE. How lucky that you come on the subject of news. I too have something of the very drollest to impart to you in that line.

Lis.   Mine is still droller, I expect.

Le.   Impossible.   What will you bet?

Lis.   Oh, bother betting! I should get nothing out of you.

Le.   Eh? You are silly! Only wait till my cousin dies. Then——

Lis.   Oh, she intends to do a good deal before her death.

Le.   You speak as if you knew already what I was going to tell you.

Lis.   Eh? Out with it then! What is it?

Le.   First let me hear your news.

Lis.   Well, listen, then. Your cousin——

Le.   My cousin.

Lis.   Is going to marry.

Le.   Is going to marry. That is what I was going to tell you too. Where the deuce have you got it from already? Only this moment Frau Oront told it to me, and promised me all possible assistance in frustrating it.

Lis.   Oh, in determinations of this kind old maids are too obstinate.

Le.   But what the deuce will my creditors say to it? They who have helped me in such a Christian spirit at twelve *per cent.*, in the hope that one day I should be the sole heir of all her property.

Lis.   That is the creditors' affair. Why do you worry yourself about that?

Le.   I am not troubled much about those who are already my creditors, but about those who might become so in future. What hopes shall I be able to hold out to them?

Lis.   None more certain than your inheritance, otherwise you run the risk of having to pay them one day.

Scene V.—Lelio, Lisette, Peter (*with a basket of cakes.*)

Pe.   Hullo! Good people! Won't you buy to-day?

Lis.   Nothing this time, Peter.

Pe.   Macaroons, tartlets, Bath buns, fritters; nothing?

Lis.   Nothing. No.

PE.   Nothing whatever.   Herr Lelio for **your** sweet tooth?   Macaroons, tartlets, Bath buns, fritters.

LE.   Be off; I have no money to-day.

PE.   Pray buy one.   Macaroons, tartlets, Bath buns, fritters.

LE.   I shall soon come in for a fortune.   If you will give me credit till then, I will take your whole basket off your hands.

PE.   Ha, ha!   You are up to the same games as the captain.   He would buy from me every day, if I would only wait till after his marriage for my money.   But, my friends, such things are easy to eat, but hard to pay for when the taste is out of the mouth.

LE.   Who is your captain?

PE.   He lives in a three pair back.

LE.   But where?

PE.   Over there in the broad street.   It is a little room with only one window.

LIS.   Well, don't you know enough yet?   The captain in the broad street, three pair up, in a little room at the back with only one window.

PE.   Yes, yes.   Quite right.   That's he.

LE.   But what is his name, then, you fool.

PE.   Oh, his name. . . . . his name is. . . . . wait . . . . . I think I shall remember.   His dog's name is Judas.   It is a big tawny mastiff.   I know that.   But he, his name is von Whack—no.   Von Kick—no.   Ah! Stamp, von Stamp.   Captain von Stamp.

LE.   You know him, then!

PE.   Why not?   I have also the honour to know his servant, too.   For he is my mother's daughter's husband.   And so, unless I am mistaken, we are actually brothers-in-law.

LIS.   Well, Peter, in that case you might do us a great service.

PE.   Done!   If it brings me in anything, it is as good as done.   Let's hear. (*Puts down his basket.*)

LIS.   Do you know whom Herr von Stamp wants to marry?

PE.   The first that comes, if only she has money.   I believe he could take you.   But——

LIS.   Oh!   I shall take care to provide for myself else-

where without that " but." Briefly, he wants to marry
our old maid.

Pe. Yes, he wants to——

Lis. Oh, and she wants it too.

Pe. So much the better! Then all is right! And, in
future I have one customer the more.

Lis. Yes, fool, but we do not want it. (*She takes hold of
the basket.*)

Pe. Well, then, nothing will come of it.

Le. It is desirable that it should not, and then I should
not lose my inheritance.

Pe. Ha, ha, ha!

Le. What are you laughing at?

Pe. Ha, ha! Does your inheritance depend on a
suitor? It's good that I still have my macaroons! But
what were you going to say to me, Lisette? (*he sees her
eating cakes*). Oh, zounds! You are a nice one! Get
away, cat! I shall catch it from my mistress. She has
counted out every one of these to me. (*Places the basket on
the other side.*)

Lis. Idiot! I want to taste. Perhaps I shall buy something, if they are good. Now, just listen. Take yourself
off with your wares to the captain. (*Goes to the other side.*)

Pe. Couldn't you stay where you were, Lisette? I can
hear as well with that ear as this one (*places the basket
again on the other side*). Well, what am I to do with him?
he won't buy anything of me.

Lis. Couldn't you in some clever manner bring the conversation round to his marriage——

Pe. In some clever manner? Do you doubt that? The
deuce, I know such beautiful turns: for instance, he says,
" I don't want any of your wares, Peter." Then perhaps
I should say—yes, what was I going to say?—yes, well,
I should say, "None at all? God protect you;" and go
my way again.

Lis. Well, fool, and what, then, would you have said
to him about the marriage? And you must not only
do that, but you must also try to put our lady out of his
head. And we will give you all necessary freedom to
shame and slander her in every way, if that will help you
at all.

LE. The idea would not be so stupid, but he who is to carry it out is so much the more stupid.

PE. Oh, no. You are mistaken, Herr Lelio. I have done something in this way before. Just to give you a little proof. Suppose you were the captain. "What?" I would say, "you want to marry? Who would have dreamed that? You who used to be such a despiser of marriage,"—but no, that would not do. It is not true. He would have married a long ago. But then. . . . . "What? You want to marry the old maid?—Well, that is not bad, she has heaps of money."

LIS. Oh! You would be a nice help to us! Go, go; I see well enough there is nothing to be done with you.

PE. Eh? How is that? Why, you haven't tried me yet? But do you imagine it would be any use if I were to say, "You want to marry that old monkey-faced woman? Why, she looks as if she had lain in the grave three years already. She will carry on your noble race well. And, in confidence, they say she is a witch. Her riches, about which people make such a fuss, are nothing but red-hot coals, which she keeps in big pots behind the cellar door, and over which a huge black dog watches; one with eyes of fire, with six rows of teeth, with a triple tail——

LIS. Oh! God preserve us! With a triple. . . . . Fellow, you make one so frightened with your talk, that one is ready to die. (*Takes hold of the basket again.*)

PE. Ha, ha! And all that would be of no use with him. "Don't be alarmed," he would say. "I shall see how to make myself master of the treasure. Just as in Silesia or Bohemia, when the peasant had buried his bits of property ever so deep——"

LIS. I have got a better idea. I am sure it will do.

PE. Well, what? . . . . The devil! are you at the basket again? I must hang it on my neck again.

LIS. Don't be a fool, it will be too heavy for you.

PE. No, no. If I let it stand too long it might become too light.

LIS. I know our mistress has never seen Herr von Stamp yet. I should think, if you were to pass yourself off for him——

Le. I understand you, Lisette. That is excellently planned.

Pe. I understand nothing yet.

Lis. Come away. We will discuss the matter in a safer place. Here we might be surprised.

ACT II.

Scene I.—Lisette, Lelio.

Lis. Don't be afraid. I fully believe our trick will succeed.

Le. I will hope so. Certainly I would let you benefit by it; and perhaps would even marry you.

Lis. Of that another time. But how firmly the marriage must be fixed in her mind you may see from this: she has immediately sent for a lace-seller, a dress-maker, a hair-dresser, and a poet.

Le. What is the poet for?

Lis. As if marriage could go off without a song! He is to make it in his own name, or in that of another, and she has put an old gulden by for him.

Scene II.—Lisette, Lelio, Clitander.

Cli. Your servant, Herr Lelio. How do you do? Did our affair yesterday agree with you? Have you had your sleep out? Will you be at the club again to-day. Haven't you been to the coffee-house yet? How did you like the wine? Didn't Valer pick out a spruce brunette?

Le. That is a host of questions, and you have not yet allowed me to answer your greeting.

Cli. The deuce! I find you two alone together again. Lelio? Lisette? No good can come of that. But what is the matter with you, Lelio? You look quite—quite—I don't know what. You want cheering up. Come with me. Ah, by-the-by, it is lucky that I think of it: do you know who the girl was that met us in the garden yesterday? Didn't you like her? Let us go there again. Perhaps we shall meet her.

LE. Won't you tell me which question I am to answer first? Or shall I answer none at all?

LIS. Oh, we have no time just now to listen to your chatter, sir.

CLI. Eh? Could not that truth be rather more politely expressed? Are your affairs very urgent? Have you nothing new to tell me, Herr Lelio?

LE. Oh dear, yes. And truly a piece of news which touches me very nearly.

CLI. Really? But do you know yet that our friend, Clarissa is betrothed? It was settled yesterday.

LE. So you do not want to hear my news?

CLI. Tell it, tell it. I am uncommonly glad to hear anything new. Only yesterday——

LE. You are already beginning again on something else. I can't even get these five words out for you, "My cousin means to marry."

CLI. Ha, ha, ha!

LE. Ah! If you were in my place you would not laugh.

CLI. Ha, ha, ha! You complain that I talk so much, and the other day I was with people who blamed me for speaking too little. Ha, ha, ha! When, then, does one speak neither too much nor too little? That is a good joke! Ha, ha, ha! But were you not going to tell me something new? What was it?

LIS. If you only were not too much occupied with yourself you would have heard it long ago. His cousin means to marry.

CLI. Is it certain already? Lelio, you will manage that I shall be present at the marriage, won't you? Has she bought the wine yet? Is it good?

LE. If you wanted to act as a friend towards me, you would rather advise me how to frustrate this unlucky marriage.

CLI. How so?

LE. Why, my inheritance will go to the deuce through it.

CLI. Oh! That is soon remedied. Get the inheritance given you in advance. Your cousin may then do as she likes.

LIS. Herr Lelio, how stupid we must be. It is true. That is the best plan; and we never hit on it. Hurrah for a quick wit.

CLI. O, my child, you are not the first to tell me that I am very happy in the advice I give.

LIS. To be sure! Your advice has no more than the one defect, that it is very absurd.

CLI. So! At least I shall think that it might supply the material for a better. But where is your cousin? I must of course, congratulate her on her excellent choice. Whom is she going to take?

LIS. You can ask her yourself. I hear somebody coming. No doubt it is she. Come, Herr Lelio, Peter might be in need of our instruction.

LE. If you want to talk with my cousin, be so kind as to tease her well.

CLI. I should have done that without being reminded. I am a master of biting and delicate satire. And if you like I will make it so bad that she shall burst with rage.

LE. So much the better.

SCENE III.—CLITANDER, FRÄULEIN OHLDINN.

CLI. Mademoiselle—mistress—bride—Madame . . . . . what the devil am I to call her? Is it true, or is it not true, that you mean to marry?

FR. OHL. Yes, it is quite true. Who can go against his fate? I assure you, Herr Clitander, there has been an extraordinary dispensation of Providence in this matter. I had thought of nothing so little as of a husband, and suddenly——

CLI. And suddenly the desire for one came upon you?

FR. OHL. You may be sure that it has by no means been my doing. Marriages are made in heaven, and who would be so impious as to oppose them here.

CLI. There you are right. The whole town, it is true, is laughing at you. But that is the fate of the pious. Don't mind that. A husband is a thoroughly useful piece of household furniture.

FR. OHL. I don't know what the town should have to

laugh at. Is a marriage such a laughable thing. The impious, wicked town!

CLI. You do the town injustice. It does not laugh at your marrying, but that you did not marry thirty years ago.

FR. OIL. Isn't that silly? Thirty years ago? Thirty years ago I was still a child.

CLI. But still, already a tolerably marriageable one. For your sex has the privilege of retaining that appellation a long time. The deuce! If I was in love with you I should still call you "my child," I suppose. But, Mademoiselle, I have said that without prejudice to myself. Pray don't imagine that I am so.

FR. OIL. I should be little proud of it. Such a wild, flighty, senseless——

CLI. Oh, good sense only comes with age. Thank your wrinkles if it has already taken up its abode with you.

FR. OIL. My wrinkles? Pray tell me through what misfortune I have come in your presence to-day? My wrinkles? . . . . . I suppose I am to believe you rather than my mirror? I am certainly the first bride to whom any one has uttered such base rudeness.

CLI. Yet it would be no small reproach to me if I did not know how to treat a bride. But in you I meet with an exception. And I should be very culpable if I were to utter the smallest pretty phrase, the slightest gallant trifling to you. But I will do you a special kindness. If you will invite me to your wedding, I promise to teach you some new dances, a dozen or so love expressions for your bridegroom, and various tender glances which are now in fashion. For in all these three matters you cannot be otherwise than very poorly versed. I will also, to fill up the cup of my kindness, introduce you to some agreeable girls, good friends of mine from whom you can soon learn the usages of society.

FR. OIL. They must be nice people who make acquaintance with you. They must certainly be girls who run after the men.

CLI. Well, not a tithe of them has the gift of waiting so long as you. A man goes along his way. Every step he comes across a girl whom he could have. She who does not put herself a little forward, remains behind. And so it has been with you. But moralising aside. I will earn gratitude at your hands and your bridegroom's. Let us see whether you can dance a minuet.

Fr. Ohl. How much further do you mean to carry your nonsense?

Cli. Pray make no ceremony. You ought to be grateful to me for it.

Fr. Ohl. That you should have an opportunity for mocking.

Cli. The deuce! You have a very pretty foot for dancing. (*Lifts her skirt up a little.*)

Fr. Ohl. For shame! I beg——

Cli. What ancient, obsolete words you use! Shame has not been in use for more than a hundred years. Come! We will first proceed with one thing at a time. How do you make a courtesy?

Fr. Ohl. Your servant! So far I will not allow your mockery to go. (*Makes a courtesy.*)

Cli. I see clearly I must attend to your deeds and not your words. The courtesy was not so bad. But raise your skirt a little. I cannot see what is going on under there.

Fr. Ohl. It is true the skirt is, really, a little too long. I must at least have so much taken off. (*Raises it a little.*)

Cli. The devil! What a foot! What a pity it does not belong to a youthful body! Just make one *pas*.

Fr. Ohl. No, Herr Clitander, I must confess to you that dancing is not my forte, and my dislike to it is not small. Instead of taking a couple of firm natural steps (*she takes two steps*) one behaves affectedly and makes a senseless *pas*, (*she makes a dancing step*). What folly.

Cli. But, upon my soul, the folly doesn't suit you ill. So you can dance already. And just as well as I can. Ah! That looks promising. You can fly round with the rest on the evening of the wedding.

Fr. Ohl. That can hardly be, and Captain von Stamp will certainly not ask it of me.

Cli. What have you to do with that scoundrel? What about Captain von Stamp? If I once get him in my power . . . . . I will teach you to play with honest people, and not pay them——

Fr. Ohl. Gently, gently! Perhaps you don't know yet
that it is Captain von Stamp who is my bridegroom.

Cli. That beggarly fellow your bridegroom? The
miserable hound has owed me five and twenty ducats for
the last three months, which I won from him at billiards.
How did you come across him?

Fr. Ohl. Herr Oront, at whose house he lives, was the
suitor's envoy. And I request you to speak a little more
moderately of him.

Cli. Eh? What? Listen, Mademoiselle, I will put
your person under arrest. And the devil fetch me if he
shall marry you until I have my money.

Fr. Ohl. He will not withhold it from you——

Cli. Yes, indeed. If I were his only creditor; but I
will just say that there are quite as many of them as
you, I, and he have hairs on our heads.

Fr. Ohl. God preserve me! Herr Oront didn't tell me that.

Cli. I will go to him this moment. I will make it
hot enough for him. He had better dare to deceive an
honourable woman!

Fr. Ohl. Do not be so angry. Stay, I implore you. I
will myself, if there is nothing else to be done, make the
five and twenty ducats——

Cli. Let me go. Rather than that cursed fellow shall
marry you, and give himself airs with your money, rather
. . . . . yes, rather will I bite at a sour apple myself,
rather will I take the trouble upon myself and marry you.
Good-bye for the present.

SCENE IV.—FRÄULEIN OHLDINN (alone.)

Fr. Ohl. Oh Heavens! How is it with me? Must all
proposals of marriage that are made to me come to nothing?
This is the twelfth time! But the captain is said to be
such a pleasant man. Why, what harm is it, if he is a
little in debt? One can't take one's money into the grave.
And who knows if it is as bad as Clitander makes out.
Ah! Dear Captain von Stamp! it is settled, then, I keep him.
And doesn't it come to the same thing whether I give my
property to him or to my dissolute cousin? He may
perhaps let me enjoy it with him; but my cousin——

Scene V.—Fräulein Ohldinn, Lisette, Herr Kräusel, a Tailor.

Lis. Mistress, I bring you two persons for whom you have sent: Mr. Tailor and Mr. Poet.

Fr. Ohl. (*to the poet*). Welcome, Mister Tailor! (*To the tailor.*) Have patience for an instant, my dear Mr. Poet; I will just get rid of him first.

Kr. What! To call me a tailor? What are you thinking of? Heavens, what an insult! To take a crowned poet for a tailor.

Tai. Eh? What? To take an honest citizen and master craftsman for a poet? For a idler of that sort? Do you not consider that a libel?

Lis. Gently, friends, gently. She does not know you yet.

Kr. What?. I a tailor?

Tai. What? I a poet.

Kr. Let him make your poem for you, if he can. Adieu.

Tai. Let him make your clothes for you, if he can. Adieu.

Lis. Wait a moment. Fancy getting angry directly about a mistake. You are both honourable upright people, whom one cannot do without.

Kr. To call a man who associates daily and nightly with the divine Muses a tailor! That is unbearable! Let me go! (*Exit.*)

Tai. Shall a man who has clothed the persons of princes allow himself to be stigmatised as a poet? I understand my profession. There is no one who can say any evil of me. And I will certainly not bear abuse. We shall see; we shall soon see. (*Exit.*)

Scene VI.—Fräulein Ohldinn, Lisette, *and afterwards* Kräusel.

Fr. Ohl. Are not they fools! I can protest before heaven that I did not know them.

Lis. Oh, the poet has his bread to get; he will come back. Here we have him.

KR. The wisest gives way; and I am he. I considered, as I was going out, that——

LIS. That a tailor can be obstinate, better than a poet——

KR. That anger does not become a wise man. I thus forgive you your error. Only learn from it that there is more hidden in many a man than one can see. But what do you require? In what can my ability serve you?

FR. OHL. I have resolved, under Providence, to marry. And, since I have heard that you can make a good verse, and since too, my bridegroom is of noble birth, and since I also should like to have a marriage-song, and since I don't know whether any one else might be so polite——.

KR. *Sapienti sat.* You have explained yourself clearly enough. The rest shall be my care. I will at once make you one with which you shall be pleased. Would you like one, *per Thesin et Hypothesin?*

FR. OHL. Yes, yes.

KR. Or merely one *per Antecedens et Consequens?*

FR. OH. Yes, yes.

KR. Choose. Choose. It is all the same to me. I will merely remind you provisionally that you will be pleased to give somewhat more for one *per Thesin et Hypothesin.* Times are dear. Meditation, too, has risen in price, and——

FR. OHL. I shall not let that be a consideration. Only see that it be neat and pretty.

KR. As true as I am an honourable poet it shall be a masterpiece. Shall the contents be of a religious character?

FR. OHL. Religious, religious! At a wedding, I should think——

KR. Or historical? Mythological? Playful? Satirical? Or of a waggish character?

FR. OHL. Waggish would, I should think, be——

KR. Oh, excellent! In waggishness is my strength. And for this purpose the best thing, I suppose, would be some innocent *Quodlibet.* Eh?

FR. OHL. As you think best.

KR. Yes, yes. An innocent *Quodlibet* will suit admirably. At the conclusion I can tack on a lively description of the bride and bridegroom. For instance, I would describe the bridegroom as a well-built handsome man, whose majestic gait, whose fiery and ravishing eyes, whose imperial nose, whose fine figure——

FR. OHL. Oh, Lisette! What a delightful man Captain von Stamp must be. Have you already seen him, sir?

KR. Is he really like that? What is his name?

FR. OHL. I believe you know him already. It is Captain von Stamp.

KR. Von Stamp? And your honoured name is——

FR. OHL. Ohldinn.

KR. Ohldinn? Under your permission, to how many husbands is he whom you are now taking the successor?

FR. OHL. What a silly question! He is the first.

KR. Oh, pardon me. I might have seen that at once by looking at you. It is true you are still in the bloom of your youth.

FR. OHL. Do you hear, Lisette?

KR. Ohldinn, Mademoiselle Ohldinn and Stamp, Herr von Stamp. Oh, what happy names! They will give occasion for excellent thoughts! Ohldinn, Stamp. What an excellent allusion I shall be able to make to coins of ancient stamp! Old maids, I can say, are like coins of an ancient stamp——

LIS. Do you hear, mistress?

FR. OHL. Oh, my good man, your thoughts are very absurd. Old maids, old coins? I don't promise myself anything remarkable from you.

KR. Well, we will drop that idea if it does not please you. When do you wish to see the poem complete?

FR. OHL. Why, as soon as possible.

KR. Good, good. I shall be here with it in an hour at the farthest.

FR. OHL. In an hour! Oh, pray be a little longer. Otherwise I fear it might be too bad.

KR. Yes, if you will allow me, I will compose it here at once. Just let me have a room to myself for a little. At home my wife and children overburden my ear with noise.

FR. OHL. Wife and children?

LIS. A poet with a wife and children?

KR. That very Corinna, whom in my youth I made
immortal by my songs, that very Corinna is now my wife.
I have sung this evil around my neck myself, and therefore I belong in reality to those great poets who, through
their art, have been rendered unhappy. The wicked
woman! 'Tis true she lies at home sick unto death, but
she has lain so for more than a week already, and will not
make up her mind to die. Ah, my dear young ladies, it
is certain that women are created for the unhappiness of
the whole world! Oh, the cursed sex!

LIS. Eh? You cursed scoundrel of a poet!

KR. Oh, pardon me! pardon me! I was in my ecstasy.
Whither shall I betake myself? *Nam Musæ secessum scri-
bentis et otia quærunt.*

FR. OHL. Oh, you can go into the next room here.

LIS. But don't be frightened. You will meet a lot of
fools in that room.

KR. How so?

LIS. Because there are a lot of mirrors there. Go.

KR. I don't see that. (*Exit.*)

SCENE VII.—FRÄULEIN OHLDINN, LISETTE.

FR. OHL. Do you now believe, Lisette, that I am in
earnest? But, good heavens, what will my cousin say to
it? He will tear his hair from his head when he hears
of it.

LIS. You are mistaken. I have already told him——

FR. OHL. Well?

LIS. As soon as he heard that Captain von Stamp was
to have you, he became calm. "Captain von Stamp," said
he, "is one of my best friends. I do not grudge it him.
And I cannot blame my cousin for it; I have already
received many benefits from her——"

FR. OHL. What? Did my cousin say that? Oh, my
dearest cousin! Come, I must speak to him at once. For
this he shall have a note for five hundred thalers from me
on the spot.

LIS. Only mind and give it him in such a way as not
to make him blush for shame.

ACT III.

SCENE I.—LISETTE, PETER (*in an old uniform, with a moustache*).

PE. Don't run like that, Lisette. I can't keep up with you. I am not used to the leg yet.

LIS. Oh, what an incomparable captain! That's the sort of husband I should like to have.

PE. You are no fool. I fancy there are more girls with your taste. And I fear, I fear, though, I have disguised myself so much that your mistress will penetrate more deeply into my real character, and desire to keep me in spite of your trick.

LIS. She would have to be mad, then.

PE. At any rate, madness of that kind would be nothing peculiar or new with old maids. I'll say this much, take care that you don't saddle me with her. I have a regular devil already at home. If the other one were to come as well, my place would be hot enough.

LIS. Don't be afraid. To make matters the safer, Lelio will behave as if this union entirely pleased him. But if you act and speak as we have bidden you, and I now and then employ my eloquence, she must have the marriage demon incarnate in her if she does not become utterly disgusted with you. I have announced Herr von Stamp in your person to her already, and she will soon be here.

PE. But Lisette, Lisette, my head is swimming dreadfully. I only hope I shan't come in for a second wife, as the other man did for a box on the ear.

LIS. Never fear if only you make it bad enough. Let us see. How will you play your part? Just imagine I am my mistress.

PE. But you are not.

LIS. Well, just imagine I am.

PE. If imagining is enough, just you imagine also how I would do it.

K 2

SCENE II.—HERR KRÄUSEL (*with a sheet of paper on which something is written*), LISETTE, PETER.

LIS. Oh! Here comes that confounded fellow to thwart our plans. Deuce take the poets!

KR. *Bene!* (*In thought, and reading his poem.*)

PE. That is Kräusel, isn't it? It is good that the scoundrel comes in my way.

KR. Well expressed.

LIS. What is the matter? What is the matter, Peter? Where are you off to?

PE. The rogue made a purchase of me six months ago, and I haven't yet got a farthing from him for it. And the worst of it is, he has actually put my name into a street-song. To put an honest cake-seller into a street song! Let me go! Now I've got the scamp.

KR. That is poetical. (*Still in thought.*)

PE. Yes, rascal, it is——

LIS. Peter! Peter! Consider, you are Captain von Stamp now.

PE. Yes, but I am Peter the cake-seller too.

LIS. You are ruining the whole affair. Leave him alone; let him go! You can get him all in good time.

KR. That is what I call expressing oneself well. (*Still in thought.*)

LIS. Come away. I will hear you go through your part somewhere else.

PE. Well, well. Lent isn't given.

SCENE III.—HERR KRÄUSEL (*reads over his poem*).

KR.   *The hen is wont to thank*
             The sprightly cock for his pains.

That is what I call waggish. There is something behind it.

             Rotten cheese is strong in smell,
             The mite it has ten feet.

A delicious passage!

             A bridegroom must bustle.

Ha, there is quite an Anacreontic delicacy in that line.

A crinoline needs many a stitch.
You playful wag ! A poet is a devil of a fellow !
A flea has large claws.
I know something of natural history too.
The ram doth call aloud ;
Methinks he soon will bear a lamb.
Here I am aiming at the freethinkers. People no doubt
will understand that.

Scene IV.—Lelio, Fräulein Ohldinn, Herr Kräusel.

Kr. Come, pray come ! I have finished ! I have
finished ! Oh, I have composed a wonderfully beautiful
poem. I have in this, so to speak, surpassed myself. I
could never have believed that I had such a gift for
joking. Hitherto my strong point has been serious
composition. Theologico-polemico-poetical subjects, especially, run easily from my pen. But you surely have
read the edifying comedy which I composed against
the nobility. Ah ! that is a piece such as has hardly ever
come on the boards. But to return to my song. Here it
is, my dear Fräulein Ohldinn. You can now have it
printed under whatever name you please.

Fr. Ohl. Very well. But I must first show it to Herr
von Stamp. Men of birth are very fastidious in such
matters. He might perhaps find something to alter here
and there.

Kr. That is as you please. Only would you be so
good as to take into consideration together, one verse
which, not without an object, I have worked in ? It is
written for the meditation of all Christian hearts.

Fr. Ohl. Which ?

Kr. Here, on the other page.
        " *I* am now smelting miseriam."

Fr. Ohl. What is that ? *Miseriam ?*

Kr. Yes, poets are very bashful. They don't like
saying too plainly where the shoe pinches them. But I
have good hope that your kind generosity will soon help
your ignorance on this point.

Le. Don't you understand yet, cousin ?

Fr. Ohl. No, indeed.

KR. Oh pray, sir, be kind enough to spare me from a clearer explanation, which would cost me too many blushes. (*Holds his hat before his face.*)

LE. Don't be afraid.   My cousin will not fail to show herself grateful to you.

FR. OHL. Was that it? Yes, yes, sir, I will not forget you, do not fear.

KR. Oh! It means nothing. Do not believe that I am so selfish. Honour, honour alone, is that which I seek through my poetry. For our work cannot be repaid us in that way. But what would you think that I have often taken for such a poem?

LE. Poets usually take what they can get. I don't know how you manage.

Scene V.—LELIO, FRÄULEIN OHLDINN, HERR KRÄUSEL, LISETTE.

LIS. Rejoice, my dear lady; your worthy bridegroom, Captain von Stamp, will be with you in an instant. He is already on the stairs with all his charms. The good man has to crawl up on all fours. The wooden leg, the tattered uniform, the warlike moustache, are plain marks of a hero who has sacrificed much for his country's sake. Oh, how enviable you are! Indeed, you have not waited in vain. What is long in coming is good when it comes.

FR. OHL. Are you mad? Send him off. It must be a beggar.

LIS. No, no. According to your description it must be he himself.

KR. How can you object so much to his external appearance? Why, you took me too for a tailor. And I must once more read you the lesson, that there is often more concealed in a man than one sees in him.

LIS. He already sighs for you from the bottom of his heart, and swears enough to bring the house down, because no one goes to meet him.

FR. OHL. And can that be the Captain?

LIS. Yes, yes. Now there you see him himself with body and soul.

SCENE VI.—PETER, LISETTE, FRÄULEIN OHLDINN, LELIO, KRÄUSEL.

PE. (*dressed as above*). What the devil! Is this the way they treat a bridegroom here? Not so much as a dog or a cat comes to meet me. What the deuce do they take me for? Do they know who I am?

LE. Oh, my most worthy Captain, compose yourself.

PE. What have I to do with you? Is that your cousin?

LE. Yes.

LIS. Sir, you are very impolite, in a strange house.

PE. In a strange house? I suppose you don't know yet that I can instantly become lord of this same house. I have taken the liberty, Mademoiselle, of offering to you the honour of becoming my spouse. You would be mad if you didn't snatch at it with might and main.

FR. OHL. Oh Lord! Lelio!

KR. Wasn't I afraid of the fellow! I thought, on my soul, it was Peter. How much alike men sometimes are to one another.

LE. My dear cousin, do not dwell on his somewhat too unsophisticated expressions. A warrior is accustomed to use such phrases.

PE. That is true. I am one of the old German school. And the wife I take must not be a hair's-breadth different. Are you so?

LIS. It is lucky for you that she isn't; otherwise she would have turned you out of doors already with all possible politeness.

FR. OHL. Hush, Lisette. Don't make him angry.

LIS. What? I really believe you are still going to take his part. You must be wrong in the head, Captain, if you think my mistress is going to take such a mad cripple for her husband. I am a poor girl, but if you were buried in gold up to the ears I wouldn't look at you over my shoulder. Ha, ha! What a charming figure! A wooden leg, a moustache through which one can see neither nose nor mouth——

PE. Stop, you chatterbox! Am I going to take you,

or your mistress? If I please her . . . . . and I do please
her, I know. Don't I?

FR. OHL. Yes . . . . . but——

PE. But . . . . . but . . . . . but! If you were already
my wife, I would make you stop that silly word. How
much does your property amount to? If it isn't three
times as great as my debts——

LIS. Your property probably consists of them.

LE. Your debts, Captain, would be the smallest hindrance to the business. But I see that my cousin, through
your behaviour——

FR. OHL. Don't give him too strong a rebuke.

LIS. (*whispers to* PETER). Make it strong, or she will still
bite at the bait. (*Aloud.*) Now, sir, what do you want?

SCENE VII.—PETER, LISETTE, FRÄULEIN OHLDINN, LELIO,
KRÄUSEL, HERR REHFUSS.

REH. You will not take it ill, my dear Mademoiselle
Ohldinn——

LIS. No, no, my good friend, you have come to the
wrong person. This is Mademoiselle Ohldinn.

REH. You will not take it ill, my dear Mademoiselle, if
I——

PE. My friend, if you have anything to say, make it
short. Must the fool needs disturb us in our important
negotiation?

REH. My dear Mademoiselle, I have been informed by
Herr von Stamp——

PE. From whom? From me?

REH. No, no. Excuse me, from Captain von Stamp; that
he is going in a few days to marry Mademoiselle Ohldinn.

LIS. Cursed mishap!

PE. What did I say to you?

REH. Now, since the Captain owes me some hundred
thalers on a bill——

PE. What did I owe you? Are you crazy?

REH. I am speaking of the Captain. The bill is due to-
day, and it would be in my power to have him arrested.

PE. Have me arrested?

LIS. Be silent, Peter, or we are discovered.

REH. But since he told me that his bride would pay

the debt for him, I desired to learn whether Mademoiselle Ohldinn——

Fr. Ohl. Captain, I don't know how you could make so many debts in anticipation on the strength of my word. If you are in debt——

Re. No, Mademoiselle, I am speaking of Captain von Stamp.

Fr. Ohl. Yes, and there he is.

Pe. Yes, yes, it is I, my friend. Do not be anxious about the payment of your bill; I will satisfy you as I am an honest man.

Reh. You are much too good, sir. I do not remember that you owed me anything.

Pe. Yes, yes. I owe you several hundred thalers. Wasn't it five hundred?

Re. No, no. Captain von Stamp owes me nine hundred. But you——

Pe. Oh, that is too much to take on oneself for another. Well, well. I owe nine hundred thalers. And you, my dear wife, will pay them, won't you?

Reh. I don't know, sir, whether you take me for a fool?

Le. And I don't know whether you take all of us for fools. You say the Captain owes you so and so, and when the Captain admits it, you want to deny it again. What does that mean?

Pe. Yes, yes, I owe him nine hundred thalers.

Reh. No, sir, I couldn't take a farthing from you.

Pe. You shall have it in full.

Reh. You owe me nothing.

Pe. Will you have patience for a week at most?

Reh. Are you the Captain?

Pe. The deuce! What is that to you? Provided I am ready to pay; I may or may not be he. And, briefly, I am he. As surely as I have borrowed of you nine hundred thalers, so surely will I return them, with interest.

Reh. But why, sir, do you acknowledge the debt of another?

Pe. Oh! I am an upright man. What I owe, I pay.

Lis. Doubtless, my good man, you have made a mistake in the names. I believe there is another captain of this name here——

PE.   Yes, yes, quite right.   There is another who has the
same name.   He is my father's elder brother's daughter's
husband ; and we are brothers' children.

FR. OHL.   My friend, you will do well to bring forward
your claim at another time.   If he whom I am going to
marry is really in your debt, no doubt a way will be
found of paying.   But I must say I don't know what I
am to think of this.

PE.   Think what you please.   And you, my friend, can
pack yourself off, or——

REH.   I beg you not to take it ill——

LIS.   No, no; we won't take it ill, if you go.   Be off
now !   (*Exit.*)

SCENE VIII.—LELIO, LISETTE, PETER, KRÄUSEL, FRÄULEIN OHLDINN.

PE.   The cursed fellow !   Now, how far had we got,
my treasure?   Oh, yes ; as far as the property.   But
first there are various points which you must consent to.
I have just put them down briefly.   (*Takes a piece of
paper from his pocket.*)   First of all, the bride promises,
since she is of middle rank, and the bridegroom is the
high well-born gentleman, Captain von Stamp, sprung from
an ancient noble stock, at all times to render her future
husband due reverence, and never to address him otherwise than as " your grace."   Well?   Do you promise that?

FR. OHL.   But——

PE.   You mustn't use that confounded word to me.
Who has to rule ?   The husband or the wife ?   I, or you ?

FR. OHL.   Excuse me, but we are not yet husband and
wife.

PE.   Oh !   What we are not, we may become.   Next,
the bride promises, since she is of middle rank, and the
bridegroom is the high and well-born gentleman, Captain
von Stamp, sprung from an ancient noble stock, to place
all her money in his hands, to be disposed of as shall
please him.   Well?   Do you promise that?

LIS.   Of course that is one of the most important points.

FR. OHL.   One might well concede that to a man of
sense.   But——

Pe. Enough. I don't want to know the rest. I am a man of sufficient sense. Thirdly, the bride promises, since she is of middle rank, and the bridegroom is the high and well-born gentleman, Captain von Stamp, sprung from an ancient noble stock, that the two children illegitimately born to him . . . . . Well, on that point we will talk in private. For no one need know of it but you. Fourthly, the bride promises, since she is of middle rank——

Kr. Excuse me for interrupting you. Would you not be so good as to allow your most worthy prospective consort to show you the poem which I have made on your—God grant that it may soon take place—your wedding! I have no time to wait any longer . . . . . and——

Pe. Where is it? Where is it?

Fr. Ohl. Here. (*She gives it to him.*)

Pe. What rubbish is this? I see from the title that it is good for nothing. Are you not aware that I am Lord of the Manor and High Sheriff of Nothingham, Beggarby, Shieldbury and Poorcaster? All that must be put in too. Also that I have served for sixteen years under the French, twelve under the Austrians, nineteen under the Dutch, seventeen under the English, and twenty-two more or less under the Saxons. . . . . Oh, the deuce! I am lost——

SCENE IX.—Lelio, Lisette, Peter, Kräusel, Fräulein Ohldinn, Herr Oront, Frau Oront, Von Stamp.

Le. Oh, what cursed ill-luck!

Lis. Now we are aground.

Fr. Ohl. You come at the right moment, Herr Oront. I owe you so far small thanks for having burdened me with Herr von Stamp.

Stamp. How, Mademoiselle? Do you already dislike me, before I have had the pleasure of speaking to you?

Fr. Ohl. You, sir? Why, you have just this moment stepped unknown into the room. How should I have to complain of you? No, I refer to Captain von Stamp.

Pe. She means me. She means me. It is a slight mistake in names.

Herr Or. What have you to do with the fellow? This is Captain von Stamp whom I now bring to you.

FR. OHL. What? So they attempted to deceive me. Ha, ha! My dear cousin.

LE. Cursed luck!

STAMP. I believe another has been playing my part here. Who are you, you good-for-nothing——

PE. Captain von Stamp I am . . . . . not; but—— (*Takes off his moustache and wooden leg*) but——

STAMP. I do believe it is Peter.

KR. Oh Lord! Yes, yes, it is Peter. I thought as much. I thought as much. What will become of me?

STAMP (*to* PETER). Stop, gallows bird!

PE. (*to* KRÄUSEL). Stop, gallows bird!

STAMP. What does this mean? To misuse my name thus! For whom was this deception intended?

PE. (*to* KRÄUSEL). What does this mean? To misuse my patience thus! When will you pay for my pastry?

STAMP (*to* PETER). Answer, you dog!

PE. (*to* KRÄUSEL). Answer, you dog!

KR. Oh that I was safe out of this!

PE. Oh that I was safe out of this!

STAMP (*to* PETER). I'll throttle you, fellow! Confess at once, what was the purpose of this disguise?

PE. (*breaks away and turns at* KRÄUSEL). I'll throttle you, fellow! Confess at once, for what purpose did you put me in a street-song?

KR. Oh! It is getting too hot to stay here. Good-bye, good-bye! (*Runs out.*)

PE. (*runs after him*). Ha, ha! You shan't escape me.

STAMP. And you shan't escape me.

SCENE X.—FRÄULEIN OHLDINN, LELIO, LISETTE, VON STAMP, HERR ORONT, FRAU ORONT.

LE. Stop, Captain; what has happened is my doing. You ruin me by your marriage. And could you blame me for doing all in my power to frustrate it?

STAMP. I should be very sorry if I were to ruin you. No, Lelio, if you will not stand in my way——

HERR OR. Oh! How can he stand in your way, provided she will have you? and she will.

FRAU OR. It is true. Mistress Ohldinn, why should you trouble yourself about a man who can play you such a trick?

LE. So? Who, then, was it, Madam, who, promised me her assistance in it, a while ago?

FRAU OR. Ah! A while ago I had fallen out with my husband.

LE. And now?

FRAU OR. We are reconciled again. A pair of honest married people must quarrel a hundred times a day, and a hundred times be reconciled again.

LE. Mistress cousin, sooner than agree to your marriage, I will myself claim your hand. For I believe I have the first claim on you——

FR. OHL. What?

LIS. What?

FR. OHL. You might have had this idea earlier. We have been in the house together for more than ten years.

STAMP (*takes* LELIO *aside*). A word in confidence. Why won't you let me share your property? I believe there will be enough for both of us. As her husband I should get possession of it. And I assure you, you shall enjoy it more at my hands than at hers. Yes, I promise you, even, to make no claim on that which remains when she dies. My debts now oblige me to take this step. Do not oppose me any longer, and we can live as firm friends.

FR. OHL. May we not hear what you are saying there so confidentially?

LE. Ok, it was nothing. The Captain has shown me that I am wrong in wishing any longer to stand in the way of your happiness. I give my consent to everything.

FR. OHL. Ah! You are an honourable man. And I assure you that your concurrence contributes in no small degree to the pleasure with which I now offer the Captain my hand.

STAMP. You make us happy, Lelio.

LIS. (*whispers*). But, Herr Lelio——

LE. (*whispers*). Never mind, Lisette. The fun is going to begin now.

FR. OHL. But, Lisette, I have a word to say to you. We must part. You can go where you please. For I know well that you are at the bottom of all this buffoonery, and that you, and you alone, led my cousin astray.

LIS. I!

STAMP. Oh, my dearest Mademoiselle, let me intercede for the poor girl. Pray keep her.

FR. OHL. No, no. She must go. She must go.

STAMP. Grant me this, the first favour I ask.

FR. OHL. No, no. It is not right. It is not right.

STAMP. Ah, it is quite right. Especially with people of rank like ourselves.

SCENE XI.—FRÄULEIN OHLDINN, LISETTE, VON STAMP, HERR ORONT, CLITANDER.

CLI. Do I find you all together here, my children? My dear Captain, I come to wish you happiness on your marriage. I have been looking for you everywhere.

STAMP. Have you, perchance, brought my five-and-twenty ducats with you?

CLI. Oh, you can forget them, now you have met with such good fortune.

FR. OHL. You owe them to him? You told me quite another story just now.

CLI. No, no. You cannot have understood me rightly. He won them from me at billiards the other day.

HERR OR. Well, then, all is settled. You, Miss bride, will be so kind as to give us a little banquet this evening, and, if possible, to make arrangements for the wedding to take place this week.

CLI. Oh, that is excellent. I could not have come at a more opportune time. Come, come. To the banquet, Lelio! To the banquet, Herr von Stamp! Lelio, take Frau Oront. I will take your cousin.

STAMP. And so, Lisette, remains for me.

HERR OR. A bad omen!

THE WOMAN-HATER.

(A COMEDY IN THREE ACTS.)

The 'Woman-hater' was written at Leipzig during the years 1746-1748, but was retouched afterwards at various times.

DRAMATIS PERSONÆ.

WUMSHATER.

LAURA, *his daughter.*

VALER, *his son. suitor of* HILARIA.

HILARIA, *in boy's clothes, under the name of* LELIO.

SOLBIST, *an advocate.*

LEANDER, *suitor of* LAURA.

LISETTE, *maid-servant.*

THE WOMAN-HATER.

ACT I.

Scene I.—Wumshäter, Lisette.

Wu. Where can I find the rascal? Johann! Johann! . . . . . These confounded women! . . . . . The women have involved me in a lawsuit, and it will bring me to a premature grave. Who knows why Herr Solbist is coming to call on me? I am all impatience to see him. I hope we have not received an unfavourable judgment again. Would that I had rather been three times hanged than three times married . . . . . Johann! Don't you hear me?

Lis. (*enters*). What are your orders?

Wu. What do you want? Did I call you?

Lis. Johann is gone out; what is he to do? Cannot I do it?

Wu. I do not wish to be served by you. How often have I told you already to spare me the annoyance of seeing you? Stay in your place, in the kitchen, and with my daughter . . . . . Johann!

Lis. You hear what I say; he is not there.

Wu. Who told him, then, to go out, just when I want him. . . . . Johann!

Lis. Johann! Johann! Johann!

Wu. Now then? What are you screaming for?

Lis. He won't hear your shouting alone three streets off.

Wu. Ugh! What a woman!

Lis. I like that! One spits at toads and not at human beings.

WU. Yes, well. . . . . As soon as you and the likes of
you reckon yourselves among human beings, I feel inclined
to quarrel with Heaven for having made me one.

LIS. Quarrel, then. Perhaps it already repents of not
having made a post of you.

WU. Out of my sight!

LIS. As you order.

WU. Will you do so at once? Or must I go?

LIS. I shall have the honour of following you.

WU. I could go mad.

LIS. (aside). He is insane already.

WU. Has not Herr Solbist, my lawyer, been here
yet?

LIS. Johann, no doubt, will tell you.

WU. Has my son gone out?

LIS. Ask your Johann.

WU. Is that an answer to my question? I want to
know whether Herr Solbist has been here yet?

LIS. You do not wish to be served by me, you know.

WU. Answer, I say.

LIS. My place is in the kitchen.

WU. Stay, and answer first.

LIS. My business is only to attend to your daughter.

WU. You shall answer. Has Herr Solbist——

LIS. I will spare you the annoyance of seeing me.
(Exit.)

SCENE II.—WUMSHÄTER, VALER.

WU. What a creature! . . . . . I will, this very day,
turn the whole pack of women out of my house; even my
daughter. She may look after herself. . . . . Good, good,
my son, that you come. I have just been asking for you.

VA. How happy I should be if I dared to think that
you had wished to anticipate my request. May I flatter
myself that I have at last received from you the permis
sion I have so often sought?

WU. Oh! You are beginning about that vexatious
matter again. Do not grieve your old father, who,
until now, has considered you the only comfort of his old
age. There is surely time enough yet.

VA. No, dearest father, there is not much time. I

have received letters to-day which oblige me to go back again as soon as possible.

Wu. Well, go, then, in God's name! Only obey me in this : don't marry. I love you too much to give my consent to your unhappiness.

Va. To my unhappiness? What different ideas we must have of happiness and unhappiness! I shall consider it the greatest unhappiness which could befall me, if I have to remain any longer without a person who is the most precious in all the world to me. And you——

Wu. And I shall consider it the greatest unhappiness which could befall you if I see you follow your blind impulse. To consider a woman the most precious object in the world! A woman? But the want of experience excuses you. Listen ; do you regard me as a true father ?

Va. I should be sorry if in this case my obedience——

Wu. You are right to plead your obedience. But have you ever repented of your obedience to me ?

Va. Never, hitherto ; but——

Wu. But you fear you will repent if you obey me in this also? Eh? But if it is the fact that I am a true father, if it is a fact that I unite prudence and experience with my fatherly affection, your fear is very unjust. People believe the unfortunate man whom storm and waves have cast on the shore, when he relates to them the terrors of the shipwreck ; and he who is prudent learns from his story how little the treacherous waters are to be trusted. All that such an unfortunate man has experienced at sea, I have experienced in my three marriages. And will you not learn from my mishaps? I was just as ardent, just as thoughtless, at your age, as you are. I saw a girl with red cheeks ; I saw her, and resolved to make her my wife. She was poor——

Va. Oh, father, spare me the repetition of your history. I have heard it so often——

Wu. And you have not yet profited by it ? . . . . She was poor, and I also had little. Now picture to yourself what trouble, anxiety, and vexation a man just commencing business, as I was then, meets with, if his hands are empty to begin with.

L 2

VA. My bride, however, is anything but poor.

WU. Listen to me ! In my difficulties, I could have no recourse to my relations. Why? They had proposed that I should marry a rich old widow, by which course I should have received immediate help in my business. So I offended them when I fell in love with a pretty face, and preferred to love happily than live happily.

VA. But in my marriage this can——

WU. Patience. The worst of it was that I loved her so blindly, that I went to all possible expense on her account. Her immoderate love of display brought me numberless debts.

VA. Do, father, spare me this unnecessary story, now, and tell me shortly, if I may hope——

WU. I tell it merely for your good. . . . . Do you suppose that I could have extricated myself from my many debts, if Heaven had not been so benevolent as to remove the cause of my ruin after the space of a year? She died ; and she had hardly closed her eyes, when mine were opened. Whichever way I looked, I was in debt. And just imagine into what a rage I fell when, after her death, I learned her cursed infidelity. My debts began to press with twofold force when I perceived that I had contracted them for love of a good-for-nothing, to please an infernal, confounded hypocrite. And are you sure, my son, that it will not also be thus with you?

VA. I can be as sure of this as I am convinced of the love of my Hilaria. Her soul is much too noble, her heart much too upright——

WU. Come, come, I don't want a panegyric on a syren, who knows how to keep her ugly scales under the water. If you were not my son, I should laugh heartily at your simplicity. In truth, you have the making of a nice husband in you! A noble soul, an upright heart, in a female body ! And even, as you tell me, in a beautiful female body. But it comes, after all, to the same thing, whether they are beautiful or ugly. The beautiful woman finds lovers, and men who will steal away your honour, everywhere, and the ugly woman seeks for them everywhere. What can you answer to this?

VA. Two things. Either it is not certain that all girls

are alike false, and in this case I feel sure that my Hilaria
is among the exceptions; or else it is certain that a
faithful wife is only a creature of the imagination, which
never has existed and never will exist; and in this case I,
as well as anyone else, must——

Wu. Fie, fie! For shame, for shame! . . . . . But you
are joking.

Va. Truly not. If a wife is an unquestionable evil,
she is also a necessary evil.

Wu. Yes, an evil which our folly makes necessary.
But how glad would I be to have been foolish if, on that
account, you could be less so! Perhaps, too, this would be
possible if you would carefully consider my experiences.
Listen. So when my first wife was dead, I tried my luck
with a rich, and somewhat elderly——

Scene III.—Lelio, Wumshäter, Valer.

Va. Come, Lelio, come. Help me to persuade my
father to stand in the way of my happiness no longer.

Wu. Come, Herr Lelio, come. My son has got his
marriage-attack. Help me to bring him to his senses.

Le. Oh! For shame, Valer, be open to reason. You
have heard often enough from your father that marriage
is a ridiculous and senseless affair. I should think you
ought to be convinced by now. One may well believe a
man who has tried it with three wives, that women are
all . . . . . all women.

Va. Is that how you take my part? Your sister will
be much obliged to you.

Le. I take your part more than you think; and my
sister herself would not speak otherwise were she present.

Wu. Yes, I too should imagine so : for if it is true that
girls do possess anything resembling reason, they must
necessarily be convinced of their own detestableness. It
is as clear as day; and you only cannot see it, because
love keeps your eyes shut.

Le. Oh, sir, you speak like reason itself. You have
quite converted me in the short time during which I have
been with you. Formerly women were not altogether
objects of indifference to me. But now . . . . yes, I ought

to be your son, Herr Wumshäter; I would propagate the race
of women-haters rarely! My sons should all be like me!

VA. I don't object to that. Such women-haters at any
rate would not let the world die out.

LE. That would be silly enough. Why, wouldn't the
women-haters, then, die out with the rest? No, no,
Valer, we must be mindful, as far as possible, of the preservation of such excellent men. Eh?

WU. That is in some degree true. Yet I would rather
see my son let others be mindful of it. I am sure that
the world will not miss his contribution. Why should he
for the sake of an uncertain posterity make his life
miserable? And, besides, it is a very poor joy to have
children if one must have as much trouble with them
as I have had. You see, my son, how I am interested in
your affairs. Compensate me, by your obedience, for the
vexation your mother caused me.

LE. She must have been a very bad wife, eh?

WU. As they all are, dear Lelio. Haven't I told you
the story of my life yet? It is a piteous thing to hear.

VA. Oh, spare him that. He has had to hear it more
than ten times already.

LE. I, Valer? You are mistaken. Do tell it me, Herr
Wumshäter, I beg you. I am sure I shall be able to draw
many a lesson from it.

WU. I like that. Oh, my son, if you too were of the
same mind! Well, listen. . . . . I have had three wives.

LE. Three wives?

VA. Don't you know that yet?

LE. (to VALER). Oh, be quiet, do! . . . . Three wives!
Then you must possess a real store of varied experiences.
I only wonder how you ever were able to overcome so
successfully your hatred of women three times.

WU. One cannot be wise all at once by oneself. But
if I had had a father such as my son has in me, a father
who would have withheld me from the brink of ruin
through his example. . . . . Truly, my son, you do not
deserve such a father——

LE. Oh, tell me, do, first of all, which of your bad
wives was Valer's mother? Surely it was the best of
them?

Wu. The best?

Le. Of the bad, I mean.

Wu. The best of the bad ! . . . . The worst, dear Lelio, the very worst.

Le. Well, now! So she didn't take after her son at all? Oh, the degenerate mother!

Va. Why do you want to pain me, Lelio? I love my father, but I have loved my mother too. My heart is rent when he does not leave her at peace even in her grave.

Wu. My son, if you take it in that way . . . . well, well. I will tell you the story afterwards, Herr Lelio, when we are alone. You cannot possibly imagine how selfish, how quarrelsome——

Va. You wish to tell it him when you are alone, so I must go.

Wu. Well, well, stay here. I won't say any more. I could not have imagined that one could be so prejudiced about one's mother. Mother or not, she remains still a woman whose faults one must abominate, if one does not wish to make oneself guilty along with her. But enough. To return to your marriage. You promise me, then, not to marry?

Va. How can I promise you that? Supposing I were able to suppress the affection which now holds me in sway, yet my household affairs would oblige me to look for a helpmate.

Wu. Oh, if it is only to be a helpmate in your household affairs, I know an excellent plan. Listen, take your sister with you. She is clever enough to manage your house, and I should in this way get rid of a burden which has long become intolerable to me.

Va. Am I to stand in the way of my sister's happiness?

Wu. You are a wonderful fellow! What happiness can you stand in the way of? People won't excite themselves about her; and whether you take her with you or not, she will find no match that will suit either her or me. For that I should deceive an honourable, upright man with her, can never happen. I will make no man unhappy, let alone one whom I esteem. And she herself is too proud to take a worthless and bad man, to whom I would most willingly grant her.

LE. But, Herr Wumshäter, do you not consider that it
would be very dangerous for me, if Valer were to take his
sister with him? Hatred of women has not struck its
roots any too deep as yet in my heart. Laura is lively
and pretty, and, what is best of all, she is the daughter of
a woman-hater, whom I have adopted as my model in all
things. How easily it might happen, that I should . . . .
I won't say marry, for that would be the least evil, but
that I should—Heaven avert the calamity—that I should
even fall in love with her. . . . . Then, good-night, hatred
of women! And, perhaps, after many misfortunes, I
should hardly come to myself again by the time I was
your age.

WU. Heaven forbid that that should arise from it!
But have more confidence in yourself, Herr Lelio; you
are too sensible. As has been said, my son, you may rely
on this, your sister shall go with you; she must go with
you. I will go at once and tell her so. (*Exit.*)

SCENE IV.—LELIO, VALER.

VA. Dearest Hilaria, what shall I do now? You see——
LE. I see that you are too impatient, Valer.
VA. Too impatient? Haven't we been here a week
already? Why was not I sufficiently thoughtless to
dispense with my father's consent altogether? Why
must Hilaria have so much complaisance towards the
weakness of his peevish age? The idea which you had
of winning his good-will beforehand, in the disguise of
a man under your brother's name, was the most ingenious
in the world, and one which promised to lead rapidly
to our end. And yet it will not help us at all.

LE. Do not say that; for I believe our affair is going on
very well. Have not I, as Lelio, obtained his friendship
and his entire confidence?

VA. And that, too, without performing any miracles.
You agree with him in everything.

LE. Must I not do so?

VA. Yes, but not so earnestly. Instead of dissuading
him from his obstinate delusion, you confirm him in it.
That cannot possibly come to good. And another thing,

dearest Hilaria; you are also carrying the masquerade much too far with my sister.

LE. But it will always remain merely acting. And as soon as she learns who I am, everthing will be right again.

VA. If she does not learn it too late. I am quite aware that since you appeared here as a man you could not refrain from a little flattery. But you ought to have given this flattery as coldly as possible, without appearing to have any serious design on her heart. My father has just gone to tell her that she is to travel with us. Mind what I say, that will be grist to her mill, as the proverb says. For us, indeed, no harm can be done by that, but all the more may be for another.

LE. I know what you mean. Leander——

VA. Leander has long been on the best terms with her; and only the lawsuit in which he is involved with our father has restrained him from asking for her hand, through fear of a contemptuous refusal. But at last Herr Solbist has obligingly undertaken to set him at ease as regards this fear. He is going to be the match-maker himself; and the turn he means to give to his petition would be the silliest in the world, if he had not to do with a man whose folly will only permit itself to be opposed by folly.

LE. A polite description of your father!

VA. It is sad enough for me that I cannot think otherwise of him in this matter. My lovely Hilaria, be kind enough to alter your manner a little. Behave with more indifference towards my sister, so that Leander may not look on you as a rival who is injuring him without himself being able in the end to use the advantage he has gained over him. You must try, too, to prepossess my father in favour of the person you really are, rather than the person you appear to be. You must begin to oppose his whims, and, by means of the influence you have obtained over him, bring him at least to consider Hilaria as the single one of her sex that deserves to be exempted from his hatred. You must——

LE. You must not always be saying "you must." My dear Valer, you promise to be a tolerably domineering

husband. Do let me have the pleasure of playing out the
part I have commenced according to my own judgment.

VA. If I could only see that you thought about
playing it out. But you are only thinking of playing
on, and are complicating the tangle more and more, and
you will end by making it so complicated that it will 'not
be possible to undo it again.

LE. Very well, if it can't be undone again, we will do
as the bad playwrights do, break it.

VA. And get hissed as the bad playwrights do.

LE. Never mind.

VA. How you torture me with this indifference,
Hilaria!

LE. You take it too seriously, Valer. I am not
really so indifferent; and to convince you of it . . . .
well . . . . I will this very day take a step in our plot for
which I did not consider that I had sufficiently prepared
the way. We will let Hilaria appear, and try what luck
she will have in her true shape.

VA. You delight me. . . . . Yes, dearest Hilaria, we
cannot be too speedy in learning our destiny. If this
does no good, we shall yet have done all that lay in our
power; and I shall at last be able to persuade my conscience to confront so strange a father. I must possess
you, cost what it may. How happy I shall be if I can
openly boast of this hand! (*Kisses her hand.*)

SCENE V.—WUMSHÄTER, LELIO, VALER.

WU. (*who sees* VALER *kissing* HILARIA'S *hand*). Eh! eh!
My son, why, you are treating your bride's brother as if
he were the bride herself. How you start!

LE. Dear Valer often forgets himself. . . . . But do
you know why that is?

WU. That I cannot know. . . . . By the bye, my son,
all is right. Your sister is going to travel with you. She
was more pleased with my proposal than I expected.
. . . . . But now, Herr Lelio, what is it that you were
going to tell me?

LE. (*softly to* VALER). Pay attention, Valer; our plot
may now be introduced.

Wu.   Tell me, Lelio, what did you mean?

Le.   You caught the ardent Valer in an ecstasy which
is a little too tender for a manly friendship. You were
surprised, and thought he must be taking me for my
sister. How penetrating is your intellect, Herr Wums-
bäter! You have hit it. He really does take me for
her frequently, in the intoxication of his passion. But
one must forgive him this *quid pro quo*, since it is
impossible for two drops of water to be more like one
another than I and my sister are. Whenever he looks me
fixedly in the face, he imagines he sees her too, and cannot
restrain himself from offering to me some of the respectful
caresses he is wont to offer to her.

Wu.   How absurd!

Le.   Not a few men of his stamp are much more absurd.
I know a certain Lidio who behaves towards a withered
nosegay which his mistress had worn in her bosom more
than a year ago, as if it were his mistress herself.
He talks with it for whole days, kisses it, kneels before
it——

Wu.   And has not been sent to Bedlam yet? My son,
my son, learn wisdom from the misfortunes of others, and
restrain your love while you are still able to do so. Just
consider, to talk with a nosegay, and kneel before it!
Could the effect of a mad dog's bite be more frightful?

Le.   Certainly not. But to return to my sister——

Wu.   Who is so like you? Now, how much is she like
you, I wonder? One can probably perceive that you are
of the same family.

Le.   Oh, that is a trifle. Our parents themselves could
not distinguish between us in our childhood, when for
fun we had exchanged clothes.

Va.   And now just consider, dearest father: if it is
true, as you have often said yourself, that even from the
outward appearance of Herr Lelio, from the form of his
face, from his features, from the modest fire of his eyes,
from his manner, one could infer the inner worth of his
soul, his intelligence, his virtue, and all the qualities
which you prize in him; consider for once, I say, whether,
in the case of his amiable sister, one can draw a different
inference from the very same external appearance, the

very same form of face, the very same features, the
very same eyes, and the very same manner? Certainly
not.

Wu. Certainly yes! But that you may not force me
to prove this at length, I venture to declare flatly that
it is impossible that his sister can be as like him as
you say.

Le. You had better prove the former for him, Herr
Wumshäter, than deny the latter, for otherwise you might,
perhaps this very day, be convinced of it by your eyes.

Wu. How by my eyes?

Le. Has not Valer told you yet that he expects my
sister to-day?

Wu. What? She is coming herself? With no dimi-
nution of the high respect which I feel for you, Herr
Lelio, I must however freely confess that I am not in the
least desirous to make the acquaintance of your female
counterpart.

Va. And just because I knew this, father, I did not
want to say anything of her coming until now. But I
will yet hope that I may have the pleasure of presenting
her to you.

Wu. Provided only you do not ask me to meet her as
my future daughter-in-law.

Va. But you will meet her as the sister of Lelio?

Wu. According as I find her. . . . . Now, Laura,
what do you want?

Scene VI.—Laura, Lelio, Valer.

La. To thank you once more, dearest father, for being
so kind as to allow me to go with my brother.

Wu. Let that be!

La. Your fatherly love has anticipated my wish.

Wu. Well, be quiet then.

La. In truth I was wishing to make the request myself.

Wu. What is that to me?

La. Only I did not know how I should express my
wish prudently. I feared——

Wu. I fear that I shall vex myself into a consumption
over your chatter.

La. I feared, I say, that you might attribute my desire to live with my brother to a false cause.

Wu. Have you not finished yet?

La. To a reprehensible weariness, perhaps, at having to remain longer with you.

Wu. I shall have to stop your mouth for you.

La. But I assure you——

Wu. Now, in truth, a mad horse is easier to stop than the chatter of such a jade. You ought to know, that I have not considered you in the least in this matter. I send you with your brother, that you may manage his household affairs for him, and because I want to get rid of you. But whether it is agreeable or disagreeable to you, is all the same to me.

La. I quite understand, father, that you are making your kindness so small and questionable only in order to spare me from a formal expression of gratitude. I will therefore be silent. But you, my dear brother——

Wu. Yes, yes! She is silent; that is, she begins to chatter to somebody else.

La. You will not, I hope, be sorry to take me with you?

Va. Dear sister——

La. Good, good, spare your assurances. I know already that you love me. How pleased I shall be in your society, which I have had to be without for so many years!

Va. I cannot possibly expect you for my sake to exchange a beloved native town, where you have so many friends and admirers, for a place quite strange to you.

Wu. But I expect it of her. I should hope you are not paying each other compliments?

La. Do you hear? And what do you mean by your quite strange place? Shall I not have you there? Will not Lelio be there? Shall I not find his excellent sister there? (*To* Lelio) Permit me, sir——

Wu. I thought so; her prating is going the whole round.

La. Permit me, I say, to regard your sister beforehand as my friend. She need only have the half of her brother's perfections, for me to love her just as much as I esteem him.

Wu. Eh ? I verily believe you are bold enough to utter
flatteries to respectable people. I am sorry, Herr Lelio,
that this thoughtless creature should make you blush.

Va. (*whispers to* LELIO). Don't answer her too cordially.

Le. Amiable Laura——

Va. (*whispers to* LELIO). Not too cordially, I say.

Le. Most lovely Laura——

Va. (*whispers to* LELIO). Take care.

La. Mademoiselle——

Wu. (*to* LAURA). Just see how embarrassed you have
made him. But it is a sign of his intelligence ; for the
more intelligent a man is, the less can he make out of
your tittle-tattle and wish-wash. Come, Lelio, let us take a
turn in the garden, and not stay here any longer with the
girl. Don't you follow us, though. But you, Valer, may
come with us. (LELIO *makes a bow to* LAURA.) Eh ?
What is that ? You surely won't feel a twinge of conscience if you turn your back on her without a salutation ?
(LAURA *returns the bow.*) And you, girl, have done with
your curtsies, or . . . . . The confounded lot ! When
their tongues are tired, they pursue one with their
grimaces.

Va. I will follow you directly.

(*Exeunt* WUMSHÄTER *and* LELIO.)

SCENE VII.—VALER, LAURA.

Va. Now, sister, just tell me what I am to think of
you?

La. Tell me first what I am to think of your Lelio?

Va. You are really resolved to go with me ?

La. Who would have supposed that Lelio did not know
how to return a compliment ! I know him better. How
many pretty things he has said to me when from time to
time he has found me alone ! But, brother, he shall not
say them to me any more alone. I will soon bring him to
say them in your father's and your presence. He has
done very rightly in playing a part before the latter up
till now. He had to make sure of his good will.
But now I should think he might gradually raise the
mask a little.

Va. I am astounded.

La. I should like to know why? Am I astounded that you have found favour in his sister's eyes?

Va. That means, I am to have the justice to refrain from astonishment that you have found favour in her brother's eyes. But Leander——

La. Say nothing to me about Leander, I beg of you. He must have known for some time now what his position was. Haven't I sent back all his letters unopened for some days past?

Va. But only for some days.

La. Sneering brother! Could it be disagreeable to you, then, to be allied doubly to the family of Lelio?

Va. I wager anything that you cannot explain yourself more clearly.

La. Don't do that; for see now if you would not have lost your wager. . . . . I know how I stand towards Lelio. He has confessed his love to me with more fervour, more tenderness than Leander has ever done. And don't you know, then, the way we girls have? When I go shopping I assure you I never buy the stuff which I have first bargained for. And if the shopman was to become annoyed at that, I should say, "Why don't you show me at once what I like best?"

Va. The shopman won't become annoyed at it, for he knows from experience that when you have considered much and long you always pitch at last on the worst thing; on a colour, on a pattern which has been out of fashion for an age. And you don't observe how you have deceived yourselves until you have inspected your purchase at home and at leisure. Then how much you wish for that which you had first bargained for.

La. You can make an excellent simile. Will you not be so good as to apply it also? It contains no bad recommendation of Lelio. Oh, he shall hear how well you speak of him; he shall hear of it this very day. Good-bye, brother.

Va. A word in earnest, sister.

La. In earnest? Have you been joking until now? Well, I will let it pass then.

Va. Listen; I tell you in plain words: Lelio cannot

possibly become yours; believe me, he cannot possibly
—not possibly.

LA. Ha, ha, ha! If I don't go at once, perhaps you
will tell me in confidence that he is already married. Ha,
ha, ha! (*Exit.*)

VA. Silly girl! . . . . . I really have not dared to say
anything to her of Herr Solbist's proposal. She would
anticipate him with my father, and then all would be lost.
We must serve her against her will, if she is to thank us
in the end. Why, here she is again.

LA. (*comes back with a serious air*). Brother——

VA. Eh? So serious?

LA. Impossible, did you say? Explain this impossibility to me.

VA. Our father is waiting for me in the garden. I
must therefore explain it very briefly. Impossible is
that . . . . . which is not possible. Good-bye for the
present, dear sister. (*Exit.*)

LA. Is that all? I am much obliged! Patience! I
must see how I can get a word with Lelio. (*Exit.*)

ACT II.

Scene I.—Lelio *or* Hilaria.

LE. I shall soon believe myself that I have made love
too boldly to the good Laura. Alas for our poor sex!
How easily we are deceived! She signed to me confidentially just now. She wants to speak to me, I suppose.
Yes, yes; I thought so. It is good that I am prepared.

Scene II.—Laura, Lelio.

LA. Poor Lelio, have you at last got away from my
father's vexatious presence? How I wish that there was
at least one person in our house whose agreeable society
could indemnify you.

LE. (*aside*). She knows excellently well how to contrive a love discourse! I hardly know how to make
the preparations for my retreat equally cleverly.

La. You do not answer me?

Le. What shall I answer?

La. It is true. What shall one answer when the answer is placed ready on one's lips? You might just as politely have told me to my face that I at any rate was not the person alluded to.

Le. Cruel Laura!

La. Merciful Lelio!

Le. Barbarous fair one!

La. Anything more? Have pity, and make me more humane.

Le. You are making fun of me. Unhappy man that I am! Oh that I had never known you, or at least had known you earlier!

La. Still no end to your ejaculations? But what do you mean by that?

Le. What have I done to you that you feed in me a flame which will consume me hopelessly?

La. Now you are gradually coming to questions, and I hope soon to understand you.

Le. How do I deserve that you should involve me in a hopeless love?

La. Inquire further. Perhaps something will come which I can answer.

Le. Was it, then, so important to you to make me an innocent victim of your charms? What pleasure did you promise yourself from my despair? Enjoy it, oh enjoy it. But that another shall enjoy it with you, who cannot possibly love you as tenderly as I do love you, that pierces me to the heart!

La. By the way, you are surely not jealous?

Le. Jealous? No. One ceases to be jealous when one has lost all hope, and one can only be envious.

La. (*aside*). What am I to think of him? . . . . . May not I know who is the fortunate person whom you envy?

Le. Pray continue to dissimulate. It is just your dissimulation which has caused my unhappiness. The lovelier a girl is, the more upright she ought to be; for only by her uprightness can she obviate the mischief which her beauty would perpetrate. Immediately after the first interchange of politeness, at any rate after the first tender glances which I directed towards you, immediately after the first sighs which my new love forced from me, you should have said to me, "I warn you, sir, be on your guard. Let not my beauty lead you too far; you come too late; my heart is already promised." You ought to have said that to me; and then I should never have presumed to covet the possession of another.

La. (*aside*). Ha! Has my brother put anything about Leander into his head?

Le. All too happy Leander!

La. (*aside*). Yes, yes! That is it. I will make him pay for that . . . . . Sir——

Le. I pray you, no excuses, Mademoiselle. You might easily make matters worse, and I might begin to believe that you at any rate pitied me. I know the sacred rights of a first love, which I suppose yours for Leander is. I will not be guilty of any foolish attempt to weaken it. All would be in vain——

La. I am astonished at your credulity.

Le. You are right to be astonished at it. Could I have imagined anything sillier than that your bewitching charms should have awaited my coming to disclose their power over a sensitive heart?

La. That credulity might have been forgiven you. But do you not perceive, then, or will you not perceive——

Le. What, most lovely Laura?

La. That it is another credulity for which I am displeased with you.

Le. Another? . . . . You are right . . . . Fool that I am.

La. What now?

Le. I can hardly raise my eyes for shame.

La. For shame?

Le. How ridiculous I must appear to you!

La. I did not know——

Le. How absurd I appear to myself!

La. You appear? . . . . And why, then?

Le. Certainly, how ridiculous, how absurd, that I should have taken politeness for tenderness, the conventional obligations for tokens of growing love! That, that is the credulity which displeases you so much in me.—a credulity which is all the more culpable the more pride it presupposes.

LA. Lelio!

LE. But forgive me; be generous, lovely Laura; judge me not with too much severity. My youth deserves your forbearance. What man of my years, of my education, of my ardent disposition, is not a bit of a coxcomb? It is our nature. Every smiling glance seems to us the reward of our desert, or the homage due to our worth, without our inquiring whether it has not fallen on us through mere absence of mind, out of pity, or even out of contempt.

LA. Oh, you make me impatient; I have no idea how it may fare at times with your small brains.

LE. Not always for the best. But trouble yourself about me no more. You have brought me back within the bounds of my own insignificance.

LA. More still? I see my father coming, I must be brief. That you should so easily have accepted as true a silly story about a certain Leander that,—that is the credulity which annoys me in you. . . . . I leave you; follow me without being noticed to the summer-house. You shall have proofs that some one is trying to deceive you. (*Exit.*)

SCENE III.—WUMSHÄTER, VALER, LELIO.

LE. I shall not follow you, my good child. I really do not know when anything has been so unpleasant to me as this interview.

WU. Why, Herr Lelio, you have slipped away from me. You can hardly think how angry my son is making me. See, through your confounded request, I have quite forgotten that Herr Solbist was coming to see me. I hope he has not been here already. My servants tell me nothing at all. Why is it? Heaven has chastised me with a lot of women to wait on me, and if once in a while I get a decent man to serve me, a month is scarcely out when that confounded hussy, Lisette, has him in her toils. Well, well, when once my daughter is gone, I won't endure even a female fly under my roof any more.

VA. Look, father, here is Herr Solbist just coming.

SCENE IV.—SOLBIST (*in a large wig, with a packet of legal documents under his arm*), WUMSHÄTER, VALER, LELIO.

WU. Ah! Is that you, my dear Herr Solbist?

SOL. Yes, it is certainly.

VA. (*aside to* LELIO). Don't let him see that you know anything of his plot, for everything must be kept secret from him.

WU. Well, what good news do you bring with you?

SOL. Hadn't I better have told you at once before the front door? . . . . Patience. I must speak with you in complete privacy.

WU. In complete privacy? You make me uneasy.

SOL. (*to* LELIO, *who is surveying him from head to foot*). Well? What are you staring at me for?

LE. I admire you.

SOL. As a bumpkin does a large house, when, for once, he comes to town.

LE. I see, you have got yourself up more than usual to-day.

SOL. I am a rogue if it was on your account.

LE. In this wig you might get yourself engraved for the Illustrated News.

SOL. Don't vex me to-day. To-day I am on professional business. Another time you can have your fun with me. To-day be so good as to respect my office.

LE. I have all respect for your official documents.

SOL. You might have dispensed with that piece of mockery. Is it my fault that I have to carry them myself? No, certainly not. I have now long enough served the ungrateful town and the dear village people as an industrious counsellor; and my deserts ought by rights to yield already at least sufficient for me to be able to keep a boy, a writer, a secretary, or something of the sort. But who, then, can compel fortune? Until now I have had to be everything myself. But as soon as I can keep a boy, or something of that sort, my generosity will not hesitate to propose you.

LE. You are joking, Herr Solbist, and with acuteness.

SOL. I never joke otherwise. But, Herr Wumshäter, please, please get these young people away. I must speak with you alone.

Le. You need only talk with him in legal style, and it will be just as good as if we were not here.

Wu. But they are my friends, you know; what you have to say to me you can certainly say in their presence.

Sol. So you don't wish to listen to me? Good (*is going*).

Le. We will not expose you to his caprice, Herr Wumshäter. Pray remain, Herr Solbist, we are going. (*Whispers to* Valer.) Come, Valer, apart from that it will soon be time for me to change my costume.

Wu. But pray don't take it ill. (*Exeunt* Valer *and* Lelio.)

Scene V.—Wumshäter, Solbist.

Wu. And now, Herr Solbist, let me hear what secrets you have to confide to me?

Sol. Are they gone? Step this way. They might be listening at the door.

Wu. Well?

Sol. Herr Leander——

Wu. Has the devil taken him?

Sol. Hush! Just listen. Herr Leander wishes . . . . (*speaking in his ear*) wishes to come to a settlement with you.

Wu. (*very loud*). What? He wishes to come to a settlement with me?

Sol. Hush! hush! Yes, he does. He has let me make a fool of him.

Wu. (*very loud*). You are a fool yourself. I do not want to come to a settlement with him. How many hundred times haven't I most decidedly assured you of that?

Sol. Hush, hush, hush! With your confounded shouting you will ruin me in honour, reputation, credit, and everything. Supposing, now, some one has heard you?

Wu. Oh, I will give you evidence before all the world that you are seeking nothing but my ruin. Come to a settlement! Have not I the best of cases?

Sol. But even the best of cases may be lost, when it stands as yours does. Your late wife let matters go too far.

Wu. The confounded woman! Doesn't all my unhappiness come from women?

SOL. Not only your unhappiness, but all the unhappiness in the world, as I shall presently show. Make haste, and listen to the proof, and tell me briefly whether it would not please you if Leander . . . . I won't say were to come to a settlement with you, since you won't hear anything of settlements . . . . but, on a trifling, quite trifling, condition, were to let the suit drop.

WU. Let it drop? As if I had won it! Yes, that would be something. But what, then, is the condition?

SOL. A condition that will be altogether after your own heart.

WU. Well?

SOL. Briefly, Leander will let the suit drop on condition . . . . on condition, Herr Wumshäter . . . . (*speaking in his ear*) that you will render him unhappy.

WU. (*very loudly*). What? Render him unhappy?

SOL. You will render me so with that treacherous, auctioneer's voice of yours. I like to manage all my affairs secretly and in silence. But you, you . . . . I'll wager Leander has heard it in his own house!

WU. Well, then, reveal to me in all secrecy in what way I can make him unhappy.

SOL. Nothing is easier. Listen now, in confidence. The man has become perfectly silly. I believe Heaven has punished him on your account. He has fallen on a most desperate idea. I will explain it to you at once.

WU. I don't see yet what you are aiming at.

SOL. (*puts his documents down, takes from his pocket a large frill, which he puts on, draws on a pair of white gloves, steps back a few paces, and begins his harangue in a pedantic manner*). Most nobly born, especially to be venerated Sir and Patron! When God had made Adam, and had placed him in a beautiful Paradise. . . . . In passing, I will remind you that up till now, no one knows exactly where Paradise was situated. Scholars contest the point very hotly. But no matter where it was. . . . . When God then had placed Adam in this, to us unknown, Paradise . . . . .

WU. Ay! Herr Solbist, Herr Solbist!

SOL. Just step a little in front of the door, that no one may come in.

Wu. I shall thank God if anyone does come, for I really am afraid you have gone out of your mind.

Sol. Do just go, and have patience a moment. . . . . When, then, I say, Adam was placed in this Paradise,— when he, I say, was placed in it; and, I will remark, was therefore in the Paradise in which he had been placed by God. He was therefore in this Paradise. . . . . Eh? This is odd! If I could only find my way out again. There it is now! That is what occurs when you interrupt an orator.

Wu. I am only sorry that I shall soon have to put pressure on you. Tell me, for goodness' sake, what you mean?

Sol. I would rather you had given me a box on the ear, than that you had broken the thread of my discourse. I must just see whether I can get hold of it again. (*Very quickly.*) Most nobly born, specially to be venerated Sir and Patron; when God had made Adam, and placed him in a beautiful Paradise. . . . . Most nobly born, specially to be venerated Sir and Patron; when God had made Adam and placed him in a beautiful Paradise. . . . . No, I really can't get further, it is as if the thread had been cut away from my lips. Well, be it so; the greatest loss is yours.

Wu. Mine?

Sol. Yes, indeed. You would have heard a truly Ciceronian masterpiece. A practised club of orators could not have composed it better. Now you will have to be satisfied with the *contenta*. Listen, then; my oration . . . . . for you must at least have perceived that I desired to make an oration . . . . . My oration, I say, had three *partes*, albeit formerly there were wont to be eight *partes orationis*. The first part, or rather the first *pars*, contained a correct list of all bad wives, from Eve downwards to the three you had.

Wu. What? A list of all bad wives? Ah! I should have been curious to hear that. . . . . It could, however, hardly have been a list of all bad wives, but only of the worst. For a list of all bad wives would be a list of all the wives that have ever lived in the world, and that it could not have been.

SOL.   Quite so. My next *pars* . . . .
WU.   Had you the wife of Job in your list?
SOL.   Certainly. My next *pars* . . . .
WU.   Had you also Tobias' wife?
SOL.   Certainly. My next *pars* . . . .
WU.   And Queen Jezebel, too?
SOL.   Also. My next *pars* . . . .
WU.   Also the Scarlet Woman of Babylon?
SOL.   Her, too. My next *pars* . . . .
WU.   You perceive that I also know a thing or two.
SOL.   I perceive that you only know the best of them.
I know quite different ones. A Hispulla, a Hippia, a
Medullina, a Saufeia, an Ogulina, a Messalina, a Cæsonia
. . . . . of all of whom more may be read in the sixth
book of the History of Juvenal. . . . . Well, lest my *contenta* should be longer than my oration would have been,
just listen to me further. My second *pars* proved as briefly
as thoroughly that a wife is the greatest misfortune in the
world, and deduced therefrom incontestably that marriage
must be a very senseless affair, a proposition which was
supported at great length by *testimonia*, especially yours.
WU.   Ah! My dear Herr Solbist, how did you come
upon such an excellent subject? I am really heartily
sorry now, that your oration came to nothing. Ay, ay!
But how is it that you desired to give me so much pleasure? It is neither my birthday to-day, nor my name-
day, that I should expect you to make me so fine a speech
of congratulation.
SOL.   All will become clear to you through my third
pars. The third *pars* contained, finally, a statement that,
notwithstanding this folly, namely, the folly of marrying,
. . . . just guess who . . . . wishes to commit——
WU.   Who? Surely not my son? For I think I have
pretty well talked it out of him.
SOL.   No, not your son.
WU.   Well, I would, then, that it were my worst enemy.
SOL.   Bravo!
WU.   I wish it were Leander.
SOL.   You have hit it.
WU.   Really? How unlucky that I can't raise one of
my three wives from the dead, and give her to him '

Sol. You can do that, Herr Wumshäter; you can do that, if only you desire it. Does not your second wife live and move in the person of your daughter? In short, you see in me the wooer for Herr Leander, and my mission, indeed, concerns the honourable and virtuous maid, Miss Laura, lawful and only daughter of the body of Herr Zacharias Maria Wumshäter. If he is fortunate in his suit, you will have won your case. *Dixi.*

Wu. What? my dearest Herr Solbist, is it possible? Leander wishes to have my daughter, and if I give her to him, shall I have won my case?

Sol. You will have won it! Don't hesitate.

Wu. Hesitate?

Sol. You must be convinced that one cannot devise a procedure more hostile to a man than to give him a wife.

Wu. I am convinced of that. He shall have her, yes; I will give her to him with joy. How miserable she shall make his life. Leander, Leander, you shall feel the vexation tenfold which you have caused to me. How delighted I shall be when I hear in a short time that my daughter is quarrelling daily with him; that she won't let him enjoy a morsel in peace; that she even lays hands on him; that she is unfaithful to him; that she is spending all his fortune; finally, that he has to give up house and home through her! I think, I think, she will bring it to that. Yes, yes, Herr Solbist, Leander shall have my daughter, he shall have her. But if I am to win the case in this way, I must have the six thousand thalers, which were deposited, paid to me.

Sol. You can have them to-morrow.

Wu. To-morrow? That would be excellent. I have just now a chance of investing them at six per cent. But I hope Leander does not fancy that he will get them back in the form of a dowry? He may just give up that idea. I can give him nothing with my daughter, nothing at all.

Sol. It will not be necessary, either; Leander is rich enough himself.

Wu. If that is the case, she is his wife this very day if he pleases. I intended her, indeed, to go with my son; but that will come to nothing now. It is better that she

should avenge me on a man who has wronged me so much.
We will go to her at once; Herr Leander may come afterwards himself. Come, Herr Solbist——

SOL. Pray go. I must first take off my lace frill, and
put my kid gloves away. But don't you tell anyone that
I have been match-maker. (*Exit* WUMSHÄTER.) It might
not be perfectly in keeping with my office, for which
reason I very wisely didn't choose to come in complete
costume. How easily people might have fancied that I
wanted to get a wooer's reward. Quick, there's someone
coming.

SCENE VI.—LISETTE, SOLBIST.

SOL. (*still taking off his frill*). Is it you, Lisette? Well,
well, you may know now what I have been doing here.

LIS. Has all gone well, Herr Solbist?

SOL. As if everything which I once undertake must not
of necessity go well. If people had taken me into their
counsels sooner, Laura might even now be the mother of
Leander's children.

LIS. One would hardly think what knaveries there
are in that little grey head!

SOL. Don't make me blush. Certainly Herr Wumshäter would have refused Leander, if the proposal had
been made for him in any other way. But it was not so
very difficult to discover this one way, especially for a
man of experience like me. For, in confidence, Lisette,
(*whispers*) do you suppose that this is the first couple that
I have brought together?

LIS. Oh dear, no. I believe on the contrary that you
are an adept at match-making.

SOL. Hush, hush! Don't shout so! It has had to
bring me in many a bright thaler. People are fright-
fully mistaken if they suppose I am the author of nothing
but quarrels. As an honourable lawyer, of course, I must
be able to make those; yet if that does not thrive well at
all times, I can also make marriages.

LIS. As if making marriages and making quarrels was
not the same thing! And from what I have heard, you
can part married folk again, just as easily as you can
bring them together. You are a sly fox. Could you have

earned so much through divorce cases if you had not laid
the foundation for them by your match-making?

Sol. The deuce! Who told you that? I do everything quietly and in silence, and don't ever like speaking
openly about such matters, and yet you have heard it.
That cannot have happened by fair means. . . . . But it is
true that it is a pleasure when I give my clients audience
in the forenoon. Every one has recourse to me. If the
peasant wants to bring an action against his master, he
comes to me. If an aged little matron wishes to get a
young healthy husband, she comes to me. If one scamp
wants to bring an action for libel against another, he
comes to me. If a young wife wants to get rid of her
decrepit old husband, she comes to me. But all these
affairs, all these, particularly those which concern marriage,
go on in such secrecy that they must only speak of them
to me in my ear. And yet you know of it? Hold your
tongue, Lisette, my dear, and don't tell anyone else.
Perhaps I can also do you a service. I don't know, though,
whether you want to be married already. But the desire
comes very quickly sometimes. Just let me know when
it does. I keep a correct list of all the marriageable
maidens and bachelors in the town. I read it over once or
twice every day, and see who is likely to have need of my
help. To tell the truth, I have already marked a few young
fellows with an asterisk, who would suit you very well.

Lis. If they are rich, young, and handsome, you can
be sure that they will suit me. My future husband has
no need of any more good qualities than these. I have
the others.

Sol. I will show you my list. You can then look out
which of those in it pleases you best. I have described
them in detail according to their external and internal
gifts, and have drawn certain tolerably good conclusions
from the proportions of their limbs; especially of the
nose, shoulders, calves. . . . . More of this at another time,
Lisette, my dear. I must go and send Herr Leander here.
Notwithstanding the lawsuit, he has always had much
love for Miss Laura.

Lis. Oh, and so has she for him. Don't forget the list.

Sol. But be sure to keep silence! Keep silence.

LIS. (*alone*). There is an upright lawyer for you! If only his plot is not too late. Laura has seemed to me much changed towards Leander during the last few days. I fear that Valer has brought his future brother-in-law with him at an unlucky time.

SCENE VII.—WUMSHÄTER, LISETTE.

WU. Where is the daughter, Lisette?

LIS. What daughter?

WU. The daughter. I have looked for her already all over the house. Where is she?

LIS. What daughter, I say?

WU. The hussy only wants me to say " my daughter;" because she knows how I dislike saying it.

LIS. Oh, so it is your own daughter you are asking for? Your own? I really don't know where she is. But what shall we bet that I know what you wish to announce to her?

WU. Perhaps she is in the garden?

LIS. That may be. You have certainly acted most wisely, in allowing Herr Leander——

WU. Don't you say I have acted wisely, or I shall think that I have committed the greatest of follies.

LIS. Well, then, I will say the latter.

WU. Say it, then, in the name of all the witches, and leave me in peace.

LIS. (*alone*). Now, certainly, if I were ever to get such a fool as that for my husband, I think I should be in my old age as great a man-hater as he is a woman-hater. But, be it observed, not before I am old.

ACT III.

SCENE I.—LISETTE *from one side, and* LAURA *from the other.*

LIS. So excited, Mamselle?

LA. Where is the worthless lawyer? The officious old match-maker! What is he meddling in? Who commissioned him to ask me from my father as an affliction for a man with whom I should be most afflicted?

Lis. By whom you would be most afflicted? Do you not love Leander? And have you not long since granted him your permission to seek your father's consent in one way or another?

La. It is lucky for you that you say "long since." For this very reason that once, long since, I loved Leander, and once, long since, desired to be his, people might as well have inquired beforehand whether I still desire it, and whether I still love him. Must one go to work so confidently, without telling me a word about it? I should think I am not the least important person in the matter.

Lis. And so you really do not love Leander any longer?

La. No; and I am ashamed of ever having loved him. Had it not been for your misleading me, I should never have honoured with my respect a man who lives in such open disagreement and strife with my father.

Lis. (makes a low courtesy). You confer too much honour on me, in confounding me and your own heart.

La. My heart cannot have taken much part in that matter. A passing fancy; that is what it was at the utmost. Otherwise it would doubtless have been more painful to me to forget him. A single trifling consideration has drawn me away from this unseemly love.

Lis. Oh! A consideration? May not one know the nature of this consideration? Surely not the consideration of Herr Lelio?

La. You are a fool.

Lis. I expected that answer. But do you know the proverb about children and fools?

La. Leander is my father's enemy. It is true he has often assured me that he is not so, and that he is unable to perceive the necessity of one man hating another because he is engaged in a lawsuit with him; one may prosecute one's right, you know, even against a man whom one esteems and loves. But I see clearly now that this is the speech of a cunning fellow, who desires to put himself in such a position that he may not lose his case even when he loses it; a selfish man, who tries to win back by a marriage-contract what he has lost through a verdict. There is my consideration! Whether Lelio has given me an opportunity of arriving at this consideration or whether he has merely strengthened it does not concern you at all, and is solely and entirely my business.

LIS. I have learnt by experience that whenever we girls defend our conduct with reasoning and by alleging ground for it, we are always wrong. So confess, therefore, to me that Lelio is the sole cause of your change of feeling. His society alone during the last few days has so captivated you, that you will neither read Leander's letters, nor grant him a secret meeting. How willingly you used to do both!

LA. I do not wish to be reminded by you of faults which, as I said before, I should not have committed but for you. I regret sufficiently that I was so weak.

LIS. To be weaker still and to give yourself up to a fickle youth whom you have only known for a week, and whose love you infer from a few meaningless flatteries. I advise you to be careful, Miss.

SCENE II.—WUMSHÄTER, LISETTE, LAURA.

WU. Well? Have you scratched poor Herr Solbist's eyes out?

LIS. If he had not already gone, who knows what she would have done?

WU. Oh I fully believe, that, like a good daughter, she wishes all ill-luck to the man who has set her honest father free from two troubles at once, from a woman and a lawsuit. But whether you grudge me this good fortune or not, I don't intend to give it up. You must become Leander's wife or cease to be my daughter.

LA. That is a hard alternative! Nevertheless I shall take the liberty of telling you that I prefer your first order, and will go with my brother. I cannot change my mind as quickly as you change yours. Perhaps, though, some one has been trying to convince you that I love Leander.

WU. That has not been considered at all; all the better if you don't love him. Woman's love is, in truth,

mere folly, and, with your sex, to love only means to hate
less. You are unable to love anyone but yourselves.

Lis. (*breaks out at him*). No, sir, no! That is too bad!
Your daughter, I agree, is wrong not to accept the husband you offer her, but you must not slander the whole
sex on that account.

Wu. Whew! Now it's time I was off. I had sooner
get between mill-wheels, than between two women.
Silence, pray, silence! My daughter can answer well
enough for herself.

Scene III.—Valer, Wumshäter, Lisette, Laura.

Va. Father, Lelio's sister has just come. She is staying
with a relative who lives here, and has already sent to me.
I am expecting her every minute. I hope you are still
willing to allow me to present her to you.

Wu. I should like to see her once, were it only for the
sake of the asserted resemblance. But not more than once.
Bring her. I will tell her myself, as gently as possible,
that she is not to count on you.

La. What, brother? Your Hilaria is here, and you
did not prepare me for her coming by a single word?

Va. You will not take it ill, sister. I did not want to
tell you anything before it was certain. . . . . You will
have far more to wonder at than her mere arrival, however; her marvellous likeness to her brother. . . . . What
do I see? Heavens! Here she is herself.

Scene IV.—Lelio (*in her true character as* Hilaria),
Valer, Wumshäter, Lisette, Laura.

Va. Oh! most lovely Hilaria, how joyful, how happy
you make me! How am I to thank you enough for deign-
ing to visit a family which is already proud in anticipation
of a nearer connection with you?

Le. Permit me, Valer, to leave your flattery unan
swered for the present, and first of all to show my respect
for one (*to* Wumshäter) who is so kind as to allow me to
love him as a father.

Wu. I am plea . . . . very displea . . . . not altogether displeased, Mademoiselle, to make your acquaintance; but I must tell you at the very commencement, that you are going a little too fast. I am already called father by two——

VA. (*to* LELIO). And his only wish is to be acknowledged as such by you also——

WU. No, my son, no.

VA. (*leading* HILARIA *to* LAURA). Permit, permit a sister, Hilaria, who can no longer restrain her joy to embrace you.

LE. (*embracing her*). I take the liberty, lovely Laura, to ask for your friendship?

LA. I am ashamed of having allowed you to anticipate me in this request.

VA. Well, father, are you not astounded at the likeness of Hilaria to her brother?

LA. Certainly, one cannot but be astounded. I cannot look at him enough. Where is Herr Lelio? Why cannot we have the pleasure of comparing him with this counterpart?

WU. If only Lelio were here; if only he were here! I don't know where your eyes can be, good people. I won't go so far as to say that you have no resemblance at all to your brother, Mademoiselle, but one really has to look closely to perceive the likeness. In the first place, Lelio is at least a hand-breadth taller, in spite of the high heels of your shoes.

LE. And yet we have measured ourselves togther a hundred times, and have not been able to discover the smallest difference.

WU. My eye does not deceive me; I can trust it. For another thing, Herr Lelio is not quite so stout; he is slenderer and better formed, though he wears no stays. I do not mean to offend you in this, Mademoiselle, but merely to do justice to your brother.

LA. I cannot agree with you, father. It is indeed true that one could hardly find a finer figure in any man than in Herr Lelio; but look carefully. Hilaria has exactly the same figure, only that, owing to the tightness of her dress, she appears rather to be slimmer than stouter.

WU. And the face——

Va. Well? The face?

Wu. I won't mention it. Lelio has a fresh natural colour, but on your face, Mademoiselle, why, the rouge lies inches deep.

Le. Though I don't think that it is unallowable for a girl to rouge a little, still I have never yet thought proper to come to the assistance of my countenance in this way. I don't wish to say this to praise myself; for perhaps what others do from pride, I have left undone from greater pride.

Wu. I understand, I understand . . . . The eyes, my son. Have you not noticed yet that these are grey eyes, while Lelio's are black?

Va. What do you say? These eyes grey?

Wu. Certainly, grey eyes, and, besides, they are just as languid as Lelio's are fiery.

La. Oh, father!——

Wu. Oh, daughter! Hold your tongue. I know quite well that hawks don't pick out hawks' een. You, of course, want her one day to call your yellow eyes black. Are you going to make me blind? And this nose . . . . Lelio hasn't a little stumpy, hooked nose like this. Will you deny that, too?

Va. I am astonished!

Wu. You must be astonished at your own delusion. The mouth, too, is twice as big as Lelio's. What a prominent lip! What a pointed chin! The right shoulder is a hand-breadth higher than the left! . . . . In a word, my son, the asserted resemblance was a trick to coax your father into giving his consent. And, in truth, it would have been a great point against me, if it had really been as you said. So much the better that it is not so, and that it is more probable now that in a body which differs so greatly from that of the brother, there will also dwell a totally different soul. Your brother, Mademoiselle, is an intelligent young man, who knows and approves of the reasons which make it impossible for me to assent to my son's marrying. He will therefore quite excuse me for treating you with so little ceremony. I cannot stay any longer now, but must give my attention to set ling matters —the sooner the better—with Leander. You, Laura, prepare yourself. I can't let her go with you now, Valer; I can win my lawsuit here by her, and that is of most importance.

LA. Do not allow yourself to be deluded, brother; I certainly shall go with you. Your lawsuit is lost, if you are to win it through me.

WU. Keep your contradictions for your husband. (*Exit.*)

SCENE V.—LELIO, VALER, LAURA, LISETTE.

LA. We must feel ashamed, brother, that so amiable a guest has been so badly received by our father. You must be very sure of your Hilaria's love, to have dared to put her patience to this painful test.

LE. You have a very kind sister, Valer; her politeness would embarrass me, did I not know in what estimation my brother has the good fortune to stand with her. You like him, sweet Laura, and this conquest was the first thing which he told me of, with an air of triumph, on my arrival. He is indeed worthy that a girl should sigh for him. But, all the same, take care; he is a little traitor, and doesn't make the least scruple of being inconstant. If you don't know how to keep a firm hold of him, he will be out of the net before you expect it. Besides, he is boastful, and I won't be certain that he will not boast of more favours than he has really received . . . . I take my leave of you for the present. Come, Valer.

SCENE VI.—LAURA, LISETTE.

LA. What is that? I think Lelio and Hilaria must be mad. How does he know that I love him? And, even if he could be sure of it, is it not a very unworthy trick to make a confidante of such an impertinent sister? Very well, my young friend, it is lucky that we have not yet gone very far! But what are you standing there like that for, Lisette? Are you petrified? Speak, do!

LIS. I cannot yet quite make out what I have seen and heard. Give me a little time to recover from my astonishment. Who was the girl?

LA. Hilaria; you were looking at her hard enough the

whole time   Wasn't she sufficiently like Lelio, that you should still doubt it?

Lis.   She was only too like him; so like, so exactly like, that I can't help wondering why you yourself have not had a suspicion——

La.   A suspicion of what?

Lis.   A suspicion which I will not be persuaded out of. Hilaria must be Lelio, or Lelio must be Hilaria.

La.   How do you mean?

Lis.   You will do well to be on your guard, Miss. I will soon fathom this secret. But, until then, think of the dog with the piece of meat. You have a lover, of whom you are sure : don't turn round to the shadow of another.

La.   Be quiet with your childish stories. Be Lelio what he may, he has lost me. He shall see; he shall see, that one can forget a bit of a face like his more easily than another.

Lis.   Quite so. Especially when there are realities with the other, which certainly are wanting with him. For the more I think of it, the more probable it appears to me . . . . Hush! Here comes the other face itself! Show now that a little dandy like Lelio hasn't got much hold on us.

Scene VII.—Wumshäter, Leander, Laura, Lisette.

Wu.   Here, daughter, I bring you the husband to whom I resign all my rights in you. It is Herr Leander.

Lea.   I flatter myself, Mademoiselle, that you will not regard me as a complete stranger.

La.   I could not have believed that the few occasions on which we have had the opportunity of meeting in public places, could have made a man of Herr Leander's refined perception so confident of success. You have applied to my father in a matter about which you unquestionably ought first to have come to an agreement with me.

Wu.   Eh? Just fancy! So he ought to have made his application to you before, ought he?

Lis. (aside).   As if he had not done so! Very well! We must dissemble a little.

Wu.   I think you are very impertinent, and if I did not

N 2

wish to spare you in the presence of your bridegroom, I would give you a very severe reprimand.

LEA. It is true, lovely Laura, that my love has been much too impatient, and that you have a right to complain of me.

WU. You surely are not going to apologize?

LA. And the way, Herr Leander, in which Solbist wooed for me——

WU. There was nothing objectionable in his way. And, in short, I wish you to obey me. Can I not demand that, my son?

SCENE VIII.—VALER, WUMSHÄTER, LEANDER, LAURA, LISETTE.

VA. If I have rightly guessed what you were speaking of, I will almost pledge myself for my sister's obedience.

LA. You are very bold, brother. I could much sooner pledge myself for your disobedience; and make a safe bet that you were more likely to give me a sister-in-law, than I to give you a brother-in-law.

LEA. Is it possible, Mademoiselle?

VA. Do not be uneasy about that.

LEA. But I hear——

VA. You hear the pruderies of a bride——

WU. And I hear a woman's nonsense! Hold your tongue, hussy! Your brother has far too much sense to be still thinking of marriage.

VA. Excuse me, father. Since I must now forego the promised help of my sister, it is so much the more necessary to abide by the determination I came to before. I certainly hope too that you will no longer be opposed to it. The whole town knows you to be a just man. But what would people say if it came out that you had highly esteemed the very same qualities and perfections in one person, which in another you depreciated? What would people say if they learnt that deep-rooted rancour against a whole sex, by whom you believe yourself to be injured, should have prevented you from recognising that which the whole world recognises? Such an obvious resemblance——

WU. Hold your tongue about your chimerical resemblance! Or will you force me to make you ridiculous in Herr Leander's eyes too? Indeed, I shall have to do it.

Herr Leander, you shall be arbitrator between us. Go, bring your Hilaria here, but bring her brother as well. We will make a fair comparison.

Va. I agree, father. Lisette, run quickly to Herr Lelio's room. You will find them together. Request them to come here. (*Exit* Lisette.)

Wu. You will see, Herr Leander, that I am right.

Lea. (*whispers to* Valer). May your trick succeed as well as mine has.

Va. (*whispers to* Leander). I hope so, my dearest friend, and I thank you.

Wu. (*seeing* Leander *and* Valer *talking together*). No, that is not fair; you mustn't talk it over together beforehand. I hope, Herr Leander, that the first test of your uprightness, which I demand from you——

Lea. Fear nothing. I shall not depart from the truth if the matter should depend on my decision. But I hope it will not do so.

Wu. How so? Do you know already what our dispute is about? The sister is said to be exactly like the brother, and because I like the brother he requires me to like the sister also.

Va. Have I not a right to require it?

Wu. Granted the likeness, you could require it with some right. But that likeness is the very point in dispute.

Va. We shall not dispute about it much longer, and I am convinced that you will at last have to acknowledge it.

Wu. I certainly shall not acknowledge it. But if I do, it will be a sure proof that I have lost sense and reason, and that therefore you are not bound to obey me in the least.

Va. Mark that, Herr Leander; that I am not bound to obey him in the least, in case he has to admit the likeness himself.

Wu. Ay, mark it! . . . . Eh? What masquerading is this?

Scene IX.—Lelio *or* Hilaria, Lisette, Wumshäter, Valer, Laura, Leander.

Le. (*attired partly as a man, partly as a woman, the dress arranged according to the taste of the actress*). You requested, sir, to see Lelio and Hilaria both at once.

Wu. Eh? My mind misgives me.

Le. Here they both are.

Wu. What?

Lis. Yes, sir, here they both are, and you were caught.

Wu. What? I caught?

Lis. (*whispers to* Laura). Wasn't I right, Miss? You start?

Wu. I caught? How am I to understand that?

Le. You will have the goodness to understand it thus: that the same person cannot be a hand-breadth taller than she really is.

Wu. Well?

Le. That the very same eyes cannot be both grey and black.

Wu. Well?   .

Le. That the very same nose——

Va. In short, dearest father (*throwing himself at his feet*), forgive my innocent trick. Lelio is Hilaria, and Hilaria only had the kindness to follow me hither in man's clothes that she might have the opportunity of gaining the goodwill of a man whose inexorable feeling against her sex she well knew.

Wu. Get up, my son, get up, and let us have an end of this nonsense. I see clearly how it is. Your Hilaria is not here at all, and that frivolous Lelio, with his girl's face, has played her part. Fie, Lelio! (*advancing towards her*). No, no! One doesn't deceive me so easily. Take off that second dress, my good . . . . (*is going to slap her on the shoulder*). Heavens! What do I see? Alas, my poor eyes! what has come to them? It is a woman! It really is a woman! And probably the most deceitful, artful, and dangerous one in the whole world. I have been deceived! I have been betrayed! My son, my son, how could you do this?

Va. Let me once more ask for pardon at your feet.

Wu. What is the good of my pardon to you, if you will no longer follow my advice? Of course I forgive you, but——

Le. I too pray most humbly for forgiveness——

Wu. Go, do; go, do; I forgive you too . . . . since I must.

.

Va. Not because you must, father. Don't let us hear such painful words. Forgive us because you love us.

Wu. Well, then, yes, because I love *you*.

Le. And will soon love me, as I sincerely hope.

Wu. You hope too much. Not to hate you will be all that I can do. I see clearly a man must fall in love, and must be foolish. What can I do against fate? Be you so too, my son. Be foolish! Through our folly we most surely become wise. Go in peace! I am glad at least that I need not be an eye-witness of your folly. See only that my daughter no longer opposes me——

La. Do not fear, father. I will not cause a second vexation. I give Herr Leander my hand, and would have given it to him even if Lelio had not been Hilaria. (*To* Hilaria.) This is for you, for your triumphant air?

Le. Are you angry with me, dearest Laura? (*To* Leander.) However did you set about it, sir, that you were able to move such a stony heart to love? If you knew what assaults I made on it in my disguise, and how sturdily it nevertheless ——

La. Stop, Hilaria, or I shall really be angry. (*To* Leander, *who is about to answer* Hilaria.) Don't answer her, Leander; I promise you that you shall never have a more dangerous rival than Lelio was.

Lea. How happy am I!

Va. And how happy I am too!

Wu. In a year or so I hope you will exclaim differently!

Lis. Differently certainly, especially if more voices join in. (*To the audience.*) Laugh, gentlemen, pray; this comedy ends like a marriage-song.

THE JEWS.

(A COMEDY IN ONE ACT.)

The 'Jews' was written at Berlin in the year 1749.

DRAMATIS PERSONÆ.

MICHEL STICH.

MARTIN KRUMM.

A TRAVELLER.

CHRISTOPH, *his servant.*

The BARON.

A YOUNG LADY, *his daughter.*

LISETTE, *a maid-servant.*

THE JEWS.

Scene I.—Michel Stich, Martin Krumm.

Krumm. You stupid Michel Stich!

Stich. You stupid Martin Krumm!

Krumm. Let's confess we have both been extremely stupid. What would it have mattered, whether we had killed one more, or not?

Stich. And how could we have managed it more prudently? Were we not well disguised? Was not the coachman on our side? and was it our fault that chance played us such a trick? Have I not said many a hundred times, "What infernal luck!" Without luck one cannot even be a good pickpocket.

Krumm. Never mind. If viewed in the right light, we have only escaped the gallows for a few days longer.

Stich. Ah, the devil take the gallows! If all thieves were hung, the gallows would have to stand thicker. One hardly sees one in two miles, and, where there is one, it stands unoccupied. I believe the judges, for politeness' sake, will abolish the things altogether. And what is the use of them, after all? None at all, except at most that, when one of us passes by, he shuts his eyes.

Krumm. Oh, I don't even do that. My father and grandfather died on the gallows; can I ask a better fate? I am not ashamed of my parents.

STICH. But honest people will be ashamed of you. You have not done nearly enough yet for one to recognise their genuine offspring in you.

KRUMM. Don't fancy that our master is going to get off in this way. And I will surely revenge myself, too, on that confounded stranger, who snatched so savoury a morsel from our mouths. His watch he shall leave me, as sure as . . . . Ha! see, there he's coming. Quick, away. I'll now perform my masterpiece.

STICH. But halves, halves!

SCENE II.—MARTIN KRUMM, *the* TRAVELLER.

KRUMM (*aside*). I will play the blockhead. (*Aloud*) Your most obedient servant, sir. I am Martin Krumm, and am the legally appointed bailiff of this property.

TRAV. I believe you, my friend. But have you not seen my servant?

KRUMM. At your service, no. But I have had the honour to hear much good of your honourable person; and I am thus much pleased that I have the honour to enjoy the honour of your acquaintance. I am told that you delivered our master from a very great danger last night. And as I cannot but rejoice at the good fortune of our master, I rejoice——

TRAV. I guess your intention. You wish to thank me for having assisted your master.

KRUMM. Yes; quite right; just so.

TRAV. You are an honest man.

KRUMM. That I am. And honesty is the best policy.

TRAV. It is no small pleasure to me to have obliged so many honest people by so trifling an action. Their gratitude is a more than sufficient reward for what I have done. Love of mankind obliged me to do it. It was my duty, and I could not but have been satisfied if it had been considered nothing more. You are too kind, my dear people, to thank me for any service which, without doubt, you would have rendered as zealously to me, if I had found myself in a similar danger. Can I serve you in anything else, my friend?

KRUMM. Oh! with serving I will not trouble you, sir.

I have my man who waits upon me, when necessary. But
.... I should like to know how it happened? Where was
it? Were there many thieves? Did they intend to murder
our good master, or did they only wish to take his money?
The latter would have been better than the former.

TRAV.   I will tell you the whole incident in a few
words.   It must be about an hour's walk from here, where
the robbers had attacked your master, in a narrow pass.
I was journeying along the same road, and his piteous
cries for help induced me to hasten towards the spot with
my servant.

KRUMM.   Ah, ah!

TRAV.   I found him in an open carriage——

KRUMM.   Ah, ah!

TRAV.   Two fellows in disguise——

KRUMM.   Disguised? Ah, ah!

TRAV.   Were already handling him roughly——

KRUMM.   Ah, ah!

TRAV.   Whether they intended to kill him, or only to
bind him in order to rob him the more securely, I don't
know.

KRUMM.   Ah, ah! No doubt they intended to kill him,
the godless wretches.

TRAV.   That I will not maintain, lest I might wrong
them.

KRUMM.   Yes, yes, believe me. They wished to kill
him. I know, I am quite certain——

TRAV.   But how can you know it?   But let it be so.
As soon as the robbers perceived me, they quitted their
booty, and escaped as fast as they could into the forest
hard by. I discharged my pistol at one of them, but as
it was already too dark, and he too far off, I doubt whether
I hit him.

KRUMM.   No; you did not hit him——

TRAV.   Do you know that?

KRUMM.   I merely fancy so, because it was already dark,
and in the dark, I am told, one cannot aim well.

TRAV.   I cannot describe to you how grateful your
master was to me. He called me his preserver a hundred
times, and obliged me to return with him to his country
seat. I sincerely wish circumstances would permit me

to remain longer with this amiable man ; but as it is, I
must proceed on my journey this very day.   And it is on
that account that I am looking for my servant.

KRUMM. Oh, do not hasten away yet. Stay a few
moments longer. Well, what else was I going to ask?
The robbers—yes, tell me, what did they look like? How
were they dressed? They were disguised ; but how?

TRAV. Your master maintains that they were Jews.
Beards they had, 'tis true; but their language was the
common dialect used among the peasantry here. If they
were disguised, as I certainly believe, twilight rendered
them a good service. But I don't understand how Jews
should be able to make the roads unsafe, since so few of
them are suffered to remain in this country.

KRUMM. Yes, yes. I believe, too, they were Jews.
You may not be well acquainted· with these wicked
people yet. All of them, without exception, are cheats,
thieves, and robbers. That is why they are a people
whom the Lord our God has cursed. If I were king,
I should not leave a single one of them alive. Oh,
may the Lord guard all honest Christians against these
people ! If the Lord our God did not hate them, why should
twice as many Jews as Christians have perished in the accident at Breslau, a short time ago? Our clergyman very
wisely reminded us of this in his last sermon. It seems
as if they had been listening to him, and wished to be
revenged for this very reason on our good master. Oh !
my dear sir, if you desire prosperity and happiness in this
world, beware of the Jews, more than of the plague.

TRAV. Would to God that this was only the language
of the vulgar !

KRUMM. For example, sir. I was once at a fair . . . . yes,
when I think of that fair, I wish I could poison the cursed
Jews all at one stroke. In the crowd they had robbed one
of his pocket-handkerchief, another of his snuff-box, a third
of his watch, and I don't know what more. They are quick,
devilish quick, when a theft is the question ; more dex-
terous than our schoolmaster ever is on his organ. For
example, sir, at first they press closely upon you, almost
as I do now upon you——

TRAV. Only with a little more politeness, my friend.

Krumm. Oh, let me just show you. Well, when they are standing close by you, do you see, like lightning shoots a hand to your watch-pocket. (*He puts his hand in the coat-pocket instead of the watch-pocket, and takes a snuff-box out of it.*) Well, they do all that so cleverly, that one would swear that the hand goes this way, when in reality it goes that. When they are talking of the snuff-box, they are aiming at the watch; and when they talk of the watch, they have designs on the snuff-box. (*He makes straight for the watch, but is caught.*)

Trav. Stop, stop, what business has your hand here?

Krumm. Well, you may now perceive what a bungling pickpocket I should be. If a Jew had made such an attempt, it would doubtless have been all over with the watch. But I see you are weary of me, and therefore I take the liberty to withdraw; and on account of the great benefit you have done my highly respected master, I shall remain my whole life your most obedient servant, Martin Krumm, legally appointed bailiff of this noble domain.

Trav. Well, go, go.

Krumm. Remember what I have told you of the Jews. They are all wicked, thieving people.

Scene III.—*The* Traveller.

Trav. Perhaps this fellow, however stupid he is, or pretends to be, is a more wicked rascal than there ever was among the Jews. If a Jew cheats, at least seven times out of nine he has been driven to it by a Christian. I doubt whether many Christians can boast of having dealt uprightly with a Jew, and they are surprised if he endeavours to render like for like. If good faith and honesty are to prevail between two different races, both must contribute equal shares. But how if the one considers it a point of religion and almost a meritorious work to persecute the other? Yet——

Scene IV.—*The* Traveller, Christoph.

Trav. Whenever one wants you, one always has to search an hour for you.

Chris. You are joking, master. I can only be in one place at one time, can I? Is it my fault that you did not go to that place? Surely you'll find me always where I am.

Trav. Indeed? And you are staggering too. I comprehend now why you are so witty. Must you get drunk at this time of the morning?

Chris. Drunk, indeed? I have hardly begun drinking. Except a couple of bottles of good country wine, a couple of glasses of gin, and a mouthful of bread, on the faith of an honest man, I have not taken anything at all. I have not broken my fast yet.

Trav. Oh, that is evident enough, and I advise you, as a friend, to double your allowance.

Chris. Excellent advice! I shall not neglect to regard it, as in duty bound, as a command.. I go, and you shall see how obedient I can be.

Trav. Be prudent. You had better go and saddle the horses, and pack up our things. I wish to depart this very morning.

Chris. If you advised me in joke to take a double breakfast, how can I imagine that you now speak in earnest? You seem to wish to make merry with me to-day. Perhaps the young lady causes you to be so humorous? Oh, she is a charming girl, only she ought to be a little older, a very little older, ought not she, master? When ladies have not attained a certain maturity——

Trav. Go and do as I ordered you.

Chris. You grow serious now. Nevertheless I'll wait for a third command. The point is of too much importance. You might have been too hasty, and I have always been accustomed to allow my masters time for consideration. Consider well before you quit a place so soon again, where we are living in clover. We arrived only yesterday, we have infinitely obliged our host, and yet have hardly enjoyed a supper and a breakfast with him.

Trav. Your impudence is insufferable. When a man resolves to go into service, he ought to accustom himself to be more tractable.

Chris. Good, sir. You begin to moralize; that is, you are getting angry. Calm yourself, I am going——

Trav. You must be little accustomed to reflect. The service we have rendered to our host loses the name of a benefit as soon as we seem to expect the least reward. I ought not even to have allowed him to bring me here with him. The pleasure of having assisted a stranger without any ulterior design, is in itself very great. And he himself would have wished us more blessings than the excessive thanks he renders us now. The man whom we put under the obligation to thank us at some length and cost, renders us a counter-service which is perhaps more troublesome to him than our good action was to us. Most men are too corrupt not to feel the presence of a benefactor burdensome to them. It seems to humble their pride.

Chris. Your philosophy, sir, deprives you of breath. Well, you shall see that I am as magnanimous as you. I go : in a quarter of an hour you shall be able to mount.

Scene V.—*The* Traveller, *the* Young Lady.

Trav. Little as I have deserved it of this fellow, he yet treats me but very rudely.

Lady. Why do you keep away from us, sir ? Why are you here alone ? Has our society already become distasteful to you in the few hours you have spent here ? I should be very sorry for that. I endeavour to please everyone, and above all others I should like to please you.

Trav. Pardon me, madam, I have merely been ordering my servant to get everything ready for our departure.

Lady. What do you say ? For your departure ; when did you arrive ? If, after a twelvemonth, a melancholy hour had suggested such an idea to you, it might be pardoned. But now ? You won't stay a single day ; that is too bad. I tell you I shall be angry if you think of it again.

Trav. You could use no threat that would affect me more deeply.

Lady. Indeed! Do you mean that? Would you really be affected if I grew angry with you?

Trav. Who could remain indifferent to the anger of an amiable young lady ?

Lady. What you say sounds almost as if you meant to laugh at me ; but I will accept it in earnest, even

though I may make a mistake in doing so. Therefore, sir
—I am tolerably amiable, I am told—I tell you once more
I shall be very angry, dreadfully angry, if you think again
of your departure between now and the new year.

TRAV. The time is fixed with much consideration. In
the midst of winter then, and the roughest weather, you
would show me the door.

LADY. Indeed, who said that? I only said, you might
then perhaps think again of your departure for decorum's
sake. But we shall not on that account allow you to go
then ; we will entreat you——

TRAV. Perhaps also for decorum's sake?

LADY. Ah! one would not have believed that so honest
a face could also ridicule . . . . But my papa is coming.
I must go. Don't tell him I have been with you, please!
He reproaches me often enough with being fond of gentlemen's society.

SCENE VI.—*The* BARON, *the* TRAVELLER.

BARON. Was not my daughter with you? Why does the
wild child run off?

TRAV. To possess such an amiable and so merry a
daughter is an inestimable fortune. She enchants one by
her conversation, which is full of the sweetest innocence
and most unaffected wit.

BARON. You judge her too favourably. She has been
little into society, and possesses but in small degree the
art of pleasing—an art which can hardly be acquired in
the country, yet which is often more powerful than Beauty
herself. Untrammelled Nature alone has been her tutor.

TRAV. And this, but seldom met with in towns, is so
much the more fascinating. There everything is feigned,
forced, and acquired. Indeed, we have made such progress
in this direction, that to be stupid, to be uncouth, and to
be natural, are considered as phrases of the same meaning.

BARON. What could be more agreable to me than to
find that our thoughts and opinions harmonize so well?
Would that I had had long ago a friend like you!

TRAV. You are unjust towards your other friends.

BARON. Towards my other friends, do you say? I am

fifty years of age . . . . acquaintances I have had, but
no friends. And friendship never appeared to me in so
charming a garb, as during the few hours in which I have
been endeavouring to obtain yours. How can I merit it?

Trav. My friendship is of so little importance, that
the mere wish for it is a sufficient merit for obtaining it.
Your request is of far more value than that which you
request.

Baron. Oh, sir! the friendship of a benefactor——

Trav. Excuse me . . . . is no friendship. If you
look at me in this false aspect, I cannot be your friend.
Suppose, for a moment, I were your benefactor; should I
not have to fear that your friendship was nothing but
gratitude?

Baron. But could not the two be united?

Trav. Hardly. A noble mind considers gratitude its
duty; friendship requires voluntary emotions of the soul
alone.

Baron. But how ought I . . . . Your nice distinctions
confuse me entirely.

Trav. Only esteem me no more than I deserve. At
most I am a man, who has done his duty with pleasure.
Duty itself does not deserve gratitude. But for having
done it with pleasure, I am sufficiently rewarded by your
friendship.

Baron. This magnanimity only confuses me the
more. But I am, perhaps, too bold. I have not dared as
yet to inquire your name, your rank. Perhaps I offer
my friendship to a man who . . . . who, if he despises it,
is——

Trav. Pardon me, sir. You . . . . you make . . . .
you think too highly of me.

Baron (*aside*). Shall I ask him? He might feel offended
at my curiosity.

Trav. (*aside*). If he asks me, what shall I answer him?

Baron (*aside*). If I do not ask him, he may consider it
rudeness.

Trav. (*aside*). Shall I tell him the truth?

Baron (*aside*). But I will take the safest way. I'll first
make inquiries of his servant.

Trav. (*aside*). How car I get out of this perplexity?

BARON. Why so thoughtful?

TRAV. I was just going to put the same question to you.

BARON. I know now and then we forget ourselves. Let us speak of something else. Do you know that they were really Jews who attacked me? Just now my bailiff told me, that some days ago he met three of them on the high road. According to his description they must have looked more like rogues than honest people. And why should I doubt it? People so intent on gain care little whether they make money by fair means or foul—by cunning or force. They seem to be born for commerce, or, to speak more plainly, for cheating. Politeness, liberality, enterprise, discretion, are qualities that would render this people estimable, if they did not use them entirely to our disadvantage. (*He pauses a moment.*) The Jews have already been to me a source of no small mischief and vexation. When I was still in military service, I was persuaded to sign a bill in favour of one of my acquaintances, and the Jew on whom it was drawn not only made me pay the bill, but pay it twice. Oh! they are the most wicked, the most base people! What do you say? You seem cast down.

TRAV. What shall I say? I must confess I have often heard similar complaints.

BARON. And is it not true, their countenance has something that prejudices one against them? It seems to me as if one could read in their eyes their maliciousness, unscrupulousness, selfishness of character, their deceit and perjury. But why do you turn away from me?

TRAV. I hear you are very learned in physiognomies; I am afraid, sir, that mine——

BARON. Oh, you wrong me! How could you entertain such a suspicion? Without being learned in physiognomies, I must tell you, I have never met with a more frank, generous, and pleasing countenance than yours.

TRAV. To tell you the truth, I do not approve of generalizations concerning a whole people. You will not feel offended at my liberty. I should think among all nations good and wicked are to be found. And among the Jews——

Scene VII.—*The* Young Lady, *the* Traveller,
the Baron.

Lady. Oh, papa!

Baron. Well, wild puss? Why did you run away from
me? What was that for?

Lady. I did not run away from you, papa; but from
your scoldings.

Baron. The difference is very subtle. But what was it
that deserved a scolding?

Lady. Oh! you know. You saw it. I was with the
gentleman——

Baron. Well? And——

Lady. And the gentleman is a man; and with men,
you have told me, I must not have too much to do.

Baron. You ought to have seen that this gentleman is
an exception. I could wish that he liked you. It will
always give me pleasure to see you in his society.

Lady. Oh, it will have been the first and the last time,
I suppose. His servant is packing up. And that is what
I came to tell you.

Baron. What! Who? His servant?

Trav. Yes, sir; I ordered him to do so. My business,
and the fear of causing you any trouble——

Baron. What in the world shall I think of this? Shall
I not have the happiness of proving to you that in me you
have obliged a grateful heart? Oh! I entreat you to add
to your benefit another, which will be not less estimable
than the preservation of my life—remain with me a little
time; for a few days, at any rate. I would never forgive
myself, if I allowed a man like you to leave me unknown,
unhonoured, unrewarded, when it lay in my power to act
otherwise. I have invited some of my relations to spend
the day with us, to share my joy with them, and to give
them the good fortune of becoming acquainted with my
guardian angel.

Trav. Sir, I am forced——

Lady. To stay, sir! To stay! I will run to tell your
servant to unpack again . . . . But there he is.

Scene VIII.—Christoph (*booted and spurred, with two portmanteaux under his arm*), the Young Lady, *the* Traveller, *the* Baron.

Chris.   Well, sir, everything is ready.   Make haste; shorten your farewell ceremonies a little.   Of what use is so much talking, if we cannot stay?

Baron.   What prevents you, then, from staying?

Chris.   Certain considerations, my Lord Baron, founded on the obstinacy of my master, but for which his magnanimity is the pretext.

Trav.   My servant is sometimes rather silly; pardon him.   But I see that your entreaties are indeed more than mere compliments.   I submit, lest, from fear of being rude, I should commit a rudeness.

Baron.   Oh, how grateful I am to you!

Trav.   You may go and unsaddle; we'll not depart until to-morrow.

Lady.   Well, don't you hear?   Why are you standing there?   You are to go and unsaddle.

Chris.   By rights I ought to be angry; and I feel almost as if my wrath would break out.   Yet since nothing worse follows than to remain here to eat and drink and be well treated, we'll let it pass.   Otherwise, I am not at all fond of being troubled unnecessarily; you know that.

Trav.   Silence! you are too insolent.

Chris.   Because I tell the truth.

Lady.   Oh, how charming, that you will stay with us! Now I like you twice as well.   Come, I will show you our garden; you will like it.

Trav.   If it will please you, it will certainly please me.

Lady.   Come, then, until dinner is ready.   Papa, you permit us, don't you?

Baron.   I will even accompany you.

Lady.   No, no! we will not trouble you to do that; you have plenty to do.

Baron.   I have now no more important business than to please my guest.

Lady.   He will not be offended—would you, sir? (*Whispering.*)   Say no, do.   I should like to go alone with you.

Trav. I should repent of having given my consent to stay so easily, if I should occasion you the least trouble. I therefore beg——

Baron. Oh! why do you take any notice of the child's words?

Lady. Child! Papa! Don't make me blush. The gentleman will imagine me ever so young. Don't mind him; I am old enough to go for a walk with you. Come. But just look, your servant is still standing there with the portmanteaux under his arm.

Chris. I should think that only concerned him who had to carry them.

Trav. Hold your tongue! People show you too much consideration.

Scene IX.—Lisette, Christoph, *the* Young Lady, *the* Traveller, *the* Baron.

Baron (*perceiving* Lisette *coming*). Sir, I shall follow you immediately, if you will be pleased to conduct my daughter to the garden.

Lady. Oh, stay as long as you please. We shall amuse ourselves. Come. (*Exeunt the* Young Lady *and the* Traveller.)

Baron. Lisette, I have something to say to you.

Lis. Well?

Baron (*whispering*). I don't know yet who our guest is. For certain reasons I don't like to ask him. Could not you learn from his servant?

Lis. Oh! I know what you want. My own curiosity has already urged me to do that, and I have come here for that very reason.

Baron. Well, try your best and let me know. You will earn my thanks.

Lis. All right; go now.

Chris. You will not be offended then, sir, that we are pleased to stay. But don't inconvenience yourself at all on my account, I beg. I am contented with everything.

Baron. Lisette, I leave him under your care. Let him want for nothing. (*Exit.*)

Chris. I recommend myself then to your care, mademoiselle, you who are to let me want for nothing. (*Is going.*)

SCENE X.—LISETTE, CHRISTOPH.

LIS. (*stopping him*). No, sir, I cannot allow you to be so impolite. Am I not woman enough to be worthy of a little conversation?

CHRIS. The deuce, mistress, you take things too literally. Whether you are woman enough, or perhaps too much, I cannot say. But judging from your loquacity I should almost affirm the latter. But be that as it may, I hope you will dismiss me now; you see my hands and arms are full. As soon as I am hungry or thirsty I'll come to you.

LIS. Our watchman does the same.

CHRIS. The deuce! He must be a clever fellow, if he does as I do.

LIS. If you would like to make his acquaintance, he is chained up in the back-yard.

CHRIS. The devil! I verily believe you mean the dog. I see, you thought I meant bodily hunger and thirst; but that was not what I meant. I spoke of the hunger and thirst of love. That, mistress, that. Are you satisfied with my explanation?

LIS. Better than with what it explains.

CHRIS. Now, in confidence; do you mean to imply by that, that a declaration of love from me would not be disagreeable to you?

LIS. Perhaps. Will you make me one? Seriously?

CHRIS. Perhaps.

LIS. Ugh! What an answer! "Perhaps!"

CHRIS. And yet there was not a hair's-breadth difference between yours and mine.

LIS. But from my mouth it means something quite different. A woman's greatest pledge is "perhaps." For however bad our cards may be, we must never allow anyone to see them.

CHRIS. Well, if that's the case! But let's come to business. (*He throws the two portmanteaux on the ground.*) I don't know why I troubled myself so long. There they lie . . . . I love you, mistress.

LIS. I call that saying much in a few words. We'll dissect it.

Chris. No, we'll rather leave whole. But, that we may acquaint each other with our thoughts at leisure, be good enough to take a seat. Standing fatigues me. Make no ceremony. (*Makes her sit upon the portmanteau.*) I love you, mistress.

Lis. But . . . . my seat is desperately hard. I believe there are books in it.

Chris. Yes; full of wit and tenderness, and nevertheless you consider it a hard seat. That is my master's travelling library. It consists of comedies moving to tears, and tragedies moving to laughter; of tender epics, and philosophic drinking songs, and I don't know what more novelties. But we'll change. Take my seat; make no ceremony; mine is the softest.

Lis. Pardon me, I will not be so rude.

Chris. Make no ceremony, no compliments. Well, if you won't go, I shall carry you.

Lis. Well, if you order it. (*Is going to change her seat.*)

Chris. Order! Good gracious, no! Order means a great deal. If you mean to take it so, you had better keep your seat. (*He sits down again.*)

Lis. (*aside*). The uncivil brute! But no matter.

Chris. Well, where did we stop? Yes! I have it; we stopped at love. I love you, then, mistress. *Je vous aime,* I should say if you were a French marquise.

Lis. The deuce! Are you a Frenchman, then?

Chris. No, I must confess, to my own disgrace, I am only a German. But I had the good luck to be able to associate with some French gentlemen, from whom I have learned how an honest fellow ought to behave. I think, too, that one can see it in me at a glance.

Lis. You have come then from France, with your master?

Chris. Oh, no!

Lis. Where from, then? Perhaps——

Chris. It is some miles further than France, where we come from.

Lis. Not from Italy?   '

Chris. Not very far from there.

Lis. From England, then?

Chris. Almost. England is a province of the country. Our home is more than two hundred miles from here. But by Jove! my horses; the poor beasts are still in their harness. Pardon me, mistress. Quick! get up! (*He takes the portmanteaux under his arm.*) In spite of my fervent love I must go, and first attend to what is necessary. We have yet the whole day before us, and, what's better still, the whole night. I see we shall get on together. I shall know where to find you again.

SCENE XI.—MARTIN KRUMM, LISETTE.

LIS. I shall not get much information from him. He is either too stupid, or too cunning; and neither quality is easy to fathom.

KRUMM. Ah, Miss Lisette! So that is the fellow who is to cut me out.

LIS. There was no need for him to do that.

KRUMM. No need? And I was fancying how firmly I was rooted in your heart.

LIS. Of course, Herr Bailiff, you were fancying. People like yourself have the right to fancy absurdities. So I am not at all angry that you thought so, but that you have told me of it. I should like to know what you have to do with my heart? With what kindness, with what presents have you acquired a right to it? We don't give away our hearts so recklessly in these days. And do you think I am in distress about mine? I do not doubt I shall find an honest man for it, before I cast it to the swine.

KRUMM. The devil! that is a tweak for my nose. I must take a pinch of snuff; perhaps it will go off again with the sneezing. (*He pulls the stolen snuff-box out of his pocket, plays a little with it, and at last takes a pinch in a grandiose fashion.*)

LIS. (*giving a sidelong glance at him*). Confound it! Where has the fellow got that snuff-box?

KRUMM. Will you take a pinch?

LIS. Oh! your most obedient servant, Herr Bailiff. (*She takes a pinch.*)

KRUMM. What power a silver snuff-box has! Could an earwig be more pliant?

LIS. Is it a silver snuff-box?

KRUMM. Were it not a silver one, Martin Krumm would not have it.

LIS. May I look at it?

KRUMM. Yes; but only in my hands.

LIS. The shape is excellent.

KRUMM. Yes; it weighs full five ounces.

LIS. If it was only for the shape, I should like to have such a box.

KRUMM. When I have it melted, the shape will be at your service.

LIS. You are much too kind, sir. Without doubt it is a present?

KRUMM. Yes, it did not cost me a farthing.

LIS. Indeed, such a present might easily dazzle a woman. You can make your fortune with it, Herr Bailiff. I at least should defend myself very badly if I were attacked with silver boxes. With such a box a sweetheart might easily win his game.

KRUMM. I understand. I understand.

LIS. As it costs you nothing, I should advise you, Herr Bailiff, to make a good friend by it.

KRUMM. I see. I see.

LIS. (*insinuatingly*). Would not you give it to me?

KRUMM. Oh, I beg your pardon. One does not give away silver snuff-boxes so recklessly in these days. And do you think, Miss Lisette, that I am in distress about mine? I do not doubt I shall meet with an honest man for it, before I cast it to the swine.

LIS. Has anyone ever heard such stupid impertinence? To compare a heart with a snuff-box!

KRUMM. Yes, a stony heart with a silver snuff-box.

LIS. It might perhaps cease to be stony if . . . . But all my talking is in vain. You are not worthy of my love. What a kind-hearted fool I am! (*Begins to cry.*) I had almost believed the bailiff was one of those honest people who mean what they say.

KRUMM. And what a kind-hearted fool I am to believe that a woman means what she says! There, my Lizzy, don't cry. (*Gives her the snuff-box.*) But now I hope I am worthy of your love. To begin with, I ask nothing but a kiss on your beautiful hand. (*He kisses her hand.*) Ah! how sweet!

Scene XII.—*The* Young Lady, Lisette, Martin Krumm.

Lady (*softly approaching pushes down his head on to Li-sette's hand*). Indeed, Herr Bailiff! Come, kiss my hand also.

Lis. Botheration!

Krumm. With all my heart, madam. (*Is going to kiss her hand.*)

Lady (*gives him a box on his ear*). You stupid clown, don't you understand a joke?

Krumm. The devil! 'Tis a queer way of joking.

Lis. (*laughing*). Ha! ha! ha! Oh, how I pity you, my dear bailiff! Ha! ha! ha!

Krumm. What, you are laughing, too, are you! Is that my reward? Very well, very well. (*Exit.*)

Lis. Ha! ha! ha!

Scene XIII.—Lisette, *the* Young Lady.

Lady. I never would have believed it, Lisette, if I had not seen it myself. You allow yourself to be kissed— and by the bailiff?

Lis. I don't know what right you have to spy on me? I thought you had gone for a walk with the stranger in the garden.

Lady. Yes; and I should be with him still, if my papa had not joined us; and then I could not speak a single reasonable word with him. My papa is much too serious.

Lis. What do you call a reasonable word? And what can you have to tell him, that your papa must not hear?

Lady. A thousand things. But I shall be angry if you ask any more questions. Let it suffice; I like the strange gentleman. That I may be permitted to confess, I suppose.

Lis. You would quarrel dreadfully with your papa, I suppose, if he were to choose such a husband for you some day? But, joking aside, who knows what he intends to do? What a pity you are not a few years older! Things might soon be settled then.

Lady. Oh, if my age is the only obstacle, papa can make me a few years older, and I certainly shall not contradict him.

Lis. No; I know of a better way. I'll give you a few of my years, and that will serve us both. I shall no longer be too old, nor you too young.

Lady. That is true; that will do.

Lis. See! the stranger's servant is coming here. I must speak to him. It is all for your good. Will you leave me alone with him? Go now.

Lady. Yes; but don't forget about the years. Do you hear, Lisette?

Scene XIV.—Lisette, Christoph.

Lis. You must be either hungry or thirsty, sir, that you come again already? Eh?

Chris. Yes, indeed. But mind how I have explained hunger and thirst. To tell you the truth, my dear young woman, as soon as I dismounted yesterday, I cast my eye on you. But thinking to remain here only a few hours, I thought it would not be worth while to make your acquaintance. What could we have done in so short a time? We should have had to begin our novel at the wrong end. And it is not safe to pull the cat out of the stove by the tail.

Lis. True enough; but now we can proceed more according to rule. You can make a proposal; I can reply to it. I can raise scruples; you can overcome them. We may deliberate at each step, and need not sell one another a pig in a poke. If you had made me your offer yesterday at once, I must confess, I should have accepted it. But only fancy how much I should have staked, if I had had no time to inquire about your rank, fortune, country, employments, and such like.

Chris. The deuce! But would that have been necessary? Such a fuss! You could not make much more, if you were going to be married.

Lis. Oh! if it had been a mere marriage, it would be

ridiculous to be so conscientious on my part. But a love
affair is quite another thing. The least trifle is of the
greatest importance. And therefore don't fancy that you
will obtain the least favour from me, if you do not satisfy
my curiosity in every respect.

Chris. Well; and how far does it go?

Lis. Since a servant is best judged by his master, before
anything else I wish to know——

Chris. Who my master is? Ha! ha! that's good.
You ask me a question which I should like to ask you,
if I thought you knew more about it than I did.

Lis. And do you really think to get off with this miserable subterfuge? In short, I must know who your master
is, or there's an end to our friendship.

Chris. I have not known my master longer than four
weeks. So long it is, since I entered his service at Hamburg. I have come with him from that place, but have
never taken the trouble to inquire for his rank or name.
But so much is quite certain; he must be rich, for he has
not let either himself or me want for anything on our
journey. And why should I care about anything else?

Lis. What can I hope from your love, if you won't even
trust such a trifle to my discretion? I should never treat
you in such a way. For example, you see this handsome
silver snuff-box——

Chris. Really! Well?

Lis. You only need to beg me, and I'll tell you from
whom I have got it.

Chris. Oh, that is not of much consequence to me. I'd
rather know who is to get it from you.

Lis. I have not exactly settled that point yet. But if
you don't get it, it will be no one's fault but your own.
I certainly should not leave your openness unrewarded.

Chris. Or rather my loquacity. But as I am an honest
fellow, if I am silent now, it is from necessity, for, indeed,
I don't know what I can tell you. Confound it! How
willingly I would pour out my secrets if I only had any!

Lis. Good-bye! I'll not assail your virtue any longer.
But I wish it may help you soon to a silver snuff-box and
a sweetheart, as it has now deprived you of them. (*Is going.*)

Chris. Come, come; patience! (*Aside.*) I see I must

tell a lie, for I really cannot let such a present escape.
Besides, what harm can it do?

Lis. Well, will you explain yourself more frankly?
But I see. You do not like it. No, no, I don't want to
know anything——

Chris. Yes, yes; you shall know everything! (*Aside.*)
What would I not give to be able to tell lies. (*Aloud.*) Well,
listen, then! My master .... is a nobleman. He comes
—we come together—from Holland. He was obliged, on
account of some vexations—a trifle—a murder—to run
for it.

Lis. What! on account of a murder?

Chris. Yes. But it was an honourable murder—was
obliged to escape in consequence of a duel—and just now
he is flying——

Lis. And you, my friend?

Chris. I am also flying. The dead one—I mean to
say, the friends of the dead one—are prosecuting us, and
on account of this prosecution .... But the rest you can
easily guess .... What the deuce can one do? Consider
for yourself: a saucy young monkey—called us names!
My master knocked him down. How could it be otherwise? If anyone calls me names, I do the same, or—
I give him a good box on the ear. An honest fellow
must not put up with such things.

Lis. Bravo! I like people of that sort; for I am a
little hasty myself. But see, there's your master coming.
Would anyone believe, from his countenance, that he was
so fierce and cruel?

Chris. Come, come; let us get out of his way. He
might perhaps see that I have betrayed him.

Lis. Just as you please.

Chris. But the silver snuff-box——

Lis. Come on. (*Aside.*) I must first see what I shall
get from my master for the secret I have discovered; if
that is worth something, he may have the box.

Scene XV.—*The* Traveller.

Trav. I miss my box. It is a trifle, yet the loss of it
would grieve me. Could the bailiff, perhaps .... But no,

I have lost it; I may have pulled it out of my pocket unawares. We ought not to injure anyone even by suspicion. Nevertheless—he pressed close up to me—he snatched at my watch .... I caught him at it .... Might he not have snatched at the box without my having caught him?

SCENE XVI.—MARTIN KRUMM, *the* TRAVELLER.

KRUMM (*perceiving the stranger, is about to retire*). Holloa!

TRAV. Well, well, my friend, approach. (*Aside.*) He is as shy as if he knew my thoughts! Well? come nearer!

KRUMM (*defiantly*). I have no time. I know well you wish to chat with me. I have more important business to attend to. I don't wish to hear your heroic deeds for the tenth time. Relate them to somebody else, who has not heard them yet.

TRAV. What do I hear! Just now the bailiff was simple and polite, now he is insolent and rude. Which is your true mask?

KRUMM. Ah! who the deuce taught you to call my face a mask? I don't want to quarrel with you .... otherwise—— (*Is going away.*)

TRAV. (*aside*). His insolent behaviour increases my suspicion. (*Aloud.*) No, no, wait a moment. I have something important to ask you.

KRUMM. And I shall have nothing to reply, however important it may be. Therefore, spare yourself the trouble of asking.

TRAV. I'll venture it. But I should be very sorry if I did him a wrong. My friend, have you not seen my snuff-box? I miss it.

KRUMM. What a question! Is it my fault that some one has stolen it? What do you take me for—the receiver or the thief?

TRAV. Who spoke of theft? You are betraying yourself.

KRUMM. I betray myself? Then you think I have

got it? But do you know, sir, what it is to accuse an honest fellow of such things? Do you know that?

Trav. Why shout so loud? I have not yet accused you of anything. You are your own accuser. Besides, I don't know whether I should be greatly in the wrong. Who was it whom I caught snatching at my watch?

Krumm. Oh! you are a man who can't understand a joke. Listen. (*Aside.*) Suppose he has seen it in Lisette's possession? But the girl has surely not been so foolish as to boast of it.

Trav. Oh, I understand your way of joking so well, that I almost believe you would like to joke with my box also. But if one carries a joke too far, it at last becomes earnest. I should be sorry for your reputation. Suppose I was convinced you had had no evil intentions, would other people too——

Krumm. Oh! other people .... other people would have long ago been weary of being charged with things of this sort. But if you think I have got it, search me, examine me.

Trav. That is not my business. Besides, one does not carry everything in one's pocket.

Krumm. Very well; but that you may see I am an honest fellow, I'll turn out my pockets myself. Look! (*Aside.*) The devil must have a hand in the game if it should tumble out.

Trav. Oh, don't trouble yourself.

Krumm. No, no! you shall see, you shall see. (*He turns one of his pockets inside out.*) Is there a box there? Crumbs of bread are in it; that precious food. (*He turns out another.*) There is nothing here either. But stop, a bit of a calendar; I keep it on account of the verses written above the months. They are very amusing. Well, to proceed. Attend now. I'll turn out the third. (*In turning it out, two large beards fall out.*) The devil! what is that? (*He stoops hastily to pick them up, but the traveller is quicker, and snatches one of them.*)

Trav. What is the meaning of these things?

Krumm (*aside*). Cursed fate! I thought I had put them away long ago.

TRAV. Why, this is a beard. (*He puts it to his face.*)
Do I look like a Jew now?

KRUMM. Give it back to me. Give it back. Who
knows what you may be fancying? I sometimes frighten
my little boy with it. That is what it is for.

TRAV. You will be kind enough to leave it me. I will
also frighten some one with it.

KRUMM. Don't let us quarrel; I must have it back.
(*Tries to snatch it from his hand.*)

TRAV. Go, or——

KRUMM (*aside*). The devil! 'Tis time now to look out
where the carpenter has left a hole. (*Aloud.*) All right, sir,
all right. I see you came here to bring me ill-luck. But
may all the devils take me if I am not an honest man! I
should like to see the man who can say anything bad of
me! Bear that in mind. Whatever may come of it, I
can swear I have not used that beard for any evil purpose!
(*Exit.*)

SCENE XVII.—*The* TRAVELLER.

TRAV. This man himself raises suspicions in me which
are very prejudicial to himself. Might he not be one of the
disguised robbers? But I will follow out my supposition
cautiously.

SCENE XVIII.—*The* BARON, *the* TRAVELLER.

TRAV. Would you not think I had been fighting
yesterday with the Jewish robbers and I had torn out one
of their beards? (*He shows him the beard.*)

BARON. What do you mean, sir?—But why did you
leave me so hastily?

TRAV. Pardon my want of politeness. I intended to
be with you again immediately. I only went to look for
my snuff-box, which I must have lost somewhere here.

BARON. I am really sorry for that. Should you, after
all, have suffered a loss in my house——

TRAV. The loss would not be so very great. But pray
just look at this curious beard.

BARON. You showed it to me before. Why?

TRAV. I will explain myself more intelligibly. I
believe . . . . But no, I will keep my supposition to myself.

BARON. Your supposition? Explain yourself!

TRAV. No, I have been too hasty. I might be mistaken.

BARON. You make me uneasy.

TRAV. What do you think of your bailiff?

BARON. No, no, we won't turn the conversation. I conjure you, by the benefit you have rendered me, to explain to me what you think, what you suppose, and in what you might be mistaken?

TRAV. A reply to my question alone can induce me to acquaint you with the whole matter.

BARON. What do I think of my bailiff? Well, I consider him a thoroughly honest and upright man.

TRAV. Then forget that I had anything to tell you.

BARON. A beard—suppositions—the bailiff .... How shall I connect these things? Are my entreaties of no avail? You might be mistaken. Suppose you are mistaken, what risk do you run with a friend?

TRAV. You press me too hard. I tell you then, that your bailiff incautiously dropped this beard; that he had another, which he hastily put back again in his pocket; that his language betrays a man who thinks that people believe as much evil of him as he is capable of doing; that I also have caught him in an attempt not very conscientious, or at least not very prudent.

BARON. It seems as if my eyes were suddenly opened I am afraid you will not be mistaken. And you hesitated to inform me of it? I shall go at once, and try all means in my power to discover the truth. Am I to harbour murderers in my own house?

TRAV. But do not be angry with me, if you should happily find my supposition to be false. You forced it from me, otherwise I should have kept it secret.

BARON. True or false, I shall always be grateful to you

SCENE XIX.—*The* TRAVELLER. *Afterwards* CHRISTOPH.

TRAV. I hope he will not proceed too hastily with him; for however well-founded the suspicion is, the man may nevertheless be innocent. I am very uneasy .... Indeed, it is no trifle to cause a master to suspect his servants. Even if he finds them to be innocent, yet he loses his confidence in them for ever. Certainly, when I consider the matter more fully, I feel I ought to have been silent. And when they hear that I have ascribed my loss to him, will they not conclude that selfishness and revenge are the causes of my suspicion? I would willingly give a good deal to postpone the investigation.

CHRIS. (*approaches laughing*). Ha! ha! ha! Do you know, sir, who you are?

TRAV. Do you know that you are a fool? What do you want?

CHRIS. Well, if you don't know it, I will tell you. You are a nobleman; you come from Holland, where you got into a scrape and fought a duel; you were so fortunate as to kill a young monkey of a fellow; the friends of the dead man have pursued you hotly; you have taken to flight; I have the honour of accompanying you on your flight.

TRAV. Are you dreaming, or are you mad?

CHRIS. Neither the one nor the other; since for a madman my discourse would be too reasonable, and for a dreamer too mad.

TRAV. Who has imposed upon you with such nonsense?

CHRIS. Oh, you may rest assured that no one imposes upon me. But don't you think it is cleverly invented in the short time they left me for lying? I'm sure I could not have hit upon anything better. So now at least you are secured against further curiosity.

TRAV. But what am I to make of all this?

CHRIS. No more than you please! Leave the remainder to me. Just listen how it happened. I was asked for your name, rank, fatherland, occupations; I did not let them ask twice. I told all I knew; that is, that I knew nothing at all. You can easily understand that this news was hardly sufficient, and that they had little cause to be contented with it. So they pressed me, but in vain; I kept silent, because I had nothing to keep silent about. But at last the offer of a present induced me to tell more than I knew; that is, I told a lie.

TRAV. You scoundrel! I see what excellent hands I am in.

Chris. What! I hope I have not accidentally lied the truth ?

Trav. You impudent liar ! you have placed me in an embarrassment out of which——

Chris. Out of which you can extricate yourself as soon as you like to make further use of the nice epithet you just now were pleased to bestow on me.

Trav. But I shall then be obliged to disclose myself?

Chris. So much the better ; then I too shall learn who you are. But judge for yourself whether, with a good conscience, I could have been conscientious in regard to this lie ? (*He pulls out the snuff-box.*) Look at this box ! Could I have earned it more easily ?

Trav. Let me look at it. (*He takes it into his hand.*) What do I see ?

Chris. Ha ! ha ! ha ! I thought you would be astonished. Why, I am sure, if you could earn such a box, you would not mind telling a lie or two yourself.

Trav. So you have robbed me of it ?

Chris. How ? What ?

Trav. Your faithlessness vexes me less than the over-hasty suspicion which I have cast upon an honest man on account of this box. And you can still be so insanely impudent as to want to persuade me that it was a present, obtained, however, hardly less disgracefully. Go ! And never come into my presence again.

Chris. Are you dreaming, or are . . . . But out of respect for you I will not say it. Surely envy cannot have led you to such extravagances? Do you mean to say this box is yours, and I have robbed you of it, *salva venia?* If it were so, I should be a stupid devil to boast of it in your very presence. Well, there is Lisette coming. Quick, come here ! Help me to bring my master back to his senses.

SCENE XX.—Lisette, *the* Traveller, Christoph.

Lis. Oh, sir, what troubles you are making among us ! What harm has our bailiff done to you ? You have made our master furious with him. They are talking of beards, and snuff-boxes, and robberies; the bailiff is crying and swearing that he is innocent, and that you say what is not true. Our master is not to be softened; and, indeed, he has now sent for the magistrate and the police to put the bailiff in irons. What is the meaning of it all?

Chris. Oh, all that is nothing at all! Only listen, listen what he intends to do with me.

Trav. Yes, indeed, my dear Lisette. I have been too hasty. The bailiff is innocent. It is my wicked servant alone who has brought me into this trouble. It is he who has stolen my box, on account of which I suspected the bailiff, and the beard may certainly have been for the children, as he said. I will go and give him satisfaction; I will confess my mistake. I will do whatever he may request.

Chris. No, no, stop; you must first give me satisfaction. In the devil's name, Lisette, why don't you speak? Tell him how it is. I wish that you and your box were both at the dickens! Am I to be called a thief for it? Did you not give it to me?

Lis. Yes, indeed, and I don't want it back again.

Trav. What? It is true, then? But the box is mine.

Lis. Yours? I did not know that.

Trav. And you found it? And my negligence is to blame for all this disturbance. (*To* Christoph.) I have wronged you also;—pardon me! I am ashamed of my hastiness.

Lis. (*aside*). The deuce! Now I begin to see. I don't think he has been over-hasty, either.

Trav. Come, we will——

Scene XXI.—*The* Baron, *the* Traveller, Lisette, Christoph.

Baron (*in a great hurry*). Lisette, restore the box to the gentleman immediately! All is discovered; he has confessed all. And you were not ashamed to accept presents from such a rascal?—Well, where is the box?

Trav. Then it is true, after all?

Lis. The gentleman got it back a long time ago. I thought I might take presents at the hands of those from

whom you accepted services. I knew as little of him as
you.

CHRIS. And so my present has gone to the deuce again.
Lightly come, lightly go.

BARON. But how can I show my gratitude to you, my
dearest friend? You have saved me a second time from
an equally great danger. I owe my life to you. Without
you I should never have discovered this misfortune that
threatened me. My agent, whom I considered the most
honest man on my whole property, was the bailiff's accom-
plice. How then could I ever have imagined it? Had
you departed to-day——

TRAV. True enough . . . . then the assistance which
I thought to have rendered you yesterday would have
been very incomplete. I therefore consider myself happy
that Heaven has chosen me to make this unlooked-for
discovery. I now rejoice as much as I feared before that
I might be mistaken.

BARON. I admire your philanthropy as much as your
magnanimity. Oh may that be true which Lisette has
told me!

SCENE XXII.—*The* YOUNG LADY, *the* BARON, *the* TRAVELLER,
LISETTE, CHRISTOPH.

LIS. And why should it not be true?

BARON. Come, my daughter, come. Unite your entreaties
with mine: request my preserver to accept your hand, and
with your hand my fortune. What more costly gift could
my gratitude present him with, than you, whom I love as
much as him? Do not wonder that I can make you such
an offer! Your servant has disclosed to us who you are.
Grant me the inestimable pleasure of showing my gratitude. My fortune is equal to my rank, and this is equal to
yours. Here you are safe from your enemies, and come
among friends who will adore you.—But you seem de-
pressed. How am I to interpret this?

LADY. Can you be distressed on my account? I assure
you I shall obey my papa with pleasure.

TRAV. Your magnanimity astonishes me. From the
greatness of the reward which you offer me, I now per-

ceive how small was my deed. But what shall I reply to you? My servant has told an untruth, and I ——

Baron. Would to Heaven you were not what he says! Would to Heaven your rank were lower than mine! Then the value of my requital would be increased a little, and you would, perhaps, feel less inclined to refuse my entreaty.

Trav. (aside). Why do I not disclose myself? (Aloud.) Sir, your nobility of mind touches my soul. Ascribe it to fate and not to me, that your offer is in vain. I am ——

Baron. Perhaps married already?

Trav. No.

Baron. Well? What then?

Trav. I am a Jew.

Baron. A Jew? Cruel fate!

Chris. A Jew?

Lis. A Jew?

Lady. Oh! what does that matter?

Lis. Hush, Miss, hush! I will tell you afterwards what it matters.

Baron. And so there are cases where Heaven itself prevents our being grateful.

Trav. Your wish to be so renders it superfluous.

Baron. I will at least do all that fate permits me to do. Accept my whole fortune. I would rather be poor and grateful than rich and thankless.

Trav. This offer, too, I must decline, for the God of my fathers has given me more than I want. For requital I ask but one thing, that you will henceforth judge of my nation in a kinder and less sweeping way. I did not conceal my race from you because I am ashamed of my religion. No! But I saw that you felt friendship for me, and enmity against my nation. And the friendship of a man, whoever he may be, has always been esteemed by me.

Baron. I am ashamed of my conduct.

Chris. I am only just coming to myself again, after my surprise. What, you are a Jew, and have been bold enough to take an honest Christian into your service? You ought to have served me. That would have been

right, according to the Bible. By my faith! You have
insulted all Christendom in my person. Now I know the
reason why the gentleman would eat no pork during our
journey, and did a hundred other follies. Don't fancy I
shall go with you any further. I shall bring an action
against you, too.

TRAV. I cannot expect of you that you should think
more kindly than other Christian people. I will not remind you from what miserable circumstances I took you
at Hamburg: nor will I force you to remain any longer
with me. But as I am pretty well satisfied with your
services, and have just now suspected you unjustly, you
may keep the object that caused my suspicion as a recom-
pense. (*He gives him the box.*) Your wages you shall also
have, and now you may go wherever you please.

CHRIS. Deuce take it! there are Jews too, I suppose,
who are no Jews. You are a good fellow. Done! I stay
with you. A Christian would have given me a kick in
the ribs, and not a snuff-box.

BARON. I am charmed with all I have seen of you. Come,
let us take steps to have the guilty ones put in safe
custody. Oh, how estimable would the Jews be, were
they all like you!

TRAV. And how amiable the Christians, if they all
possessed your qualities!

(*Exeunt the* BARON, *the* YOUNG LADY, *and the* TRAVELLER.)

SCENE XXIII.

LISETTE, CHRISTOPH.

LIS. And so, my friend, you told me a lie.

CHRIS. Yes; and for two reasons. Firstly, because
I did not know the truth; and secondly, because one cannot tell many truths for a box which one is obliged to give
back again.

LIS. And perhaps, if one only knew it, you are a Jew
yourself, too, however you may disguise it.

CHRIS. You are too inquisitive for a young lady. Come
along with me.

(*Exeunt arm-in-arm.*)

THE FREETHINKER.

(A COMEDY IN FIVE ACTS.)

———————

The 'Freethinker' was written at Berlin in the year 1749.

DRAMATIS PERSONÆ.

ADRAST, *the Freethinker.*

THEOPHAN, *a young Clergyman.*

LISIDOR.

ARASPE, *cousin of* THEOPHAN.

JOHANN *and* ⎫
MARTIN, ⎭ *servants.*

A BANKER.

JULIANE *and* ⎫
HENRIETTE, ⎭ *daughters of* LISIDOR.

FRAU PHILANE, *mother of* LISIDOR.

LISETTE, *maid-servant.*

The scene is at LISIDOR'S *house.*

THE FREETHINKER.

ACT I.

SCENE I.—ADRAST, THEOPHAN.

THEOPH. Will you be offended, Adrast, if at last I find fault with the haughty reserve which you still continue to show towards me? We have already been many months in the same house, awaiting the same good fortune. Two amiable sisters are about to make us happy. Consider then, Adrast, can there exist a greater inducement for us to love one another and to form such a friendship as there should be between brothers? How often have I not maintained——

ADR. Just as often have you perceived that I do not wish to enter into such a friendship. Friendship, indeed! Friendship between us! Do you know, I would ask, what friendship is?

THEOPH. Do I know?

ADR. A question always surprises, when it is put unexpectedly. Granted that you do know—but my way of thinking and your own, I suppose, you also know?

THEOPH. I understand you; so we are to be enemies, I suppose?

ADR. You seem to have understood me nicely! Enemies! Is there no medium, then? Must one always either love or hate? We will remain indifferent to each other; and I know that is what you in reality wish yourself. Learn frankness at least from me.

THEOPH. That I am ready to do. But will you teach me this virtue in all its purity?

ADR. Ask yourself, in the first place, if in all its purity it would be agreeable to you?

THEOPH. Certainly. And to prove to you that your future scholar has some capacity for it, will you let me make the trial?

ADR. Most willingly.

THEOPH. Take care that my attempt does not prove a masterpiece. Hear, then, Adrast .... But permit me to begin by a little flattery of myself. Hitherto I have always set some value on my friendship; I have been cautious, I have been sparing of it. You are the first person to whom I have offered it; and you are the only one upon whom I shall urge it. In vain does your look of contempt tell me that I shall not succeed. Yes, I shall succeed. Your own heart is my surety : your own heart, Adrast, which is infinitely better than your judgment, perhaps wishes it to be, enamoured, as it is, of certain high-sounding opinions.

ADR. I detest flattery, Theophan; and especially that flattery which is paid to my heart at the expense of my understanding. I really do not know what weaknesses (for weaknesses they must be) can have made you so well satisfied with my heart : but this I know, that I will not rest till I have utterly expelled them by the help of my understanding.

THEOPH. Scarcely have I begun the proof of my sincerity, when your sensibility takes fire. I shall not get far.

ADR. As far as you please. Proceed, I pray.

THEOPH. Indeed! Your heart, then, is as good as can be found. It is too good to be subservient to your understanding, which some new and extraordinary doctrines have blinded, which an appearance of solidity has hurried on to palpable errors, and which, from an eager desire to be conspicuous, is forcibly making of you that which only enemies of virtue and unprincipled men should be. Call such what you will—freethinkers, sceptics, deists ; or, if you would misapply honourable appellations, call them philosophers — monsters they are, and a disgrace to humanity. And you, Adrast, whom nature intended to be an ornament of our race, who have but to follow your

natural feelings to become so; you, with such a groundwork of all that is noble and great, you wilfully belie
your character. You deliberately throw yourself down
from your exalted position, to gain a reputation amongst
the *canaille* of minds, than which I would rather choose a
world-wide ignominy.

Adr. You forget yourself, Theophan; and if I do not
interrupt you, you will eventually begin to imagine that
you are in that place from which your fraternity are
allowed to babble by the hour undisturbed.

Theoph. No, Adrast, you are interrupting no impor-
tunate preacher; think but a little, you interrupt only a
friend—contrary to your wish, I so call myself—who was
to give you a specimen of his frankness.

Adr. And who has given me a specimen of his flattery;
—but of a concealed flattery, a flattery which assumes a
certain asperity in order the less to appear like flattery.
You will at last make me despise you also. If you knew
what frankness was, you would have told me openly what
in your heart you think of me. Your lips would not have
attributed good qualities to me which your inward conviction does not acknowledge. You would have directly
reproached me with being an impious profligate, who seeks
to withdraw himself from religion only that he may indulge his inclinations in greater security. To express
oneself more forcibly, you would have called me a brand
of hell! an incarnate fiend! You would have spared no
curse; in short, you would have conducted yourself as a
clergyman must, against a despiser of his superstition,
and consequently of his reputation.

Theoph. I am astounded. What conceptions!

Adr. Conceptions which I have selected from a
thousand examples. But we are going too far. I know
what I know, and have long learnt to distinguish the
mask from the face. Carnivals show us that the more
beautiful the former is, the more hideous is the latter.

Theoph. You mean thereby to say——

Adr. I mean to say nothing thereby, except that I
have not as yet sufficient reason to limit on your account
the general opinion which I hold of the members of your
profession. I have sought in vain for exceptions too long

to expect to find the first in you. I should have to have known you longer, and have seen you under various circumstances, before——

THEOPH. Before you would do my face the justice of not taking it for a mask. Very well! But how can you arrive at that sooner, than by allowing me a more intimate acquaintance with you? Make me your friend; put me to the proof.

ADR. Gently! The proof would come too late, if I had already made you my friend. In my opinion, the proof should come first.

THEOPH. There are different degrees of friendship, Adrast, and I do not yet ask for the closest.

ADR. Of the most distant even you are not capable.

THEOPH. Incapable? Where is the impossibility?

ADR. You know, Theophan, a book, I suppose, which is said to be the book of all books, which is said to contain all our duties, and which is said to give us the surest prescriptions for all virtues, but which at the same time makes no mention of friendship? Do you know the book, I say?

THEOPH. I see your drift, Adrast. From what ignoramus have you borrowed that poor objection?

ADR. Whether I have borrowed it, or discovered it myself, is much the same. It must be a small mind which is ashamed of borrowing truths.

THEOPH. Truths, indeed! Are the rest of your truths of equal value? Can you listen to me for one moment?

ADR. More preaching?

THEOPH. Do not you force me to it? Or do you wish that I shall leave your shallow scoffs unanswered, so that it may appear as if one was unable to answer them?

ADR. And what can you answer, then?

THEOPH. This: tell me, is love included in friendship, or friendship in love? Doubtless the latter. He, therefore, who has enjoined love in its very widest compass, has he not enjoined friendship also? I should think so; and so little is it the truth that our Lawgiver has not considered friendship worthy of his command, but on the contrary his injunction extends to friendship for the whole world.

ADR. You charge him with absurdities. Friendship for the whole world! What is that? My friend must not be the friend of the whole world.

THEOPH. Nothing, then, in your opinion, is friendship, I suppose, but that accordance of dispositions, that innate harmony of minds, that secret drawing together, that invisible chain which unites two souls of similar opinions and tastes.

ADR. Yes, that alone I call friendship.

THEOPH. That alone? Then you contradict yourself.

ADR. Oh, how you people find contradictions everywhere, except just where they really are!

THEOPH. Just consider; if this certainly not arbitrary agreement of minds, this innate accordance with one single other being alone constitutes true friendship, how can you require that it should be the object of a law? Where it exists it need not be enjoined; and where it does not exist it would be enjoined in vain. And how can you lay to the charge of our Teacher, that he has passed over friendship in this sense? He has enjoined a more exalted friendship, which can dispense with that blind inclination, which even the unreasoning animals are not without, a friendship communicated agreeably to laws of acknowledged perfection, a friendship which is not governed by, but which governs, nature itself.

ADR. Oh, what talk!

THEOPH. This I must tell you, Adrast. though you might know it as well as I do, and also ought to know it. What would you yourself think of me, if I did not endeavour by every means to avert the suspicion that religion could make me despise friendship, the religion which you would be only too ready to find some sound reason for despising? Do not look at me so contemptuously, do not turn from me so insultingly.

ADR. (aside). Wretched parson!

THEOPH. I see you require time to suppress the first feeling of ill-will which the refutation of a favourite opinion naturally creates. I will leave you. I have just heard too that one of my relations had arrived. I will go and meet him, and shall have the honour of introducing him to you.

SCENE II.—ADRAST.

ADR. Would that I need never see him again! Is there one of you black-coated gentry who is not a hypocrite? I have to thank the clergy for my misfortunes. They have oppressed me and persecuted me; however nearly we may have been allied by blood. I will hate you, Theophan, and all your order. Am I here also to become related to the priesthood? This sneaking fellow, this dull renouncer of his understanding, to become my brother-in-law! And my brother-in-law through Juliane!—through Juliane! What cruel destiny pursues me everywhere? An old friend of my deceased father offers me the hand of one of his daughters. I hasten to him, but arrive too late; and I find her, who at first sight took captive my whole heart, and with whom alone I could live happily, already promised! Ah, Juliane! You were not destined for me! You whom I love! And am I to content myself with a sister whom I do not love?

SCENE III.—LISIDOR, ADRAST.

LIS. That is it! Alone again, Adrast? Tell me, pray, must philosophers creep thus into corners? I would rather not be one—and, if I heard correctly, you were actually talking to yourself. Well, well, perhaps so; you whimsical fellows certainly could not talk with anybody cleverer than yourselves. But still such as we are no fools either. I will join in, be the subject what it may.

ADR. I beg your pardon——

LIS. How pardon? Why, you have not done anything to hurt me yet. I like to see people merry; and as sure as I am an honest man, the idea of having for my son-in-law the merry scapegrace, as they used to call you formerly at home, gave me true pleasure. Certainly since that time you are grown-up; you have travelled; seen distant countries and peoples. But that you would return such an altered gentleman was what I never would have dreamt. You argue now about what is, and what is not; about what might be, and if it might be why then it might not be; about necessity, partial necessity, and complete necessity; about necessary necessity, and necessity which is not necessary; about at—at—what do you call those little things that fly about in the rays of the sun?—about at—at— What are they, Adrast?

Adr. Atoms I suppose you mean.

Lis. Yes, yes, atoms, atoms. So called because one gets at 'em by the thousand when one draws a breath.

Adr. Ha! ha! ha!

Lis. You laugh, Adrast! Yes, my young friend, you must not imagine that I understand nothing at all about the matter. I have heard you and Theophan quarrelling often enough over it. I retain the pith of it. While you are knocking your heads together, I am fishing in the dark. Many a crumb falls which neither of you know how to use; and those are for me. You must not be envious of me for this, for I take from you both impartially. I take one idea from you, my good Adrast, and one from Theophan, and then from them all I afterwards make a complete——

Adr. Which must be something monstrous.

Lis. Why so?

Adr. Because you mingle day and night if you unite my ideas with those of Theophan.

Lis. Very well! And an agreeable twilight springs therefrom. Besides, it is not at all true that you differ so much from each other. Fancies! fancies! On the contrary, how often have I not considered you both in the right at the same moment? Indeed, I am thoroughly convinced that all honourable people believe alike.

Adr. Should do so, should do so, that is true.

Lis. There, see now! what difference is there in that? Believe, or should believe; it comes to the same thing. Who can measure every word with compasses? And I wager a trifle, when you are once brothers-in-law, no egg will be more like another——

Adr. Than I to Theophan, and he to me?

Lis. Certainly: you do not yet know what it is to be relations. For relationship's sake, one will yield an inch, and the other will yield an inch; one inch and one inch, that makes two inches; two inches make . . . . well, I'll be hanged if you are that distance apart. And then

nothing in the world, I think, could give me so much
pleasure as the thought, that my daughters suit each of
you so exactly. Juliane was born for a clergyman's wife;
and as for Henriette, there is not to be found in the whole
land, Adrast, a girl that would suit you better. Pretty,
lively, but firm in character; she sings, dances, and plays;
in short, she is a daughter after my own heart. Juliane,
on the other hand, is pious simplicity itself.

Adr. Juliane? Do not say that. Her perfections,
perhaps, strike the eye less. Her beauty does not dazzle;
but it touches the heart. One is willingly led captive by
her silent charms, and submits deliberately to her yoke,
which others must throw on one in a fit of gay thoughtlessness. She speaks little; but then there is sense in
each word she utters.

Lis. And Henriette?

Adr. Henriette can certainly express herself wittily
and with freedom. But could not Juliane do the same,
if only she wished, and if she did not prefer truth and
feeling to that ostentatious parade? All virtues seem to
have united in her soul——

Lis. And Henriette?

Adr. Far be it from me to deny to Henriette the possession of any virtue. But there is a certain manner
which would hardly allow one to attribute them to her
if one had not better grounds for doing so. Juliane's
sedate sweetness, her natural modesty, her quiet joyous-
ness, her——

Lis. And Henriette's——

Adr. Henriette's pleasant freedom, her becoming confidence, her gay transport, contrast admirably with the
solid qualities of her sister. But by the comparison Julia
gains——

Lis. And Henriette?

Adr. Loses nothing by it. Only that Juliane——

Lis. Ho! ho! Herr Adrast, I trust you are not suffer-
ing from an attack of that folly which makes people consider nothing good or charming but what they cannot
possess. Who the deuce has been bribing you to praise
Juliane?

Adr. Think nothing unpleasant. I only wished to

show that love for my Henriette does not make me blind
to the superior charms of her sister.

Lis. Well, well, if that is so, let it pass. She is certainly a good child also, is Juliane. She is her grand-
mother's darling. And the good old lady has said a
hundred times that the pleasure she takes in her little
Julie keeps her alive.

Adr. Ah!

Lis. Why, how you sigh! What troubles you now?
Nonsense! A young man in robust health, just about to
marry, and sigh? Spare your sighing till you have got
your wife.

Scene IV.—Johann, Adrast, Lisidor.

Joh. Hist! hist!

Lis. Well? well?

Joh. Hist! hist!

Adr. What is the matter?

Joh. Hist! hist!

Lis. Hist! hist! Johann! Cannot the blockhead come
nearer?

Joh. Hist! Herr Adrast! a word in your ear.

Adr. Come here, then!

Joh. In your ear, Herr Adrast.

Lis. (*going near him*). Well, what do you want?

Joh. (*passing over to the other side*). Hist! Herr
Adrast, only one word, quite privately!

Adr. Come here, then, and speak.

Lis. Speak! speak! What can concern the son-in-law,
that the father-in-law ought not to hear?

Joh. Herr Adrast—(*pulling him aside by the sleeve.*)

Lis. You rascal, will you send me forcibly from the
spot. Speak, do! I am going.

Joh. Oh! you are really too polite. Only just be kind
enough to walk into the corner for one minute, and you
can remain in the room.

Adr. Stay, I beg.

Lis. Well! if you wish—(*approaching them*).

Adr. Now speak; what do you want?

Joh. (*seeing Lisidor near him*). Nothing.

Adr. Nothing?

Joh.   Nothing whatever.

Lis.   That word in private; have you already forgotten it again?

Joh.   Dickens! are you here?   I thought you were safe in the corner, there.

Lis.   Fool! the corner has come nearer.

Joh.   In that it has done very wrong.

Adr.   Detain me no longer, but speak.

Joh.   Herr Lisidor, my master is getting angry?

Adr.   I have no secrets for him; speak!

Joh.   Then I have no secrets for you, either.

Lis.   Scoundrel!—so I must let you have your way.   I am going into my study, Adrast, if you wish to come——

Adr.   I shall follow you directly.

Scene V.—Johann, Adrast.

Joh.   Has he gone?

Adr.   Well, what have you to say to me?   I wager it is some trifle, and the old man will imagine it is a matter of life and death.

Joh.   A trifle?   In one word, Herr Adrast, we are lost: and you could wish me to say it in the presence of Lisidor?

Adr.   Lost!   How so?   Explain yourself.

Joh.   What is there to explain?   In a word, we are lost. But certainly I should never have imagined that you had so little prudence that you even wished to let your future father-in-law hear——

Adr.   Let me hear it, at any rate.

Joh.   Truly, he might have lost the desire of ever becoming your father.   A nice trick!

Adr.   Come! what is the trick then?   How long will you continue to torture me?

Joh.   A cursed trick.   Yes, yes! if the servant was not often more cautious than the master, pretty things might come to pass.

Adr.   Worthless scamp——

Joh.   Oh! oh! are these my thanks?   If I had but said it when the old gentleman was present.   We should have seen, we should have seen——

Adr. May the devil——

Joh. Ha! ha! Don't mention him. You talk of the devil, but I know there is none. I must have learnt little from you if I couldn't do that (*snapping his fingers*) at all the inhabitants of hell!

Adr. I believe you are playing the Freethinker. It is enough to disgust an honourable man with it when he sees how every low fellow tries to assume the character. But I forbid you to say another word to me of this secret. I know it is nothing.

Joh. What, not tell you? Let you run on to your own destruction? We will see about that.

Adr. Get out of my sight!

Joh. Patience! patience! You remember, I suppose, pretty well how you left your affairs at home?

Adr. I do not want to hear anything.

Joh. Well, I am not telling you anything yet. Still you surely remember the bills you gave Herr Araspe, twelve months ago?

Adr. Silence! I do not want to hear anything about them.

Joh. Without doubt, because you wish to forget them? If they only got paid by that means! But are you aware that they have been dishonoured?

Adr. I am aware that it is no business of yours.

Joh. I can brook that also. You think, perhaps, "out of sight out of mind;" and that Herr Araspe has no need to be in a hurry. But what would you think if Herr Araspe——

Adr. Well, what?

Joh. Was this moment seen getting off the coach.

Adr. What do you say? I am astonished.

Joh. So was I, when I saw him.

Adr. You have seen Araspe? Araspe here?

Joh. Sir, I have taught myself to recognise your creditors and my own at the first glance. Yes, I smell them when they are still a hundred paces off.

Adr. (*after thinking*). I am lost!

Joh. That is just what I said at first.

Adr. What is to be done?

Joh. The best thing will be, to pack up and be off.

ADR. That is impossible.

JOH. Then make up your mind to pay.

ADR. I cannot do that; the sum is too large.

JOH. Ah! that is what I said again. You are thinking?

ADR. Still, who knows if he is come hither expressly on my account. He may have other business.

JOH. Still, he will settle your business at the same time. We shall be talked about at any rate.

ADR. You are right. I could go mad when I think of all the freaks which an unjust fate unceasingly plays me. Yet against what do I rail? Against a deaf chance, against a blind fate, which, without design and without purpose, overwhelms us! Ah! worthless life!

JOH. Oh! you need not abuse life; to wish to quarrel with it for such a trifle would be clever indeed.

ADR. Well, advise me then if you look upon it as such a trifle.

JOH. Does no plan really occur to you? I shall soon cease to consider you that great genius for which I have always taken you. Run you won't; pay you can't: what then remains?

ADR. To allow myself to be sued.

JOH. Nonsense. What I should first think of, even if I could pay——

ADR. What is that, then?

JOH. Swear the bills are not of your drawing.

ADR. (*with bitter contempt*). Scoundrel!

JOH. How? What am I? Such fraternal advice——

ADR. Yes, truly. Fraternal advice, which you should only give to your own brethren, to scamps like yourself.

JOH. Is this Adrast? I never heard you turn an oath into ridicule, I suppose?

ADR. An oath, as an oath, but not as a mere asseveration of one's word. To a man of honour, his word must ever be sacred, even though there be neither heaven nor hell. To me, to have denied my signature, would be an eternal shame; and I could never write my name again without feeling contempt for myself.

JOH. Superstition on superstition! You have driven it out at one door, and you let it in again at the other.

Adr. Silence! I don't care to hear your tiresome prating. I will go to Araspe. I will remonstrate with him; I will tell him of my marriage; and I will promise him interest on interest. I suppose I shall still find him where the coach stops.

Joh. Perhaps .... There he goes, a soft-hearted boaster. His words are big enough; but when it comes to prove by actions, what he believes, then the old woman trembles. Happy the man who can live up to his convictions. He does get something from them. I should like to be in his place. However, I must just see what he is after.

ACT II.

Scene I.—Juliane, Henriette, Lisette.

Lis. First of all, my dear young ladies, before I smooth your little difference, let us settle to which of you I belong to-day. You know your authority over me is to be by turns. For since it is said to be impossible to serve two masters, therefore your estimable papa—make me a courtesy for that, young ladies—your estimable papa, I say, has considerately wished to spare me the possibility of doing what is impossible. He has made each of you my commandress-in-chief on alternate days; so that on Monday I am to be the modest maid of the gentle Juliane, and on Tuesday the sprightly Henriette's unruly Lisette. But now, since the strange gentlemen have been in the house——

Hen. Our admirers you mean——

Lis. Yes, yes; your admirers now, soon to be your ruling lords. Since, I say, these gentlemen have been in the house, everything is at sixes and sevens; I am tossed from one to the other of you; and, alas! our charming regularity lies together with your work-boxes, which you have not looked at from the same day, under the dressing-table. Out with it again. I must know whereabouts I am, if I am to pronounce an impartial judgment.

HEN. We will soon settle that. You remember, don't you, the last saint's-day when my sister dragged you with her to afternoon service, much as you would have liked to drive out with me to the farm. You were very strict then, Juliane!

JUL. Well, at all events, I did not cause a worthy person to take an idle journey.

HEN. Lisette——

LIS. Hush, Miss! No tales out of school, or——

HEN. Don't threaten, girl! You know I have a good conscience.

LIS. And so have I. But don't let us chatter so much. Well, I remember the saint's-day. It was the last orderly day; for on that very evening Theophan arrived.

HEN. Therefore, with my sister's permission, you are mine to-day.

JUL. Without doubt.

LIS. Huzza! Missy. So to-day I am yours. Huzza!

JUL. Is that your watch-word under her flag?

LIS. Without more ado then, tell me your difference. . . . . In the meantime I will put on the face of a judge.

JUL. Difference? a weighty difference? You are both joking. I won't hear anything more of it.

HEN. Oh, oh! You will not acknowledge an umpire? A clear proof that you are in the wrong. Now listen, Lisette! we have been quarrelling about our admirers. I will still call them so, whatever the finish of it may be.

LIS. As I thought. About what else could two sisters quarrel? It is certainly vexatious to hear one's future lord disparaged.

HEN. Stuff! You are quite on the wrong tack. Neither has disparaged the admirer of the other; but our quarrel arose because one extolled the admirer of the other too much.

LIS. A new kind of quarrel, truly, a new kind.

HEN. Can you deny it, Juliane?

JUL. Oh, spare me more of this!

HEN. Hope for no mercy unless you retract. Say Lisette, have you ever compared our young lovers? What

do you think! Juliane cries down her poor Theophan as
if he was a young monster.

JUL.   Unkind sister!   When did I do that?   Must you
draw such conclusions from a casual remark, which you
ought not even to have mentioned.

HEN.   I see, one must make you angry before you will
speak out.   You call it a casual remark, do you?   Why
did you contend for its reasonableness then?

JUL.   What foolish expressions you use!   Did you not
begin the whole business yourself?   I thought I should
please you, if I said that your Adrast had the finest figure
I had ever seen.   You ought to have thanked me for my
opinion, and not have contradicted it.

HEN.   See how strange you are!   What else was my
contradiction, but thanks?   For how could I express my
thanks more emphatically, than by applying the unde-
served praise to your Theophan.

LIS.   She is right.

JUL.   No, she is not.   For that very thing vexed me.
Should she treat me in such a childish manner?   Did
not I feel like a little girl at play, who had said to her,
"Your doll is the prettiest;" and to whom she therefore answered, to prevent crying, "No, yours is the
prettiest."

LIS.   Now *she* is right.

HEN.   Oh! go along!   You are a fine judge.   Have you
forgotten already that you belong to me to-day?

LIS.   So much the more strict shall I be towards you
for fear of being partial.

JUL.   Believe me only that I know how to value other
qualities in a man than his figure.   And it is enough,
that I find these superior qualities in Theophan.   His
mind——

HEN.   That is not the question at all.   At present we
are concerned with the figure, and Theophan's is finer,
say what you will.   Adrast is taller: well; he has a
neater foot, I do not deny it.   But when we come to the
face——

JUL.   I did not deal with the subject so in detail.

HEN.   That is just your fault.   What pride, what contempt for everybody else shows itself in each feature of

Adrast's countenance. You will call it noble; but does
that make it beautiful? It is in vain that his features
are so regular; his caprice, his love of scoffing has added
certain lines to them, which make him truly ugly in my
eyes. But I will smooth them out for him as soon as the
honeymoon is over! Your Theophan, on the contrary, has
the most amiable countenance in the world. A sweetness
reigns in it which never belies itself.

Jul. You need not tell me what I have remarked just
as well as yourself. But still this very sweetness is not
so much the natural property of his face, as the result of
his inward peace of mind. The beauty of the mind adds
charms even to an ill-favoured body; just as the deformity
of it creates a something even in the most perfect face
and beautiful figure, which causes an inexplicable disgust.
If Adrast was the same pious man that Theophan is, if his
soul was enlightened by the same heavenly rays of truth,
which he forcibly strives to misunderstand, he who is now
scarcely a man among men would then be an angel among
men. Do not be angry, Henriette, that I speak so slight-
ingly of him. If he falls into good hands he may still
become all that which he now is not, because he has
never endeavoured to be so. His conceptions of honour
and natural justice are admirable.

Hen. (mockingly). Oh, you cry him down much too
seriously. But may not I now say that you treat me like
the child at play? I am not anxious for you to make me
satisfied with him. He is as he is, and good enough
for me. You spoke of good hands into which he must
fall, if anything is to be made of him. Since, however, he has fallen into mine, I suppose he will not alter
much. To accommodate myself to him will be my only
artifice to make our life supportable. His discontented
looks, however, must be laid aside; and I shall propose to
him the countenance of your Theophan as a pattern.

Jul. Theophan and his amiable looks again already.

Lis. Hist! Miss——

SCENE II.—THEOPHAN, JULIANE, HENRIETTE, LISETTE.

HEN. (*springing forward to meet* THEOPHAN). Come Theophan, pray come. Can you believe that I have had to take your part against my sister? Admire my disinterestedness. I praised you up to the skies, although I know that you are not to be my husband, but are destined for my sister, who does not know your value. Imagine! She maintains that your figure is not to be compared with Adrast's. I don't know how she can say such a thing. Of course I look at Adrast with the eyes of a lover, that is, I fancy him ten times handsomer than he really is, and yet, in my opinion, you are in no respect inferior to him. She says, indeed, that you have the advantage in respect of genius; but what do we young girls know about genius?

JUL. The tell-tale! But you know her, Theophan; do not believe her.

THEOPH. Not believe her, fairest Juliane? Why will you not have me remain in the happy conviction that she has spoken of me so favourably? I thank you, kind Henriette, for your defence of me; I thank you so much the more from being myself thoroughly convinced that you have had to defend a bad cause. Still——

HEN. Oh, Theophan, I do not ask you to justify me. There is a certain person——

JUL. Do that certain person justice. Theophan; you know my sentiments, I trust——

THEOPH. Do not treat me as a stranger, dearest Juliane. Use no arguments in my favour; I should only lose by every comparison. Over books, in a confined and dusty study, one easily forgets the body, and you know the body must be trained just as much as the soul, if both are to acquire those perfections of which they are capable. Adrast has been brought up in the world of fashion; he possesses everything which gains favour there.

HEN. Even the faults——

THEOPH. I did not mean to say that, at any rate. . . . . But have patience! A great mind cannot be for ever the slave of such faults. Adrast, in time, will see the littleness of them, which is always betrayed by the void they leave in the heart. So certain am I of his reformation, that I already love him for it in anticipation. How happy you will be with him, you fortunate Henriette!

HEN. Adrast never speaks so generously of you, Theophan.

JUL. That again is a very unkind remark, my dear sister. What object have you in saying that to Theophan? It is always better not to know who speaks ill of us. A knowledge of our calumniators causes, even in the most generous hearts, a sort of coolness towards them, which only renders a reconciliation the more difficult.

THEOPH. I am delighted to hear you say that, Juliane. But fear nothing. Just in this shall sooner or later be my triumph—that I have forced Adrast to have a better opinion of me, contemptuously as he now thinks of me. But should I not destroy this triumph entirely, if I should myself entertain any resentment against him? He has not yet taken the trouble to know me intimately. Perhaps I may find means of enabling him to do so. Let us now quit the subject; and allow me to announce to you the arrival of one of my nearest relations, who has been pleased to take me here by surprise.

JUL. A relation?

HEN. And who is he?

THEOPH. Araspe.

JUL. Araspe?

HEN. Ah! that is delightful! Where is he?

THEOPH. He has just got off the coach and promised to follow me here without delay.

HEN. Does papa know?

THEOPH. I believe not.

JUL. And grandmamma?

HEN. Come, sister, we must be the first to take them this good news. You are not angry with me, are you?

JUL. Angry with you, you flatterer! Come, let us go.

THEOPH. Let me wait for him here.

HEN. But bring him soon. Do you hear!

Lis. I remain, Herr Theophan, to pay you a little great compliment. You really are the luckiest man in the world. And I believe if Herr Lisidor had two more daughters, they would all four be in love with you.

Theoph. What do you mean, Lisette?

Lis. I mean that if all four would be, then the present two must be.

Theoph. (smiling). Still more in the dark.

Lis. Your smile does not say that. If, however, you really do not know your own merits, you are so much the more deserving of love. Juliane loves you, and that is all right, because she ought to love you. It is only a pity that her love has such a very discreet appearance. But what shall I say of Henriette? She certainly loves you too; and the worst of it is, she loves you—out of love. If only you could marry them both.

Theoph. You mean it well, Lisette.

Lis. Yes, certainly! Then you should also keep me into the bargain.

Theoph. Better still. But, I see, Lisette has sense.

Lis. Sense? To that compliment I unfortunately do not know how to reply. To another one, "Lisette is pretty," I think I have learned how to answer. "Oh! sir, you are joking." I do not know whether this answer will do here too.

Theoph. But to my purpose. Lisette can render me a great service if she will tell me her real opinion about Juliane. I am sure she will not be far from the mark even in her conjectures. There are certain things which the eye of a woman sees quicker than those of a hundred men.

Lis. Good gracious! You can't have got that knowledge from books. But if you had paid attention to what I said, I have already told you my real opinion of Juliane. Did not I tell you, that to my mind her love has rather too discreet an appearance? That is all I think about it. Consideration, duty, superior beauties of the mind..... To tell you the truth, a lover may always be distrustful of such excellent words in the mouth of a woman. And there

is another little observation I would make at the same
time, that she made use of these excellent words far more
sparingly when Herr Theophan was the only gentleman
in the house.

THEOPH. Indeed!

LIS. (*after looking at him for a minute*). Herr Theophan,
Herr Theophan! You said that word *indeed* in a tone . . . .
in a tone——

THEOPH. In what sort of tone?

LIS. Yes, now it is different again. These men, these
men, even the most pious.—Still I will not be misled!
Since Herr Adrast has been in the house, I was going to
say, looks now and then pass between him and Juliane.

THEOPH. Looks? you alarm me, Lisette.

LIS. And you can express your alarm so calmly, so
calmly.—Yes, I say, looks pass between them; looks
which are as like as two pins to the looks which now and
then pass between Fräulein Henriette and the fourth
person of the party.

THEOPH. What fourth?

LIS. Do not get angry. Though I call you the fourth,
you really are to all intents and purposes the first.

THEOPH. (*aside*). Cunning girl! I am ashamed of my
curiosity, and I have got my deserts. (*Aloud.*) You are
wrong, however, Lisette, prodigiously wrong!

LIS. Fie! You just paid me such a pretty compliment,
and now you suddenly repent of having done so, I couldn't
have any of that sense which you attributed to me if I
could be so prodigiously wrong.

THEOPH. (*uneasy and absent*). Where, then, can he be?

LIS. Where can what be? My sense? Anywhere. But
this much is certain, that Herr Adrast is not in Henriette's best books, although she appears to conform so
well to his opinions. She can bear everything but being
lightly valued; and that she cannot bear. She knows only
too well what Adrast considers us women; creatures who
are here for no other purpose than to please the men. And
that is a very mean way of thinking. But there, one can
see into what impious errors your unbelievers fall. Well?
Aren't you listening to me, Herr Theophan? Why so
absent? Why so uneasy?

THEOPH.   I cannot think what detains my cousin.

LIS.   Oh! he will come.

THEOPH.   I must really just go to meet him.   Farewell, Lisette.

SCENE IV.—LISETTE.

LIS.   That is what I call an abrupt break-off.   I hope he is not vexed that I just sounded him a little.   An excellent young fellow!   I shall like to see what will come of it.   I really wish him well; and, if it depended upon me, I know what I would do.   (*Looking round her.*) Who is coming along the passage there?   Oh! it is you, is it?   A pretty pair of gabies, Adrast's Johann and Theophan's Martin; true likenesses of their masters, from the ugly side.   One is a freethinking rogue, the other a pious blockhead.   I must do myself the pleasure of listening to them a bit (*steps back*).

SCENE V.—LISETTE (*half hidden behind the scene*), JOHANN, MARTIN.

JOH.   As I tell you.

MAR.   You must take me for a great stupid.   Your master an atheist?   The deuce may believe that.   Why he looks just like you and me.   He has got hands and feet and a mouth across and a nose down his face, like a man; and he talks like a man and eats like a man—and he is an atheist?

JOH.   Well?   Are not atheists men, then?

MAR.   Men?   Ha! ha! ha!   Now I see that you don't know yourself what an atheist is.

JOH.   The deuce!   You know better, I suppose.   Pray teach your ignorant neighbour.

MAR.   Listen then!   An atheist is a child of hell, who can assume a thousand shapes, like the Devil.   Now he is a cunning fox, now a savage bear; now he takes the shape of an ass, now that of a philosopher; now he becomes a dog, now a coarse poet.   In short, he is a monster, that is already burning alive with Satan in hell; a pest on earth; a detestable creature; a beast, which is more senseless than a beast; a devourer of souls; an antichrist; a frightful prodigy——

JOH. It has cloven feet, has it? two horns? a tail?

MAR. Very likely. It is a changeling lustfully begotten of hell with the wisdom of this world; it is—yes, that is an atheist. Our parson described him just so, he knows all about him from great books.

JOH. Simple dolt! Just look at me.

MAR. Well!

JOH. What do you see in me?

MAR. Nothing but what I can see ten times better in myself.

JOH. Do you find anything frightful, anything dreadful, in me? Am I not a man like yourself? Did you ever see me like a fox, or a donkey, or a cannibal?

MAR. Leave out the donkey, if I must answer you as you wish. But why do you ask?

JOH. Because I am an atheist myself; that is, a strong-minded man, as every honest fellow must be to be in the fashion. You say, an atheist burns alive in hell. Now, just smell: do you smell any burning in me?

MAR. Just for that reason you are not one.

JOH. I am not one? Do not disgrace me by doubting it—or . . . . But really pity prevents my getting angry. You are indeed to be pitied, poor knave!

MAR. Poor! Just let us see who had the biggest number of tips last week (*putting his hand into his pocket*). You are a careless devil, you spend everything in drink——

JOH. Let your money alone! I speak of quite a different poverty, the poverty of the mind, which must be fed with mere miserable crumbs of superstition, and clothed with wretched rags of stupidity. But so it is with you people who never go further than four miles at the most, from your own kitchen fire. If you had travelled as I have——

MAR. You have travelled, have you? Let us hear; where have you been?

JOH. I have been——in France.

MAR. In France? with your master?

JOH. Yes, my master was with me.

Mar. Is that the country where the French live? I
once saw one; that was a droll frog; he could turn round
on his heel seven times in a wink, and whistle into the
bargain.

Joh. Oh! Yes, there are great geniuses among them.
It was there that I first became clever myself.

Mar. Did you learn Francish?

Joh. French, you mean. Perfectly.

Mar. Indeed! do speak.

Joh. I'll soon do that. Quelle heure est-il, maraut?
Le père est la mère, une fille, des coups de bâton. Comment,
coquin? Diantre, diable, carogne à vous servir.

Mar. That sounds funny! And the folks there can
understand that stuff? Now just say, what is that in
German?

Joh. In German, indeed. You poor simpleton, that
cannot be expressed so in German. Such fine thoughts can
only be expressed in French.

Mar. Zounds! Well, where have you been besides?

Joh. Besides? Why in England——

Mar. In England! Can you speak Englandish, too?

Joh. What can't I speak?

Mar. Do speak then.

Joh. You must know it is just the same as French.
It is French—understand me, spoken in English. What
will you gain by hearing it? I will tell you very different things, if you will listen to me: things which cannot have their like. For example, to return to our former
subject—don't be a fool, and think that an atheist is such
an awful thing. An atheist is nothing more than a man
who does not believe in a God.

Mar. Does not believe in a God! Why that is much
more wicked still! No God! What does he believe,
then?

Joh. Nothing.

Mar. That must be a great deal of trouble.

Joh. What! trouble! If it was a trouble to believe
nothing, why my master and I would certainly believe
everything. We are sworn enemies of everything that
gives trouble. Man is in the world to live merry and
jolly. Pleasure, laughter, courting, drinking, are his

R 2

duties. Trouble hinders these duties, and therefore it is also necessarily his duty to avoid trouble. There, that is a conclusion which contains more logic than the whole Bible.

MAR. No doubt. But, tell me, what is there in the world without labour?

JOH. All that one inherits or marries. My master inherited from his father and from two rich cousins no small sums; and I must bear him witness that he has got through all like a brave fellow. Now he is going to get a rich young lady, and if he is wise, he will begin again where he left off. For some time he has not been exactly to my mind; and I see that even Freethinking does not always remain wise when it goes courting. However, I shall soon bring him into gear again. And hear, Martin; I will make your fortune, too. I have an idea; but I do not think that I can well impart it, except—over a glass. You were thinking your money just now; and certainly you run a risk of not getting any more, if it is seen that you do not use it for the purpose for which it was given you. To the tavern, good Martin, to the tavern; that is what tips are for.

MAR. Gently, Johann, gently! You already owe me one. Did I not treat you the other evening? But let us hear what the good fortune is which I may expect from you.

JOH. Well, then, when my master marries, he must take another servant. A jug of ale, and you shall have the preference with me. You only grow sour with your stupid parson. With Adrast you shall have better wages, and more liberty; and into the bargain, I will make a shrewd fellow of you, able to cope with the Devil and his grand-dam, if there be such a thing.

MAR. What? If there be such a thing! Ho! Ho! Is not it enough that you don't believe in a God? Will you not believe in a Devil either? Talk of the Devil, and he is sure to appear! *He* won't be so long-suffering as God is. God is too good, and laughs at such a poor fool as thou art. But the Devil . . . . his anger is soon raised, and then there is a pretty fuss; no, no, I shall not stay with you. I shall go——

Joh. (*holding him back*). Oh! you cheat! you cheat!
Do you think I don't see your trick? You are more afraid
of the jug of ale which you are to stand, than of the Devil.
Stop! I cannot possibly allow **you** to remain in such
superstition. Only think a little. The Devil! The
Devil! Ha! ha! ha! And it does not seem laughable
to you? Laugh, do!

Mar. If there was no Devil, where would those go to
who scoff at him? Just answer me that! Untie that
knot for me! You see, I know too how to show up you
fellows!

Joh. Another error! How can you be so sceptical about
my words? They are the utterings of wisdom—the oracles
of reason. It is proved. I tell you, in books it is proved,
that there is neither Devil nor hell. Do you know
Balthasar? He was a celebrated baker in Holland.

Mar. What are the bakers in Holland to me? Who
knows whether he could make such good rolls as the man
at the corner here.

Joh. Ah! that was a clever baker! His ' Enchanted
World!' .... Ha! that is a book! My master read it
once. In short, I recommend you that book, as it was re-
commended to me, and will now assure you, in confidence,
that he must be an ox, a beast, an old woman, who can
believe in a Devil. Shall I take an oath that there is not
one? May I be——

Mar. Pooh! an oath won't be much to you.

Joh. Well, hear; may I be .... may I be .... struck
blind on the spot, if there is a Devil.

(Lisette *springs quickly forward, and puts her hands over his
eyes from behind, making a sign at the same time to*
Martin.)

Mar. That certainly would be some proof; but then
you know very well that it won't happen.

Joh. (*in terror*). Oh, Martin! Oh!

Mar. What is the matter?

Joh. Martin, what has happened to me? What has
happened, Martin?

Mar. Well! what is the matter?

Joh. Do I see? .... or .... Ah! .... Oh God! ....
Martin! Martin! how dark it has suddenly grown!

MAR. Dark! What do you mean by dark?

JOH. Oh, dear! Is not it dark? Help! Martin, help!

MAR. Help, what about? What do you want?

JOH. Oh! I am blind! I am blind! It is on my eyes, on my eyes .... O Lord! I tremble all over——

MAR. You are blind? You don't mean that? Stay, let me hit you over the eyes, to strike fire out of them, and you will soon see.

JOH. Ah! I am punished, I am punished. And you can still laugh at me! Help! Martin, help! (*falling on his knees*). Indeed I will reform! What a wicked wretch I have been!

LIS. (*lets him go suddenly and springs forward, giving him a box on the ear*). You scamp!

MAR. Ha! ha! ha!

JOH. Oh! I breathe again (*getting up*). Lisette, you vixen.

LIS. Are you lions so easily turned into hares? Ha! ha! ha!

MAR. I shall laugh myself into a fit. Ha! ha! ha!

JOH. Laugh away! laugh away! You are mighty stupid, if you think I did not see it. (*Aside.*) The confounded girl, what a fright she put me in! I must recover myself. (*Exit slowly.*)

MAR. Are you going? Oh! laugh at him! Yes, laugh on, Lizzie, laugh on. Ha! ha! ha! You did that capitally; beautiful! beautiful! I could kiss you for it.

LIS. Go along, silly Martin!

MAR. Come, do; I will take you to the alehouse. Come, I will treat you to the jug which that rascal wanted to cheat me out of. Come.

LIS. Wouldn't you like it! I will go and tell my young mistresses the joke.

MAR. Yes, and I my master. He got it! he got it this time.

ACT III.

Scene I.—Theophan. Araspe.

Ar. As I told you, my dear cousin, the pleasure of
surprising you, and the desire of being present at your
wedding, are certainly the principal causes of my journey,
but they are not the only ones. Having at last found out
that Adrast was sojourning here, I was glad in this way,
as the saying is. to kill two birds with one stone. Adrast's
bills have been dishonoured ; and I have not the least desire
to grant him the smallest consideration. I am indeed
astonished to find him—a thing I could never have conceived—in the house of your future father-in-law, and to
find him here on the same footing as you, Theophan ; but,
notwithstanding, even if fortune could make him more
closely allied to me——

Theoph. I entreat you, my good cousin, be careful what
you say.

Ar. Why ? You know very well, Theophan, I am not
generally the man to oppress my debtors cruelly.

Theoph. I do know it ; so much the more therefore——

Ar. No *so much the more* will apply here. Adrast, this
man who endeavours to distinguish himself from others
in a manner equally absurd and impious, deserves that
some one, in return, should distinguish him from others.
He must not enjoy the favour which an honourable man
is willing to allow a neighbour in difficulties. One does
not even return like for like. in making the present life of a
scoffing Freethinker somewhat disagreeable to him when he
would willingly rob us of the noblest privileges we possess,
and would destroy all hopes of a future more blessed
life. I know the blow which I give Adrast will be final ; he
will not be able to re-establish his credit. Yes, I should
be rejoiced if I could thereby prevent his marriage. If I
was only concerned about my money, you must see that I
should rather help to forward this alliance, because he will
get something in his pocket again through it. But, no—
and even if, at the meeting of the creditors. which must
take place, I come off without a son, nevertheless I am

determined to bring him to the worst. Yes, when I weigh
everything I really believe I shall be doing him a kindness by this severity. Difficulties may perhaps make him
reflect seriously, a thing he has never thought it worth
while to do in prosperity; and perhaps, as very frequently
happens, his character may alter with his luck.

THEOPH. I have allowed you to finish. I trust you will
now have the kindness to listen to me also.

AR. I will, certainly. But I should never have expected to find a defender of Adrast in my pious cousin.

THEOPH. I am less so than appears; and there are so
many unpleasant circumstances connected with this business, that henceforward, I think, I shall only attend to
my own affairs. Adrast, as I am thoroughly convinced, is
one of those Freethinkers who really deserve to be something better. It is also quite conceivable that in youth a
person may be something of the kind even contrary to inclination. But then he is only so until the understanding
has attained a certain state of maturity, and the boiling
blood has cooled down. Adrast is now at this critical junc-
ture, but still with uncertain step: a gentle wind, a breath,
may hurl him down again. The misfortune with which
you threaten him would render him deaf to conviction;
he would give himself up to raging despair, and fancy he
had good reason not to trouble himself about a religion,
the followers of which had made no scruple of working
his destruction.

AR. There is something in that; but——

THEOPH. No, for a man of your mind, my dear cousin,
there should be more than something, there should be very
much in it. You have not yet viewed the matter in this
light; you have only considered Adrast as a lost man, for
whom one must attempt a desperate cure as the last resource.
On this ground, the warmth with which you speak against
him is excusable. But let me teach you to judge of him more
impartially. He is already more rational in his conversation
than he is described to me as having formerly been. In
arguing, he no longer scoffs, but takes great pains to advance proofs. He begins to reply to the counter-evidence
which one brings forward, and I have remarked that he
is ashamed if he cannot reply satisfactorily. Certainly

he now and then strives to hide his shame under some contemptuous word of abuse; but have patience! it is a good deal that he no longer directs this abuse against the sacred things which one is defending, but only against their defenders. His contempt for religion is gradually changing into a poor opinion of those who teach it.

Ar. Is that true, Theophan?

Theoph. You will soon have an opportunity of convincing yourself of it. You will perceive, indeed, that his contempt of the clergy is now directed chiefly against me; but I entreat you beforehand, not to be more irritated at it than I am myself. I have firmly resolved not to repay him in his own coin; but rather to extort his friendship from him, let it cost what it may.

Ar. If you act so generously under personal insults——

Theoph. Stop! We will not call it generosity. It may be egoism, or a species of ambition to overcome his prejudice against the members of my order. But whatever it may be, you are much too good, I know, to oppose me in my purpose. Adrast would be sure to consider it a preconcerted plot, if he saw that my cousin was so sharp upon him. His anger would fall entirely on me, and he would proclaim me everywhere as a mean fellow, who with a thousand assurances of friendship had plunged a dagger in his heart. I should be sorry that he should be able, with any appearance of truth, to increase through me the number of examples of knavish parsons, as he calls them.

Ar. My dear friend, I should be a thousand times more grieved at it than you yourself.

Theoph. Permit me, then, to make a proposition; or no—I should rather say a request.

Ar. Speak without restraint. I am, you know, at your disposal.

Theoph. Would you be so good, then, as to give me the bill, and receive the payment of it from me.

Ar. Receive the payment of it from you! You are within an ace of making me angry! What do you mean by payment? If I had not already told you that I do not care about the money, you might at least have known that anything I have is yours.

THEOPH. I recognise my cousin in this.

AR. I hardly recognised mine. My nearest relation, my sole heir, treats me as a stranger, with whom he may make a bargain (*taking out his pocket-book*). Here is the bill. It is yours; do with it what you please.

THEOPH. But let me observe that I shall not be able to act so freely with it, if I have not made it my own property in due form.

AR. What then is "due form" between us, except that I give, and you accept? However, to remove all your scruples, let it be so! You shall sign a bond, that you will not again require the sum of this bill from my property after my death (*smiling*). Singular cousin! do you not see that I do nothing more than pay in advance?

THEOPH. You perplex me——

AR. (*still holding the bill in his hand*). Relieve me of the scrap without further delay.

THEOPH. Accept my thanks for it.

AR. What a waste of breath! (*Looking round him.*) Hide it quickly; here comes Adrast himself.

SCENE II.—ADRAST. THEOPHAN. ARASPE.

ADR. (*with surprise*). Good heavens! Araspe here!

THEOPH. Adrast, let me have the pleasure of introducing my cousin to you in the person of Araspe.

ADR. What! Is Araspe your cousin?

AR. Oh! we are already acquainted! I am delighted, Adrast, to meet you here.

ADR. I have already been all over the town in search of you. You know how we stand with each other, and I wished to save you the trouble of looking for me.

AR. It was not necessary. We will talk over our business another time. Theophan has taken it upon himself.

ADR. Theophan? Oh! then it is clear——

THEOPH. (*calmly*). What is clear, Adrast?

ADR. Your deceit—your cunning——

THEOPH. (*to ARASPE*). We have been here too long already. Lisidor will be anxiously awaiting you, my cousin. Allow me to conduct you to him. (*To* ADRAST:) May I request, Adrast, that you will stay here a moment? I will just accompany Araspe, and be back here immediately.

AR. If I may be allowed to advise you, Adrast, do not act unjustly towards my cousin.

THEOPH. He will not do so, I am sure. Come.

(*Exeunt* THEOPHAN *and* ARASPE.)

SCENE III.—ADRAST.

ADR. (*bitterly*). No, certainly, I shall not do so. Of all his cloth that I have as yet known, he is the most detestable. In this I will certainly do him justice. He has got Araspe here expressly on my account; that is not to be denied. I am glad now that I have never given him credit for having one drop of honest blood in his veins, and have always held his soft speeches for what they are.

SCENE IV.—ADRAST. JOHANN.

JOH. Well! have you seen Herr Araspe?

ADR. (*still bitterly*). Yes.

JOH. Is all well?

ADR. Excellent.

JOH. Ah! I should like to have given him a bit of my mind too, if he had made any difficulty.—Then I suppose he has taken his departure again.

ADR. Wait a bit. He will soon make us take ours.

JOH. He—ours? Where is he?

ADR. With Lisidor.

JOH. Araspe with Lisidor? Araspe?

ADR. Yes, Theophan's cousin.

JOH. What have I to do with that fool's cousin? I mean Araspe.

ADR. I mean Araspe too.

JOH. But——

ADR. But don't you see that I shall soon go raving mad? Why do you keep plaguing me? You hear, don't you, that Theophan and Araspe are cousins?

JOH. For the first time in my life. Cousins! Well,

so much the better; your bill will remain in the family; and your new brother-in-law will persuade his old cousin——

ADR. You blockhead! He will persuade him to have no respect for my happiness. Are you so stupid as to consider it accidental that Aras]e is here? Do you not see that Theophan must have learnt how I stand with his cousin? that he has informed him of my circumstances? that he has compelled him, at all hazards, to take this long journey, not to miss the opportunity of making my ruin public, and thus destroying my last chance, namely, Lisidor's favour?

JOH. Confound it! now I see it. You are right. Can I be such an ass as not at once to think the worst where a parson is concerned? Oh! that I could grind the black-coats into powder, and scatter them to the winds! What tricks they have played us already! One did us out of some thousands; that was the honourable husband of your own sister. Another——

ADR. Oh! do not begin to enumerate my disasters. I will soon see the end of them. And then let me see what fortune will be able to rob me of when I have nothing left.

JOH. What it will still rob you of, when you have nothing more left? Well, I can tell you: it will then take *me* away from you.

ADR. I understand you, rogue!——

JOH. Don't waste your rage on me. Here comes one against whom you may direct it better.

SCENE V.—THEOPHAN. ADRAST. JOHANN.

THEOPH. Here I am again, Adrast. You let slip something about "deceit" and "cunning" just now.

ADR. I never let accusations slip. When I make them, I do so with design, and after reflexion.

THEOPH. But a clearer explanation——

ADR. You must demand from yourself.

JOH. (*the first sentence aside*). Here I must come in. Yes, yes, Herr Theophan! it is well known that my master is a thorn in your side.

Theoph. Adrast, have you given your servant orders to answer in your place?

Joh. What? do you mean to grudge him my countenance too? I shall like to see who will prevent me taking my master's part.

Theoph. Let him see it, Adrast.

Adr. Hold your tongue!

Joh. I should——

Adr. (threatening). Another word, and——

Theoph. Well! Now, I suppose, I may repeat my request for a clearer explanation of your words? I am not able to give it myself.

Adr. Are you willing, then, to give *me* a clearer explanation, Theophan?

Theoph. With pleasure, when asked.

Adr. Tell me, then, what did Araspe mean, on that occasion of which you know, by the words " Theophan has taken it upon himself?"

Theoph. Araspe should by rights explain that. Still, I can do it in his place. He meant to say, that he has given your bill to me to see to.

Adr. At your request?

Theoph. That may be.

Adr. And what do you intend to do with it?

Theoph. You have not yet been called upon for it, have you? Can we determine anything before we know what you would then do?

Adr. A poor shift! Your cousin knows already what I can do.

Theoph. He knows that you can pay it. And then there is an end of it, isn't there?

Adr. You are mocking.

Theoph. I am not, Adrast.

Adr. But supposing the case—and you may well suppose it—that I should not be in a situation to pay; what have you determined to do then?

Theoph. In that case nothing is yet determined upon.

Adr. But what might be determined upon?

Theoph. That rests with Araspe. Still I should think that a single appeal, or a mere civil request, with such a man as Araspe, might effect much.

Joh.   That depends how his whisperers advise.

Adr.   Must I tell you once more to be silent?

Theoph.   I shall be really glad if by my interference in the business I can render you any service.

Adr.   And do you expect me to ask this favour of you in a humble tone, with fawning adulation, and mean flattery? No, I will not augment your triumph over me. Having promised me on your word of honour to do everything in your power, you would return to me after a few moments in a sorrowful plight, and lament that all the trouble you had taken had been useless. How your eyes would feast on the sight of my distress!

Theoph.   You will not, then, give me the opportunity of proving the reverse to you? It will cost you but one word.

Adr.   No, I will not waste one word even. For hear —and this is my clearer explanation of the matter— Araspe would never have come here, but on your instigation. And now that you have dug your mine so dexterously to destroy me, is it likely that you would be induced by one single word not to spring it? Pray execute your honourable work.

Theoph.   Your suspicions do not astonish me. Your temper has shown me the same before. But it is a positive fact that I had as little knowledge that Araspe was your creditor, as you had of his being my cousin.

Adr.   That remains to be proved.

Theoph.   To your satisfaction, I trust.—Look a little more cheerful, and let us join the others.

Adr.   I do not wish to see them again.

Theoph.   A strange determination. Your friend, and her you love——

Adr.   It will cost me little to part from her. But do not be afraid that this will happen until you have been satisfied. I do not wish that you should lose anything by me, and will go directly to make a final attempt——

Theoph.   Stop, Adrast. I am sorry that I did not at once release you from your anxiety. Learn to appreciate my cousin better (*taking out the bill*), and be assured, however meanly you may think of me. that he at any rate is a man who deserves your esteem. He is only desirous of seeing you perfectly happy, and therefore he gives you your bill back again (*holding it out to him*). You are yourself to keep it until you can conveniently discharge it. He thinks that it is quite as safe in your hands as under his own lock. You have the reputation of an honourable man, if you have not that of a religious one.

Adr. (*starting, and pushing back* Theophan's *hand*). What new trap is this which you threaten me with? The favour of an enemy!——

Theoph. By this "enemy" you mean me; but what has Araspe done to merit your hatred? It is he, not I, who wishes to show you this slight favour; if, indeed, such a poor act deserves the name. Why do you still hesitate? Here, Adrast, take your bill back again.

Adr. That I will not do.

Theoph. Do not let me return with my mission unaccomplished, to a man who wishes only to act honourably towards you. He would throw the blame of his slighted offer on me. (*Whilst he again holds out the bill,* Johann *snatches it from him.*)

Joh. Ha! ha! ha! in whose hands is the bill now?

Theoph. (*composedly*). In yours, without doubt. Keep it for your master.

Adr. (*advancing in a rage towards his servant*). Wretch! it is as much as your life is worth——

Theoph. Not so hasty, Adrast.

Adr. Give it back this instant. (*Takes it away from him.*) Get out of my sight!

Joh. Well, really!——

Adr. If you stay another minute—(*pushes him out.*)

Scene VI.—Theophan. Adrast.

Adr. I am ashamed, Theophan; but I do not think that you will go quite so far as to confound me with my servant.—Take back what he wished to rob you of.

Theoph. It is in the hands in which it ought to be.

Adr. No; I feel far too much contempt for you to deter you from committing a base action.

Theoph. This is not bearable. (*Takes the bill back.*)

ADR. I am glad that you have not compelled me to throw it at your feet. If it is to come into my possession again, I shall find a more suitable mode of obtaining it. But if I can find none, it is all the same. You will be glad to cause my ruin, and I shall be glad to be able to hate you from the bottom of my heart.

THEOPH. But it is really your bill, Adrast, is not it? *(opening it and showing it to him.)*

ADR. You think, perhaps, that I shall disown it.

THEOPH. No! I do not think that; I merely wish to be certain. *(Tears it coolly in pieces.)*

ADR. What are you doing, Theophan?

THEOPH. *(throwing the pieces away).* Nothing. Merely destroying a trifle, which can, however, mislead a man like Adrast into such petty calumny.

ADR. But it does not belong to you.

THEOPH. Never mind that. What I do I can answer for. Have you still suspicions? *(Exit.)*

SCENE VII.—ADRAST.

ADR. *(looking for some time after him).* What a man! I have met with many of his profession, who have deceived under the mask of sanctity, but never before one who did so under the mask of generosity. He is either endeavouring to make me ashamed, or to gain me over: he shall not succeed in either. By good luck I have just bethought me of a banker who lives here, with whom I formerly had dealings under more prosperous circumstances. He will imagine that I am still in the same position, I hope, and advance me the necessary sum without hesitation. Not that I intend to make him the goat, on whose horns I may spring safely out of the well. I have still some land which I may sell advantageously, if I can but gain time. I must seek him out.

SCENE VIII.—HENRIETTE. ADRAST.

HEN. Wherever have you been, Adrast? They have been asking for you twenty times. You ought to be

ashamed to let me look for you at a time that you should
be seeking me. You are playing the husband part too
soon. Never mind! perhaps you will play the lover when
others usually cease to do so.

ADR. Pardon me, but I have just a little business of
consequence to transact out-of-doors.

HEN. What can you have to do at present of more
consequence than to attend upon me?

ADR. You are jesting.

HEN. I am jesting?—What a pretty compliment!

ADR. I never pay compliments.

HEN. Dear me! what a surly physiognomy! Do you
know, I think we shall quarrel about these morose looks,
even before the marriage ceremony allows us to do so.

ADR. Do you know that such a remark from you is not
the most pleasing?

HEN. Perhaps because you think that frivolous remarks
suit your lips only! But I did not know that you had
the peculiar privilege of making them.

ADR. You play your part excellently. A young lady
who is so ready with her answers, is invaluable.

HEN. That is true; for we weak creatures at the best
are endowed with little power of tongue.

ADR. Would to God!

HEN. Your heartfelt "would to God" makes me laugh,
though I certainly ought to be angry. I am good again
now, Adrast.

ADR. You are twice as charming when you want to be
angry; for you seldom get further than a grave look, and
that makes your countenance all the more beautiful, because it is seldom seen there! Perpetual cheerfulness and
eternal smiling grow insipid.

HEN. (gravely). Oh! my good sir, if that is the case
with you, I will make my face sufficiently to your
taste.

ADR. I could wish—for as yet I have no right to
dictate to you——

HEN. Your "as yet" saves me. But what could you
wish?

ADR. That you would comport yourself somewhat
more after the manner of your elder sister. I do not ask

that you should assume her modest manner in its entirety.
Who knows whether it would become you?

HEN. Out of the fulness of the heart the mouth speaketh;
let us see if mine does so equally.

ADR. Go on.

HEN. It is well that you have arrived at the chapter
of examples: I also have a little verse from the same on
which I shall be glad to preach to you.

ADR. What a curious mode of expressing yourself!

HEN. You think so, perhaps, because you do not believe
in preaching. But you will find that I am a lover of it.
Just listen (*imitating his tone*). I could wish . . . . for as
yet I have no right to dictate to you——

ADR. And never will.

HEN. Very well.—Leave that out then. I could
wish that you would comport yourself somewhat more
after the manner of Herr Theophan. I do not ask that
you should assume his pleasing manner in its entirety,
because I would not ask anything that is impossible; but
a small portion of it would render you a great deal more
bearable. Theophan, who acts on principles much stricter
than those of a certain Freethinker, is at all times agreeable and communicative. His virtue, and another quality,
at which you will doubtless laugh, his piety . . . . . Do you
not laugh?

ADR. Do not be alarmed. Continue your talking. In
the mean time I will go and settle my business, and return
presently. (*Exit.*)

HEN. You need not hurry. Come when you will, you
will not find me again as heretofore . . . . . What rudeness!
Shall I get angry about it? I must think about this. (*Exit
on the opposite side.*)

ACT IV.

SCENE I.—JULIANE, HENRIETTE, LISETTE.

HEN. Say what you will, his conduct is inexcusable.

JUL. I cannot give you an opinion on it until I
have heard his motives too. But, my dear Henriette,

you will not take it ill if I give you a little sisterly advice?

HEN. I cannot promise that till I know what it is. If it should refer, as I rather fancy——

JUL. Oh! if you begin with your fancies——

HEN. I am quite satisfied with the correctness of my fancies. I cannot say they have ever led me far wrong as yet.

JUL. What do you mean by that?

HEN. Must I always mean something? You know very well I can chatter with pleasure the whole day long, and am always astonished myself if by chance I hit upon the very subject which people are not willing to hear discussed.

JUL. Now just listen, Lisette!

HEN. Yes, Lisette, let us hear what the sisterly advice is, which she wishes to give me.

JUL. I give you advice?

HEN. I thought you said so.

JUL. I should do quite wrong in giving you the least.

HEN. Oh! I beg——

JUL. Leave me alone.

HEN. The advice, dear sister.

JUL. You do not deserve it.

HEN. Let me hear it without deserving it.

JUL. You will make me angry.

HEN. And I . . . . I am so already. But do not imagine I am angry with you. I am angry with nobody but Adrast; and what makes my anger against him implacable, is this—that my sister acts unjustly towards me on his account.

JUL. Of what sister do you speak?

HEN. Of what sister? . . . . Of the one I used to have.

JUL. I have never seen you so touchy. You know, Lisette, what I said.

LIS. Yes, I do; and it was really nothing but a little harmless praise of Adrast, with which I had no fault to find, except that it might make Fräulein Henriette jealous.

JUL. Praise of Adrast?

HEN. I jealous?

B 2

LIS. Not so stormy! That is what people always get who speak the truth; they please nobody.

HEN. I jealous? jealous about Adrast? From this day I shall pray heaven for nothing more earnestly, than to escape from the clutches of that man.

JUL. I? Praise Adrast? Is it praise to say that a man cannot be equally good-tempered one day with another? When I say that the austerity, which my sister finds fault with in Adrast is not natural to him, and that some galling vexation must have created it in him; when I say that a man like Adrast, who perhaps has occupied himself too much with gloomy reflexions——

SCENE II.—ADRAST. JULIA. HENRIETTE, LISETTE.

HEN. You come as if called, Adrast. You left me just now rudely enough, in the midst of my encomium on Theophan; but that does not prevent my permitting you the opportunity of listening to a repetition of your own. You look round? doubtless in search of your panegyrist. It is not I: indeed it is not I; it is my sister. A bigot the panegyrist of a sceptic! What a contradiction! Either the conversion of Adrast or the perversion of my sister is at hand.

JUL. How frivolous she is again.

HEN. (to ADRAST). Do not stand there stock still.

ADR. I call you to witness, Juliane, how contemptuously she treats me.

HEN. Come, Lisette, we will leave them by themselves. Adrast certainly does not require our presence, either to pour forth his own thanks, or his charges against me.

JUL. Lisette may remain here.

HEN. No, she may not.

LIS. You know I belong to-day to Fräulein Henriette.

HEN. But take care, sister, for all this! If I should meet with your Theophan you will see what may take place. Do not imagine, Adrast, that I say this to make you jealous. In verity I feel that I am beginning to dislike you.

ADR. You would hardly succeed in making me jealous.

Hen. Oh! it would be capital if you resembled me
in that respect. Then, indeed, our marriage would be a
happy one. Rejoice, Adrast! How scornful we will be
to one another! You wish to speak, sister? Now is the
time. Come Lisette. (*Exeunt.*)

Scene III.—Adrast, Juliane.

Jul. Adrast, you must have patience with her. Indeed
she deserves it; for she has the best heart in the world,
though her tongue would make it seem doubtful.

Adr. Too indulgent Juliane! She has the good fortune
to be your sister; but to how bad an account does she turn
this good fortune. I can pardon a girl who has not grown
up free from all serious faults, if she has been brought up
without education, or good examples; but to excuse one
who has had a Juliane as a pattern, and then has become a
Henriette—so far my courtesy does not reach.

Jul. You are provoked, Adrast! and therefore do not
judge fairly.

Adr. I do not know what I am now; but I know that I
speak as my feelings prompt.

Jul. Which are too violent to last long.

Adr. Then you prophesy unhappiness for me.

Jul. What! Do you forget how you stand towards
my sister?

Adr. Ah! Juliane, why must I tell you that I do not
love your sister?

Jul. You startle me.

Adr. And I have only told you the smallest half of
what I must tell you.

Jul. Permit me, to spare myself hearing the rest.
(*Is going.*)

Adr. Where would you go? I have made known to
you the change in my feelings, and you will not listen
to the reasons that have caused it? You will quit me
with the suspicion, that I am an inconstant and fickle
deceiver?

Jul. You are wrong. Not I—my father—my sister,
alone have a right to hear your vindication.

Adr. They alone? . . . . Alas——

Jul. Detain me no longer.

Adr. I entreat you but for one minute. The greatest criminal is heard.

Jul. By his judge, Adrast; but I am not your judge.

Adr. But I implore you to be so now. Your father, lovely Juliane, and your sister, will condemn, and not judge me. From you alone can I depend upon receiving that justice which can pacify me.

Jul. (*aside*). I believe he will persuade me to listen to him. . . . . Well, tell me then, Adrast, what has prejudiced you so much against my sister.

Adr. She has herself been the cause of it. She is not woman enough for me to love her as a woman. If her features did not mark her sex, one would take her for a disguised hair-brained boy, too unskilled to play well the part he had assumed. What a tongue! and what a spirit must that be which keeps that tongue constantly going. Do not say that her tongue and her understanding may have little or no connection with each other. So much the worse. This disagreement, whereby voice and mind each takes its own course, makes the offences of such a person less culpable, it is true; but it destroys all the good qualities which she otherwise may possess. If her cutting derision, her offensive observations, are to be overlooked, because, as the saying is, she means no harm, is one not entitled, on the same grounds, to consider any praiseworthy or obliging words she may utter, as mere words by which she perhaps means no good. How are you to judge of what is a person's mode of thinking, if you are not to do it by their mode of speaking. And if the dependence of the speech upon the mind in one instance is not to be valid, why should it be so in the other? She says openly that she begins to dislike me; and am I to imagine that she still loves me? Then I must also think that she dislikes me, should she say that she begins to love me.

Jul. Adrast, you think too much of her trifling raillery, and mistake thoughtlessness for falsehood. She may be guilty of the former a hundred times a day, and still be far from the latter. You must learn to see from her actions, and not from her conversation, that she has at the bottom a most amiable and tender disposition.

ADR. Ah Juliane! words are the forerunners of deeds, in fact their very elements. How can one expect she will act considerately and properly, if she is not even accustomed to speak considerately and properly? Her tongue spares nothing, not even that which ought to be most sacred in the world to her. Duty, virtue, propriety, religion, everything is subject to her ridicule.

JUL. Hold, Adrast! You should be the last person to say that.

ADR. Why so?

JUL. Why so! Shall I speak openly?

ADR. As if you could speak otherwise.

JUL. What if the whole conduct of my sister, her endeavours to appear more volatile than she really is, her desire to be satirical, only date from a certain period? What if this period is exactly that of your stay here, Adrast?

ADR. What do you say?

JUL. I will not say that you have set her a bad example. Still, how far will not the desire to please lead us? Even if you had expressed your opinions less openly—and you have often expressed them but too plainly—Henriette would yet have divined them. And as soon as she discovered them, so soon she determined, by the adoption of the same sentiments, to gain your affections; a very natural thing for a spirited girl to do. Will you now be so cruel as to consider that a fault for which you ought rather to thank her as for a compliment?

ADR. I can thank no one who is so small-minded as to relinquish her natural character on my account; and that woman pays me a bad compliment who looks upon me as a fool, who is pleased with no manner but his own, and who would wish to behold on every side faint copies and imitations of himself.

JUL. But if this is your view you will make few proselytes.

ADR. What an opinion you have of me, dear Juliane! I make proselytes! Mad undertaking! On whom have I ever wished to force or intrude my opinions? I should be sorry to see them become general. If I have often defended them loudly, and with a certain amount of warmth, it was done with the motive of vindicating myself, and not of converting others. If my opinions were to become too general, I should be the first to quit them, and to adopt the opposite.

JUL. Then you seek only to be singular?

ADR. No, I do not admire singularity, but truth; and I cannot help it if, unfortunately, the former is a consequence of the latter. I can never believe that truth can be common, any more than I could believe daylight to exist throughout the world at the same moment. That which passes current amongst all nations under the form of truth, and is accepted as such by the most weak-minded, is assuredly no truth; and it only requires courage to lay hands on it, and divest it of its covering, and one sees the most frightful errors naked before one.

JUL. What wretched creatures are men, and how unjust is their Creator, if you are right, Adrast, in what you say! Either there must be no such thing as truth, or else it must be of such a nature, that it may be perceived by the majority, indeed by all, at least in matters of consequence.

ADR. It is not the fault of truth that it cannot be perceived, but of men. We are to live happily in the world; for that purpose we are created; and for that purpose alone. As often as truth is opposed to this great end, one is obliged to set it aside; for few minds can find their happiness in truth itself. Let us therefore leave their errors to the multitude, and leave them for this reason— that they are the groundwork of their happiness, and the support of the State in which they find their security, wealth and happiness. To deprive the multitude of religion would be like turning loose a horse from a rich pasture—as soon as it feels its freedom it prefers to roam in unproductive forests and to suffer want, rather than gain what it requires by an easy service even. But not for the people alone, for another part also of the human species must religion be maintained. For the fairest part, I mean, to whom it is a kind of adornment, as it is a bridle to the people. Religion becomes feminine modesty very well; it gives to beauty a certain noble, solid, and devout appearance.

JUL. Stop, Adrast, you do my sex as little honour as you do religion. The former you class with the populace, cunning as was your turn of words; and the second you consider at best as a kind of rouge, to be kept on a lady's dressing-table. No, Adrast, religion is an adornment for all men, and must be their most real adornment. Alas! you mistake it, through pride—but through a false pride. What can fill the soul with more sublime conceptions, than religion? And in what can the beauty of the soul consist, but in such conceptions—in worthy conceptions of God, of ourselves, of our duties, and of our final destination? What can cleanse and tranquillize the heart, that fountain of corrupt and unruly passions, like religion? What can support us in our misfortunes, as it can? What can make of us more honest men, more useful citizens, and more sincere friends than it does? I am almost ashamed, Adrast, to speak so seriously to you. It is doubtless not the tone which is pleasing to you in a young woman, although apparently an opposite one pleases you as little. You might hear the same thing from more eloquent lips—namely, those of Theophan.

SCENE IV.—HENRIETTE, JULIANE, ADRAST.

HEN. (*pauses in entering and listens.*) Hush!

ADR. Do not speak to me of Theophan. One word from you has more influence than a lecture of an hour's length from him. Are you surprised? Can it be otherwise, with the power which a person whom alone I love, whom I adore, must have over me? . . . Yes, whom I love. . . . . I have said the word. I have told the secret which would have tormented me for ever if I had kept it, but from the disclosure of which I have nothing more to hope. You grow pale!

JUL. What have I heard, Adrast?

ADR. (*kneeling to her*). Let me swear to you on my knees that you have heard the truth. . . . . I love you, dearest Juliane, and will love you for ever. Now, now is my heart open and laid bare before you. In vain have I endeavoured

to persuade myself and others that my indifference towards
Henriette was the result of my remarking her displeasing
qualities; when it was nothing but the result of a pre-
engaged affection. Ah! perhaps our lovely Henriette has
no other fault than that she has a still more lovely
sister——

HEN. Bravo! I must let Theophan interrupt this
scene. (*Exit.*)

SCENE V.—JULIANE. ADRAST.

ADR. (*rising in haste*). Who spoke there?

JUL. Heavens! it was Henriette's voice.

ADR. Yes. it was she. What curiosity! what inquisitiveness! No. no. I retract nothing; she has all the
faults which I have laid to her charge. and many more.
I could not love her. even if I was quite free. and perfectly
indifferent towards everybody else in the world.

JUL. What trouble, Adrast. you will bring on me.

ADR. Fear not! I shall spare you all vexation by
departing immediately.

JUL. By departing?

ADR. Yes, I have fully determined on doing so. My
affairs are in such a state that I should but abuse the goodness of Lisidor if I stayed any longer. And. besides. I
would rather take my departure freely, than be required
to do so.

JUL. You do not consider what you are saying. Adrast.
By whom should you be required to go?

ADR. I know what fathers are. and I know. too. what
Theophan is. Do not ask me to explain myself more
clearly. Oh! if I could flatter myself that Juliane.....
But I will say no more. I will not flatter myself with
an impossibility. No, Juliane cannot love Adrast; she
must hate him——

JUL. I hate nobody, Adrast.

ADR. You hate me: for in this case to hate is the same
as not to love. You love Theophan. Ah!— here he
comes.

Scene VI.—Theophan, Adrast, Juliane.

Jul. (*aside*). What will he say? What shall I answer?

Adr. I can conceive at whose instigation you come. But what does she expect to gain thereby? To embarrass me? To draw me after her again? How fitting for you, Theophan, and how becoming your honourable character, to be the tool of feminine jealousy. Or you come to catechise me perhaps? I will confess everything to you; I am even proud of it.

Theoph. Of what are you speaking, Adrast? I do not understand a word.

Jul. Allow me to leave you. Theophan, I flatter myself your good opinion of me is such that you will put no unjust construction upon my actions, and at least believe that I know my duty, and that it is too sacred to me to violate even in thought.

Theoph. Wait a moment. .... What does all this mean? I understand you as little as I have understood Adrast.

Jul. I am glad that you do not wish to attach importance to an innocent and trifling matter. But permit me——(*Exit*).

Scene VII.—Adrast, Theophan.

Theoph. It was Henriette, your love, Adrast, who sent me: she said my presence was required here. I hasten to you, and hear nothing but riddles.

Adr. My love? Oh! how craftily have you brought in that word. Certainly you could not express your reproaches more laconically.

Theoph. My reproaches? With what then have I to reproach you?

Adr. I suppose you wish to hear the confirmation from my lips.

Theoph. Tell me only what you wish to confirm. I stand here in perplexity.

Adr. That is too much. What grovelling dissimulation! But lest it should become too troublesome to you to maintain, I will force you to lay it aside. .... Yes, all that Henriette has made known to you is perfectly true. She was mean enough to listen to us. . . . . I love Juliane, and have confessed my love to her.

THEOPH. You love Juliane?

ADR. (*scornfully*). And what is worse, without asking permission from Theophan to do so.

THEOPH. Make yourself easy on that score. You have only dispensed with a slight formality.

ADR. Your composure, Theophan, in this matter is not astonishing. You think you are sure of your game.— Ah! would that you were less so! Would that I could add, with the least probability of truth, that Juliane also loves me. What rapture would the dismay cause me which would betray itself in your countenance. What balm to me, to hear you sigh, and to see you tremble. How should I be delighted when you vented your whole rage upon me, and, in utter despair, wished me I know not where.

THEOPH. Cannot good fortune enrapture you, unless it be seasoned with another's misery? I pity Adrast, truly. Love must have showered upon him all its pernicious power, since he can speak so unbecomingly.

ADR. True, from that look, from that language, I remember what I am. It is true I am your debtor, Theophan: and towards one's debtors one is entitled to . . . . But patience! I hope not to be so much longer. I have found an honourable man who will rescue me from this dilemma. I do not know why he delays. In accordance with his promise, he should have been here with the money already. I had better fetch him.

THEOPH. One word more, Adrast. I will disclose my whole heart to you——

ADR. The disclosure would not gratify me much. I go now, and I shall soon be able to appear before you with a bolder countenance. (*Exit.*)

THEOPH. (*alone*). Unyielding spirit! I almost despair of my undertaking. Everything is useless with him. But what would he have said, had he given me time to repay his confession by another of a similar nature? . . . . She is coming!

Scene VIII.—Henriette, Lisette, Theophan.

Hen. Well, Theophan, did not I help you to a nice sight?

Theoph. You are merry, dear Henriette. But what sight do you mean? After much difficulty and trouble, I have scarcely been able to make out the outline of the matter.

Hen. What a pity!—Then you came too slowly, and Adrast was no longer on his knees before my sister.

Theoph. Was he kneeling before her?

Lis. Alas! for both of you!

Hen. And my sister stood there. . . . . I cannot describe it to you. . . . . stood there, almost as if she beheld him with pleasure in that uncomfortable position. I feel for you, Theophan.

Theoph. Shall I also pity you, compassionate girl?

Hen. What! pity me? Wish me good luck.

Lis. No! this indeed cries out for vengeance.

Theoph. How does Lisette mean, that one should be revenged?

Lis. Do you wish to be?

Theoph. Perhaps.

Lis. And you also, Fräulein?

Hen. Perhaps.

Lis. Good! those are two perhapses, out of which one may make something.

Theoph. But it is still very doubtful whether Juliane returns Adrast's love; and if that is not the case, I should be thinking of revenge too soon.

Lis. Oh! the good Christian soul! It only just remembers that it is not right to take revenge .

Theoph. Not so satirical, Lisette; the question here is concerning a very innocent revenge.

Hen. That is my opinion also; concerning a very innocent revenge.

Lis. Who denies that? So innocent that it may be taken into consideration with a good conscience. Just listen! Your revenge, Herr Theophan, is doubtless a male revenge, is it not? and your revenge, Fräulein Henriette,

is doubtless a female revenge. Now, a male revenge and a
female revenge—let me see ; how shall I manage it?

HEN.   You are a simpleton with your males and
females.

LIS. Come, help me a little, Herr Theophan. . . . . What
do you think of it? If two people must travel the same
road, do you not think it advisable that they should keep
each other company?

THEOPH.   Certainly : provided that the two persons can
put up with each other.

HEN.   That is the point!

LIS. (aside). Will neither of them bite?—Then I must
try another tack. (Aloud.) It is true, as Herr Theophan
said just now, that it is still very uncertain whether
Fräulein Juliane loves Herr Adrast. And I add, that it
is still very uncertain whether Herr Adrast really loves
Fräulein Juliane.

HEN.   Oh! be quiet, you unhappy sceptic. It must be
certain now.

LIS. Men now and then have certain attacks of a
certain weathercock illness, which arises from a certain
overcharge of the heart.

HEN. From a certain overcharge of the heart.
Granted.

LIS. I will tell you directly what that is. As persons
who have overeaten themselves, do not rightly know any
more what suits and what does not suit their palate, so is
it with those who have overcharged the heart. They no
longer know on which side the overcharged heart lies,
and then it often happens that trifling mistakes of persons
arise. Am I not right, Herr Theophan?

THEOPH.   I will consider it.

LIS. You indeed are a better sort of man ; and I look
upon you as too prudent to overload your heart in that
fashion. But do you know, a thought strikes me
whereby we may easily get at the truth respecting Herr
Adrast and Fräulein Juliane.

THEOPH.   Well?

HEN. You would make me curious, if I had not got at
the truth already.

LIS. How if we created a false alarm?

Hen. What do you mean by that?

Lis. A false alarm is an alarm for which there is no real cause, but which still has the power of attracting the enemy's attention to a certain extent. For example: to discover whether Fräulein Juliane loves Adrast, Herr Theophan would have to feign to be in love with someone else; and to discover whether Adrast loves Fräulein Juliane, you would have to feign to be in love with someone else. And since it would not do at all that Herr Theophan should pretend to be in love with me, and still less that you should pretend to be in love with his servant Martin, the long and short of my advice is, that you pretend to be in love with each other. I only speak of pretending to be—remark particularly what I say, only pretending to be, otherwise the false alarm might turn out to be true. Now tell me, both of you, is not the idea a good one?

Theoph. (aside). If I do not go away she will make me declare my sentiments. (Aloud.) The idea is not so bad, but——

Lis. You must only pretend, you know.

Theoph. The pretending is the very part that does not please me.

Lis. And you, Fräulein?

Hen. I do not like pretending either.

Lis. Are you both afraid that you would play your parts too naturally? What are you about, Herr Theophan? Why are you so absorbed, Fräulein?

Hen. O dear! It must be the first time in my life if I am.

Theoph. I must leave you a few moments, dear Henriette——

Lis. You need not do that. You shall not say of me that I have talked you away. Come, Fräulein Henriette.

Hen. Your chattering is really very annoying sometimes. Come, Theophan, shall I say that you will not be absent long?

Theoph. If you will be so good. (Henriette and Lisette go off on one side. Whilst Theophan is leaving on the other he his met by the Banker.)

Scene IX.—Theophan. Banker.

Bank. I beg your pardon, sir; I wish to speak a word with Herr Adrast.

Theoph. He has just gone out. Will you entrust your message to me?

Bank. If I may take the liberty. He wished to borrow a sum of money of me, which at first I promised to let him have; but I now have scruples on the subject, and am come to decline advancing it; that is all.

Theoph. Scruples, sir? What scruples? Surely none as to Adrast's character.

Bank. Why not?

Theoph. Is not his credit good?

Bank. Credit, sir, you know what that is. A man may have credit to-day, without being sure of having it to-morrow. I have been made acquainted with his present circumstances.

Theoph. (aside). I must do all I can that this is not made public. (Aloud.) You must have been misinformed. Do you know me, sir?

Bank. By sight, no; perhaps when I hear your name.

Theoph. Theophan.

Bank. A name of which I have never heard anything but good.

Theoph. If you are not willing to advance the required sum to Herr Adrast, on his personal security, would you do it on mine?

Bank. With pleasure.

Theoph. Have the goodness then to accompany me into my study—I will give you the necessary security— so that the surety which I give may remain a secret from Adrast.

Bank. From him?

Theoph. By all means; to spare him the annoyance which your mistrust would cause to him——

Bank. You are truly a noble friend.

Theoph. Let us not delay any longer. (Exeunt.)

ACT V.

Scene I.—*The* Banker *enters on one side;* Adrast *on the other.*

Adr. (*to himself*).   I cannot find the man.

Bank. (*to himself*).   That will do for me.

Adr.   Why there he is!   Ah! sir, do I find you here? We have missed each other, then.

Bank.   I am glad, Herr Adrast, that I have found you at last.

Adr.   I have been to your house in search of you.   The matter admits of no delay.   I may trust to you still, I suppose?

Bank.   Yes, now you may.

Adr.   Now?   What do you mean?

Bank.   Nothing.   Yes, you may trust to me.

Adr.   I hope you do not mistrust me?

Bank.   Not in the least.

Adr.   Or, that any one has insinuated aught to you?

Bank.   Still less.

Adr.   We have had dealings together before, and I trust you will always find me an honourable man.

Bank.   I have no fear.

Adr.   My honour is concerned in putting those to shame who are malicious enough to destroy my credit.

Bank.   I find people do quite the reverse.

Adr.   Oh! do not say that.   I know I have my enemies.

Bank.   But you have friends also.

Adr.   At the most by name.   I should deserve ridicule if I trusted to them.   And I assure you, sir, I am not pleased that you have been in this house during my absence.

Bank.   And yet you ought to be pleased.

Adr.   It is true the house is one where I should expect nothing but good; and yet a certain person therein, sir, a certain person. . . . I know I should have suffered had you met with him.

Bank.   I have not really spoken with anyone; but the one person from whom I made inquiries concerning you, showed the greatest regard for you.

Adr.   I will tell you who the man is whose ill-report of me I fear in some measure.   It may be as well for you to know, that you may be aware who is the author, should any reports to my detriment reach your ears.

Bank.   I shall not need to listen to them.

Adr.·   But still. . . . in a word, it is Theophan.

Bank. (*astonished*).   Theophan ?

Adr.   Yes, Theophan.   He is my enemy.

Bank.   Theophan your enemy?

Adr.   You appear astonished !

Bank.   Not without good reason.

Adr.   Because, doubtless, you think that a man of his profession cannot be otherwise than generous and noble.

Bank.   Sir——

Adr.   He is the most dangerous hypocrite that I have ever met with amongst his profession.

Bank.   Sir——

Adr.   He knows that I see through him, and on that account does all he can to undermine my character.

Bank.   I beg, sir,——

Adr.   If you have a good opinion of him, you are much mistaken.   Perhaps, indeed, you are only acquainted with him through his fortune, and on that score I have nothing to say ; he is rich, but just his riches give him the opportunity to do mischief in the most subtle manner.

Bank.   What do you say ?

Adr.   He employs indescribable intrigues to drive me from this house ; intrigues to which he can give such an innocent appearance, that I am myself astonished.

Bank.   This is too much !   I cannot longer keep silence. Sir, you deceive yourself in the most astonishing manner.

Adr.   I deceive myself?

Bank.   Theophan cannot possibly be the man you give him out to be.   You shall hear all : I came here to retract the promise I formerly made you ; I had heard particulars respecting you, from good authority, but not from Theophan, which induced me to take this step.   I found him here, and I thought there would be no objection to my telling him my business.

Adr.   Theophan !   How the base fellow must have chuckled !

Bank. Chuckled! He spoke for you most decidedly. And, in short, it is entirely through him that I keep to my first promise.

Adr. Through him! What do I hear?

Bank. He has given me an assurance, under his hand, which I may consider as security for you. It is true he forbad me to speak a word on the subject to any one; but it was impossible for me to stand by and hear an honest man so undeservedly reviled. You may send for the required sum when you please. But you will have the goodness not to let him know anything about it. He showed so much sincerity and friendship for you throughout the whole transaction, that he must be a monster if he can carry dissimulation so far. Farewell! (*Exit.*)

Scene II.—Adrast.

Adr. What new trick is this? I cannot collect my thoughts! It is not to be endured! Slights, insults — insults through the object which must be dearest to him —all is in vain; nothing makes him feel. What can render him so callous? Malice alone: nought but his wish to bring his revenge to maturity. Whom would not this man deceive? I hardly know what to think. He forces his favours upon one in a manner. . . . . But cursed be both his favours and his manner. Even if no snake lay concealed beneath these flowers, still I could not do otherwise than hate him. Hate him I will, even if he should save my life. He has robbed me of that which is more precious than life—the heart of Juliane; a theft which he cannot replace; no, not if he gave me his life. But he will not attempt to atone for it. I give him credit for too much.

Scene III.—Theophan, Adrast.

Theoph. In what violent excitement I find you again, Adrast!

Adr. It is your doing.

Theoph. Then it must be one of those deeds which we perform against our inclination, and when we are earnestly

striving to effect the reverse. I wish nothing more than
to see you tranquil, that you may discuss with me, in cool
blood, a matter which affects us both most closely.

ADR. Confess, Theophan, is it not the highest degree
of cunning, when a man can so execute his designs that
those against whom they are aimed do not themselves
know what reproaches they can make in return for them?

THEOPH. Without doubt.

ADR. Congratulate yourself then, for you have reached
that point.

THEOPH. What do you mean now?

ADR. I promised you to pay the acknowledged bill.
(*Ironically.*) You must not take it ill, it cannot now be
done. I will write you another bill in place of the one
you have destroyed.

THEOPH. (*in the same ironical tone*). It is true, I destroyed
it for no other purpose than to have another one from you.

ADR. That may or may not have been your intention;
but you shall have it. Would you **not** also like to hear
why it is no longer in my power to pay you?

THEOPH. Well, why?

ADR. Because I am not fond of sureties.

THEOPH. Sureties?

ADR. Yes; and because I do not wish to pay into your
right hand what I have been obliged to take from your
left.

THEOPH. (*aside*). The Banker has not kept his word
with me.

ADR. Do you understand me?

THEOPH. I cannot say with certainty.

ADR. I take every possible trouble to be under no obligation to you: must it not then annoy me that you make
it appear as if I had good reason to be under much?

THEOPH. I am astonished at your skill in viewing
everything in the worst light.

ADR. And as you have heard, I am also astonished at
yours, in concealing the bad side so excellently. In fact,
I scarcely know myself what I am to think of it.

THEOPH. Because you will not take the most natural
view of the subject.

ADR. This most natural view, you perhaps mean, is,

that I should think that you have taken this step from
generosity, from an anxiety for my good name. But, with
your permission, that would just be the most unnatural.

THEOPH. Yet you are right: for how would it be
possible that a man of my profession could ever possess
sentiments half so humane?

ADR. Let us for once set aside your profession.

THEOPH. Can you do that?

ADR. Suppose then, that you are not one of those who,
to maintain a character for piety, conceal their passions as
much as possible; who at first learn hypocrisy for decency's
sake, and eventually retain it as a second nature; who are
bound by their principles to withdraw themselves from
the society of honourable people, whom they call children
of the world, or at least to have communication with them
with no other view than the mean one of drawing them
over to their own way of thinking: suppose, I say, you
are not one of these; you are at least a man who can
feel an insult, I suppose? And, to sum up all in one word,
are you not a lover, who can feel jealousy?

THEOPH. I am much pleased that you have at last
come on to that subject.

ADR. But do not imagine that I shall speak on it
with any moderation.

THEOPH. Then I must endeavour to employ so much
the more.

ADR. You love Juliane, and I. . . . I. . . . But why do
I search for words? I hate you on account of this love,
although I have indeed no title to the beloved object: and
should not you hate me also, you who have a right, which
I envy?

THEOPH. Certainly I should not. But let us examine
the right which you or I may have to Juliane.

ADR. If this right depended upon the strength of our
love, perhaps I might still contest it with you. It is your
good fortune that it rests upon the consent of a father
and the obedience of a daughter.

THEOPH. Upon that, however, I will not let it depend.
Love alone shall decide. But, observe, not our love only,
but principally hers, which you think I possess. If you can
convince me that you are loved in return by Juliane----

Adr.   You will resign your claims in my favour?

Theoph.   I must.

Adr.   How contemptuously you deal with me. You are sure of your game, and satisfied that you risk nothing by this rodomontade.

Theoph.   You cannot tell me then whether Juliane loves you?

Adr.   If I could, do you think I would refuse to annoy you with this advantage?

Theoph.   Stay! you make yourself more inhuman than you really are. Well! I will—I will tell you: Juliane loves you.

Adr.   What do you say? — But I had almost forgotten, in the rapture of this assurance, from whose mouth I hear it. Oh! yes, Theophan, yes! one may mock one's enemies: but will you not also assure me, to make this mockery perfect, that you do not love Juliane either?

Theoph. (*vexed*).   It is quite impossible to speak a reasonable word with you. (*Turns to go.*)

Adr. (*aside*).   Is he angry? (*Aloud.*) Stop, Theophan, do you know that the first angry look which I have ever seen on your face, makes me curious to hear this reasonable word.

Theoph. (*angry*).   And do you know, I begin to be tired of your abusive manner.

Adr. (*aside*).   He appears to be in earnest.

Theoph. (*still angry*).   I shall endeavour to let you find Theophan such as you fancy him to be.

Adr.   Pardon me; but I think I see more sincerity in your resentment than I ever did in your friendship.

Theoph.   Extraordinary man! Must one put one's-self on your level? must one be equally proud, equally suspicious, equally insolent with yourself, to win your pitiful confidence?

Adr.   I must pardon you this language on account of its novelty.

Theoph.   It shall become common enough for you.

Adr.   But to speak truth, you completely puzzle me. Must you tell me, with a smiling countenance, that on which all my happiness depends? I entreat you, tell me again what I just now took for mockery.

THEOPH. If I repeat it, do not imagine that I do it on your account.

ADR. Then I shall put all the more faith in what you say.

THEOPH. But without interrupting me, I beg.

ADR. Proceed then.

THEOPH. In the first place, I will give you the key to what you are going to hear. My affection has not deceived me less than yours has deceived you; I perceive and admire all the virtues which make Juliane an ornament to her sex; but . . . . I do not love her.

ADR. You do not——

THEOPH. It is quite immaterial whether you believe me or not. I have taken the greatest trouble to convert my esteem into love. But whilst doing so, I have had many opportunities of remarking that Juliane has experienced the same difficulty. She wished to love me, but she did not love me. The heart cannot be reasoned into anything; and in this case, as in others, maintains its independence of the understanding. One may act the tyrant over it, but not constrain it. And what good does it do, to make one's-self a martyr to one's reason, when one knows at the same time that no peace of mind is to be gained by it? I therefore pitied Juliane—or rather, I pitied myself. I no longer restrained my growing preference for another person, and saw with pleasure that Juliane was too weak or too kind to restrain hers. But it was for a man who is as unworthy of her as he is unworthy to have a true friend. Adrast would long ago have been aware that his happiness lay in her, if he had been calm enough to take a right view of anything. He observes everything through the coloured glass of his own preconceived opinions, and that but superficially ; and would often rather belie his senses than renounce his prejudices. Since Juliane considered him amiable, I could not possibly conceive him depraved beyond remedy. I sought for the best means of making known to both of them that they need not consider me as a hindrance to their union. I came here now with this purpose, but Adrast only allowed me to enter upon the subject after the most unseemly opposition. I should have left him without a word more, if I had not constrained myself, for

the sake of her for whom, from the bottom of my heart, I
wish everything which she herself desires. I have nothing
more to say. (*Is going.*)

ADR. Where are you going, Theophan? Judge by my
silence how great my astonishment must be! It is a
human weakness easily to be convinced of that which one
ardently wishes. Shall I indulge this weakness? or shall
I suppress it?

THEOPH. I have no wish to be present at your deliberation.

ADR. Woe to him who would jest with me in so cruel
a manner!

THEOPH. May your torturing uncertainty, then, revenge
me on you.

ADR. (*aside*). Now I will catch him. (*Aloud.*) Allow me
to say one word more, Theophan. How can you be angry
with a man who doubts more through astonishment at his
own good fortune than through mistrust of you?

THEOPH. Adrast, I will confess my shame at having
been angry for one moment, as soon as you express a wish
to talk rationally.

ADR. If it be true that you do not love Juliane, will it
not be necessary to let Lisidor know it?

THEOPH. Certainly.

ADR. And that is really your intention?

THEOPH. Yes; and the sooner the better.

ADR. You will tell Lisidor that you do not love
Juliane?

THEOPH. Why not?

ADR. And that you love another?

THEOPH. By all means! So that he may have no reason
to charge Juliane with breaking off the engagement.

ADR. Will you indeed do all this immediately?

THEOPH. Immediately?

ADR. (*aside*). Now I have him. (*Aloud.*) Yes! immediately.

THEOPH. But will you also take the same step! Will
you also tell Lisidor that you do not love Henriette?

ADR. I am most anxious.

THEOPH. And that you love Juliane?

ADR. Do you doubt it?

Theoph. Very well; come then.

Adr. (*aside*). He really will?

Theoph. Come, quick!

Adr. Consider it well.

Theoph. What shall I consider?

Adr. There is still time.

Theoph. It is you that hesitate. Come—(*going on first.*) You linger? You are lost in thought? Why do you look at me with such astonishment?

Adr. (*after a pause*). Theophan!

Theoph. Well; am I not ready?

Adr. (*affected*). Theophan! You are really an honourable man after all.

Theoph. Why do you think that now? What has that to do with the matter?

Adr. Why do I think so now? Can I require a stronger proof that my happiness is not a matter of indifference to you?

Theoph. You acknowledge this very late, but still you do acknowledge it. My dear Adrast, give me your hand.

Adr. I am ashamed.—Leave me to myself, I will follow you shortly.

Theoph. No, I will not leave you alone. Is it possible that I have overcome your dislike? that I have overcome it by a sacrifice which costs me so little? Ah! Adrast, you do not know yet how selfishly I am acting; perhaps I shall again lose all your regard . . . . I love Henriette.

Adr. You love Henriette? Good heavens! Then we may both be happy yet. Why did we not explain ourselves sooner? Oh, Theophan! Theophan! I should then have regarded your conduct with very different eyes. You would not have been exposed to the acrimony of my reproaches, of my suspicion.

Theoph. No excuses, Adrast. Prejudice and an unfortunate attachment are two evils, either of which is sufficient to change a man's nature completely. But why do we delay here any longer?

Adr. Yes, Theophan, let us hasten now. But if Lisidor opposes us—if Juliane loves another——

Theoph. Fear not.—Here is Lisidor.

SCENE IV.—LISIDOR, THEOPHAN, ADRAST.

LIS. You are pretty fellows! Am I always to be left alone with your cousin, who is quite a stranger to me?

THEOPH. We were on the point of coming to you.

LIS. What have you been about now? Quarrelling again? Believe me, one gets nothing by arguing. You are both right, doubtless both right. For example—(*to* THEOPHAN)—this man says reason is weak; and this man—(*looking at* ADRAST)—says reason is strong. The first proves with strong argument that reason is weak, the latter with weak argument that reason is strong. Now, is that not just the same? Weak and strong, or strong and weak: pray what is the difference?

THEOPH. Excuse me, but we have not been speaking either of the strength or the weakness of reason.

LIS. Well! then it was perhaps of something else, equally indifferent. Perhaps of liberty. Whether a hungry donkey stuck between two bundles of hay, precisely like each other, has the power of eating from the first that comes, or whether the donkey is such a donkey that he prefers to starve!

ADR. No, that was not our discussion either. We were occupied about a matter that concerns you principally.

LIS. Me?

THEOPH. You, in whose hands our happiness lies.

LIS. Oh! You will do me a kindness if you will take it into your own as soon as possible. You mean your happiness with my girls? I have already long wished to get them off. A man is a man, and a girl is a girl; and as for happiness, it is like a glass, easily broken.

THEOPH. We can never be sufficiently grateful for the near alliance with which you deign to favour us. There is still, however, one great difficulty.

LIS. What?

ADR. A difficulty which it was impossible to see before.

LIS. How now?

THEOPH. *and* ADR. We must confess to you——

LIS. Both at once? What is it? I must interrogate you in order. What have you to confess, Theophan?

THEOPH. I must confess to you that I do not love Juliane.

LIS. Not love her? Do I hear right? And what is your confession, Adrast?

ADR. I must confess to you that I do not love Henriette.

LIS. Not love her? You not love, and you not love; it is not possible. You wranglers, who have never yet agreed on any point, are going to do so now for the first time when it is a question of leaving me in the lurch? Ah! you are joking, now I begin to see it.

ADR. We? Joking?

LIS. Or else you are not right in your heads. You do not love my daughters? Why the girls will cry their eyes out. But why not, let me ask? What is the matter with Juliane that you cannot love her?

THEOPH. To tell you the truth, I believe her heart is occupied with thoughts of another.

ADR. And that is just what I suspect of Henriette—not without reason.

LIS. Oh! oh! I must get to the bottom of this. Halloa! Lisette! Lisette! So you are both jealous, are you, and only wish to threaten?

THEOPH. Threaten? Where we have the greatest need of your kindness.

LIS. Halloa there! Lisette!

SCENE V.—LISETTE, LISHOR, THEOPHAN, ADRAST.

LISE. Well! Here I am! What is the matter?

LIS. Tell them to come here directly.

LISE. Who?

LIS. Both of them; do you not hear?

LISE. My young Mistresses?

LIS. Of course.

LISE. I will fetch them immediately. (*Turning round again.*) Cannot I tell them beforehand what they are to come for.

LIS. No!

LISE. (*Goes out and returns*). But if they ask me?

LIS. Will you go!

LISE. I am going. (*Returns again.*) Is it anything particular?

LIS. I think it is you, you monkey, who wish to know it before they do!

LISE. Gently! I am not so curious. (*Exit.*)

SCENE VI.—LISIDOR, THEOPHAN, ADRAST.

LIS. You have completely confounded me all of a sudden. But patience! patience! I will soon put the matter right again. A pretty business it would be if I had to look about for another pair of sons-in-law. You were just to my mind; and I shall not get such a pair together again, even if I have them made to order.

ADR. Look about for other sons-in-law? With what misfortune do you threaten us?

LIS. Why you would not marry the girls without loving them? You will excuse me there.

THEOPH. Without loving them?

ADR. Who said that?

LIS. Then what did you say?

ADR. I adore Juliane.

LIS. Juliane!

THEOPH. I love Henriette, more than myself.

LIS. Henriette! Humph! now my heart suddenly grows light again. Is that the difficulty? Then it is nothing more than that you have fallen in love with one another's sweethearts? Well, an exchange will set the whole affair right again.

THEOPH. You are very kind, Lisidor.

ADR. You consent then?

LIS. What am I to do? It is certainly better that you change before marriage than after. If my daughters are satisfied, so am I.

ADR. We flatter ourselves they will be so. But after the good will which you have shown us, there is still a confession which I cannot withhold from you.

LIS. Another one?

ADR. I should not act like an honourable man, if I concealed the state of my finances from you.

LIS. What about your finances?

ADR. My fortune is so wasted, that when I have paid all my debts I shall have nothing left.

LIS. Oh! do not talk about that : did I ask you what fortune you had? I know well enough that you have been a wild blade, and squandered everything; but just for this reason I give you my daughter, that you may have something again. Hold! here they come; now let me speak——

SCENE VII.—JULIANE, HENRIETTE, LISETTE, LISIDOR,
THEOPHAN, ADRAST.

LISE. Here they are, Herr Lisidor; we are most curious to know what you have to say.

LIS. Cheer up, my girls! I have good news for you. To-morrow it shall be all right. Think of that.

LISE. What shall be all right?

LIS. Nothing will be all right for you. Cheer up, my girls! Weddings! Weddings! Why, you look as doleful . . . . What is the matter, Juliane?

JUL. You shall always find me an obedient daughter; but just this once, let me represent to you that you would be hurrying me. Heavens! to-morrow?

LIS. And you, Henriette?

HEN. I, dear father! Oh! I shall be ill to-morrow—sick unto death.

LIS. Put it off till the day after.

HEN. It cannot be; Adrast knows my reasons.

ADR. I know, lovely Henriette, that you do not like me.

THEOPH. And you, dearest Juliane, do you mean to obey? How near do I appear to be to my happiness, and how far am I perhaps from it still. With what countenance shall I tell you that I am not worthy of your hand? that, with all the esteem which I cannot but feel for such a faultless being, I do not dare to feel that for you which I can feel for one person alone in the whole world.

LISE. Why, that is a flat refusal. It is not allowed for men too to give such things. So, quick, Juliane, out with it.

THEOPH. My explanation could give offence to none

but a vain woman ; and I know that Juliane is so far
above such weakness——

JUL. Ah ! Theophan, I perceive you have read my
heart too well.

ADR. Well, you are free, lovely Juliane. I have no
further avowal to make than what I have already made.
What may I hope ?——

JUL. My dear father—Adrast—Sister—Theophan——

LISE. Now I see it all. Their grandmamma must
know it at once. (LISETTE *runs off.*)

LIS. (*to* JULIANE.) Do you see, girl, what a pretty
business you have made?

THEOPH. And what do you say, dearest Henriette?
Is not Adrast a faithless lover ? Ah ! would you but cast
your eyes on a truer one ! We talked just now of revenge,
an innocent revenge.

HEN. It is a bargain, Theophan : I will be revenged.

LIS. Take care, Henriette ! Have you forgotten the
illness you are going to have to-morrow ?

HEN. I shall not be at home, if it comes.

LIS. Now, are not you strange people ? I wished to
bring together birds of the same feather; but I see you
have a piebald taste. The serious was to have the serious,
and the lively the lively; but no, the serious wants the
lively, and the lively the serious.

SCENE VIII.—FRAU PHILANE, *with* LISETTE. (*The rest
as before.*)

FRAU PHI. Children, what do I hear? is it possible ?

LIS. Yes, mamma, it is ; and I suppose you will not say
nay. They want——

FRAU PHI. I say nay? This change has been my
wish, my prayer. Ah, Adrast! Ah, Henriette ! often
have I trembled for you. You would have been an unhappy couple. You both require a companion who knows
the path of duty better than yourselves. Theophan, you
have long had my blessing ; but if you court more than
this, if you court the blessing of heaven, make such a
character of Henriette as is worthy of you. And Adrast,
I have hitherto considered you a bad man, but we will

hope. He who can love a pious woman, must already be on the road to piety himself. For this I rely upon you, Juliane. And above all things, induce him not to treat honest people—good clergymen, so contemptuously as he has treated Theophan.

ADR. Madam, do not remind me of my injustice. Oh! if I am always in the wrong in the same degree as I have been in my conduct to you, Theophan, what a man, or rather, what a wretch I must be.

Lis. Now, did I not say that you would be the best friends in the world, as soon as you became brothers-in-law? This is but the beginning.

THEOPH. I repeat it, Adrast, you are a better man than you imagine; better than till now you have wished to appear.

FRAU PHI. Well, it is a comfort too, to hear that. (*To* LISIDOR.) Come, my son, give me your arm. I am tired of standing, and my joy has made me forget that I left Araspe alone.

LIS. Ah! to be sure, this is something to tell him. Come, mother. But no more changing, no more changing!

LISE. Poor me! how badly I come off, with nothing to change.

THE TREASURE.

(A COMEDY IN ONE ACT.)

The ' Treasure ' was written in the year 1750

U

DRAMATIS PERSONÆ.

LEANDER.

STALENO, LEANDER'S *Guardian.*

PHILTO, *An old Man.*

ANSELMUS.

LELIO, *Son of* ANSELMUS.

MASKARILL, LELIO'S *Servant.*

RAPS.

A PORTER.

The Scene is in a Street.

THE TREASURE.

SCENE I.—LEANDER, STALENO.

STAL. What! Leander, so young, and you have already found a girl to your taste?

LEAN. She will be so much the more pleased that I am young: and yet not very young either. If I was twice as old, I might already have children as old as I am.

STAL. And I am to let you have her?

LEAN. Yes, my dear Guardian, if you will have the kindness.

STAL. Dear Guardian! It is long since I have heard that. If you will have the kindness! How polite one suddenly becomes when one is in love. But what sort of a person is she? for you have not told me that yet.

LEAN. A most delightful girl!

STAL. Has she money? How much will she have?

LEAN. She is beauty itself; and as innocent, too—as innocent—as I am.

STAL. Does she also talk already of the children she might have? But tell me, how much will she have?

LEAN. If you saw her, you would fall in love with her yourself. An oval, plump face, but nothing childish in it; a figure like a reed——

STAL. And how much will she have?

LEAN. As straight as a reed. Not thin, and yet not stout either. You doubtless know that a young lady to be really beautiful, must be neither one nor the other.

STAL. And how much will she have?

U 2

LEAN. She carries herself in such a manner; ah! dear Herr Staleno, in such a manner .... And I assure you she never learnt to dance; it came to her by nature.

STAL. And how much will she have?

LEAN. If her face was not out-and-out the most lovely one to be conceived, her manners alone would make her the most agreeable person under the sun. I cannot conceive who can have taught her them.

STAL. Will you listen! I am asking you about her marriage-portion? How much will she have?

LEAN. And talks .... She can talk like an angel.

STAL. How much will she have?

LEAN. You will hardly meet with more intelligence and virtue than she possesses in any other of her sex.

STAL. Very good, very good; but how much will she have?

LEAN. Moreover, she comes of a good family, dear Guardian; of a very good family.

STAL. The good families are not always the richest. How much will she have?

LEAN. By-the-by, I forgot to tell you, that she also sings very well.

STAL. The Devil! Don't let me ask the same question a hundred times. First and foremost, I wish to know how much she will have.

LEAN. It was only yesterday evening I heard her sing for the first time. How enchanted I was!

STAL. Do not make fun of your guardian. If you will not give me an answer, go your way, and let me go mine.

LEAN. Why, you are quite angry, dearest Guardian. I was on the point of answering your question.

STAL. Well, do so, then.

LEAN. What was it? Yes, I recollect. You asked if she was a good housewife. Oh! an incomparable one! I am convinced she will save her husband thousands every year.

STAL. There is something in that; but that was not what I asked. I asked—don't you understand your native language—I asked, is she rich? whether she will have a good dowry?

LEAN. (*sorrowfully*). A dowry?

STAL. Yes, a dowry. What is she worth? the young gentleman has never troubled himself about that. Oh! youth! youth! that hair-brained youth should be so indifferent about that which is of the very utmost consequence! Well, if you do not know yet what your young lady will have—why go and find out. Then we can talk more of the matter.

LEAN. We may do that at once, if you are not averse to it. I have not been so thoughtless; I have already made inquiries.

STAL. Then you know what she is to have?

LEAN. To a fraction.

STAL. And how much is it?

LEAN. Not a great deal, certainly.

STAL. Well, who wants a great deal? Only what is just. You have plenty yourself, you know.

LEAN. Oh! you are an excellent man, my dear Guardian. It is true I am rich enough to be able to dispense with money in her.

STAL. Will the girl have the half of your fortune?

LEAN. The half? No, not the half.

STAL. A third part?

LEAN. Nor a third part.

STAL. Surely a fourth?

LEAN. Hardly.

STAL. At any rate, I suppose, it is an eighth? then it would be a few thousand thalers, which on commencing house-keeping are soon enough gone.

LEAN. I have told you already it is not much, not in any way much.

STAL. But *not much* is still something. How much?

LEAN. Little, dear Guardian.

STAL. How little, then?

LEAN. Little. You know yourself what little means.

STAL. Now out with it. I must have a name. Express it by numbers.

LEAN. Why the little, Herr Staleno, is . . . . nothing at all.

STAL. Nothing at all! Indeed! You are right; nothing is little enough. But, seriously, are you not ashamed,

Leander, to be so foolish as to choose a girl for a wife who has nothing?

Lean. What do you say? Has nothing! She has everything which belongs to a perfect woman; money is the only thing she has not.

Stal. That is to say, she has everything which could make a perfect woman, if she only had that which does make a perfect woman.—Say no more, I must know best what is good for you. But may I know who this beautiful, amiable, accomplished beggar is? what her name is?

Lean. That is wrong of you, Herr Staleno. If it depended on merit we should all be poor, and this beggar would alone be rich.

Stal. Tell me her name, then, that I may know what else to call her.

Lean. Camilla.

Stal. Camilla! Surely not the sister of the dissolute Lelio?

Lean. The same. Her father is one of the most honourable men in the world.

Stal. Is, or was. It is now nine years since he left this place; and for four years nobody has had any tidings at all of him. Who knows where the honest Anselmus is lying? It is as well for him, perhaps, that he does not return; for if he did come, and saw the state his family is in, he would vex himself to death.

Lean. You knew him, then?

Stal. I should think so. He was my most intimate friend.

Lean. And you will be so cruel to his daughter? You would prevent my placing her again in the position she deserves.

Stal. Leander, if you were my son, I would not say a word against the match; but, remember, you are only my ward. Your feelings might alter when you grew older, and if you become tired of the pretty face—for the best foundation is here wanting—all the blame would fall on me.

Lean. What! My feelings alter? I cease to love Camilla? I——

Stal. Wait till you are your own master, then you can act as you please. If, indeed, the young lady was still in the same circumstances in which her father left her—if her brother had not squandered everything—if old Philto, to whom Anselmus entrusted the care of his children, had not been an old rogue—why then I would certainly myself do all in my power that nobody but you should win Camilla. But, since that is not the case, I will have nothing to do with it. Go home again.

Lean. But, my dear Herr Staleno.

Stal. Your flattery is all to no purpose. What I have said, I have said. I was just going to old Philto, who in other respects is a good friend of mine, to read him a lesson on his behaviour towards Lelio. He has even bought the house from this dissolute youth now—the last thing they had left. That is too bad; that is not to be defended. Go, Leander; do not detain me longer. We can speak more of this at home.

Lean. In the hope that you will think better of the matter, I will go. You will come back soon, I suppose.

Stal. Yes.

Scene II.—Staleno.

Stal. It certainly does not answer to tell people the truth, and upbraid them with their own bad deeds; one generally makes enemies thereby. But be it so. I will not have that man for a friend who has so little conscience. Could I ever have imagined that Philto, the man in whom I had such confidence. . . . Ah! there he comes, just in the nick of time.

Scene III.—Staleno, Philto.

Stal. Good day, Herr Philto.

Phil. What, is that you, Herr Staleno! How are you, my dear old friend? Where were you going?

Stal. I was just in the act of coming to you.

Phil. To me? Why, that is capital. Come, I will turn back with you directly.

Stal. It is not necessary, if only I can speak with you. It is all the same to me whether it is in your house or in

the street. I would rather talk with you in the open air
to be clear of contagion.

PHIL. What do you mean by contagion? Have I had
the plague since I saw you?

STAL. Something worse than the plague. Oh! Philto!
Philto! are you the honourable Philto, whom the town
has hitherto numbered amongst the few men of real
weight and value?

PHIL. That is a capital beginning to a castigatory
sermon. How do I come by it?

STAL. What pretty stories are told about you in the
town! An old knave, a skin-flint, a leech—these are the
best of your titles.

PHIL. Mine?

STAL. Yes, yours.

PHIL. I am sorry for it. But what is to be done?
One must let people talk. I cannot prevent any person
from thinking or speaking ill of me; enough if I am
conscious they do me injustice.

STAL. Are you so indifferent about it? I was not so
indifferent when I heard it. But this coolness is not
enough to justify you. One is often cool, because one
feels that one has no right to be hasty and angry.
Should any one speak so of me . . . . I would break the
neck of the first who did. I trust, however, that I should
never, by my actions, give occasion for it.

PHIL. May I then hear what is the crime that I am
accused of?

STAL. You must have come to an understanding with
your conscience that it does not occur to you immediately.
Tell me, was Anselmus your friend?

PHIL. He was, and is so still, far as we now are from
each other. Do you know that on his departure he
entrusted his son and daughter to my care? Would he
have done that, if he had not considered me his true
friend?

STAL. Ah! honest Anselmus, how have you deceived
yourself!

PHIL. I trust he has not deceived himself.

STAL. No? Well, well, if I had a son whom I wished
to see in a state of extreme depravity, I certainly would

entrust him to your guardianship. He has become a pretty fellow, has Lelio!

Phil. Now you lay that to my charge of which you have always hitherto acquitted me. Lelio committed his dissolute excesses without my knowledge; and when I heard of them, it was already too late to prevent them.

Stal. I no longer believe that! for your last trick betrays your intentions.

Phil. What trick?

Stal. To whom has Lelio sold his house?

Phil. To me.

Stal. Welcome, Anselmus! You may now sleep in the streets. Shame, Philto!

Phil. I have fairly paid the three thousand thalers for it.

Stal. Fairly to lose the name of an honourable man.

Phil. Ought I not to have paid the money then?

Stal. Oh! Don't pretend to be so silly. You ought not to have bought anything from Lelio. To help such a man to money—is not that putting a knife into the hand of a madman, that he may cut his own throat? Is not that entering into partnership with the son, to ruin the father without mercy?

Phil. But Lelio had the greatest need of the money. With part of it he had to free himself from a disgraceful imprisonment. And if I had not bought the house, somebody else would.

Stal. Others might have done as they pleased. But do not excuse yourself; one cannot but see your real reason. The house is worth about four thousand thalers; it was to be sold for three thousand, and I have the best claim, thought you, to the profit. I am fond of money likewise: but look you, Philto, I would sooner have had this right hand of mine cut off than have been guilty of so mean an action, even could I have gained a million by it. In short, to finish the business, our friendship is at an end.

Phil. Now truly, Staleno, you press me hard. I believe you will induce me, by your invectives, to trust a secret to you which no other person on earth should have learnt from me.

STAL.   Do not be anxious about anything you may
entrust to me.   It is as safe with me as with yourself.

PHIL.   Just look round about, and see that nobody is
listening.—Look well!—Are you sure nobody is peeping
out of those windows?

STAL.   This really must be a most secret secret.   I do
not see anybody.

PHIL.   Well, listen.   On the very day that Anselmus
took his departure, he drew me aside, and led me to a
particular spot in his house.   My dear Philto, said he,
I have one thing more to make known to you.   Here, in
this . . . . Wait a little, Staleno, I see somebody there;
we will let him pass first.

STAL.   He has gone now.

PHIL.   Here, said he, in this cellar, under one of the
. . . . Stop! there comes a——

STAL.   It is only a child.

PHIL.   Children are curious.

STAL.   It has gone.

PHIL.   Under one of the stones of the floor, said he, I
have . . . . There is something running there again.

STAL.   It is nothing but a dog.

PHIL.   But it has ears!   I have, said he (*looking
anxiously from side to side*), buried a small sum of money.

STAL.   What!

PHIL.   Hist! hist! Who would say such a thing twice?

STAL.   A sum of money!   A treasure!

PHIL.   Yes; but, I say, if any one heard!

STAL.   Perhaps a sparrow, flying over our heads.

PHIL.   I have, continued he, been saving long enough,
and have put up with much for it.   I am now going to
travel.   I leave my son sufficient to live upon, I dare not
leave him a farthing more.   He has every disposition to
be a dissolute man, and the more he had, so much the
more would he squander.   What would then remain
for my daughter?   I must be prepared for any event; my
journey is a long and dangerous one: who knows if I may
ever return.   A certain part, therefore, of this sum shall
be a dowry for my Camilla, if a good opportunity present
itself for her to marry.   My son shall have the remainder;
but not before you have certain intelligence of my death.

Till that time, I entreat you, Philto, with tears I entreat
you, my good friend, to let Lelio know nothing about it;
keep it moreover a secret from everyone, lest by chance
he hear it from a third person. I promised my friend all,
and took an oath upon it. Now tell me, Staleno, when I
heard that Lelio was determined to sell the house, the
very house in which the money is concealed, tell me, I
say, what could I do?

STAL. What do I hear? By my faith! the matter
now assumes a different aspect.

PHIL. Lelio had advertised the house for sale while I
was absent in the country.

STAL. Ha! ha! The wolf had observed that the sheep-
dog was away from the flock.

PHIL. You may imagine that I was not a little alarmed
when I returned to town. It was done. Could I then
betray my friend, and disclose the treasure to the dissolute
Lelio? Or should I let the house go into the hands of a
stranger, from whom perhaps Anselmus would never
have recovered it? To take the treasure away—that was
not to be done. In a word, I saw no other remedy than
to purchase the house myself, to save both one and the
other. Anselmus may now return to-day or to-morrow;
I can give both over to him. You must see that I do not
want the house I have bought; I have turned out son and
daughter, and shut it up. No one shall enter it again
but its lawful owner. I perceived beforehand that the
people would abuse me; but I prefer appearing dishonest
for a short time, to really being so. Am I still in your
eyes an old cheat, a leech?

STAL. You are an honourable man, and I am a fool.—
I wish the people who must needs know all the gossip,
and go about with stories which have neither head nor
tail, were hanged. What stuff have they not whispered
to me about you! But why was I such an old ass as to
believe it all? Do not take it ill of me, Philto; I was too
hasty.

PHIL. I take nothing ill where I see the intention is
good. You had my good name at heart, and that pleases
me. Much you would have troubled yourself about it if
you had not been my friend.

STAL. Indeed, I am quite angry with myself.

PHIL. Do not be so.

STAL. I am quite distressed that I could have imagined any dishonesty on your part for a single instant.

PHIL. And I am quite pleased with you, that you have been so open with me. A friend, who tells one to one's face anything objectionable that he notices in one, is now very rare; one must not quarrel with him, even if he be only right once in ten times. Only be equally kind to me in the future.

STAL. That is what I call spoken as a man ought to speak! Agreed! we are friends, and will remain so.

PHIL. Agreed! Have you anything else to say to me?

STAL. I think not. Oh! yes, I have. (*Aside.*) Perhaps I can give my ward an unexpected pleasure.

PHIL. What is it?

STAL. Did you not say that a part of the hidden treasure was to be a dowry for the young Camilla?

PHIL. Yes.

STAL. To what will that part amount?

PHIL. To six thousand thalers.

STAL. Not so bad. And if a suitable match for the six thousand thalers—for Miss Camilla, I should say—were to offer, would you have a mind to say yes to it?

PHIL. If the match was suitable, why not?

STAL. For example—my ward. What do you think?

PHIL. What! young Herr Leander? Has he an eye on her?

STAL. That he has, both eyes. He is so wrapt up in her, that he would rather marry her to-day than to-morrow, even if she came to him without clothes on her back.

PHIL. That is what I call love! Truly, Herr Staleno, your proposal is not to be despised. If you are in earnest——

STAL. Quite in earnest! I should not joke about six thousand thalers.

PHIL. But will Camilla have Leander?

STAL. At any rate he will have her. When twenty thousand thalers wish to marry six thousand, why the six will not be mad and give the twenty their *congé*. The girl can surely count.

Phil.   I believe if Anselmus should return home to-day he could not wish to see his daughter better provided for.   Very well, I take the responsibility upon myself. Consider the matter settled, Herr Staleno.

Stal.   If the six thousand thalers are forthcoming.

Phil.   Oh! confound it! The greatest difficulty only just occurs to me.   Must Leander have the six thousand thalers at once—down?

Stal.   He need not, but then he must not have Camilla at once, either.

Phil.   Pray give me your advice, then.   The money is concealed; if I take it out, where shall I say that I got it from?   If I tell the truth, Lelio will smell a rat, and not be talked over to believe that more money cannot lie in the same place where the six thousand have lain.   Shall I say that I give the money from my own fortune? That I should not care to do; for the people would only find a fresh inducement to slander me in that. "Philto," they would perhaps say, "would not be so generous, did not his conscience whisper to him that he had cheated the poor children out of too much."

Stal.   That is true.

Phil.   And for that reason I should think it would be as well if the dowry could remain till Anselmus's return. Leander is quite sure of having it.

Stal.   Leander, as I have said, would care nothing about it.   But, my dear Philto, I, who am his guardian, must be just as careful of calumny as you. "Yes! yes!" would be muttered, " the rich ward is in good hands! A girl without a farthing is now tacked to him, and the poor creature, to show her gratitude, will understand how she must behave towards the guardian.   Staleno is cunning; such an account as he has against Leander is not likely to be readily paid off.   A female intercessor, who will keep her husband's eyes shut when he wishes to look into matters, is not so bad."   Such comments I beg to decline.

Phil.   You are right.   But how is the matter to be managed?   Do think a little.

Stal.   You think, too.

Phil.   What if we——

STAL. Well?

PHIL. No! that will not do.

STAL. Oh! I tell you what! Supposing . . . . That will not do either.

PHIL. Could not one——   *Spoken at the same moment,*
STAL. One would have to—— *after they have been thinking*
for some time.

PHIL. What did you mean?

STAL. What were you going to say?

PHIL. Go on.

STAL. No, you.

PHIL. I should like to hear your ideas first.

STAL. And I yours. Mine are not quite ripe.

PHIL. And mine . . . . mine have slipped away again.

STAL. What a pity! But stop! mine begin to ripen . . . . Now they are ripe.

PHIL. That is good!

STAL. What if we got some fellow privately, for a good bribe, who was impudent enough, and had sufficient gift of the gab, to tell ten lies in a breath?

PHIL. How could he help us?

STAL. Why, he would have to disguise himself, and give out that he came from some out-of-the-way country or other.

PHIL. And——

STAL. And that he has spoken with Anselmus——

PHIL. And——

STAL. And that Anselmus has made him the bearer of letters, one to his son, and one to you.

PHIL. And what then?

STAL. Why, do you not see what I intend? In the letter to his son must be written—that Anselmus cannot return yet; that Lelio in the meantime shall look after the house, and husband his income well, and more of the same kind. In your letter it must be written—that Anselmus has reflected upon the age of his daughter; that he would willingly know that she was married; that he has sent her such and such a sum for her marriage-portion, in case a good offer should arise.

PHIL. And the fellow must pretend that he has brought the money for the dowry with him, eh!

Stal. Exactly so.

Phil. That will do admirably!—But what if the son know his father's handwriting? What, if he remembers his seal?

Stal. Oh! there are a thousand ways to manage that. Do not alarm yourself before your time. I have this moment bethought me of a man who will be able to play the part to perfection.

Phil. Indeed! Go then at once and settle what is necessary with him. I will see about the money immediately; for the present I would rather take it from my own, until I can disinter it with safety.

Stal. Do so! Do so! In half an hour the man shall be at your house. (*Exit.*)

Phil. (*alone*). It is disagreeable enough to me that I am obliged in my old age to practise such devices, and particularly on that scamp Lelio's account. There he comes himself, with the friend who leads him into all the mischief. They appear to be talking earnestly; without doubt some creditor is after them again. (*Retires a little.*)

Scene IV.—Lelio, Maskarill, Philto.

Lelio. And that is all that remains from the three thousand thalers? (*Counts.*) Ten, twenty, thirty, forty, fifty, five-and-fifty. Only fifty-five left!

Mask. It appears almost incredible to me. Let me count them. (*Lelio gives him the money.*) Ten, twenty, thirty, forty, five-and forty. Yes, sure enough! five-and-forty, and not one fraction more. (*Gives him the money back.*)

Lelio. Five-and-forty! Five-and-fifty you mean.

Mask. Oh! I think I have counted better than you.

Lelio. (*after he has counted the money to himself*). Ha! ha! You conjuror! you have used your hands as pockets? Allow me just——

Mask. What do you please to wish?

Lelio. Your hand, Herr Maskarill.

Mask. Oh! nonsense!

Lelio. I beg——

MASK. No, no! I—I—feel ashamed——

LELIO. Ashamed? That would be something new for you. Without further fuss, rascal, show me your hand.

MASK. I tell you, Herr Lelio, I am ashamed; for the fact is—I have not yet washed my hands to-day.

LELIO. There it is ! It is no wonder, then, that everything remains sticking to the dirt. (*Opens his hand and finds the money between his fingers.*) Do you see what a necessary virtue cleanliness is? You were within an ace of being taken for a dishonest fellow, whereas you are only a dirty one. But, in earnest : if you have taken your ten thalers discount from every fifty, why then, from the three thousand—let us see—not more than six hundred have crept into your pocket.

MASK. Zounds! one would hardly believe that a spendthrift could reckon so well.

LELIO. And even then I do not rightly see how the whole sum is to be accounted for. Just think, three thousand thalers——

MASK. Are soon disposed of. In the first place, the bill drawn that was sued for——

LELIO. That does not make it.

MASK. The housekeeping of your sister——

LELIO. Is a trifle.

MASK. To Herr Stiletti, for oysters and French wines——

LELIO. Were a hundred and twenty thalers.

MASK. Debts of honour paid——

LELIO. They cannot have amounted to much more.

MASK. Another kind of debts of honour, which were not contracted at play—and yet they were, too—due to the good and honest Frau Lelane and her amiable nieces.

LELIO. Pass over that. For a hundred thalers one can buy a great many ribbons, shoe-buckles, and lace cuffs.

MASK. But your tailor——

LELIO. What, was he paid out of it?

MASK. Why no! he is not paid yet. And I——

LELIO. And you ? Yes, truly, I must reckon more for you than for the bill, or for Herr Stiletti, or for Frau Lelane.

MASK. No, no, sir; I was going to say that I have not

yet been paid, either. I have let my wages run on un-
paid for seven years.

Lelio. You have thereby had a seven years' licence to
cheat me in every possible way, and have known so well
how to make use of it——

Phil. (*coming up to them*). That finally the master
will have to wear the livery of the servant.

Mask. A prophecy! It surely came from heaven.
(*Looking round him.*) Ha! ha! Herr Philto, did it come
from you? I am too generous to wish you the fate of the
modern prophets. But if you have been listening to us,
say yourself, is it permitted that a poor servant, looking
for his wages for seven long years——

Phil. You should find your wages at the gallows.
Lelio, I would speak a word with you.

Lelio. Anything but reproaches, Herr Philto; I may
deserve them, but they are now too late.

Phil. Leander has made an offer, through his guardian,
Herr Staleno, to your sister.

Lelio. To my sister? That is good news indeed.

Phil. Undoubtedly it would be good news; but there
is a difficulty about the settlements. Staleno did not
know that you had got through everything. As soon as
I told him he withdrew his consent.

Lelio. What do you say?

Phil. I say that you have made your sister miserable.
The poor girl must now remain single through your
fault.

Mask. Not through his fault; but through the fault
of an old miser. I wish the deuce would fetch all selfish
guardians, and everything that looks like one (*looking
at* Philto.) Must a girl, then, have money, to become the
honourable wife of an honourable gentleman? And, at
all events, I know who might well give her a dowry.
There are people who are accustomed to buy houses cheap.

Lelio. (*thoughtful.*) Camilla is indeed to be pitied.
Her brother is a good-for-nothing vagabond.

Mask. You must settle that matter with yourself, if
you choose to abuse yourself. But, Herr Philto, a small
gift of a thousand thalers, in consideration of the cheap
purchase——

PHIL. Adieu, Lelio. You appear to be struck by the news I have given you. I will not interrupt good reflections.

MASK. And not willingly indulge in any yourself. Isn't that the case? Otherwise the small gift I spoke of would furnish an excellent subject.

PHIL. Maskarill, take care of my small gifts. The coin may not be of the sort to please you. (*Exit.*)

MASK. It must be worthless coin if it has not some value at the gaming table.

SCENE V.—MASKARILL, LELIO.

MASK. What is the matter now? Why, you hardly make such a sour phiz even when you count your trumps in a confounded bad hand . . . . And yet what will you bet that I don't know your thoughts? . . . . "Now, it is a cursed unlucky thing," think you, "that my sister should not marry the rich Leander." How I would like to have fleeced my new brother-in-law!

LELIO. (*still in thought*). Listen, Maskarill!

MASK. Well?—but I cannot hear you think, you must speak.

LELIO. Are you inclined to make good the numerous acts of roguery you have practised upon me, by one single honest deed?

MASK. A droll question! For what, then, do you take me? For a deceiver who is an honest man; or for an honest man who is a deceiver?

LELIO. My good, honest Maskarill, I take you for a man who might lend me a few thousand thalers, at least, were he only willing to lend me as much as he has robbed me of.

MASK. Oh! good, honest Maskarill! And what would you do with these few thousand thalers?

LELIO. Give them to my sister for her marriage portion, and afterwards I would shoot myself through the head.

MASK. Shoot yourself through the head! It is true that would not be running away with the money from me; but yet—— (*As if meditating.*)

Lelio.   You know, Maskarill, I love my sister.   I must therefore do all in my power for her now, if she is not to think ill of her brother for the rest of her life.   Be generous, and do not refuse me your assistance.

Mask.   You take me on my weak side.   I have a deuced propensity for generosity; and your fraternal affection, Herr Lelio, really quite enchants me.   It is altogether noble, altogether grand! and then your sister deserves it so truly.   And I feel myself constrained——

Lelio.   Oh! my good Maskarill! let me embrace you. Heaven grant that you may have cheated me out of a good large sum, that you may be able to lend me a good deal.   Could I ever have conceived that you possessed such a tender heart.   But tell me, how much can you lend me?

Mask.   I lend you, sir!

Lelio.   You need not say, "Sir."   Call me your friend; I at least shall consider you my best and only friend, till the day of my death.

Mask.   Heaven forbid!   Should I forget the respect which I owe to you on account of such a paltry trifling obligation?

Lelio.   What, Maskarill, you are not only generous you are modest also?

Mask.   Do not put my modesty to the blush.   I will lend you then, for ten years——

Lelio.   For ten years?   What unbounded kindness! For five years is sufficient, Maskarill; or for two years if you please.   Only lend me money, and make the time for payment as near as you will.

Mask.   Well then, I will lend you, for fifteen years——

Lelio.   I must let you have your own way, noble Maskarill.

Mask.   For fifteen years will I lend you, without any interest——

Lelio.   Without interest!   To that I can never consent. I will not pay less than fifty per cent. for the sum you lend.

Mask.   Without any interest, I say.

Lelio.   I am most thankful, Maskarill but forty per cent. you must take at any rate.

Mask.   Without any interest whatever——

Lelio.   Do you think I am mean enough to abuse your kindness? If you will be satisfied with thirty per cent., I shall consider it a proof of the greatest disinterestedness.

Mask.   Without interest, I say.

Lelio.   But I beg, Maskarill — consider, the most Christian of Jews would take twenty per cent.

Mask.   In a word, without interest, or else——

Lelio.   Well, then——

Mask.   Or the loan falls to the ground altogether.

Lelio.   Well, well, as you are determined that your kindness to me shall have no bounds whatever——

Mask.   Without interest——

Lelio.   Without interest! I really feel ashamed! Without interest, then, you lend me for fifteen years . . . . what? How much?

Mask.   I will lend you, without interest, for fifteen years, the hundred and seventy-five thalers which are owing to me from you for seven years' wages.

Lelio.   What do you say! the hundred and seventy-five thalers which I owe you——

Mask.   Constitute my whole fortune; and I am willing to let you have them, from the bottom of my heart, for fifteen years longer, without interest, without any interest!

Lelio.   And you really mean it, rascal?

Mask.   Rascal? That does not sound at all grateful.

Lelio.   I see now how we stand, you dishonourable, worthless, infamous rogue and deceiver.

Mask.   A wise man is equally indifferent to praise or blame, flattery or reproach. You have seen that before, and you see it again.

Lelio.   With what face can I go into the presence of my sister?

Mask.   With a shameless one, is my advice. One has never done anything dishonest, so long as one has the heart to justify one's conduct. "It is a misfortune for you, sister, I allow. But who can help it? May I die if I ever thought for a moment in my extravagance that I was spending your money at the same time." Something of that sort you must say to her, sir.

Lelio. (*after thinking a little time.*) Yes, that is the only thing. I will propose it to Staleno myself. Come, knave!

Mask. The way to your club where I am to accompany you is here.

Lelio. The devil take your club! But is not that Herr Staleno himself that I see coming this way?

SCENE VI.—STALENO, LELIO, MASKARILL.

Lelio. Sir, I was about to take the liberty of calling on you. I have learnt from Herr Philto the sentiments of your ward towards my sister. Do not consider me so depraved that it would not pain me beyond measure if she should remain single through my fault. It is true my excesses have brought me down terribly; but poverty which threatens me alarms me much less than the reproaches which I should have to make myself, on my beloved sister's account, if I did not endeavour, by all means in my power, to ward off from her, as much as is still possible, the misfortune which I have brought upon her through my folly. Consider, therefore, Herr Staleno, whether the offer which I am about to make deserves any attention. Perhaps it is not unknown to you, that my aged godmother left me in her will a tolerably comfortable farm. This I still have—though, as you may readily imagine, there is a mortgage on it—notwithstanding which it still brings in so much per annum that I could contrive to live upon it. I will give it over to my sister with pleasure. Your ward has money enough to pay the mortgage and make considerable improvements on it, of which it is capable. It might then be considered as no mean dowry, for want of which, as Herr Philto has told me, you alone oppose the match.

Mask. (*in a whisper to* Lelio). Are you mad, Herr Lelio?

Lelio. Silence!

Mask. The only property you still have left!

Lelio. Have I to account to you for it?

Mask. Are you going begging afterwards?

LELIO. I will do as I please.

STAL. (*aside*). I see how it is. Yes, Herr Lelio, it is true that I had to oppose the match on account of the total absence of dowry, willingly as I otherwise should have seen the marriage take place. So, if you are really in earnest in this proposition, I might still consider the matter.

LELIO. It is my settled determination, Herr Staleno.

MASK. Pray take back your word!

LELIO. Will you——

MASK. Just consider.——

LELIO. A word more, and——

STAL. First of all, Herr Lelio, you must make a plan of the farm to me, and an exact account of every debt you have on it. Then we will talk further of it.

LELIO. Certainly. I will go this instant and prepare both documents. When can I speak with you again?

STAL. You will always find me at home.

LELIO. Farewell for the present. (*Exit.*)

SCENE VII.—STALENO, MASKARILL.

MASK. (*aside*). Now I must do him a kindness against his will. How shall I begin? Hem! . . . . Stay for one moment, Herr Staleno——

STAL. What is it?

MASK. I look upon you as a man who knows how to set a proper value on a well-meant warning.

STAL. Then you look upon me as being what I am.

MASK. And for a man who does not imagine that a servant is betraying his master when he does not want to take part with him in everything.

STAL. Why certainly a servant should have as little share as possible in the evil his master does. But why do you say that? Has Lelio any design against me?

MASK. Be upon your guard; I beg, I conjure you. I conjure you, by everything that is dear to you in the world; by the happiness of your ward; by the honour of your grey hairs——

STAL. You speak indeed as one who conjures. But why am I to be upon my guard?

Mask. Because of the offer that Lelio has made you.

Stal. But why?

Mask. In short, you and your ward are both lost if you accept the farm. In the first place, I must tell you that he has mortgaged it for almost as much as the whole concern is worth.

Stal. Well, Maskarill, if it is only almost as much——

Mask. Right; something would be still to be gained from it. But only listen to what I have to tell you. The spot where the farm lies must be the very place where all the curses that ever have been uttered against the earth have flowed together.

Stal. You alarm me!

Mask. Whilst all the farmers in the neighbourhood have the most plentiful harvest, the fields belonging to this farm scarce return the seed. A murrain every year quite clears out the cattle sheds.

Stal. Then one must not keep cattle on the farm.

Mask. Herr Lelio thought so too, and for that reason, sold the bullocks and sheep, horses and pigs, poultry and pigeons a long time ago. But when the murrain cannot find cattle—what do you think?—it attacks the men.

Stal. You do not mean it!

Mask. Yes, indeed. No ploughboy has held out for half a year there, even with an iron constitution. Herr Lelio hired the strongest fellows that were to be found in the Wend country. But what use? The spring came; they were all dead.

Stal. Well, then, one must try the Pomeranians. They are people who can stand more than the Wends; men of stone and iron.

Mask. And the timber on the farm, Herr Staleno——

Stal. Well, the timber?

Mask. In the whole estate there is no tree to be found which has not either been struck by lightning——

Stal. Struck by lightning!

Mask. Or on which some one has not, at some time or other, hanged himself. Lelio is so enraged with the abominable timber that he is having it thinned every day. And—would you believe it?—he sells the wood which is cut there for half-price.

STAL.   That is bad.

MASK.   Why, he cannot do otherwise; for those who buy it, and attempt to burn it, are monstrous venture-some.   With some people it has blown up the ovens, with others it has sent such a pestiferous fume that the kitchen-maid, standing on the hearth, has fallen fainting into the arms of the cook.

STAL.   But, Maskarill, are you not telling me a parcel of lies?

MASK.   I do not tell a lie, sir, when I tell you that I cannot lie. . . .   And the ponds——

STAL.   What, the farm has ponds too?

MASK.   Yes, but ponds in which more men have been drowned than there are drops of water in them.   And so since the fish feed chiefly upon human bodies, you may easily conceive what sort of fish they must be.

STAL.   Large and fat fish, doubtless.

MASK.   Fish which, from the nature of their food, have acquired human reason, and therefore are not so silly as to be caught any more; if one lets the water off they dis-appear.   In a word, there can be no corner in the whole world where disadvantages, and misfortunes of all kinds, are to be met with, so certainly and in such numbers, as at this miserable farm.   Tradition tells us also, and history confirms it, that for some three hundred and fifty years— or even four hundred years—no one possessor of the pro-perty has died a natural death.

STAL.   Except the old godmother who left it to Lelio.

MASK.   One does not like to speak of it, but even the old godmother——

STAL.   Well?

MASK.   The old godmother was smothered at night by a black cat which she always had about her: and it is very probable—very probable—that this black cat was the devil!   Heaven knows how it will fare with my master.   It has been foretold to him that robbers would murder him.   I must allow, he takes the greatest pains to render this prophecy false, and to keep off the thieves from him by a generous sacrifice of all his property, but still——

STAL.   But still, Maskarill, I shall accept his offer.

Mask.   You will ? Oh, no, that I am sure you will not.

Stal.   Assuredly I will.

Mask. (*aside*).   The old fox.

Stal. (*aside*).   How I torture him ! The rogue ! (*Aloud*)
But, Maskarill, I thank you for your advice.   It may so far
profit me, that I may accept the farm for my ward and sell
it again directly.

Mask.   The best thing would be to have nothing to do
with it.   I have not told you nearly all yet.

Stal.   Save yourself the trouble ; I have no leisure
now.   Another time, Maskarill, I may listen to your nonsense again.   (*Exit.*)

Scene VIII.—Maskarill.

Mask.   All to no purpose.   Was I too stupid or he too
sharp ? Ah, well, I shall be the least loser.   If Lelio
wishes to part with everything, he may if he likes.   I can at
length manage without such a master as he is   My sheep
are safe in their fold.   What I now do for him, I shall do
out of pity.   He was always a trump ; and I should not
like him to fare so badly at last.   But march !—Ah ! Why,
there is a stranger.   I have not so much to do that I
cannot trouble myself about now people.   A useful thing
is curiosity.

Scene IX.—Anselmus, a Porter, Maskarill.

Ansel.   Heaven be praised, that I see my house, my
dear home, again at length !

Mask.   His house ?

Ansel. (*to the* Porter).   Put the trunk down here, my
good man.   I will have it taken in presently.—I have
paid you, haven't I ?

Por.   Oh, yes, sir ! Oh, yes ! But. . . . doubtless you
are pleased—very happy to be at home again.

Ansel.   That I am.

Por.   I have known people who would give a trifle
extra to a poor devil, when they were very happy.   But
you have paid me, sir, you have paid me.

Ansel.   Well, there ; I will give you a trifle extra.

Por. Ah! ah! I am right glad that I did not deceive myself: I took you at first sight for a generous gentleman. Oh! I can trust myself there. Heaven reward you. (*Exit.*)

Ansel. No one is visible about the house. I must knock.

Mask. The man is clearly mistaken.

Ansel. It seems as if all the household was dead. God forbid!

Mask. (*approaching him*). Sir, I beg pardon. Excuse me—(*falling back*). The deuce!.... I ought to know that face.

Ansel. May heaven forgive you your stupidity! But what do you want?

Mask. I wished. ... I wished——

Ansel. Well, what are you marching round me for?

Mask. I wished——

Ansel. To discover, perhaps, where my purse may best be got at.

Mask. I am wrong; if it was he, he would certainly know me too. I am curious, sir, but my curiosity is not uncivil, and with all modesty I beg to inquire what you want at this house?

Ansel. Fellow!.... But now I look at him. Mas——

Mask. Herr An——

Ansel. Maska——

Mask. Ansel——

Ansel. Maskarill.

Mask. Herr Anselmus.

Ansel. Is it really you?

Mask. It is I; there is no doubt of it. But you——

Ansel. No wonder that you doubt whether it is I.

Mask. Can it possibly be?—surely not! Herr Anselmus has been absent nine years; and it would be really extraordinary if he should return just to-day! Why should he return just to-day?

Ansel. You might ask that question every day; and at that rate I should never return at all.

Mask. That is true!— Well, then, a thousand welcomes, my dear Herr Anselmus. And yet, after all, it surely is not you?

Ansel. Really it is. And now answer me quick;
is all well? Are my children yet alive—Lelio, Camilla?

Mask. Now, indeed, I can no longer doubt if it be you.
They live, they both live. (*Aside*) If he could but hear
the rest of the story from some one else.

Ansel. God be thanked! that they both live still.
They are at home, I suppose? Quick, let me clasp them
in my aged arms! Bring the trunk after me, Maskarill.

Mask. Where to, Herr Anselmus, where to?

Ansel. Into the house.

Mask. Into this house?

Ansel. Into my house.

Mask. That won't exactly do. (*Aside*.) What shall
I say next?

Ansel. And why not?

Mask. This house, Herr Anselmus, is shut up.

Ansel. Shut up?

Mask. Shut up, yes; and for this reason — because
nobody lives in it.

Ansel. Nobody lives in it? Where, then, do my children live?

Mask. Herr Lelio, and Fräulein Camilla? They live
. . . . live in another house.

Ansel. Come! You speak so oddly, so enigmatically.

Mask. You do not know then what has happened
lately?

Ansel. How should I know?

Mask. True, you were not here; and in nine years
many changes may have taken place. Nine years! a long
time! And yet it is certainly very singular . . . . Nine
years, nine whole years away, and to return just at this
time! Now if that was to happen in a play, every one
would say, It is not probable that the old man would
return just at that time. And yet it is true! It was
possible that he should return at this time, and returned
at this time he has . . . . Singular, very singular!

Ansel. Oh, you infernal chatterer, detain me no longer,
but tell me——

Mask. I will tell you where your children are. Your
daughter is . . . . with your son; and your son is——

Ansel. And my son——

MASK. Has left this house, and lives . . . . there. do you see, down the street, that new corner-house? Your son lives there.

ANSEL. And why does not he live here still? Here, in the family mansion?

MASK. The family mansion was too large for him—too small. too roomy—too confined.

ANSEL. Too large, too small, too roomy, too confined. What does that mean?

MASK. In truth, you may learn better from himself how that is. So much you must at least have heard, that he has become a great merchant!

ANSEL. My son a great merchant?

MASK. A very great one! He has lived for more than a year upon nothing but what he has sold.

ANSEL. What do you say? Perhaps, then, he required a large house as a magazine for his goods?

MASK. Exactly so. exactly so.

ANSEL. That is excellent! I have also brought merchandise with me; valuable Indian goods.

MASK. That will be a grand sale!

ANSEL. Quick, Maskarill! Take the trunk upon your back and lead me to him.

MASK. The trunk, Herr Anselmus, is very heavy. I expect. Wait one moment. I will fetch a porter directly.

ANSEL. You can carry it yourself; it contains nothing but manuscripts and linen.

MASK. I have lately put my arm out.

ANSEL. Your arm? Poor devil! Then go and fetch some one.

MASK. (aside). Come, I got well out of that. Herr Lelio! Herr Lelio! what will you say to the news? (Exit, but returns.)

ANSEL. Well. have not you gone yet?

MASK. I must take one more look at you, to see if it really is you.

ANSEL. Doubt on, you desperate doubter!

MASK. (going). Yes. yes. it is he. Nine years away, and then to return just at this particular time!

Scene X.—Anselmus.

Ansel. I must wait here in the open air, I suppose. It is well the street is somewhat retired, and that very few people will recognise me. Still it will be as well to keep an eye to my trunk. Suppose I make a seat of it. Soon, very soon now, I trust I shall sit more at my ease. I have gone through so many dangers and difficulties that I can make my last days, days of rest and pleasure with a good conscience. Yes, yes, that they shall be. And who will blame me? I will just make a slight calculation : I possess—(*Speaking lower and lower, and finally counting on his fingers in silence.*)

Scene XI.—Raps (*in a strange foreign costume*), Anselmus.

Raps. One must be able to play every character. I should like to see the man who would know Drummer Raps in this get-up? I look like, I hardly know myself what ; and am meant to be, I do not know myself who. A foolish commission! foolish indeed ; but never mind that, I am paid for it. Staleno told me that I was to look for my man in this street. He lives near his old house; and that is it there.

Ansel. What hobgoblin is that?

Raps. How the people stare at me!

Ansel. This figure must belong to the mushroom tribe. His hat reaches half a yard on all sides beyond his body.

Raps. Good sir, you stare at me, are you less a stranger here than myself?— He won't hear. . . . . You, sir, sitting on the box, could you have the kindness to put me right? I am looking for a young gentleman of the name of Lelio ; and a baldpate of your kind, who answers to the name of Philto.

Ansel. Lelio! Philto! (*Aside.*) Why, these are the names of my son, and my good old friend.

Raps. If you can show me the house of these people you will gain the thanks of a man who will have it in his power to trumpet out your politeness at all the four

corners of the world—of a traveller who has been seven
times round the world, once by sea, twice by coach, and
four times on foot.

ANSEL. May I not know, sir, who you are—what is
your name—whence you came — what you want with
those you mention?

RAPS. That is a good deal at once. Which question
shall I answer first? If you would ask me each one separately, with politeness, I might, perhaps, impart some
information. For I am communicative, sir, very communicative. (*Aside.*) I may as well rehearse my part a
little with him.

ANSEL. Well then, sir, suppose we begin with the
shortest. What is your name?

RAPS. With the shortest? My name? Out, quite
out!

ANSEL. How so?

RAPS. Yes, my good old gentleman, I must tell you—
now attend to me: if you were to begin quite early, as
soon as the dawn begins to gray, with my first name, and
go on and on as quick as you could, I wager that the sun
would be down before you could arrive at the first letter
of my last name.

ANSEL. Indeed; then one wants a lantern and a wallet
with provisions for your name!

RAPS. Just so.

ANSEL. (*aside*). The fellow can talk! (*Aloud.*) But
what do you want with young Lelio, and old Philto?
Doubtless you have dealings with the former; Lelio is a
great merchant, I understand.

RAPS. A great merchant! I did not know that. No,
sir, I have only two or three letters for him.

ANSEL. Ah! ah! Advices, perhaps, of goods, which
have been dispatched to him, or something of that kind.

RAPS. Nothing of that kind. They are letters which
his father intrusted to me for him.

ANSEL. Who?

RAPS. His father.

ANSEL. Lelio's father?

RAPS. Yes, Lelio's father, now abroad. He is a great
friend of mine.

ANSEL. (*aside*). This man is, to put it politely, a scoundrel. Stop, I will soon catch you. (*Aloud.*) I gave him letters for my son?

RAPS. What do you say, sir?

ANSEL. Nothing. So you know Lelio's father?

RAPS. If I did not know him, should I have letters from him to his son Lelio, do you think, and letters to his friend Philto? There they are. He is my most intimate friend.

ANSEL. Your most intimate friend! And where was he, then, this your most intimate friend, when he gave you the letters?

RAPS. He was . . . . he was . . . . in capital health.

ANSEL. I am very glad to hear it. But where was he, where?

RAPS. Sir, he was . . . . on the coast of Paphlagonia.

ANSEL. Was he? You have told me you know him; of course you mean personally?

RAPS. To be sure. Have not I finished many a bottle of Cape wine with him, on the spot where it is grown? You know where I mean, on the promontory of Capua, where Hannibal, in the Thirty Years' War, drank so much that he could not march upon Rome.

ANSEL. You are a scholar, I see.

RAPS. In a small way.

ANSEL. Can you tell me what Lelio's father is like?

RAPS. What he is like! You are very inquisitive. But I am fond of inquisitive people. He is about a head taller than you are.

ANSEL. (*aside*). That is good! I am taller absent than I am present. You have not yet told me his name. What is it?

RAPS. He calls himself—precisely as an honourable man should call himself.

ANSEL. But let me hear——

RAPS. His name is. . . . his name is not the same as his son. . . . it would have been better if he had had the same name, but his name is. . . . Confound it.

ANSEL. Well?

RAPS. I believe I have forgotten his name.

ANSEL. What! the name of your friend?

RAPS. Only have patience. I have it at the tip of my tongue. Just mention any name that sounds something like it. It begins with an A.

ANSEL. Arnold, perhaps?

RAPS. No, not Arnold.

ANSEL. Anton?

RAPS. Nor Anton. Ans—Ansa—Ansi—Asi—Asinus. No! not Asinus, not Asinus. Confounded name! An—Ansel——

ANSEL. Not Anselmus?

RAPS. Right! Anselmus. Deuce take the rascally name!

ANSEL. That is not spoken like a friend.

RAPS. Then why does it stick between one's teeth so. Is that friendly, to let one hunt for it so long? I forgive it this once. Anselmus is his name, didn't you say? Yes, right! Anselmus. As I said, the last time I saw him was on the coast of Paphlagonia, in the harbour of Gibraltar. He was about to pay a short visit to the kings of Gallipoli.

ANSEL. The kings of Gallipoli? Who are they?

RAPS. What, sir, do you not know the far-famed brothers who reign in Gallipoli, the illustrious Dardanelles? Some twenty years back they made the tour of Europe, and he was then introduced to them.

ANSEL. (aside). This nonsense goes on too long; but I must discover the drift of it all.

RAPS. The court of the Dardanelles, sir, is one of the most splendid in all America; I am certain my friend Anselmus will be extremely well received there. He will not get away from it very soon either. Foreseeing this, and knowing that I was travelling here direct, he gave me some letters, to satisfy his family as to the cause of his long absence.

ANSEL. That was wisely done. But I have still one question to ask.

RAPS. As many as you will.

ANSEL. If, then, O most strange gentleman with the long name——

RAPS. My name is long, certainly; but I also have a very short one, the quintessence of the long one.

Ansel. May I venture to ask it?

Raps. Raps.

Ansel. Raps?

Raps. Yes, Raps, at your service.

Ansel. Much obliged by the offer of your services, Herr Raps.

Raps. Raps means, properly, the son of Rap. My father's name was Rap; my grandfather, Rip, from which my father was often wont to be called Rips; so that, if I wished to show off my descent, I might call myself Rips Raps.

Ansel. Well, Herr Riff Raff—to return to my question —if anyone was to show you your friend Anselmus now, would you know him again?

Raps. If I retained my eyesight, doubtless. But it seems as if you did not believe yet that I know Anselmus. Listen, therefore, to a proof which is above proof. Not only has he given me letters, but also six thousand thalers, which I am to hand over to Herr Philto. Would he have done that if I were not his second self?

Ansel. Six thousand thalers!

Raps. In good coins of full weight.

Ansel. (aside). I know not what to think of the fellow now. An impostor who brings money is a most extraordinary impostor.

Raps. But, sir, we chat here too long. I perceive you either cannot or will not show me my man.

Ansel. One word more! Herr Raps, have you the money about you which Herr Anselmus gave you?

Raps. Yes. Why?

Ansel. And it is a fact, that Anselmus, Lelio's father, gave you six thousand thalers.

Raps. Sure enough.

Ansel. Then give them back to me, Herr Raps.

Raps. Give what back to you?

Ansel. The six thousand thalers you got from me.

Raps. I six thousand thalers from you!

Ansel. You said so yourself.

Raps. What did I say? You are . . . . who are you, then?

Ansel. I am that person who gave six thousand thalers to Herr Raps. I am Anselmus.

RAPS.   You Anselmus?

ANSEL.   Do you not know me?   The kings of Gallipoli, the illustrious Dardanelles, have had the goodness to allow me to depart sooner than I expected.   And since I am now here myself, I will save Herr Raps any further trouble.

RAPS. *(aside).*   Now wouldn't one swear this man was a greater swindler than I am myself.

ANSEL.   Don't stand considering, but return me the money.

RAPS.   Who would believe that an old man could be so crafty!   As soon as he hears that I have money in my pocket; bang! he is Anselmus.   But, my good old gentleman, quick as you have Anselmised yourself, so quickly must you un-Anselmise yourself again.

ANSEL.   Who am I then, if I am not he whom I am?

RAPS.   What is that to me?   Be who you will, provided you are not he whom I don't wish you to be.   Why were you not at first he whom you are?   And why do you wish now to be he whom you were not at first?

ANSEL.   Go on, do!

RAPS.   What shall I do?

ANSEL.   Give me my money again.

RAPS.   Do not put yourself to any further inconvenience. I told a lie.   The money is not in gold, but only in paper.

ANSEL.   I shall soon begin in a different tone with you. You shall know in earnest, Herr Riff Raff, that I am Anselmus—and if you do not hand over to me instanter both the letters and the money that you had declared you had received from me, I will soon call together sufficient people to hold such an impostor fast.

RAPS.   Then you know for a certainty that I am an impostor?   And you are yourself for a certainty Herr Anselmus?   I have the honour then to wish Herr Anselmus good-day. *(Going.)*

ANSEL.   You shall not escape so easily, my friend.

RAPS.   Oh! pray, Sir . . . . (*When* ANSELMUS *endeavours to seize him,* RAPS *pushes him back, on to the trunk again.*) The old rascal might raise a tumult.   I will send someone to you who knows you better. *(Exit.)*

ANSEL. Here I sit again! Where is he gone, the rogue? .... where is he gone? .... I see nobody .... Have I fallen asleep on the trunk, and dreamt all this stuff? or .... hang it, dreamt or not, poor I! there is something in it; something in it without doubt! .... And Maskarill! Maskarill does not come back! .... That is not right either. .... What shall I do? I will call the first man I find. Hullo! my friend! hullo, there!

SCENE XII.—ANSELMUS, a PORTER.

POR. What do you want, Sir?

ANSEL. Do you wish to earn a good tip?

POR. That is just my business.

ANSEL. Take this trunk then quickly, and go with me to Lelio the merchant.

POR. To Lelio the merchant?

ANSEL. Yes. He lives in this street, I am told, in the new corner house.

POR. I know no merchant Lelio in all the town. Quite another sort of gentleman lives in the new corner house there.

ANSEL. Surely not! Lelio must live there. Otherwise he would have dwelt in this house, which also belongs to him.

POR. Now I see who you mean. You mean Lelio the rake. Oh! I know him, well!

ANSEL. What? Lelio the rake?

POR. Yes! so all the town calls him; why should I call him otherwise? Old Anselmus was his father. He was a nasty shabby chap, who could never get enough. He left here on his travels many years since: heaven knows for what place. Meantime, while he is toiling abroad, or perhaps is already under the ground, his son is enjoying himself here. He must now be getting gradually down to the dregs of his purse; but that is all right. A collector must have a distributor. I hear he has sold this house, too.

ANSEL. What! Sold? Now it's all clear! Ah! thou cursed Maskarill! .... Wretched father that I am! And, oh! wicked degenerate son!

Por.   Eh?   You surely are not old Anselmus himself!
Don't take it ill of me if you are.   I really did not know
you, or, I should have been careful not to call you a
nasty shabby chap.   It is not written on a man's forehead who he is.   I don't mind if you don't let me earn
the money you spoke of.

Ansel.   You shall earn it, my good man, you shall
earn it.   But tell me directly; is it really true that he
has sold this house?   And to whom has he sold it?

Por.   Old Philto has bought it.

Ansel.   Philto?   Oh! dishonourable man!   Is that thy
friendship? . . . . I am betrayed!   I am undone! . . . .
He will now deny everything.

Por.   The people looked upon it as bad enough on his
part that he had anything to do with the sale.   Was he
not to have acted as guardian to your son in your
absence?   A pretty guardian!   That is what I call giving
the goose into the care of the fox.   All his life he has
been considered a selfish man ; and a harpy always remains
a harpy. . . . . Why there he comes!   I must leave my
money behind for the present; people are so strange when
they hear that they are known.   (*Exit.*)

Scene XIII.—Anselmus, Philto.

Ansel.   Misfortune upon misfortune!   Come here,
traitor!

Phil.   I must see who has the insolence to pass himself
off for Anselmus. . . . . Ah! what do I see?   It is indeed
he. . . . . Your hand, my dearest friend.   So you have at
length returned again.   Heaven be praised! . . . . But
why so downcast?   Don't you know your friend, Philto,
again?

Ansel.   I know all, Philto!   I know all.   Is that a
trick which one expects from a friend?

Phil.   Not a word more, Anselmus.   I understand; an
officious slanderer has preceded me. . . . . This is not the
place to enter into explanations.   Come into your house.

Ansel.   Into my house?

Phil.   Yes, it is yours still, and never shall belong
to another against your will.   Fortunately I have the key

with me . . . . This is your trunk, I suppose? Take hold
we will carry it in ourselves; no one will see us.

Ansel. But my treasure?

Phil. That you will also find as you left it. (*They*
enter the house, pulling the trunk after them.)

Scene XIV.—Lelio, Maskarill.

Mask. Well! Have you seen him? Is it not Ansel
mus?

Lelio. It is he, Maskarill.

Mask. If the first meeting was but over!

Lelio. I never had such a lively sense of my own
worthlessness as now, when it prevents me going gladly
into the presence of a father who has always loved me so
tenderly. What shall I do? Shall I fly from him'
or shall I go and fall at his feet?

Mask. The last is not much use; but the first, no use
at all.

Lelio. Advise me, then! Name someone at least who
will intercede for me.

Mask. Someone who shall speak to your father in you
favour? . . . . Why, Herr Stiletti.

Lelio. Are you mad?

Mask. Or . . . . Frau Lelane.

Lelio. Villain!

Mask. One of her nieces.

Lelio. I will break your head!

Mask. Yes, that would be a great pleasure for you
father to find a murderer in his son.

Lelio. I dare not apply to old Philto. I have despised
his instruction, his warnings, his advice too often to b
able to lay any claim now to his good offices.

Mask. But does it not occur to you to ask me?

Lelio. You will have to seek an intercessor for your
self.

Mask. I have done that already, and you are the man

Lelio. I?

Mask. You! And out of gratitude to me, for providing
you with an advocate such as you might seek for ever in vain.

Lelio. If you do that, Maskarill——

Mask. Just come aside; the old folks might come out again.

Lelio. But name the intercessor, than whom I might for ever seek in vain for a better.

Mask. Why, your father shall be your intercessor with Herr Anselmus.

Lelio. What do you mean?

Mask. I mean that I have a plan which I cannot here explain to you. Come! (*Exeunt.*)

Scene XV.—Anselmus, Philto (*coming out of the house*).

Ansel. Well, that is true, Philto. A more trusty and prudent friend than yourself could not be found in the world. I thank you a thousand times, and only wish I could repay your services.

Phil. They are sufficiently repaid if they have your approval.

Ansel. I am aware that you must have suffered much calumny on my account.

Phil. What do calumnies matter, when one feels convinced one has not deserved them! I hope also you approve of the trick which I intended to make use of, with regard to the dowry?

Ansel. It was capitally planned; I am only sorry nothing can come of the affair.

Phil. Nothing come of it! Why not? Ah! it is well you come, Herr Staleno.

Scene XVI.—Staleno, Anselmus, Philto.

Stal. Is it indeed true that Anselmus has returned at length? Welcome! welcome!

Ansel. I am glad to see a good old friend again in health. But I am not glad that the first thing which I must say to him should be a refusal of his proposal. Philto has told me of your ward's wishes with respect to my daughter. Without knowing him I should say "yes" to it, merely out of regard for you, if I had not already promised my daughter to the son of an old friend who died abroad some short time back. I gave him my

word, upon his death-bed, that I would make his son,
who lives here somewhere, mine also. He has even left
his request in writing, and it must be one of my first acts
to find out young Leander, and give him this intelligence.

Stal.   Who? young Leander? Ah! that is my ward.

Ansel.   Leander your ward? Old Pandolfo's son?

Stal.   Leander, old Pandolfo's son, is my ward.

Ansel.   And this Leander was to marry my daughter?

Phil.   The same.

Ansel.   What good luck! Could I have wished it
better? Now then, I confirm the promise Philto made you
in my name. Come, let me see your ward, and embrace
my dear daughter. Ah! if I had not such a dissolute
son, what an enviable man I should be!

Scene XVII.—Maskarill, Anselmus, Philto, Staleno.

Mask.   Oh! ill luck! unexpressible ill luck! Where
shall I find poor Anselmus?

Ansel.   Is not that Maskarill? What says the rascal?

Mask.   Oh! unhappy father, what will you say to this
news?

Ansel.   To what news?

Mask.   Ah! ill-fated Lelio!

Ansel.   Well, what has happened to him?

Mask.   Ah! miserable accident!

Ansel.   Maskarill!

Mask.   Ah! tragic occurrence!

Ansel.   Tragic? Torture me no longer, fellow, but
tell me what is the matter.

Mask.   Ah! Herr Anselmus, your son——

Ansel.   Well? my son!

Mask.   When I went to announce your happy arrival,
I found him supported on his arm in an arm-chair——

Ansel.   At the last gasp, perhaps?

Mask.   Gasping he was, for he had just finished a long
draught of Hungarian wine. " Rejoice, Herr Lelio," said
I, " your dear, and anxiously longed-for father has just
returned." " What, my father?"—Here the bottle fell
from his hand through alarm ; it broke in pieces, and the

costly contents flowed upon the dusty floor.—"What," he
exclaimed again, "my father returned! What will become of me now?" "What you have deserved?" said I.
He sprang on his feet, ran to the window that looks
over the river, tore it open——

ANSEL. And threw himself out?

MASK. And looked what sort of a day it was. "Quick,
my sword!"—I did not wish to give him his sword, because one has examples that much evil has been done with
a sword. "What do you want with your sword, Herr
Lelio?" "Detain me not, or——" He spake the "or"
with such a terrific tone of voice, that I gave him the
sword out of fear. He took it, and——

ANSEL. And turned it against himself?

MASK. And——

ANSEL. Ah! unhappy father that I am!

SCENE XVIII.—LELIO (*at the back of the stage*), *the rest
as before.*

MASK. And buckled it on. "Come, Maskarill," he
cried, "my father will be enraged against me, and his
anger is not to be supported. I will not live longer without being reconciled to him." He rushed down the staircase, dashed helter-skelter out of the house, and threw
himself not far from here (*whilst* MASKARILL *speaks, and*
ANSELMUS *is turned towards him,* LELIO *falls at his feet on the
other side*)—at his father's feet.

LELIO. Forgive me, dearest father, for trying by such
means whether your heart can still feel any compassion
towards me. The most dreadful fate which you feared
on my account will surely happen to me, if I must rise
from your feet without obtaining your forgiveness. I
acknowledge that I am not worthy of your affection, but
without it I will not live. Youth and inexperience may
excuse much.

PHIL. Allow yourself to be moved, Anselmus.

STAL. I also petition for him. He will reform.

ANSEL. Could I but think so. Rise, I will give you
another trial. If, however, you hereafter commit an
unworthy action, consider that I have forgiven you no-

thing; the least excess of which you may be guilty, will
bring certain punishment for all the rest with it.

Mask.   That is just.

Ansel.   You must forthwith send that worthless Maskarill packing.

Mask.   That is unjust! . . . . However, send me away or
keep me, it is all one; only pay me first the money which
I have already lent you for seven years, and which I
generously offered to lend you for ten more.

———————————

MINNA VON BARNHELM;

OR,

THE SOLDIER'S FORTUNE.

(A COMEDY IN FIVE ACTS.)

Minna von Barnhelm, on which Lessing had been working for some time, was completed during his fourth residence in Berlin, in the year 1765. It was first acted in Hamburg in 1767, but met with little success. In the following year, however, when acted in Berlin, it immediately became very popular. In 1789 it was produced at the Haymarket Theatre, under the title of ' The Disbanded Officer,'

DRAMATIS PERSONÆ.

MAJOR VON TELLHEIM, *a discharged officer.*

MINNA VON BARNHELM.

COUNT VON BRUCHSAL, *her uncle.*

FRANZISKA, *her lady's maid.*

JUST, *servant to the* MAJOR.

PAUL WERNER, *An old Sergeant of the* MAJOR'S.

The LANDLORD *of an Inn.*

A LADY.

An ORDERLY.

RICCAUT DE LA MARLINIÈRE.

The scene alternates between the Parlour of an Inn, and a Room adjoining it.

MINNA VON BARNHELM.

ACT I.

SCENE I.—JUST.

JUST. (*sitting in a corner, and talking while asleep*). Rogue of a landlord! *You* treat *us* so? On, comrade! hit hard! (*He strikes with his fist, and wakes through the exertion.*) Ha! there he is again! I cannot shut an eye without fighting with him. I wish he got but half the blows. Why, it is morning! I must just look for my poor master at once; if I can help it, he shall not set foot in the cursed house again. I wonder where he has passed the night?

SCENE II.—LANDLORD, JUST.

LAND. Good-morning, Herr Just; good-morning! What, up so early! Or shall I say—up so late?

JUST. Say which you please.

LAND. I say only—good-morning! and that deserves, I suppose, that Herr Just should answer "Many thanks."

JUST. Many thanks.

LAND. One is peevish, if one can't have one's proper rest. What will you bet the Major has not returned home, and you have been keeping watch for him?

JUST. How the man can guess everything!

LAND. I surmise, I surmise.

JUST. (*turns round to go*). Your servant!

LAND. (*stops him*). Not so, Herr Just!

JUST. Very well, then, not your servant!

LAND. What, Herr Just, I do hope you are not still

angry about yesterday's affair! Who would keep his anger over night?

JUST. I; and over a good many nights.

LAND. Is that like a Christian?

JUST. As much so as to turn an honourable man who cannot pay to a day, out of doors, into the street.

LAND. Fie! who would be so wicked?

JUST. A Christian innkeeper.—My master! such a man! such an officer!

LAND. I thrust him from the house into the streets? I have far too much respect for an officer to do that, and far too much pity for a discharged one! I was obliged to have another room prepared for him. Think no more about it, Herr Just. (*Calls*)—Hullo! I will make it good in another way. (*A lad comes.*) Bring a glass; Herr Just will have a drop; something good.

JUST. Do not trouble yourself, Mr. Landlord. May the drop turn to poison, which .... But I will not swear; I have not yet breakfasted.

LAND. (*to the lad, who brings a bottle of spirits and a glass*). Give it here; go! Now, Herr Just; something quite excellent; strong, delicious, and wholesome. (*Fills, and holds it out to him.*) That can set an over-taxed stomach to rights again!

JUST. I hardly ought!—And yet why should I let my health suffer on account of his incivility? (*Takes it, and drinks.*)

LAND. May it do you good, Herr Just!

JUST. (*giving the glass back*). Not bad! But, Landlord, you are nevertheless an ill-mannered brute!

LAND. Not so, not so! .... Come, another glass; one cannot stand upon one leg.

JUST. (*after drinking*). I must say so much — it is good, very good! Made at home, Landlord?

LAND. At home, indeed! True Dantzig, real double distilled!

JUST. Look ye, Landlord; if I could play the hypocrite, I would do so for such stuff as that; but I cannot, so it must out.—You are an ill-mannered brute all the same.

LAND. Nobody in my life ever told me that before. .... But another glass, Herr Just; three is the lucky number!

Just. With all my heart! — (*Drinks.*) Good stuff indeed, capital! But truth is good also, and indeed, Landlord, you are an ill-mannered brute all the same!

Land. If I was, do you think I should let you say so?

Just. Oh! yes; a brute seldom has spirit.

Land. One more, Herr Just: a four-stranded rope is the strongest.

Just. No, enough is as good as a feast! And what good will it do you, Landlord? I shall stick to my text till the last drop in the bottle. Shame, Landlord, to have such good Dantzig, and such bad manners! To turn out of his room, in his absence—a man like my master, who has lodged at your house above a year; from whom you have had already so many shining thalers; who never owed a heller in his life—because he let payment run for a couple of months, and because he does not spend quite so much as he used.

Land. But suppose I really wanted the room and saw beforehand that the Major would willingly have given it up if we could only have waited some time for his return! Should I let strange gentlefolk like them drive away again from my door? Should I wilfully send such a prize into the clutches of another innkeeper? Besides, I don't believe they could have got a lodging elsewhere. The inns are all now quite full. Could such a young, beautiful, amiable lady remain in the street? Your master is much too gallant for that. And what does he lose by the change? Have not I given him another room?

Just. By the pigeon-house, at the back, with a view between a neighbour's chimneys.

Land. The view was uncommonly fine, before the confounded neighbour obstructed it. The room is otherwise very nice, and is papered——

Just. Has been!

Land. No, one side is so still. And the little room adjoining, what is the matter with that? It has a chimney which, perhaps, smokes somewhat in the winter——

Just. But does very nicely in the summer. I believe, Landlord, you are mocking us into the bargain!

Land. Come, come; Herr Just, Herr Just——

JUST.   Don't make Herr Just's head hot——

LAND.   I make his head hot ?   It is the Dantzig does that.

JUST.   An officer, like my master!   Or do you think that a discharged officer is not an officer, who may break your neck for you?   Why were you all, you Landlords, so civil during the war?   Why was every officer an honourable man then, and every soldier a worthy, brave fellow?   Does this bit of a peace make you so bumptious?

LAND.   What makes you fly out so, Herr Just!

JUST.   I will fly out.

SCENE III.—MAJOR VON TELLHEIM, LANDLORD, JUST.

MAJ. T. (*entering*).   Just!

JUST. (*supposing the* LANDLORD *is still speaking*).   JUST? Are we so intimate ?

MAJ. T.   Just!

JUST.   I thought I was "Herr Just" with you.

LAND. (*seeing the* MAJOR).   Hist! hist!   Herr Just, Herr Just, look round ; your master——

MAJ. T.   Just, I think you are quarrelling!   What did I tell you?

LAND.   Quarrel, your honour?   God forbid!   Would your most humble servant dare to quarrel with one who has the honour of being in your service?

JUST.   If I could but give him a good whack on that cringing cat's back of his!

LAND.   It is true Herr Just speaks up for his master, and rather warmly ; but in that he is right. I esteem him so much the more : I like him for it.

JUST.   I should like to knock his teeth out for him !

LAND.   It is only a pity that he puts himself in a passion for nothing.   For I feel quite sure that your honour is not displeased with me in this matter, since— necessity—made it necessary——

MAJ. T.   More than enough, sir !   I am in your debt ; you turn out my room in my absence.   You must be paid, I must seek a lodging elsewhere.   Very natural.

LAND.   Elsewhere?   You are going to quit, honoured sir ?   Oh unfortunate stricken man that I am.   No, never !

Sooner shall the lady give up the apartments again. The
Major cannot and will not let her have his room. It is
his; she must go; I cannot help it. I will go, honoured
sir——

Maj. T. My friend, do not make two foolish strokes
instead of one. The lady must retain possession of the
room——

Land. And your honour could suppose that from distrust, from fear of not being paid, I . . . . As if I did not
know that your honour could pay me as soon as you pleased.
The sealed purse . . . . five hundred thalers in louis d'ors
marked on it—which your honour had in your writing-desk
. . . . is in good keeping.

Maj. T. I trust so; as the rest of my property. Just
shall take them into his keeping, when he has paid your
bill——

Land. Really, I was quite alarmed when I found the
purse. I always considered your honour a methodical
and prudent man, who never got quite out of money . . . .
but still, had I supposed there was ready money in the
desk——

Maj. T. You would have treated me rather more
civilly. I understand you. Go, sir; leave me. I wish
to speak with my servant.

Land. But, honoured sir——

Maj. T. Come, Just; he does not wish to permit me
give my orders to you in his house.

Land. I am going, honoured sir! My whole house is
at your service. (*Exit.*)

Scene IV.—Major von Tellheim, Just.

Just. (*stamping with his foot and spitting after the* Landlord). Ugh!

Maj. T. What is the matter?

Just. I am choking with rage.

Maj. T. That is as bad as from plethora.

Just. And for you, sir, I hardly know you any longer.
May I die before your eyes, if you do not encourage
this malicious, unfeeling wretch. In spite of gallows,

axe, and torture I could . . . . yes, I could have throttled
him with these hands, and torn him to pieces with these
teeth!

MAJ. T.   You wild beast!

JUST.   Better a wild beast than such a man!

MAJ. T.   But what is it that you want?

JUST.   I want you to perceive how much he insults
you.

MAJ. T.   And then——

JUST.   To take your revenge. . . . . No, the fellow is
beneath your notice!

MAJ. T.   But to commission you to avenge me?   That
was my intention from the first.   He should not have
seen me again, but have received the amount of his bill
from your hands.   I know that you can throw down a
handful of money with a tolerably contemptuous mien.

JUST.   Oh! a pretty sort of revenge!

MAJ. T.   Which, however, we must defer.   I have not
one heller of ready money, and I know not where to
raise any.

JUST.   No money!   What is that purse then with five
hundred dollars' worth of louis d'ors, which the Landlord
found in your desk?

MAJ. T.   That is money given into my charge.

JUST.   Not the hundred pistoles which your old sergeant
brought you four or five weeks back?

MAJ. T.   The same.   Paul Werner's; right.

JUST.   And you have not used them yet?   Yet, sir,
you may do what you please with them.   I will answer
for it that——

MAJ. T.   Indeed!

JUST.   Werner heard from me, how they had treated
your claims upon the War Office.   He heard——

MAJ. T.   That I should certainly be a beggar soon, if
I was not one already.   I am much obliged to you, Just.
And the news induced Werner to offer to share his little
all with me.   I am very glad that I guessed this.   Listen,
Just; let me have your account, directly too; we must part.

JUST.   How! what!

MAJ. T.   Not a word.   There is someone coming.

SCENE V.—LADY *in mourning*, MAJOR VON TELLHEIM, JUST.

LADY. I ask your pardon, sir.

MAJ. T. Whom do you seek, Madam?

LADY. The worthy gentleman with whom I have the honour of speaking. You do not know me again? I am the widow of your late captain.

MAJ. T. Good heavens, Madam, how you are changed!

LADY. I have just risen from a sick bed, to which grief on the loss of my husband brought me. I am troubling you at a very early hour, Major von Tellheim, but I am going into the country, where a kind, but also unfortunate friend, has for the present offered me an asylum.

MAJ. T. (*to* JUST). Leave us.

SCENE VI.—LADY, MAJOR VON TELLHEIM.

MAJ. T. Speak freely, Madam! You must not be ashamed of your bad fortune before me. Can I serve you in any way?

LADY. Major——

MAJ. T. I pity you, Madam! How can I serve you? You know your husband was my friend; my friend, I say, and I have always been sparing of this title.

LADY. Who knows better than I do how worthy you were of his friendship—how worthy he was of yours? You would have been in his last thoughts, your name would have been the last sound on his dying lips, had not natural affection, stronger than friendship, demanded this sad prerogative for his unfortunate son, and his unhappy wife.

MAJ. T. Cease, Madam! I could willingly weep with you; but I have no tears to-day. Spare me! You come to me at a time when I might easily be misled to murmur against Providence. Oh! honest Marloff! Quick, Madam, what have you to request? If it is in my power to assist you, if it is in my power——

LADY. I cannot depart without fulfilling his last wishes. He recollected, shortly before his death, that he was dying a debtor to you, and he conjured me to discharge his debt with the first ready money I should have. I have sold his carriage, and come to redeem his note.

MAJ. T. What, Madam! Is that your object in coming?

LADY. It is. Permit me to count out the money to you.

MAJ. T. No, Madam. Marloff a debtor to me! that can hardly be. Let us look, however. (*Takes out a pocket-book, and searches.*) I find nothing of the kind.

LADY. You have doubtless mislaid his note; besides, it is nothing to the purpose. Permit me——

MAJ. T. No, Madam; I am careful not to mislay such documents. If I have not got it, it is a proof that I never had it, or that it has been honoured and already returned by me.

LADY. Major!

MAJ. T. Without doubt, Madam; Marloff does not owe me anything—nor can I remember that he ever did owe me anything. This is so, Madam. He has much rather left me in his debt. I have never been able to do anything to repay a man who shared with me good and ill luck, honour and danger, for six years. I shall not forget that he has left a son. He shall be my son, as soon as I can be a father to him. The embarrassment in which I am at present——

LADY. Generous man! But do not think so meanly of me. Take the money, Major, and then at least I shall be at ease.

MAJ. T. What more do you require to tranquillize you, than my assurance that the money does not belong to me? Or do you wish that I should rob the young orphan of my friend? Rob, Madam; for that it would be in the true meaning of the word. The money belongs to him: invest it for him.

LADY. I understand you; pardon me if I do not yet rightly know how to accept a kindness. Where have you learnt that a mother will do more for her child than for the preservation of her own life? I am going——

MAJ. T. Go, Madam, and may you have a prosperous journey! I do not ask you to let me hear from you. Your news might come to me when it might be of little use to

me. There is yet one thing, Madam ; I had nearly forgotten that which is of most consequence. Marloff also had
claims upon the chest of our old regiment. His claims
are as good as mine. If my demands are paid, his must
be paid also. I will be answerable for them.

LADY. Oh! Sir .... but what can I say ? Thus to purpose future good deeds is, in the eyes of heaven, to have
performed them already. May you receive its reward, as
well as my tears. (*Exit.*)

Scene VII.—Major von Tellheim.

MAJ. T. Poor, good woman! I must not forget to
destroy the bill. (*Takes some papers from his pocketbook
and destroys them*). Who would guarantee that my own
wants might not some day tempt me to make use of it?

Scene VIII.—Just, Major von Tellheim.

MAJ. T. Is that you, Just?

JUST. (*wiping his eyes*). Yes.

MAJ. T. You have been crying?

JUST. I have been writing out my account in the
kitchen, and the place is full of smoke. Here it is, sir.

MAJ. T. Give it to me.

JUST. Be merciful with me, sir. I know well that
they have not been so with you; still——

MAJ. T. What do you want?

JUST. I should sooner have expected my death, than
my discharge.

MAJ. T. I cannot keep you any longer: I must learn
to manage without servants. (*Opens the paper, and reads*).
" What my master, the Major, owes me :—Three months
and a half wages, six thalers per month, is 21 thalers.
During the first part of this month, laid out in sundries—
1 thaler 7 groschen 9 pfennigs. Total, 22 thalers 7gr.
9pf." Right; and it is just that I also pay your wages, for
the whole of the current month.

JUST. Turn over, sir.

MAJ. T. Oh! more? (*Reads.*) " What I owe my
master, the Major :—Paid for me to the army-surgeon,

twenty-five thalers. Attendance and nurse during my cure, paid for me, thirty-nine thalers. Advanced, at my request, to my father—who was burnt out of his house and robbed—without reckoning the two horses of which he made him a present, fifty thalers. Total 114 thalers. Deduct the above 22 thalers, 7gr. 9pf.; I remain in debt to my master, the Major, 91 thalers, 16gr. 3pf." You are mad, my good fellow!

JUST. I willingly grant that I owe you much more; but it would be wasting ink to write it down. I cannot pay you that: and if you take my livery from me too, which, by the way, I have not yet earned,—I would rather you had let me die in the workhouse.

MAJ. T. For what do you take me? You owe me nothing; and I will recommend you to one of my friends, with whom you will fare better than with me.

JUST. I do not owe you anything, and yet you turn me away!

MAJ. T. Because I do not wish to owe you anything.

JUST. On that account? Only on that account? As certain as I am in your debt, as certain as you can never be in mine, so certainly shall you not turn me away now. Do what you will, Major, I remain in your service; I must remain.

MAJ. T. With your obstinacy, your insolence, your savage boisterous temper towards all who you think have no business to speak to you, your malicious pranks, your love of revenge,——

JUST. Make me as bad as you will, I shall not think worse of myself than of my dog. Last winter I was walking one evening at dusk along the river, when I heard something whine. I stooped down, and reached in the direction whence the sound came, and when I thought I was saving a child, I pulled a dog out of the water. That is well, thought I. The dog followed me; but I am not fond of dogs, so I drove him away—in vain. I whipped him away—in vain. I shut him out of my room at night; he lay down before the door. If he came too near me, I kicked him; he yelped, looked up at me, and wagged his tail. I have never yet given him a bit of bread with my own hand; and yet I am the only person whom he will obey, or who dare touch him. He jumps about me, and shows off his tricks to me, without my asking for them. He is an ugly dog, but he is a good animal. If he carries it on much longer, I shall at last give over hating him.

MAJ. T. (*aside*). As I do him. No, there is no one perfectly inhuman. Just, we will not part.

JUST. Certainly not! And you wanted to manage without servants! You forget your wounds, and that you only have the use of one arm. Why, you are not able to dress alone. I am indispensable to you; and I am—without boasting, Major,—I am a servant who, if the worst comes to the worst, can beg and steal for his master.

MAJ. T. Just, we will part.

JUST. All right, Sir!

SCENE IX.—SERVANT, MAJOR VON TELLHEIM, JUST.

SER. I say, comrade!

JUST. What is the matter?

SER. Can you direct me to the officer who lodged yesterday in that room? (*pointing to the one out of which he is coming*).

JUST. That I could easily do. What have you got for him?

SER. What we always have, when we have nothing— compliments. My mistress hears that he has been turned out on her account. My mistress knows good manners, and I am therefore to beg his pardon.

JUST. Well, then, beg his pardon; there he stands.

SER. What is he? What is his name?

MAJ. T. I have already heard your message, my friend. It is unnecessary politeness on the part of your mistress, which I beg to acknowledge duly. Present my compliments to her. What is the name of your mistress?

SER. Her name! We call her my lady.

MAJ. T. The name of her family?

SER. I have not heard that yet, and it is not my business to ask. I manage so that I generally get a new master every six weeks. Hang all their names!

JUST. Bravo, comrade!

SER. I was engaged by my present mistress a few

days ago, in Dresden. I believe she has come here to look for her lover.

MAJ. T. Enough, friend. I wished to know the name of your mistress, not her secrets. Go!

SER. Comrade, he would not do for my master.

SCENE X.—MAJOR VON TELLHEIM, JUST.

MAJ. T. Just! see that we get out of this house directly! The politeness of this strange lady affects me more than the churlishness of the host. Here, take this ring—the only thing of value which I have left—of which I never thought of making such a use. Pawn it! get eighty louis d'ors for it: our host's bill can scarcely amount to thirty. Pay him, and remove my things. . . . . Ah, where? Where you will. The cheaper the inn, the better. You will find me in the neighbouring coffee-house. I am going; you will see to it all properly?

JUST. Have no fear, Major!

MAJ. T. (*comes back*). Above all things, do not let my pistols be forgotten, which hang beside the bed.

JUST. I will forget nothing.

MAJ. T. (*comes back again*). Another thing: bring your dog with you too. Do you hear, Just?

SCENE XI.—JUST.

JUST. The dog will not stay behind, he will take care of that. Hem! My master still had this valuable ring! and carried it in his pocket instead of on his finger! My good landlord, we are not yet so poor as we look. To him himself, I will pawn you, you beautiful little ring! I know he will be annoyed that you will not all be consumed in his house. Ah!——

SCENE XII.—PAUL WERNER, JUST.

JUST. Hullo, Werner! good-day to you, Werner. Welcome to the town.

WER. The accursed village! I can't manage to get

at home in it again. Merry, my boys, merry; I have got some more money! Where is the Major?

JUST. He must have met you; he just went down stairs.

WER. I came up the back stairs. How is he? I should have been with you last week, but——

JUST. Well, what prevented you?

WER. Just, did you ever hear of Prince Heraclius?

JUST. Heraclius? Not that I know of.

WER. Don't you know the great hero of the East?

JUST. I know the wise men of the East well enough, who go about with the stars on New Year's Eve.*

WER. Brother, I believe you read the newspapers as little as the Bible. You do not know Prince Heraclius? Not know the brave man who seized Persia, and will break into the Ottoman Porte in a few days? Thank God, there is still war somewhere in the world! I have long enough hoped it would break out here again. But there they sit and take care of their skins. No, a soldier I was, and a soldier I must be again! In short (*looking round carefully, to see if anyone is listening*), between ourselves, Just, I am going to Persia, to have a few campaigns against the Turks, under his Royal Highness Prince Heraclius.

JUST. You?

WER. I myself. Our ancestors fought bravely against the Turks; and so ought we too, if we would be honest men and good Christians. I allow that a campaign against the Turks cannot be half so pleasant as one against the French; but then it must be so much the more beneficial in this world and the next. The swords of the Turks are all set with diamonds.

JUST. I would not walk a mile to have my head split with one of their sabres. You will not be so mad as to leave your comfortable little farm!

WER. Oh! I take that with me. Do you see? The property is sold.

JUST. Sold?

WER. Hist! Here are a hundred ducats, which I received yesterday towards the payment: I am bringing them for the Major.

* This refers to an old German custom.

JUST.   What is he to do with them?

WER.   What is he to do with them? Spend them ; play them, or drink them away, or whatever he pleases.   He must have money, and it is bad enough that they have made his own so troublesome to him.   But I know what I would do, were I in his place.   I would say—"The deuce take you all here ; I will go with Paul Werner to Persia!" Hang it! Prince Heraclius must have heard of Major von Tellheim, if he has not heard of Paul Werner, his late sergeant.   Our affair at Katzenhäuser——

JUST.   Shall I give you an account of that?

WER.   You give me! I know well that a fine battle array is beyond your comprehension.   I am not going to throw my pearls before swine.   Here, take the hundred ducats ; give them to the Major : tell him, he may keep these for me too.   I am going to the market now.   I have sent in a couple of loads of rye ; what I get for them he can also have.

JUST.   Werner, you mean it well ; but we don't want your money.   Keep your ducats ; and your hundred pistoles you can also have back safe, as soon as you please.

WER.   What, has the Major money still?

JUST.   No.

WER.   Has he borrowed any?

JUST.   No.

WER.   On what does he live, then?

JUST.   We have everything put down in the bill ; and when they won't put anything more down, and turn us out of the house, we pledge anything we may happen to have, and go somewhere else.   I say, Paul, we must play this landlord here a trick.

WER.   If he has annoyed the Major, I am ready.

JUST.   What if we watch for him in the evening, when he comes from his club, and give him a good thrashing?

WER.   In the dark! Watch for him! Two to one! No, that won't do.

JUST.   Or if we burn his house over his head?

WER.   Fire and burn! Why, Just, one hears that you have been baggage-boy and not soldier.   Shame!

JUST.   Or if we ruin his daughter? But she is cursedly ugly.

WER. She has probably been ruined long ago. At any rate you don't want any help there. But what is the matter with you? What has happened?

JUST. Just come with me, and you shall hear something to make you stare.

WER. The devil must be loose here, then?

JUST. Just so; come along.

WER. So much the better! To Persia, then; to Persia.

ACT II.

SCENE I.—*Minna's Room.* MINNA, FRANZISKA.

MIN. (*in morning dress, looking at her watch*). Franziska, we have risen very early. The time will hang heavy on our hands.

FRAN. Who can sleep in these abominable large towns? The carriages, the watchmen, the drums, the cats, the soldiers, never cease to rattle, to call, to roll, to mew, and to swear; just as if the last thing the night is intended for was for sleep. Have a cup of tea, my lady!

MIN. I don't care for tea.

FRAN. I will have some chocolate made.

MIN. For yourself, if you like.

FRAN. For myself! I would as soon talk to myself as drink by myself. Then the time will indeed hang heavy. For very weariness we shall have to make our toilets, and try on the dress in which we intend to make the first attack?

MIN. Why do you talk of attacks, when I have only come to require that the capitulation be ratified.

FRAN. But the officer whom we have dislodged, and to whom we have apologized, cannot be the best bred man in the world, or he might at least have begged the honour of being allowed to wait upon you.

MIN. All officers are not Tellheims. To tell you the truth, I only sent him the message in order to have an opportunity of inquiring from him about Tellheim.

Franziska, my heart tells me my journey will be a successful one and that I shall find him.

FRAN. The heart, my lady! One must not trust to that too much. The heart echoes to us the words of our tongues. If the tongue was as much inclined to speak the thoughts of the heart, the fashion of keeping mouths under lock and key would have come in long ago.

MIN. Ha! ha! mouths under lock and key. That fashion would just suit me.

FRAN. Rather not show the most beautiful set of teeth, than let the heart be seen through them every moment.

MIN. What, are you so reserved?

FRAN. No, my lady; but I would willingly be more so. People seldom talk of the virtue they possess, and all the more often of that which they do not possess.

MIN. Franziska, you made a very just remark there.

FRAN. Made! Does one make it, if it occurs to one?

MIN. And do you know why I consider it so good? It applies to my Tellheim.

FRAN. What would not, in your opinion, apply to him?

MIN. Friend and foe say he is the bravest man in the world. But who ever heard him talk of bravery? He has the most upright mind; but uprightness and noble-ness of mind are words never on his tongue.

FRAN. Of what virtues does he talk then?

MIN. He talks of none, for he is wanting in none.

FRAN. That is just what I wished to hear.

MIN. Wait, Franziska; I am wrong. He often talks of economy. Between ourselves, I believe he is extrava-gant.

FRAN. One thing more, my lady. I have often heard him mention truth and constancy towards you. What, if he be inconstant?

MIN. Miserable girl! But do you mean that seriously?

FRAN. How long is it since he wrote to you?

MIN. Alas! he has only written to me once since the peace.

FRAN. What—A sigh on account of the peace? Sur-prising! Peace ought only to make good the ill which war causes; but it seems to disturb the good which the

latter, its opposite, may have occasioned. Peace should
not be so capricious! . . . . How long have we had peace?
The time seems wonderfully long, when there is so little
news. It is no use the post going regularly again; nobody writes, for nobody has anything to write about.

Min. "Peace has been made," he wrote to me, "and I
am approaching the fulfilment of my wishes." But since
he only wrote that to me once, only once——

Fran. And since he compels us to run after this fulfilment of his wishes ourselves. . . . . If we can but find him,
he shall pay for this! Suppose, in the meantime, he
may have accomplished his wishes, and we should learn
here that——

Min. (*anxiously*). That he is dead?

Fran. To you, my lady; and married to another.

Min. You teaze, you! Wait, Franziska, I will pay
you out for this! But talk to me, or I shall fall asleep.
His regiment was disbanded after the peace. Who knows
into what a confusion of bills and papers he may thereby
have been brought? Who knows into what other regiment, or to what distant station, he may have been sent?
Who knows what circumstances——There's a knock at the
door.

Fran. Come in!

Scene II.—Landlord, Minna, Franziska.

Land. (*putting his head in at the door*). Am I permitted,
your ladyship?

Fran. Our landlord?—Come in!

Land. (*A pen behind his ear, a sheet of paper and an ink-
stand in his hand*). I am come, your ladyship, to wish you
a most humble good-morning; (*to* Franziska) and the same
to you, my pretty maid.

Fran. A polite man!

Min. We are obliged to you.

Fran. And wish you also a good-morning.

Land. May I venture to ask how your ladyship has
passed the first night under my poor roof?

Fran. The roof is not so bad, sir; but the beds might
have been better.

LAND. What do I hear! Not slept well! Perhaps the over-fatigue of the journey——

MIN. Perhaps.

LAND. Certainly, certainly, for otherwise . . . . Yet, should there be anything not perfectly comfortable, my lady, I hope you will not fail to command me.

FRAN. Very well, Mr. Landlord, very well! We are not bashful; and least of all should one be bashful at an inn. We shall not fail to say what we may wish.

LAND. I next come to . . . . (*taking the pen from behind his ear*).

FRAN. Well?

LAND. Without doubt, my lady, you are already acquainted with the wise regulations of our police.

MIN. Not in the least, sir.

LAND. We landlords are instructed not to take in any stranger, of whatever rank or sex he may be, for four-and-twenty hours, without delivering, in writing, his name, place of abode, occupation, object of his journey, probable stay, and so on, to the proper authorities.

MIN. Very well.

LAND. Will your ladyship then be so good . . . . (*going to the table, and making ready to write*).

MIN. Willingly. My name is——

LAND. One minute! (*He writes*) "Date, 22nd August, A.D., &c.; arrived at the King of Spain hotel." Now your name, my lady.

MIN. Fräulein von Barnhelm.

LAND. (*writes*). "Von Barnhelm." Coming from . . . . where, your ladyship?

MIN. From my estate in Saxony.

LAND. (*writes*). "Estate in Saxony." Saxony! Indeed, indeed! In Saxony, your ladyship? Saxony?

FRAN. Well, why not? I hope it is no sin in this country to come from Saxony!

LAND. A sin? Heaven forbid! That would be quite a new sin! From Saxony then? Yes, yes, from Saxony, a delightful country, Saxony! But if I am right, your ladyship, Saxony is not small, and has several—how shall I call them?—districts, provinces. Our police are very particular, your ladyship.

Min. I understand. From my estate in Thuringia, then.

Land. From Thuringia! Yes that is better, your ladyship; that is more exact. (*Writ nd reads*) " Fräulein von Barnhelm, coming from her tate in Thuringia, together with her lady in waiting and two men servants."

Fran. Lady in waiting! That means me, I suppose!

Land. Yes, my pretty maid.

Fran. Well, Mr. Landlord, instead of "lady in waiting," write "maid in waiting." You say, the police are very exact; it might cause a misunderstanding, which might give me trouble some day when my banns are read out. For I really am still unmarried, and my name is Franziska, with the family name of Willig : Franziska Willig. I also come from Thuringia. My father was a miller, on one of my lady's estates. It is called Little Rammsdorf. My brother has the mill now. I was taken very early to the manor, and educated with my lady. We are of the same age—one-and-twenty next Candlemas. I learnt everything my lady learnt. I should like the police to have a full account of me.

Land. Quite right, my pretty maid; I will bear that in mind, in case of future inquiries. But now, your ladyship, your business here?

Min. My business here?

Land. Have you any business with His Majesty the King?

Min. Oh! no.

Land. Or at our courts of justice?

Min. No.

Land. Or——

Min. No, no. I have come here solely on account of my own private affairs.

Land. Quite right, your ladyship; but what are those private affairs?

Min. They are .... Franziska, I think we are undergoing an examination.

Fran. Mr. Landlord, the police surely do not ask to know a young lady's secrets!

Land. Certainly, my pretty maid; the police wish to know everything, and especially secrets.

FRAN. What is to be done, my lady? .... Well, listen,
Mr. Lan lord—but take care that it does not go beyond
ourselves and the police.

MIN. What is the simpleton going to tell him?

FRAN. We come to carry off an officer from the king.

LAND. How? What? My dear girl!

FRAN. Or to let ourselves be carried off by the officer.
It is all one.

MIN. Franziska, are you mad? The saucy girl is
laughing at you.

LAND. I hope not! With your humble servant
indeed she may jest as much as she pleases; but with
the police——

MIN. I tell you what; I do not understand how to
act in this matter. Suppose you postpone the whole
affair till my uncle's arrival. I told you yesterday why
he did not come with me. He had an accident with his
carriage ten miles from here, and did not wish that I
should remain a night longer on the road, so I had to
come on. I am sure he will not be more than four-and-
twenty hours after us.

LAND. Very well, madam, we will wait for him.

MIN. He will be able to answer your questions better.
He will know to whom, and to what extent, he must give
an account of himself—what he must relate respecting
his affairs, and what he may withhold.

LAND. So much the better! Indeed one cannot expect
a young girl (*looking at* FRANZISKA *in a marked manner*)
to treat a serious matter with serious people in a serious
manner.

MIN. And his rooms are in readiness, I hope?

LAND. Quite, your ladyship, quite; except the one——

FRAN. Out of which, I suppose, you will have to turn
some other honourable gentleman!

LAND. The waiting maids of Saxony, your ladyship,
seem to be very compassionate.

MIN. In truth, sir, that was not well done. You
ought rather to have refused us.

LAND. Why so, your ladyship, why so?

MIN. I understand that the officer who was driven out
on our account——

LAND.   Is only a discharged officer, your ladyship.

MIN.   Well, what then?

LAND.   Who is almost done for.

MIN.   So much the worse! He is said to be a very deserving man.

LAND.   But I tell you he is discharged.

MIN.   The king cannot be acquainted with every deserving man.

LAND.   Oh! doubtless he knows them; he knows them all.

MIN.   But he cannot reward them all.

LAND.   They would have been rewarded if they had lived so as to deserve it.   But they lived during the war as if it would last for ever; as if the words "yours" and "mine" were done away with altogether.   Now all the hotels and inns are full of them, and a landlord has to be on his guard with them.   I have come off pretty well with this one.   If he had no more money, he had at any rate money's worth; and I might indeed have let him remain quiet two or three months longer.   However, it is better as it is.   By-the-by, your ladyship, you understand about jewels, I suppose?

MIN.   Not particularly.

LAND.   Of course your ladyship must.   I must show you a ring, a valuable ring.   I see you have a very beautiful one on your finger; and the more I look at it, the more I am astonished at the resemblance it bears to mine.   There! just look, just look! (*taking the ring from its case, and handing it to her.*) What brilliancy! The diamond in the middle alone weighs more than five carats.

MIN. (*looking at it*).   Good heavens! What do I see? This ring——

LAND.   Is honestly worth fifteen hundred thalers.

MIN.   Franziska! look!

LAND.   I did not hesitate for a moment to advance eighty pistoles on it.

MIN.   Do not you recognise it, Franziska?

FRAN.   The same! Where did you get that ring, Mr. Landlord?

LAND.   Come, my girl! you surely have no claim to it?

FRAN.   We have no claim to this ring! My mistress's

monogram must be on it, on the inner side of the setting.
Look at it, my lady.

MIN.   It is! it is! How did you get this ring?

LAND.   I! In the most honourable way in the world.
You do not wish to bring me into disgrace and trouble,
your ladyship! How do I know where the ring properly
belongs? During the war many a thing often changed
masters, both with and without the knowledge of its
owner. War was war. Other rings will have crossed the
borders of Saxony. Give it me again, your ladyship;
give it me again!

FRAN.   When you have said from whom you got it.

LAND.   From a man whom I cannot think capable of
such things; in other respects a good man——

MIN.   From the best man under the sun, if you have it
from its owner. Bring him here directly! It is himself,
or at any rate he must know him.

LAND.   Who? who, your ladyship?

FRAN.   Are you deaf? Our Major!

LAND.   Major! Right! he is a Major, who had this
room before you, and from whom I received it.

MIN.   Major von Tellheim!

LAND.   Yes, Tellheim. Do you know him?

MIN.   Do I know him! He is here! Tellheim here!
He had this room! He! he pledged this ring with
you! What has brought him into this embarrassment?
Where is he? Does he owe you anything? Franziska,
my desk here! Open it! (FRANZISKA *puts it on the table
and opens it*). What does he owe you? To whom else
does he owe anything? Bring me all his creditors! Here
is gold: here are notes. It is all his!

LAND.   What is this?

MIN.   Where is he? Where is he?

LAND.   An hour ago he was here.

MIN.   Detested man! how could you act so rudely, so
hardly, so cruelly towards him?

LAND.   Your ladyship must pardon——

MIN.   Quick! Bring him to me.

LAND.   His servant is perhaps still here. Does your
ladyship wish that he should look for him?

MIN.   Do I wish it? Begone, run. For this service

alone I will forget how badly you have behaved to him.

FRAN. Now then, quick, Mr. Landlord! Be off! fly! fly! (*Pushes him out.*)

SCENE III.—MINNA, FRANZISKA.

MIN. Now I have found him again, Franziska! Do you hear? Now I have found him again! I scarcely know where I am for joy! Rejoice with me, Franziska. But why should you? And yet you shall; you must rejoice with me. Come, I will make you a present, that you may be able to rejoice with me. Say, Franziska, what shall I give you? Which of my things would please you? What would you like? Take what you will; only rejoice with me. I see you will take nothing. Stop! (*Thrusts her hand into the desk.*) There, Franziska (*gives her money*), buy yourself what you like. Ask for more, if it be not sufficient; but rejoice with me you must. It is so melancholy to be happy alone. There, take it, then.

FRAN. It is stealing it from you, my lady. You are intoxicated, quite intoxicated with joy.

MIN. Girl, my intoxication is of a quarrelsome kind. Take it, or (*forcing money into her hand*) . . . . and if you thank me . . . . Stay, it is well that I think of it. (*Takes more money from the desk.*) Put that aside, Franziska, for the first poor wounded soldier who accosts us.

SCENE IV.—LANDLORD, MINNA, FRANZISKA.

MIN. Well, is he coming?

LAND. The cross, unmannered fellow!

MIN. Who?

LAND. His servant. He refuses to go for him.

FRAN. Bring the rascal here, then. I know all the Major's servants. Which of them was it?

MIN. Bring him here directly. When he sees us he will go fast enough. (*Exit LANDLORD.*)

SCENE V.—MINNA, FRANZISKA.

MIN. I cannot bear this delay. But, Franziska, how cold you are still! Why will you not share my joy with me?

FRAN. I would from my heart, if only——

MIN. If only what?

FRAN. We have found him again. But how have we found him? From all we hear, it must go badly with him. He must be unfortunate. That distresses me.

MIN. Distresses you! Let me embrace you for that, my dear playmate! I shall never forget this of you. I am only in love, *you* are good.

SCENE VI.—LANDLORD, JUST, *and the above.*

LAND. With great difficulty I have brought him.

FRAN. A strange face! I do not know him.

MIN. Friend, do you live with Major von Tellheim?

JUST. Yes.

MIN. Where is your master?

JUST. Not here.

MIN. But you could find him?

JUST. Yes.

MIN. Will you fetch him quickly?

JUST. No.

MIN. You will be doing me a favour

JUST. Indeed!

MIN. And your master a service.

JUST. Perhaps not.

MIN. Why do you suppose that?

JUST. You are the strange lady who sent your compliments to him this morning, I think?

MIN. Yes.

JUST. Then I am right.

MIN. Does your master know my name?

JUST. No; but he likes over-civil ladies as little as over-uncivil landlords.

LAND. That is meant for me, I suppose?

JUST. Yes.

LAND. Well, do not let the lady suffer for it then; but bring him here directly.

MIN. (*to* FRANZISKA.) Franziska, give him something——

Fran. (*trying to put some money into* Just's *hand*). We do not require your services for nothing.

Just. Nor I your money without services.

Fran. One in return for the other.

Just. I cannot. My master has ordered me to pack up. That I am now about, and I beg you not to hinder me further. When I have finished, I will take care to tell him that he may come here. He is close by, at the coffeehouse; and if he finds nothing better to do there, I suppose he will come. (*Going.*)

Fran. Wait a moment! My lady is the Major's . . . . sister.

Min. Yes, yes, his sister.

Just. I know better; the Major has not a sister. He has sent me twice in six months to his family in Courland. It is true there are different sorts of sisters——

Fran. Insolent!

Just. One must be so to get the people to let one alone. (*Exit.*)

Fran. That is a rascal!

Land. So I said. But let him go! I know now where his master is. I will fetch him instantly myself. I only beg your ladyship, most humbly, that you will make an excuse for me to the Major, that I have been so unfortunate as to offend a man of his merit against my will.

Min. Pray go quickly. I will set all that right again. (*Exit the* Landlord.) Franziska, run after him, and tell him not to mention my name! (*Exit* Franziska.)

SCENE VII.—Minna, *and afterwards* Franziska.

Min. I have found him again!—Am I alone?—I will not be alone to no purpose.—(*Clasping her hands.*) Yet I am not alone! (*Looking upwards.*) One single grateful thought towards heaven, is the most perfect prayer! I have found him! I have found him! (*With outstretched arms.*) I am joyful and happy! What can please the Creator more than a joyful creature! (*Franziska returns.*) Have you returned, Franziska? You pity him! I do not pity him. Misfortune too is useful. Perhaps heaven deprived him of everything—to give him all again, through me!

FRAN. He may be here any moment.—You are still in your morning dress, my lady. Ought you not to dress yourself quickly?

MIN. Not at all. He will now see me more frequently so, than dressed out.

FRAN. Oh! you know, my lady, how you look best.

MIN. (*after a pause*). Truly, girl, you have hit it again.

FRAN. I think women who are beautiful, are most so when unadorned.

MIN. Must we then be beautiful? Perhaps it was necessary that we should think ourselves so. Enough for me, if only I am beautiful in his eyes. Franziska, if all women feel as I now feel, we are—strange things. Tender-hearted, yet proud; virtuous, yet vain; passionate, yet innocent. I dare say you do not understand me. I do not rightly understand myself. Joy turns my head.

FRAN. Compose yourself, my lady, I hear footsteps.

MIN. Compose myself! What! receive him composedly?

SCENE VIII.—MAJOR VON TELLHEIM, LANDLORD, *and the above.*

MAJ. T. (*walks in, and the moment he sees* MINNA *rushes towards her*). Ah! my Minna!

MIN. (*springing towards him*). Ah! my Tellheim!

MAJ. T. (*starts sudden'y, and draws back*). I beg your pardon, Fräulein von Barnhelm; but to meet you here——

MIN. Cannot surely be so very unexpected! (*Approaching him, whilst he draws back still more.*) Am I to pardon you because I am still your Minna? Heaven pardon you, that I am still Fräulein von Barnhelm!

MAJ. T. Fräulein. . . . (*Looks fixedly at the* LANDLORD, *and shrugs his shoulders.*)

MIN. (*sees the* LANDLORD, *and makes a sign to* FRANZISKA). Sir——

MAJ. T. If we are not both mistaken——

FRAN. Why, Landlord, whom have you brought us here? Come, quick! let us go and look for the right man.

LAND. Is he not the right one? Surely!

Fran. Surely not! Come, quick! I have not yet wished your daughter good morning.

Land. Oh! you are very good (*still does not stir*).

Fran. (*takes hold of him*). Come, and we will make the bill of fare. Let us see what we shall have.

Land. You shall have first of all——

Fran. Stop, I say, stop! If my mistress knows now what she is to have for dinner, it will be all over with her appetite. Come, we must talk that over in private. (*Drags him off.*)

SCENE IX.—MINNA, MAJOR VON TELLHEIM.

Min. Well, are we still both mistaken?

Maj. T. Would to heaven it were so!—But there is only one Minna, and you are that one.

Min. What ceremony! The world might hear what we have to say to one another.

Maj. T. You here? What do you want here, Madam?

Min. Nothing now (*going to him with open arms*). I have found all that I wanted.

Maj. T. (*drawing back*). You seek a prosperous man, and one worthy of your love; and you find—a wretched one.

Min. Then do you love me no longer? Do you love another?

Maj. T. Ah! he never loved you, who could love another afterwards.

Min. You draw but one dagger from my breast; for if I have lost your heart, what matters whether indifference or more powerful charms than mine have robbed me of it? You love me no longer; neither do you love another? Wretched man indeed, if you love nothing!

Maj. T. Right; the wretched must love nothing. He merits his misfortunes, if he cannot achieve this victory over himself—if he can allow the woman he loves to take part in his misfortune....Oh! how difficult is this victory!.... Since reason and necessity have commanded me to forget Minna von Barnhelm, what pains have I taken! I was just beginning to hope that my trouble would not for ever be in vain—and you appear.

MIN. Do I understand you right? Stop, sir; let us see what we mean, before we make further mistakes. Will you answer me one question?

MAJ. T. Any one.

MIN. But will you answer me without shift or subterfuge? With nothing but a plain " Yes," or " No?"

MAJ. T. I will—if I can.

MIN. You can. Well, notwithstanding the pains which you have taken to forget me, do you love me still, Tellheim?

MAJ. T. Madam, that question——

MIN. You have promised to answer Yes, or No.

MAJ. T. And added, If I can.

MIN. You can. You must know what passes in your heart. Do you love me still, Tellheim? Yes, or No?

MAJ. T. If my heart——

MIN. Yes, or No?

MAJ. T. Well, Yes!

MIN. Yes?

MAJ. T. Yes, yes! Yet——

MIN. Patience! You love me still; that is enough for me. Into what a mood have we fallen! an unpleasant, melancholy, infectious mood! I assume my own again. Now, my dear unfortunate, you love me still, and have your Minna still, and are unhappy? Hear what a conceited, foolish thing your Minna was—is. She allowed —allows herself, to imagine that she makes your whole happiness. Declare all your misery at once. She would like to try how far she can outweigh it.—Well?

MAJ. T. Madam, I am not accustomed to complain.

MIN. Very well. I know nothing in a soldier, after boasting, that pleases me less than complaining. But there is a certain cold, careless way of speaking of bravery and misfortune——

MAJ. T. Which at the bottom is still boasting and complaining.

MIN. You disputant! You should not have called yourself unhappy at all then. You should have told the whole, or kept quiet. Reason and necessity commanded you to forget me? I am a great stickler for reason; I have a great respect for necessity. But let me hear how reasonable this reason, and how necessary this necessity may be.

Maj. T. Listen then, Madam. You call me Tellheim; the name is correct. But you suppose I am that Tellheim whom you knew at home ; the prosperous man, full of just pretensions, with a thirst for glory ; the master of all his faculties, both of body and mind ; before whom the lists of honour and prosperity stood open ; who, if he was not then worthy of your heart and your hand, dared to hope that he might daily become more nearly so. This Tellheim I am now, as little as I am my own father. They both have been. Now I am Tellheim the discharged, the suspected, the cripple, the beggar. To the former, Madam, you promised your hand ; do you wish to keep your word?

Min. That sounds very tragic. . . . . Yet, Major Tellheim, until I find the former one again—I am quite foolish about the Tellheims—the latter will have to help me in my dilemma. Your hand, dear beggar! (*taking his hand*).

Maj. T. (*holding his hat before his face with the other hand, and turning away from her*). This is too much ! . . . . What am I? . . . . Let me go, Madam. Your kindness tortures me ! Let me go.

Min. What is the matter? Where would you go?

Maj. T. From you !

Min. From me (*drawing his hand to her heart*)? Dreamer !

Maj. T. Despair will lay me dead at your feet.

Min. From me?

Maj. T. From you. Never, never to see you again. Or at least determined, fully determined, never to be guilty of a mean action ; never to cause you to commit an imprudent one. Let me go, Minna ! (*Tears himself away, and Exit.*)

Min. (*calling after him.*) Let you go, Minna? Minna, let you go? Tellheim ! Tellheim !

ACT III.

SCENE I.—*The Parlour.* JUST (*with a letter in his hand.*)

JUST. Must I come again into this cursed house! A note from my master to her ladyship that would be his sister. I hope nothing will come of this, or else there will be no end to letter carrying. I should like to be rid of it; but yet I don't wish to go into the room. The women ask so many questions, and I hate answering— Ah! the door opens. Just what I wanted, the waiting puss!

SCENE II.—FRANZISKA AND JUST.

FRAN. (*calling through the door by which she has just entered*). Fear not; I will watch. See! (*observing* JUST) I have met with something immediately. But nothing is to be done with that brute.

JUST. Your servant.

FRAN. I should not like such a servant.

JUST. Well, well, pardon the expression! . There is a note from my master to your mistress—her ladyship— his sister, wasn't it?—sister.

FRAN. Give it me! (*Snatches it from his hand.*)

JUST. You will be so good, my master begs, as to deliver it. Afterwards you will be so good, my master begs, as not to think I ask for anything!

FRAN. Well?

JUST. My master understands how to manage the affair. He knows that the way to the young lady is through her maid, methinks. The maid will therefore be so good, my master begs, as to let him know whether he may not have the pleasure of speaking with the maid for a quarter of an hour.

FRAN. With me?

JUST. Pardon me, if I do not give you your right title. Yes, with you. Only for one quarter of an hour; but alone, quite alone, in private, tête-à-tête. He has something very particular to say to you.

FRAN. Very well! I have also much to say to him.
He may come; I shall be at his service.

JUST. But when can he come? When is it most con-
venient for you, young woman? In the evening?

FRAN. What do you mean? Your master can come
when he pleases; and now be off.

JUST. Most willingly! (*Going.*)

FRAN. I say! one word more! Where are the rest of
the Major's servants?

JUST. The rest? Here, there, and everywhere.

FRAN. Where is William?

JUST. The valet? He has let him go for a trip.

FRAN. Oh! and Philip, where is he?

JUST. The huntsman? Master has found him a good
place.

FRAN. Because he does not hunt now, of course. But
Martin?

JUST. The coachman? He is off on a ride.

FRAN. And Fritz?

JUST. The footman? He is promoted.

FRAN. Where were you then, when the Major was
quartered in Thuringia with us that winter? You were
not with him, I suppose!

JUST. Oh! yes, I was groom; but I was in the
hospital.

FRAN. Groom! and now you are——

JUST. All in all; valet and huntsman, footman and
groom.

FRAN. Well, I never! To turn away so many good,
excellent, servants, and to keep the very worst of all! I
should like to know what your master finds in you!

JUST. Perhaps he finds that I am an honest fellow.

FRAN. Oh! one is precious little if one is nothing more
than honest. William was another sort of a man! So
your master has let him go for a trip!

JUST. Yes, he . . . . let him—because he could not
prevent him.

FRAN. How so?

JUST. Oh! William will do well on his travels. He
took master's wardrobe with him.

FRAN. What! he did not run away with it?

JUST. I cannot say that exactly; but when we left Nürnberg, he did not follow us with it.

FRAN. Oh! the rascal!

JUST. He was the right sort! he could curl hair and shave—and chatter—and flirt—couldn't he?

FRAN. At any rate, I would not have turned away the huntsman, had I been in the Major's place. If he did not want him any longer as huntsman, he was still a useful fellow. Where has he found him a place?

JUST. With the Commandant of Spandau.

FRAN. The fortress! There cannot be much hunting within the walls either.

JUST. Oh! Philip does not hunt there.

FRAN. What does he do then?

JUST. He rides—on the treadmill.

FRAN. The treadmill!

JUST. But only for three years. He made a bit of a plot amongst master's company, to get six men through the outposts.

FRAN. I am astonished; the knave!

JUST. Ah! he was a useful fellow; a huntsman who knew all the foot-paths and by-ways for fifty miles round, through forests and bogs. And he could shoot!

FRAN. It is lucky the Major has still got the honest coachman.

JUST. Has he got him still?

FRAN. I thought you said Martin was off on a ride: of course he will come back!

JUST. Do you think so?

FRAN. Well, where has he ridden to?

JUST. It is now going on for ten weeks since he rode master's last and only horse—to water.

FRAN. And has not he come back yet? Oh! the rascal!

JUST. The water may have washed the honest coachman away. Oh! he was a famous coachman! He had driven ten years in Vienna. My master will never get such another again. When the horses were in full gallop, he only had to say " Wo!" and there they stood, like a wall. Moreover, he was a finished horse-doctor!

Fran. I begin now to be anxious about the footman's promotion.

Just. No, no; there is no occasion for that. He has become a drummer in a garrison regiment.

Fran. I thought as much!

Just. Fritz chummed up with a scamp, never came home at night, made debts everywhere in master's name, and a thousand rascally tricks. In short, the Major saw that he was determined to rise in the world (*pantomimically imitating the act of hanging*), so he put him in the right road.

Fran. Oh! the stupid!

Just. Yet a perfect footman, there is no doubt of that. In running, my master could not catch him on his best horse if he gave him fifty paces; but on the other hand, Fritz could give the gallows a thousand paces, and, I bet my life, he would overhaul it. They were all great friends of yours, eh, young woman? . . . . William and Philip, Martin and Fritz! Now, Just wishes you good-day. (*Exit.*)

Scene III.—Franziska, *and afterwards the* Landlord.

Fran. (*looking after him seriously*). I deserve the hit! Thank you, Just. I undervalued honesty. I will not forget the lesson. Ah! our unfortunate Major! (*Turns round to enter her mistress's room, when the* Landlord *comes*).

Land. Wait a bit, my pretty maid.

Fran. I have not time now, Mr. Landlord.

Land. Only half a moment! No further tidings of the Major? That surely could not possibly be his leave-taking!

Fran. What could not?

Land. Has not her ladyship told you? When I left you, my pretty maid, below in the kitchen, I returned accidentally into this room——

Fran. Accidentally—with a view to listen a little.

Land. What, girl! how can you suspect me of that? There is nothing so bad in a landlord as curiosity. I had not been here long, when suddenly her ladyship's door burst open: the Major dashed out; the lady after him; both in such a state of excitement; with looks—in

attitudes—that must be seen to be understood. She seized
hold of him ; he tore himself away ; she seized him again—
" Tellheim." " Let me go, Madam." " Where ?" Thus he
drew her as far as the staircase. I was really afraid he would
drag her down ; but he got away. The lady remained on
the top step ; looked after him ; called after him ; wrung
her hands. Suddenly she turned round ; ran to the
window ; from the window to the staircase again ; from
the staircase into the room, backwards and forwards.
There I stood ; she passed me three times without seeing
me. At length it seemed as if she saw me ; but heaven
defend us ! I believe the lady took me for you. " Franziska," she cried, with her eyes fixed upon me, " am I
happy now ?" Then she looked straight up to the ceiling,
and said again—" Am I happy now ?" Then she wiped
the tears from her eyes, and smiled, and asked me again—
" Franziska, am I happy now ?" I really felt, I know not
how. Then she ran to the door of her room, and turned
round again towards me, saying — " Come, Franziska,
whom do you pity now ?" and with that she went in.

FRAN. Oh ! Mr. Landlord, you dreamt that.

LAND. Dreamt ! No, my pretty maid ; one does not
dream so minutely. Yes, what would not I give —I am
not curious : but what would not I give—to have the
key to it !

FRAN. The key ? Of our door ? Mr. Landlord, that
is inside ; we took it in at night ; we are timid.

LAND. Not that sort of key ; I mean, my dear girl, the
key—the explanation, as it were ; the precise connexion of
all that I have seen.

FRAN. Indeed ! Well, good-bye Mr. Landlord. Shall
we have dinner soon ?

LAND. My dear girl, not to forget what I came to
say——

FRAN. Well ? In as few words as possible.

LAND. Her ladyship has my ring still. I call it
mine——

FRAN. You shall not lose it.

LAND. I have no fear on that account : I merely put
you in mind. Do you see, I do not wish to have it again
at all. I can guess pretty well how she knew the ring,

WER. Is he not a good man? Do you like him?

FRAN. From the bottom of my heart.

WER. Indeed! I tell you what, little woman, you
are twice as pretty now as you were before. But what are
the services, which the landlord says he has rendered our
Major?

FRAN. That is what I don't know; unless he wished
to take credit to himself for the good result which fortunately has arisen from his knavish conduct.

WER. Then what Just told me is true? (*Towards
the side where the* LANDLORD *went off*.) A lucky thing for
you that you are gone! He did really turn him out of his
room?—To treat such a man so, because the donkey
fancied that he had no more money! The Major no
money!

FRAN. What! has the Major any money?

WER. By the load. He doesn't know how much he
has. He doesn't know who is in his debt. I am his
debtor, and have brought him some old arrears. Look,
little woman, in this purse (*drawing it out of one pocket*)
are a hundred louis d'ors; and in this packet (*drawing it
out of another pocket*) a hundred ducats. All his money!

FRAN. Really! Why then does the Major pawn his
things? He pledged a ring, you know——

WER. Pledged! Don't you believe it. Perhaps he
wanted to get rid of the rubbish.

FRAN. It is no rubbish; it is a very valuable ring;
which, moreover, I suspect, he received from a loving
hand.

WER. That will be the reason. From a loving hand!
Yes, yes; such a thing often puts one in mind of what one
does not wish to remember, and therefore one gets rid
of it.

FRAN. What!

WER. Odd things happen to the soldier in winter
quarters. He has nothing to do then, so he amuses himself,
and to pass the time he makes acquaintances, which he only
intends for the winter, but which the good soul with whom
he makes them, looks upon for life. Then, presto! a ring is
suddenly conjured on to his finger; he hardly knows himself how it gets there; and very often he would willingly

give the finger with it, if he could only get free from it again.

FRAN. Oh! and do you think this has happened to the Major?

WER. Undoubtedly. Especially in Saxony. If he had had ten fingers on each hand, he might have had all twenty full of rings.

FRAN. (aside). That sounds important, and deserves to be inquired into. Mr. Freeholder, or Mr. Sergeant——

WER. Little woman, if it makes no difference to you, I like " Mr. Sergeant " best.

FRAN. Well, Mr. Sergeant, I have a note from the Major to my mistress. I will just carry it in, and be here again in a moment. Will you be so good as to wait? I should like very much to have a little talk with you.

WER. Are you fond of talking, little woman? Well, with all my heart. Go quickly. I am fond of talking too: I will wait.

FRAN. Yes, please wait. (Exit.)

SCENE VI.—PAUL WERNER.

WER. That is not at all a bad little woman. But I ought not to have promised her that I would wait, for it would be most to the purpose, I suppose, to find the Major. He will not have my money, but rather pawns his property. That is just his way. A little trick occurs to me. When I was in the town, a fortnight back, I paid a visit to Captain Marloff's widow. The poor woman was ill, and was lamenting that her husband had died in debt to the Major for four hundred thalers, which she did not know how to pay. I went to see her again to-day; I intended to tell her that I could lend her five hundred thalers, when I had received the money for my property; for I must put some of it by, if I do not go to Persia. But she was gone; and no doubt she has not been able to pay the Major. Yes, I'll do that; and the sooner the better. The little woman must not take it ill of me; I cannot wait.

(Is going in thought, and almost runs against the MAJOR, who meets him.)

Scene VII.—Major von Tellheim, Paul Werner.

Maj. T. Why so thoughtful, Werner?

Wer. Oh! that is you. I was just going to pay you a visit in your new quarters, Major.

Maj. T. To fill my ears with curses against the Landlord of my old one. Do not remind me of it.

Wer. I should have done that by the way; yes. But more particularly, I wished to thank you for having been so good as to take care of my hundred louis d'ors. Just has given them to me again. I should have been very glad if you would have kept them longer for me. But you have got into new quarters, which neither you nor I know much about. Who knows what sort of place it is? They might be stolen, and you would have to make them good to me; there would be no help for it. So I cannot ask you to take them again.

Maj. T. (smiling). When did you begin to be so careful, Werner?

Wer. One learns to be so. One cannot now be careful enough of one's money. I have also a commission for you, Major, from Frau Marloff; I have just come from her. Her husband died four hundred thalers in your debt; she sends you a hundred ducats here, in part payment. She will forward you the rest next week. I believe I am the cause that she has not sent you the whole sum. For she also owed me about eighty thalers, and she thought I was come to dun her for them—which, perhaps, was the fact—so she gave them me out of the roll which she had put aside for you. You can spare your hundred thalers for a week longer, better than I can spare my few groschens. There, take it! (Hands him the ducats.)

Maj. T. Werner!

Wer. Well! Why do you stare at me so? Take it, Major!

Maj. T. Werner!

Wer. What is the matter with you? What annoys you?

Maj. T. (angrily striking his forehead, and stamping with his foot.) That . . . . the four hundred thalers are not all there.

WER. Come! Major, did not you understand me?

MAJ. T. It is just because I did understand you! Alas, that the best men should to-day distress me most!

WER. What do you say?

MAJ. T. This only applies partly to you. Go, Werner! (*Pushing back* WERNER's *hand with the money in it.*)

WER. As soon as I have got rid of this.

MAJ. T. Werner, suppose I tell you that Frau Marloff was here herself early this morning——

WER. Indeed?

MAJ. T. That she owes me nothing now——

WER. Really?

MAJ. T. That she has paid me every penny—What will you say then?

WER. (*thinks for a minute*). I shall say that I have told a lie, and that lying is a low thing, because one may be caught at it.

MAJ. T. And you will be ashamed of yourself?

WER. And what of him who compels me to lie? Should not he be ashamed too? Look ye, Major; if I was to say that your conduct has not vexed me, I should tell another lie, and I won't lie any more.

MAJ. T. Do not be annoyed, Werner. I know your heart, and your affection for me. But I do not require your money.

WER. Not require it! Rather sell, rather pawn, and get talked about!

MAJ. T. Oh! people may know that I have nothing more. One must not wish to appear richer than one is.

WER. But why poorer? A man has something as long as his friend has.

MAJ. T. It is not proper that I should be your debtor.

WER. Not proper! On that summer day which the sun and the enemy made hot for us, when your groom, who had your canteen, was not to be found, and you came to me and said—"Werner, have you nothing to drink?" and I gave you my flask, you took it and drank, did you not? Was that proper? Upon my life, a mouthful of dirty water at that time was often worth more than such filth (*taking the purse also out of his pocket, and holding out both to him*). Take them, dear Major! Fancy it is water. God has made this, too, for all.

MAJ. T. You torment me: don't you hear, I will not be your debtor.

WER. At first, it was not proper; now, you will not. Ah! that is a different thing. (*Rather angrily.*) You will not be my debtor? But suppose you are already, Major? Or, are you not a debtor to the man who once warded off the blow that was meant to split your head; and, at another time, knocked off the arm which was just going to pull and send a ball through your breast? How can you become a greater debtor to that man? Or, is my neck of less consequence than my money? If that is a noble way of thinking, by my soul it is a very silly one too.

MAJ. T. To whom do you say that, Werner? We are alone, and therefore I may speak; if a third person heard us, it might sound like boasting. I acknowledge with pleasure, that I have to thank you for twice saving my life. Do you not think, friend, that if an opportunity occurred I would have done as much for you, eh?

WER. If an opportunity occurred! Who doubts it, Major? Have I not seen you risk your life a hundred times for the lowest soldier, when he was in danger?

MAJ. T. Well!

WER. But——

MAJ. T. Why cannot you understand me? I say, it is not proper that I should be your debtor; I will not be your debtor. That is, not in the circumstances in which I now am.

WER. Oh! so you would wait till better times. You will borrow money from me another time, when you do not want any; when you have some yourself, and I perhaps none.

MAJ. T. A man ought not to borrow, when he has not the means of repaying.

WER. A man like yourself cannot always be in want.

MAJ. T. You know the world. . . . . Least of all should a man borrow from one who wants his money himself.

WER. Oh! yes; I am such a one! Pray, what do I

want it for? When they want a sergeant, they give him enough to live on.

MAJ. T. You want it, to become something more than a sergeant—to be able to get forward in that path in which even the most deserving, without money, may remain behind.

WER. To become something more than a sergeant! I do not think of that. I am a good sergeant; I might easily make a bad captain, and certainly a worse general.

MAJ. T. Do not force me to think ill of you, Werner! I was very sorry to hear what Just has told me. You have sold your farm, and wish to rove about again. Do not let me suppose that you do not love the profession of arms so much as the wild dissolute way of living which is unfortunately connected with it. A man should be a soldier for his own country, or from love of the cause for which he fights. To serve without any purpose—to-day here, to-morrow there—is only travelling about like a butcher's apprentice, nothing more.

WER. Well, then, Major, I will do as you say. You know better what is right. I will remain with you. But, dear Major, do take my money in the meantime. Sooner or later your affairs must be settled. You will get money in plenty then; and then you shall repay me with interest. I only do it for the sake of the interest.

MAJ. T. Do not talk of it.

WER. Upon my life, I only do it for the sake of the interest. Many a time I have thought to myself—" Werner, what will become of you in your old age? when you are crippled? when you will have nothing in the world? when you will be obliged to go and beg!" And then I thought again—"No, you will not be obliged to beg: you will go to Major Tellheim; he will share his last penny with you; he will feed you till you die; and with him you can die like an honest fellow."

MAJ. T (*taking* WERNER'S *hand*). And, comrade, you do not think so still?

WER. No, I do not think so any longer. He who will not take anything from me, when he is in want, and I have to give, will not give me anything when he has to give, and I am in want. So be it. (*Is going.*)

Maj. T. Man, do not drive me mad! Where are you
going? (*Detains him.*) If I assure you now, upon my
honour, that I still have money—If I assure you, upon
my honour, that I will tell you when I have no more—
that you shall be the first and only person from whom I
will borrow anything—will that content you?

Wer. I suppose it must. Give me your hand on it,
Major.

Maj. T. There, Paul! And now enough of that. I
came here to speak with a certain young woman.

Scene VIII.—Franziska (*coming out of* Minna's *room*),
Major von Tellheim, Paul Werner.

Fran. (*entering*). Are you there still, Mr. Sergeant?
(*Seeing* Tellheim.) And you there too, Major? I will be
at your service instantly. (*Goes back quickly into the
room.*)

Scene IX.—Major von Tellheim, Paul Werner.

Maj. T. That was she! But it seems you know her,
Werner.

Wer. Yes, I know her.

Maj. Yet, if I remember rightly, when I was in
Thuringia you were not with me.

Wer. No; I was seeing after the uniforms in Leipsic.

Maj. T. Where did you make her acquaintance, then?

Wer. Our acquaintance is very young. Not a day
old. But young friendship is warm.

Maj. T. Have you seen her mistress, too?

Wer. Is her mistress a young lady? She told me you
are acquainted with her mistress.

Maj. T. Did not you hear? she comes from Thuringia.

Wer. Is the lady young?

Maj. T. Yes.

Wer. Pretty?

Maj. T. Very pretty.

Wer. Rich?

Maj. T. Very rich.

WER. Is the mistress as fond of you as the maid is?
That would be capital!

MAJ. T. What do you mean?

SCENE X.—FRANZISKA (*with a letter in her hand*), MAJOR
VON TELLHEIM, PAUL WERNER.

FRAN. Major——

MAJ. T. Franziska, I have not yet been able to give you
a "Welcome" here.

FRAN. In thought, I am sure that you have done it.
I know you are friendly to me; so am I to you. But it is
not at all kind to vex those who are friendly to you so much.

WER. (*aside*). Ah! now I see it. It is so!

MAJ. T. My destiny, Franziska! Did you give her the
letter?

FRAN. Yes; and here I bring you . . . . (*holding out a
letter*).

MAJ. T. An answer!

FRAN. No, your own letter again.

MAJ. T. What! She will not read it!

FRAN. She would have liked, but—we can't read
writing well.

MAJ. T. You are joking!

FRAN. And we think that writing was not invented for
those who can converse with their lips whenever they please.

MAJ. T. What an excuse! She must read it. It
contains my justification—all the grounds and reasons——

FRAN. My mistress wishes to hear them all from you
yourself, not to read them.

MAJ. T. Hear them from me myself! That every
look, every word of hers, may embarrass me; that I may
feel in every glance the greatness of my loss.

FRAN. Without any pity! Take it. (*Giving him his
letter.*) She expects you at three o'clock. She wishes to
drive out and see the town; you must accompany her.

MAJ. T. Accompany her!

FRAN. And what will you give me to let you drive out
by yourselves? I shall remain at home?

MAJ. T. By ourselves!

FRAN. In a nice close carriage.

Maj. T. Impossible!

Fran. Yes, yes, in the carriage, Major. You will have to submit quietly; you cannot escape there! And that is the reason. In short, you will come, Major, and punctually at three .... Well, you wanted to speak to me too alone? What have you to say to me? Oh! we are not alone. (*Looking at* Werner.)

Maj. T. Yes, Franziska; as good as alone. But as your mistress has not read my letter, I have nothing now to say to you.

Fran. As good as alone! Then you have no secrets from the Sergeant?

Maj. T. No, none.

Fran. And yet I think you should have some from him.

Maj. T. Why so?

Wer. How so, little woman?

Fran. Particularly secrets of a certain kind. . . . . All twenty, Mr. Sergeant! (*Holding up both her hands, with open fingers.*)

Wer. Hist! hist! girl.

Maj. T. What is the meaning of that?

Fran. Presto! conjured on to his finger, Mr. Sergeant (*as if she was putting a ring on her finger.*)

Maj. T. What are you talking about?

Wer. Little woman, little woman, don't you understand a joke.

Maj. T. Werner, you have not forgotten, I hope, what I have often told you; that one should not jest beyond a certain point with a young woman!

Wer. Upon my life I may have forgotten it! Little woman, I beg——

Fran. Well, if it was a joke, I will forgive you this once.

Maj. T. Well, if I must come, Franziska, just see that your mistress reads my letter beforehand? That will spare me the pain of thinking again—of talking again, of things which I would willingly forget. There, give it to her! (*He turns the letter in giving it to her, and sees that it has been opened.*) But do I see aright? Why it has been opened.

Fran. That may be. (*Looks at it.*) True, it is open.

Who can have opened it? But really we have not read it,
Major; really not. And we do not wish to read it, because
the writer is coming himself. Come; and I tell you what,
Major! don't come as you are now—in boots, and with
such a head. You are excusable, you do not expect us.
Come in shoes, and have your hair fresh dressed. You look
too soldierlike, too Prussian for me as you are.

MAJ. T. Thank you, Franziska.

FRAN. You look as if you had been bivouacking last
night.

MAJ. T. You may have guessed right.

FRAN. We are going to dress, directly too, and then have
dinner. We would willingly ask you to dinner, but your
presence might hinder our eating; and observe, we are
not so much in love that we have lost our appetites.

MAJ. T. I will go. Prepare her somewhat, Franziska,
beforehand, that I may not become contemptible in her eyes,
and in my own. Come, Werner, you shall dine with me.

WER. At the table d'hôte here in the house? I could
not eat a bit there.

MAJ. T. With me, in my room.

WER. I will follow you directly. One word first with
the little woman.

MAJ. T. I have no objection to that. (*Exit.*)

SCENE XI.—PAUL WERNER, FRANZISKA.

FRAN. Well, Mr. Sergeant!

WER. Little woman, if I come again, shall I too come
smartened up a bit?

FRAN. Come as you please; my eyes will find no fault
with you. But my ears will have to be so much the more
on their guard. Twenty fingers, all full of rings. Ah!
ah! Mr. Sergeant!

WER. No, little woman; that is just what I wished to
say to you. I only rattled on a little. There is nothing in
it. One ring is quite enough for a man. Hundreds and
hundreds of times I have heard the Major say—" He must
be a rascally soldier, who can mislead a young girl." So
think I too, little woman. You may trust to that! I must
be quick and follow him. A good appetite to you. (*Exit.*)

Fran. The same to you! I really believe, I like that man! (*Going in, she meets* Minna *coming out*).

Scene XII.—Minna, Franziska.

Min. Has the Major gone already, Franziska? I believe I should have been sufficiently composed again now to have detained him here.

Fran. And I will make you still more composed.

Min. So much the better! His letter! oh! his letter! Each line spoke the honourable noble man. Each refusal to accept my hand declared his love for me. I suppose he noticed that we had read his letter. I don't mind that, if he does but come. But are you sure he will come? There only seems to me to be a little too much pride in his conduct. For not to be willing to be indebted for his good fortune, even to the woman he loves, is pride, unpardonable pride! If he shows me too much of this, Franziska——

Fran. You will discard him!

Min. See there! Do you begin to pity him again already! No, silly girl, a man is never discarded for a single fault. No; but I have thought of a trick—to pay him off a little for this pride, with pride of the same kind.

Fran. Indeed, you must be very composed, my lady, if you are thinking of tricks again.

Min. I am so; come. You will have a part to play in my plot. (*Exeunt.*)

ACT IV.

Scene I. Minna's *Room.* Minna (*dressed handsomely and richly, but in good taste*), Franziska.

(*They have just risen from a table, which a servant is clearing.*)

Fran. You cannot possibly have eaten enough, my lady.

Min. Don't you think so, Franziska? Perhaps I had no appetite when I sat down.

Fran. We had agreed not to mention him during dinner.
We should have resolved likewise, not to think of him.

Min. Indeed, I have thought of nothing but him.

Fran. So I perceived. I began to speak of a hundred
different things, and you made wrong answers to each.
(*Another servant brings coffee.*) Here comes a beverage
more suited to fancies—sweet, melancholy coffee.

Min. Fancies! I have none. I am only thinking of
the lesson I will give him. Did you understand my plan,
Franziska?

Fran. · Oh! yes; but it would be better if he spared us
the putting it in execution.

Min. You will see that I know him thoroughly. He
who refuses me now with all my wealth, will contend
for me against the whole world, as soon as he hears that
I am unfortunate and friendless.

Fran. (*seriously*). That must tickle the most refined
self-love.

Min. You moralist! First you convict me of vanity
—now of self-love. Let me do as I please, Franziska.
You, too, shall do as you please with your Sergeant.

Fran. With my Sergeant?

Min. Yes. If you deny it altogether, then it is true.
I have not seen him yet; but from all you have said
respecting him, I foretell your husband for you.

SCENE II.—RICCAÚT DE LA MARLINIÈRE, MINNA,
FRANZISKA.

Ric. (*before he enters*). Est-il permis, Monsieur le
Major?

Fran. Who is that? Any one for us? (*going to the door*).

Ric. Parbleu! I am wrong. Mais non—I am not
wrong. C'est la chambre——

Fran. Without doubt, my lady, this gentleman expects
to find Major von Tellheim here still.

Ric. Oui, dat is it! Le Major de Tellheim; juste, **ma**
belle enfant, c'est lui que je cherche. Où est-il?

Fran. He does not lodge here any longer.

Ric. Comment? Dere is four-and-twenty hour ago

he did lodge here, and not lodge here any more? Where
lodge he den?

Min. (*going up to him*). Sir——

Ric. Ah! Madame, Mademoiselle, pardon, lady.

Min. Sir, your mistake is quite excusable, and your
astonishment very natural. Major von Tellheim has had
the kindness to give up his apartments to me, as a stranger,
who was not able to get them elsewhere.

Ric. Ah! voilà de ses politesses! C'est un très-galant
homme que ce Major!

Min. Where has he gone now?—truly I am ashamed
that I do not know.

Ric. Madame not know? C'est dommage; j'en suis
fâché.

Min. I certainly ought to have inquired. Of course his
friends will seek him here.

Ric. I am vary great his friend, Madame.

Min. Franziska, do you not know?

Fran. No, my lady.

Ric. It is vary nécessaire dat I speak him. I come
and bring him a nouvelle, of which he will be vary much
at ease.

Min. I regret it so much the more. But I hope to see
him perhaps shortly. If it is a matter of indifference from
whom he hears this good news, I would offer, sir,——

Ric. I comprehend. Mademoiselle parle français?
Mais sans doute; telle que je la vois! La demande était
bien impolie; vous me pardonnerez, Mademoiselle.

Min. Sir——

Ric. No! You not speak French, Madame?

Min. Sir, in France I would endeavour to do so; but
why here? I perceive that you understand me, sir; and
I, sir, shall doubtless understand you; speak as you
please.

Ric. Good, good! I can also explain me in your
langue. Sachez donc, Mademoiselle, you must know,
Madame, dat I come from de table of de ministre, ministro
de, ministre de .... What is le ministre out dere, in
de long street, on de broad place?

Min. I am a perfect stranger here,

Ric. Si, le ministre of de war departement. Dere I

have eat my dinner; I ordinary dine dere, and de conversation did fall on Major Tellheim; et le ministre m'a
dit en confidence, car Son Excellence est de mes amis, et
il n'y a point de mystères entre nous; Son Excellence, I
say, has trust to me, dat l'affaire from our Major is on de
point to end, and to end good. He has made a rapport to
de king, and de king has resolved et tout à fait en faveur
du Major. "Monsieur," m'a dit Son Excellence, "vous
comprenez bien, que tout dépend de la manière, dont on
fait envisager les choses au roi, et vous me connaissez.
Cela fait un très-joli garçon que ce Tellheim, et ne sais-je
pas que vous l'aimez? Les amis de mes amis sont aussi
les miens. Il coûte un peu cher au Roi ce Tellheim, mais
est-ce que l'on sert les rois pour rien? Il faut s'entr'aider
en ce monde; et quand il s'agit de pertes, que ce soit le
Roi qui en fasse, et non pas un honnête homme de nous
autres. Voilà le principe, dont je ne me dépars jamais."
But what say Madame to it? N'est pas, dat is a fine
fellow! Ah! que Son Excellence a le cœur bien placé!
He assure me au reste, if de Major has not reçu already
une lettre de la main—a royal letter, dat to-day infaillible-
ment must he receive one.

MIN. Certainly, sir, this news will be most welcome
to Major von Tellheim. I should like to be able to name the
friend to him, who takes such an interest in his welfare.

RIC. Madame, you wish my name? Vous voyez en
moi—you see, lady, in me, le Chevalier Riccaut de la
Marlinière, Seigneur de Prêt-au-val, de la branche de
Prens d'or. You remain astonished to hear me from so
great, great a family, qui est véritablement du sang
royal. Il faut le dire; je suis sans doute le cadet le plus
aventureux que la maison n'a jamais eu. I serve from
my eleven year. Une affaire d'honneur make me flee.
Den I serve de holy Papa of Rome, den de Republic
St. Marino, den de Poles, den de States General, till
enfin I am brought here. Ah! Mademoiselle, que je
voudrais n'avoir jamais vu ce pays-ci. Had one left me
in de service of de States General, should I be now at
least colonel. But here always to remain capitaine, and
now also a discharged capitaine.

MIN. That is ill luck.

ᴿɪᴄ. Oui, Mademoiselle, me voilà réformé, et par là
ѕ sur le pavé !

Mɪɴ. I am very sorry for you.

ᴿɪᴄ. Vous êtes bien bonne, Mademoiselle. . . . . No,
rit have no reward here. Réformer a man, like me !
man who also have ruin himself in dis service! I have
t in it so much as twenty thousand livres. What have
ow ? Tranchons le mot; je n'ai pas le sou, et me voilà
ictement vis-à-vis de rien.

Mɪɴ. I am exceedingly sorry.

ᴿɪᴄ. Vous êtes bien bonne, Mademoiselle. But as one
r— misfortune never come alone! qu'un malheur ne
nt jamais seul : so it arrive with me. What ressource
ts for an honnête homme of my extraction, but play ?
w, I always played with luck, so long I not need her.
w I very much need her, je joue avec un guignon,
demoiselle, qui surpasse toute croyance. For fifteen
ys, not one is passed, dat I always am broke. Yester-
r, I was broke dree times. Je sais bien, qu'il y avait
elque chose de plus que le jeu. Car parmi mes pontes
trouvaient certaines dames. I will not speak more.
e must be very galant to les dames. Dey have invite
again to-day, to give me revanche ; mais—vous m'en-
dez, Mademoiselle,—one must first have to live, before
e can have to play.

Mɪɴ. I hope, sir,——

ᴿɪᴄ. Vous êtes bien bonne, Mademoiselle.

Mɪɴ. (*Takes* Fʀᴀɴᴢɪѕᴋᴀ *aside.*) Franziska, I really feel
the man. Would he take it ill, if I offer him some-
ng ?

Fʀᴀɴ. He does not look to me like a man who would.

Mɪɴ. Very well ! Sir, I perceive that—you play,
it you keep the bank ; doubtless in places where some-
ing is to be won. I must also confess that I . . . . am
ry fond of play.

ᴿɪᴄ. Tant mieux, Mademoiselle, tant mieux ! Tous
s gens d'esprit aiment le jeu à la fureur.

Mɪɴ. That I am very fond of winning; that I like to
trust my money to a man, who—knows how to play.
Are you inclined, sir, to let me join you ? To let me
have a share in your bank ?

RIC. Comment, Mademoiselle, vous voulez être
moitié avec moi? De tout mon cœur.

MIN. At first, only with a trifle. (*Opens her d
and takes out some money.*)

RIC. Ah! Mademoiselle, que vous êtes charmante!

MIN. Here is what I won a short time back; only
pistoles. I am ashamed, so little——

RIC. Donnez toujours, Mademoiselle, donnez. (*T*
it.)

MIN. Without doubt, your bank, sir, is very consid
able.

RIC. Oh! yes, vary considerable. Ten pistoles! I
shall have, Madame, an interest in my bank for one th
pour le tiers. Yes, one third part it shall be—someth
more. With a beautiful lady one must not be too ex
I rejoice myself, to make by that a liaison with Mada
et de ce moment je recommence à bien augurer de
fortune.

MIN. But I cannot be present, sir, when you play.

RIC. For why it nécessaire dat you be present?
other players are honourable people between us.

MIN. If we are fortunate, sir, you will of course br
me my share. If we are unfortunate——

RIC. I come to bring recruits, n'est pas, Madame?

MIN. In time recruits might fail. Manage our mo
well, sir.

RIC. What does Madame think me? A simpleto
stupid devil?

MIN. I beg your pardon.

RIC. Je suis des bons, Mademoiselle. Savez vous
que cela veut dire? I am of the quite practised——

MIN. But still, sir,——

RIC. Je sais monter un coup——

MIN. (*amazed*). Could you?

RIC. Je file la carte avec une adresse.

MIN. Never!

RIC. Je fais sauter la coupe avec une dextérité.

MIN. You surely would not, sir!——

RIC. What not, Madame; what not? Donnez moi un
pigeonneau à plumer, et——

MIN. Play false! Cheat!

quarters before it began to strike three; but the paymaster met us on the way; and because conversation with those gentlemen has no end, the Major made me a sign to report the case to your ladyship.

Min. Very well, Mr. Sergeant. I only hope the paymaster may have good news for him.

Wer. Such gentlemen seldom have good news for officers.—Has your ladyship any orders? (*Going.*)

Fran. Why, where are you going again, Mr. Sergeant? Had not we something to say to each other?

Wer. (*In a whisper to* Franziska, *and seriously*). Not here, little woman; it is against respect, against discipline. . . . . Your ladyship——

Min. Thank you for your trouble. I am glad to have made your acquaintance. Franziska has spoken in high praise of you to me. (Werner *makes a stiff bow, and goes.*)

Scene V.—Minna, Franziska.

Min. So that is your Sergeant, Franziska?

Fran. (*aside*). I have not time to reproach her for that jeering *your*. (*Aloud.*) Yes, my lady, that is my Sergeant. You think him, no doubt, somewhat stiff and wooden. He also appeared so to me just now; but I observed, he thought he must march past you as if on parade. And when soldiers are on parade, they certainly look more like wooden dolls than men. You should see and hear him when he is himself.

Min. So I should indeed!

Fran. He must still be in the next room; may I go and talk with him a little?

Min. I refuse you this pleasure unwillingly: but you must remain here, Franziska. You must be present at our conversation. Another thing occurs to me. (*Takes her ring from her finger.*) There, take my ring; keep it for me, and give me the Major's in the place of it.

Fran. Why so?

Min. (*whilst* Franziska *is fetching the ring*). I scarcely know, myself; but I fancy I see, beforehand, how I may make use of it. Some one is knocking. Give it to me, quickly. (*Puts the ring on.*) It is he.

2 c 2

SCENE VI.—MAJOR VON TELLHEIM (*in the same coat, but otherwise as* FRANZISKA *advised*), MINNA, FRANZISKA.

MAJ. T. Madam, you will excuse the delay.

MIN. Oh! Major, we will not treat each other in quite such a military fashion. You are here now; and to await a pleasure, is itself a pleasure. Well (*looking at him and smiling*) dear Tellheim, have we not been like children?

MAJ. T. Yes, Madam; like children, who resist when they ought to obey quietly.

MIN. We will drive out, dear Major, to see a little of the town, and afterwards to meet my uncle.

MAJ. T. What!

MIN. You see, we have not yet had an opportunity of mentioning the most important matters even. He is coming here to-day. It was accident that brought me here without him, a day sooner.

MAJ. T. Count von Bruchsal! Has he returned?

MIN. The troubles of the war drove him into Italy: peace has brought him back again. Do not be uneasy, Tellheim; if we formerly feared on his part the greatest obstacle to our union——

MAJ. T. To our union!

MIN. He is now your friend. He has heard too much good of you from too many people, not to become so. He longs to become personally acquainted with the man whom his heiress has chosen. He comes as uncle, as guardian, as father, to give me to you.

MAJ. T. Ah! dear lady, why did you not read my letter? Why would you not read it?

MIN. Your letter! Oh! yes, I remember you sent me one. What did you do with that letter, Franziska? Did we, or did we not read it? What was it you wrote to me, dear Tellheim?

MAJ. T. Nothing but what honour commands me.

MIN. That is, not to desert an honourable woman who loves you. Certainly that is what honour commands. Indeed, I ought to have read your letter. But what I have not read, I shall hear, shall not I?

MAJ. T. Yes, you shall hear it.

MIN. No, I need not even hear it. It speaks for itself.
As if you could be guilty of such an unworthy act, as not
to take me! Do you know that I should be pointed at for
the rest of my life? My countrywomen would talk about
me, and say, "That is she, that is the Fräulein von Barnhelm, who fancied that because she was rich she could
marry the noble Tellheim; as if such men were to be
caught with money." That is what they would say, for
they are all envious of me. That I am rich, they cannot
deny; but they do not wish to acknowledge that I am also
a tolerably good girl, who would prove herself worthy of
her husband. Is that not so, Tellheim?

MAJ. T. Yes, yes, Madam, that is like your countrywomen. They will envy you exceedingly a discharged
officer, with sullied honour, a cripple, and a beggar.

MIN. And are you all that? If I mistake not, you
told me something of the kind this forenoon. Therein
is good and evil mixed. Let us examine each charge
more closely. You are discharged? So you say. I
thought your regiment was only drafted into another.
How did it happen that a man of your merit was not
retained?

MAJ. T. It has happened, as it must happen. The
great ones are convinced that a soldier does very little
through regard for them, not much more from a sense of duty,
but everything for his own advantage. What then can
they think they owe him? Peace has made a great many,
like myself, superfluous to them; and at last we shall all
be superfluous.

MIN. You talk as a man must talk, to whom in return
the great are quite superfluous. And never were they
more so than now. I return my best thanks to the great
ones that they have given up their claims to a man whom
I would very unwillingly have shared with them. I am
your sovereign, Tellheim; you want no other master.
To find you discharged, is a piece of good fortune I dared
scarcely dream of! But you are not only discharged;
you are more. And what are you more? A cripple, you
say! Well! (*looking at him from head to foot*), the cripple
is tolerably whole and upright — appears still to be
pretty well, and strong. Dear Tellheim, if you expect to
go begging on the strength of your limbs, I prophesy

that you will be relieved at very few doors; except at the door of a good-natured girl like myself.

MAJ. T. I only hear the joking girl now, dear Minna.

MIN. And I only hear the "dear Minna" in your chiding. I will not joke any longer; for I recollect that after all you are something of a cripple. You are wounded by a shot in the right arm; but, all things considered, I do not find much fault with that. I am so much the more secure from your blows.

MAJ. T. Madam!

MIN. You would say, "You are so much the less secure from mine." Well, well, dear Tellheim, I hope you will not drive me to that.

MAJ. T. You laugh, Madam. I only lament that I cannot laugh with you.

MIN. Why not? What have you to say against laughing? Cannot one be very serious even whilst laughing? Dear Major, laughter keeps us more rational than vexation. The proof is before us. Your laughing friend judges of your circumstances more correctly than you do yourself. Because you are discharged, you say your honour is sullied; because you are wounded in the arm, you call yourself a cripple. Is that right? Is that no exaggeration? And is it my doing that all exaggerations are so open to ridicule? I dare say, if I examine your beggary that it will also be as little able to stand the test. You may have lost your equipage once, twice, or thrice; your deposits in the hands of this or that banker may have disappeared together with those of other people; you may have no hope of seeing this or that money again which you may have advanced in the service; but are you a beggar on that account? If nothing else remained to you but what my uncle is bringing for you——

MAJ. T. Your uncle, Madam, will bring nothing for me.

MIN. Nothing but the two thousand pistoles which you so generously advanced to our government.

MAJ. T. If you had but read my letter, Madam!

MIN. Well, I did read it. But what I read in it, on this point, is a perfect riddle. It is impossible that any one should wish to turn a noble action into a crime. But explain to me, dear Major.

MAJ. T. You remember, Madam, that I had orders to

collect the contribution for the war most strictly in cash
in the districts in your neighbourhood. I wished to
forego this severity, and advanced the money that was
deficient myself.

MIN. 1 remember it well. I loved you for that deed
before I had seen you.

MAJ. T. The government gave me their bill, and I
wished, at the signing of the peace, to have the sum
entered amongst the debts to be repaid by them. The
bill was acknowledged as good, but my ownership of the
same was disputed. People looked incredulous, when 1
declared that I had myself advanced the amount in cash.
It was considered as bribery, as a douceur from the
government, because I at once agreed to take the smallest
sum with which I could have been satisfied in a case of
the greatest exigency. Thus the bill went from my
possession, and if it be paid, will certainly not be paid to
me. Hence, Madam, I consider my honour to be suspected! not on account of my discharge, which, if I had
not received, I should have applied for. You look serious,
Madam! Why do you not laugh? Ha! ha! ha! I am
laughing.

MIN. Oh! stifle that laugh, Tellheim, I implore you!
It is the terrible laugh of misanthropy. No, you are
not the man to repent of a good deed, because it may
have had a bad result for yourself. Nor can these consequences possibly be of long duration. The truth must
come to light. The testimony of my uncle, of our government——

MAJ. T. Of your uncle! Of your government! Ha!
ha! ha!

MIN. That laugh will kill me, Tellheim. If you
believe in virtue and Providence, Tellheim, do not laugh
so! 1 never heard a curse more terrible than that laugh!
But, viewing the matter in the worst light, if they are
determined to mistake your character here, with us you
will not be misunderstood. No, we cannot, we will not,
misunderstand you, Tellheim. And if our government
has the least sentiment of honour, I know what it
must do. But 1 am foolish; what would that matter?
Imagine, Tellheim, that you have lost the two thousand

pistoles on some gay evening. The king was an unfortunate card for you: the queen (*pointing to herself*) will be so much the more favourable. Providence, believe me, always indemnifies a man of honour—often even beforehand. The action which was to cost you two thousand pistoles, gained you me. Without that action, I never should have been desirous of making your acquaintance. You know I went uninvited to the first party where I thought I should meet you. I went entirely on your account. I went with a fixed determination to love you—I loved you already! with the fixed determination to make you mine, if I should find you as dark and ugly as the Moor of Venice. So dark and ugly you are not; nor will you be so jealous. But, Tellheim, Tellheim, you are yet very like him! Oh! the unmanageable, stubborn man, who always keeps his eye fixed upon the phantom of honour, and becomes hardened against every other sentiment! Your eyes this way! Upon me, me, Tellheim! (*He remains thoughtful and immovable, with his eyes fixed on one spot.*) Of what are you thinking? Do you not hear me?

MAJ. T. (*absent*). Oh, yes; but tell me, how came the Moor into the service of Venice? Had the Moor no country of his own? Why did he hire his arm and his blood to a foreign land?

MIN. (*alarmed*). Of what are you thinking, Tellheim? It is time to break off. Come! (*taking him by the hand*). Franziska, let the carriage be brought round.

MAJ. T. (*disengaging his hand, and following* FRANZISKA). No, Franziska; I cannot have the honour of accompanying your mistress. Madam, let me still retain my senses unimpaired for to-day, and give me leave to go. You are on the right way to deprive me of them. I resist it as much as I can. But hear, whilst I am still myself, what I have firmly determined, and from which nothing in the world shall turn me. If I have not better luck in the game of life; if a complete change in my fortune does not take place; if——

MIN. I must interrupt you, Major. We ought to have told him that at first, Franziska.—You remind me of nothing.—Our conversation would have taken quite a

different turn, Tellheim, if I had commenced with the
good news which the Chevalier de la Marlinière brought
just now.

Maj. T. The Chevalier de la Marlinière! Who is he?

Fran. He may be a very honest man, Major von Tellheim, except that——

Min. Silence, Franziska! Also a discharged officer
from the Dutch service, who——

Maj. T. Ah! Lieutenant Riccaut!

Min. He assured us he was a friend of yours.

Maj. T. I assure you that I am not his.

Min. And that some minister or other had told him,
in confidence, that your business was likely to have the
very best termination. A letter from the king must now
be on its way to you.

Maj. T. How came Riccaut and a minister in company? Something certainly must have happened concerning my affair; for just now the paymaster of the forces
told me that the king had set aside all the evidence
offered against me, and that I might take back my promise, which I had given in writing, not to depart from
here until acquitted. But that will be all. They wish
to give me an opportunity of getting away. But they are
wrong, I shall not go. Sooner shall the utmost distress
waste me away before the eyes of my calumniators,
than——

Min. Obstinate man!

Maj. T. I require no favour; I want justice. My
honour——

Min. The honour of such a man——

Maj. T. (warmly). No, Madam, you may be able to
judge of any other subject, but not of this. Honour is not
the voice of conscience, not the evidence of a few honourable men——

Min. No, no, I know it well. Honour is . . . .
honour.

Maj. T. In short, Madam . . . . You did not let me finish.
—I was going to say, if they keep from me so shamefully
what is my own; if my honour be not perfectly righted
—I cannot, Madam, ever be yours, for I am not worthy,
in the eyes of the world, of being yours. Minna von

Barnhelm deserves an irreproachable husband. It is a worthless love which does not scruple to expose its object to scorn. He is a worthless man, who is not ashamed to owe a woman all his good fortune; whose blind tenderness——

MIN. And is that really your feeling, Major? (*turning her back suddenly*). Franziska!

MAJ. T. Do not be angry.

MIN. (*aside to* FRANZISKA). Now is the time! What do you advise me, Franziska?

FRAN. I advise nothing. But certainly he goes rather too far.

MAJ. T. (*approaching to interrupt them*). You are angry, Madam.

MIN. (*ironically*). I? Not in the least.

MAJ. T. If I loved you less——

MIN. (*still in the same tone*). Oh! certainly, it would be a misfortune for me. And hear, Major, I also will not be the cause of your unhappiness. One should love with perfect disinterestedness. It is as well that I have not been more open! Perhaps your pity might have granted to me what your love refuses. (*Drawing the ring slowly from her finger.*)

MAJ. T. What does this mean, Madam?

MIN. No, neither of us must make the other either more or less happy. True love demands it. I believe you, Major; and you have too much honour to mistake love.

MAJ. T. Are you jesting, Madam?

MIN. Here! take back the ring with which you plighted your troth to me. (*Gives him the ring.*) Let it be so! We will suppose we have never met.

MAJ. T. What do I hear!

MIN. Does it surprise you! Take it, sir. You surely have not been pretending only!

MAJ. T. (*takes the ring from her*). Heavens! can Minna speak thus!

MIN. In one case you cannot be mine; in no case can I be yours. Your misfortune is probable; mine is certain. Farewell! (*Is going.*)

MAJ. T. Where are you going, dearest Minna?

Min.   Sir, you insult me now by that term of endearment.

Maj. T.   What is the matter, Madam? Where are you going?

Min.   Leave me. I go to hide my tears from you, deceiver! (*Exit.*)

Scene VII.—Major von Tellheim, Franziska.

Maj. T.   Her tears? And I am to leave her. (*Is about to follow her.*)

Fran.   (*holding him back.*) Surely not, Major. You would not follow her into her own room!

Maj. T.   Her misfortune? Did she not speak of misfortune?

Fran.   Yes, truly; the misfortune of losing you, after——

Maj. T.   After? After what? There is more in this. What is it, Franziska? Tell me! Speak!

Fran.   After, I mean, she has made such sacrifices on your account.

Maj. T.   Sacrifices for me!

Fran.   Well, listen. It is a good thing for you, Major, that you are freed from your engagement with her in this manner.—Why should I not tell you? It cannot remain a secret long. We have fled from home. Count von Bruchsal has disinherited my mistress, because she would not accept a husband of his choice. On that every one deserted and slighted her. What could we do? We determined to seek him, whom——

Maj. T.   Enough! Come, and let me throw myself at her feet.

Fran.   What are you thinking about! Rather go, and thank your good fortune.

Maj. T.   Pitiful creature! For what do you take me? Yet no, my dear Franziska, the advice did not come from your heart. Forgive my anger!

Fran.   Do not detain me any longer. I must see what she is about. How easily something might happen to her. Go now, and come again, if you like. (*Follows* Minna.)

SCENE VIII.—MAJOR VON TELLHEIM.

MAJ. T. But, Franziska! Oh! I will wait your return here.—No, that is more torturing!—If she is in earnest, she will not refuse to forgive me.—Now I want your aid, honest Werner!—No, Minna, I am no deceiver! (*Rushes off.*)

ACT V.

SCENE I.—MAJOR VON TELLHEIM (*from one side*), WERNER (*from the other.*)

MAJ. T. Ah! Werner! I have been looking for you everywhere. Where have you been?

WER. And I have been looking for you, Major; that is always the way.—I bring you good news.

MAJ. T. I do not want your news now; I want your money. Quick, Werner, give me all **you** have; and then raise as much more as you can.

WER. Major! Now, upon my life, that is just what I said—"He will borrow money from me, when he has got it himself to lend."

MAJ. T. You surely are not seeking excuses!

WER. That I may have nothing to upbraid you with, take it with your right hand, and give it me again with your left.

MAJ. T. Do not detain me, Werner. It is my intention to repay you; but when and how, God knows!

WER. Then you do not know yet that the treasury has received an order to pay you your money? I just heard it at——

MAJ. T. What are you talking about? What nonsense have you let them palm off on you? Do you not see that if it were true I should be the first person to know it? In short, Werner, money! money!

WER. Very well, with pleasure. Here is some! A hundred louis d'ors there, and a hundred ducats there. (*Gives him both.*)

Maj. Werner, go and give Just the hundred louis d'ors. Let him redeem the ring again, on which he raised the money this morning. But whence will you get some more. Werner? I want a good deal more.

Wer. Leave that to me. The man who bought my farm lives in the town. The date for payment is a fortnight hence, certainly; but the money is ready, and by a reduction of one half per cent——

Maj. T. Very well, my dear Werner! You see that I have had recourse to you alone—I must also confide all to you. The young lady you have seen is in distress——

Wer. That is bad!

Maj. T. But to-morrow she shall be my wife.

Wer. That is good!

Maj. T. And the day after, I leave this place with her. I can go; I will go. I would sooner throw over everything here! Who knows where some good luck may be in store for me. If you will, Werner, come with us. We will serve again.

Wer. Really? But where there is war, Major!

Maj. T. To be sure. Go, Werner, we will speak of this again.

Wer. Oh! my dear Major! The day after to-morrow! Why not to-morrow? I will get everything ready. In Persia, Major, there is a famous war; what do you say?

Maj. T. We will think of it. Only go, Werner!

Wer. Hurrah! Long live Prince Heraclius! (*Exit.*)

Scene II.—Major von Tellheim.

Maj. T. How do I feel! . . . . My whole soul has acquired a new impulse. My own unhappiness bowed me to the ground; made me fretful, short-sighted, shy, careless: her unhappiness raises me. I see clearly again, and feel myself ready and capable of undertaking anything for her sake. Why do I tarry? (*Is going towards* Minna's *room, when* Franziska *comes out of it.*)

Scene III.—Franziska, Major von Tellheim.

Fran. Is it you? I thought I heard your voice. What do you want, Major?

Maj. T. What do I want! What is she doing? Come!

Fran. She is just going out for a drive.

Maj. T. And alone? Without me? Where to?

Fran. Have you forgotten, Major?

Maj. T. How silly you are, Franziska! I irritated her, and she was angry. I will beg her pardon, and she will forgive me.

Fran. What! After you have taken the ring back, Major!

Maj. T. Ah! I did that in my confusion. I had forgotten about the ring. Where did I put it? (*Searches for it.*) Here it is.

Fran. Is that it? (*Aside, as he puts it again in his pocket.*) If he would only look at it closer!

Maj. T. She pressed it upon me so bitterly. But I have forgotten that. A full heart cannot weigh words. She will not for one moment refuse to take it again. And have I not hers?

Fran. She is now waiting for it in return. Where is it, Major? Show it to me, do!

Maj. T. (*embarrassed*). I have . . . . forgotten to put it on. Just—Just will bring it directly.

Fran. They are something alike, I suppose; let me look at that one. I am very fond of such things.

Maj. T. Another time, Franziska. Come now.

Fran. (*aside*). He is determined not to be drawn out of his mistake.

Maj. T. What do you say? Mistake!

Fran. It is a mistake, I say, if you think that my mistress is still a good match. Her own fortune is far from considerable; by a few calculations in their own favour her guardians may reduce it to nothing. She expected everything from her uncle; but this cruel uncle——

Maj. T. Let him go! Am I not man enough to make it all good to her again!

Fran. Do you hear? She is ringing; I must go in again.

Maj. T. I will accompany you.

FRAN. For heaven's sake, no! She forbad me expressly to speak with you. Come in at any rate a little time after me. (*Goes in.*)

SCENE IV.—MAJOR VON TELLHEIM.

MAJ. T. (*Calling after her.*) Announce me! Speak for me, Franziska! I shall follow you directly. What shall I say to her? Yet where the heart can speak, no preparation is necessary. There is one thing only which may need a studied turn . . . . this reserve, this scrupulousness of throwing herself, unfortunate as she is, into my arms; this anxiety to make a false show of still possessing that happiness which she has lost through me. How she is to exculpate herself to herself—for by me it is already forgiven—for this distrust in my honour, in her own worth. . . . . Ah! here she comes.

SCENE V.—MINNA, FRANZISKA, MAJOR VON TELLHEIM.

MIN. (*speaking as she comes out, as if not aware of the* MAJOR's *presence*). The carriage is at the door, Franziska, is it not? My fan!

MAJ. T. (*advancing to her.*) Where are you going, Madam?

MIN. (*with forced coldness*). I am going out, Major. I guess why you have given yourself the trouble of coming back: to return me my ring.—Very well, Major von Tellheim, have the goodness to give it to Franziska.—Franziska, take the ring from Major von Tellheim!—I have no time to lose. (*Is going.*)

MAJ. T. (*stepping before her*). Madam! Ah! what have I heard? I was unworthy of such love.

MIN. So, Franziska, you have——

FRAN. Told him all.

MAJ. T. Do not be angry with me, Madam. I am no deceiver. You have, on my account, lost much in the eyes of the world, but not in mine. In my eyes you have gained beyond measure by this loss. It was too sudden. You feared it might make an unfavourable impression on me; at first you wished to hide it from me. I do not

complain of this mistrust. It arose from the desire to retain my affection. That desire is my pride. You found
me in distress; and you did not wish to add distress to
distress. You could not divine how far your distress would
raise me above any thoughts of my own.

MIN. That is all very well, Major, but it is now over.
I have released you from your engagement; you have, by
taking back the ring——

MAJ. T. Consented to nothing! On the contrary, I
now consider myself bound more firmly than ever. You
are mine, Minna, mine for ever. (*Takes off the ring.*) Here,
take it for the second time—the pledge of my fidelity.

MIN. I take that ring again! That ring?

MAJ. T. Yes, dearest Minna, yes

MIN. What are you asking me? that ring?

MAJ. T. You received it for the first time from my
hand, when our positions were similar and the circumstances propitious. They are no longer propitious, but are
again similar. Equality is always the strongest tie of
love. Permit me, dearest Minna! (*Seizes her hand to put
on the ring.*)

MIN. What! by force, Major! No, there is no power
in the world which shall compel me to take back that
ring! Do you think that I am in want of a ring? Oh!
you may see (*pointing to her ring*) that I have another
here which is in no way inferior to yours.

FRAN. (*aside*). Well, if he does not see it now!

MAJ. T. (*letting fall her hand*). What is this? I see
Fräulein von Barnhelm, but I do not hear her.—You are
pretending.—Pardon me, that I use your own words.

MIN. (*in her natural tone*). Did those words offend you,
Major?

MAJ. T. They grieved me much.

MIN. (*affected*). They were not meant to do that, Tellheim. Forgive me, Tellheim.

MAJ. T. Ah! that friendly tone tells me you are yourself again, Minna; that you still love me.

FRAN. (*exclaims*) The joke would soon have gone a
little too far.

MIN. (*in a commanding tone*). Franziska, you will not
interfere in our affairs, I beg.

Fran. (*aside, in a surprised tone*). Not enough yet!

Min. Yes, sir, it would only be womanish vanity in me to pretend to be cold and scornful. No! Never! You deserve to find me as sincere as yourself. I do love you still, Tellheim, I love you still; but notwithstanding-——

Maj. T. No more, dearest Minna, no more! (*Seizes her hand again, to put on the ring.*)

Min. (*drawing back her hand*). Notwithstanding, so much the more am I determined that that shall never be, —never!—Of what are you thinking, Major?—I thought your own distress was sufficient. You must remain here; you must obtain by obstinacy—no better phrase occurs to me at the moment—the most perfect satisfaction, obtain it by obstinacy. . . . . And that even though the utmost distress should waste you away before the eyes of your calumniators——

Maj. T. So I thought, so I said, when I knew not what I thought or said. Chagrin and stifling rage had enveloped my whole soul; love itself, in the full blaze of happiness, could not illumine it. But it has sent its daughter, Pity, more familiar with gloomy misfortune, and she has dispelled the cloud, and opened again all the avenues of my soul to sensations of tenderness. The impulse of self preservation awakes, when I have something more precious than myself to support, and to support through my own exertions. Do not let the word "pity" offend you. From the innocent cause of our distress we may hear the term without humiliation. I am this cause; through me, Minna, have you lost friends and relations, fortune and country. Through me, in me, must you find them all again, or I shall have the destruction of the most lovely of her sex upon my soul. Let me not think of a future in which I must detest myself.—No, nothing shall detain me here longer. From this moment I will oppose nothing but contempt to the injustice which I suffer. Is this country the world? Does the sun rise here alone? Where can I not go? In what service shall I be refused? And should I be obliged to seek it in the most distant clime, only follow me with confidence, dearest Minna—we shall want for nothing. I have a friend who will assist me with pleasure.

SCENE VI.—*An* ORDERLY, MAJOR VON TELLHEIM, MINNA,
FRANZISKA.

FRAN. (*seeing the* ORDERLY). Hist, Major!

MAJ. T. (*to the* ORDERLY). Who do you want?

ORD. I am looking for Major von Tellheim. Ah! you
are the Major, I see. I have to give you this letter from
His Majesty the King (*taking one out of his bag*).

MAJ. T. To me?

ORD. According to the direction.

MIN. Franziska, do you hear? The Chevalier spoke
the truth after all.

ORD. (*whilst* TELLHEIM *takes the letter*). I beg your pardon,
Major; you should properly have had it yesterday, but
I could not find you out. I learnt your address this
morning only from Lieutenant Riccaut, on parade.

FRAN. Do you hear, my lady?—That is the Chevalier's
minister. " What is the name of de ministre out dere, on
de broad place?"

MAJ. T. I am extremely obliged to you for your
trouble.

ORD. It is my duty, Major. (*Exit.*)

SCENE VII.—MAJOR VON TELLHEIM, MINNA, FRANZISKA.

MAJ. T. Ah! Minna, what is this? What does this
contain?

MIN. I am not entitled to extend my curiosity so far.

MAJ. T. What! You would still separate my fate
from yours? — But why do I hesitate to open it? It
cannot make me more unhappy than I am : no, dearest
Minna, it cannot make us more unhappy—but perhaps
more happy! Permit me. (*While he opens and reads the
letter, the* LANDLORD *comes stealthily on the stage.*)

SCENE VIII.—LANDLORD, *the rest as before.*

LAND. (*to* FRANZISKA). Hist! my pretty maid! A word!

FRAN. (*to the* LANDLORD). Mr. Landlord, we do not yet
know ourselves what is in the letter.

LAND. Who wants to know about the letter! I come

about the ring. The lady must give it to me again, directly.
Just is there, and wants to redeem it.

Min. (*who in the meantime has approached the* Landlord).
Tell Just that it is already redeemed; and tell him by
whom—by me.

Land. But——

Min. I take it upon myself.   Go!   (*Exit* Landlord.)

Scene IX.—Major von Tellheim, Minna, Franziska.

Fran. And now, my lady, make it up with the poor
Major.

Min. Oh! kind intercessor! As if the difficulties must
not soon explain themselves.

Maj. T. (*after reading the letter, with much emotion.*)
Ah! nor has he herein belied himself! Oh! Minna,
what justice! what clemency! This is more than I expected; more than I deserve!—My fortune, my honour,
all is re-established!—Do I dream? (*Looking at the letter,
as if to convince himself.*) No, no delusion born of my own
desires! Read it yourself, Minna; read it yourself!

Min. I would not presume, Major.

Maj. T. Presume! The letter is to me; to your
Tellheim, Minna. It contains—what your uncle cannot
take from you. You must read it! Do read it.

Min. If it affords you pleasure, Major. (*Takes the letter
and reads.*)

"My dear Major von Tellheim,

"I hereby inform you, that the business which
caused me some anxiety on account of your honour, has been
cleared up in your favour. My brother had a more detailed
knowledge of it, and his testimony has more than proved
your innocence. The Treasury has received orders to
deliver again to you the bill in question, and to reimburse
the sum advanced. I have also ordered that all claims
which the Paymaster's Office brings forward against your
accounts be nullified. Please to inform me whether
your health will allow of your taking active service again.
I can ill spare a man of your courage and sentiments.
I am your gracious King," &c.

Maj. T. Now, what do you say to that, Minna?

2 d 2

Min. (*folding up and returning the letter*). I? Nothing.

Maj. T. Nothing?

Min. Stay—yes. That your king, who is a great man, can also be a good man.—But what is that to me! He is not my king.

Maj. T. And do you say nothing more? Nothing about ourselves?

Min. You are going to serve again. From Major, you will become Lieutenant-Colonel, perhaps Colonel. I congratulate you with all my heart.

Maj. T. And you do not know me better? No, since fortune restores me sufficient to satisfy the wishes of a reasonable man, it shall depend upon my Minna alone, whether for the future I shall belong to any one else but her. To her service alone my whole life shall be devoted! The service of the great is dangerous, and does not repay the trouble, the restraint, the humiliation which it costs. Minna is not amongst those vain people who love nothing in their husbands beyond their titles and positions. She will love me for myself; and for her sake I will forget the whole world. I became a soldier from party feeling— I do not myself know on what political principles—and from the whim that it is good for every honourable man to try the profession of arms for a time, to make himself familiar with danger, and to learn coolness and determination. Extreme necessity alone could have compelled me to make this trial a fixed mode of life, this temporary occupation a profession. But now that nothing compels me, my whole and sole ambition is to be a peaceful and a contented man. This with you, dearest Minna, I shall infallibly become; this in your society I shall unchangeably remain. Let the holy bond unite us to-morrow; and then we will look round us, and in the whole wide habitable world seek out the most peaceful, the brightest, most smiling nook which wants but a happy couple to be a Paradise. There we will dwell; there shall each day . . . . What is the matter, Minna? (Minna *turns away uneasily, and endeavours to hide her emotion.*)

Min. (*regaining her composure*). It is cruel of you, Tellheim, to paint such happiness to me, when I am forced to renounce it. My loss——

Maj. T. Your loss! Why name your loss? All that
Minna could lose is not Minna. You are still the sweetest,
dearest, loveliest, best creature under the sun ; all goodness and generosity, innocence and bliss! Now and then
a little petulant; at times somewhat wilful—so much the
better! So much the better! Minna would otherwise be
an angel, whom I should honour with trepidation, but not
dare to love. (*Takes her hand to kiss it.*)

Min. (*drawing away her hand*). Not so, sir. Why this
sudden change? Is this flattering impetuous lover, the cold
Tellheim!—Could his returning good fortune alone create
this ardour in him? He will permit me during his passionate excitement to retain the power of reflection for us both.
When he could himself reflect, I heard him say—"it is a
worthless love which does not scruple to expose its object
to scorn"—True; and I aspire to as pure and noble a
love as he himself. Now, when honour calls him, when a
great monarch solicits his services, shall I consent that he
shall give himself up to love-sick dreams with me? that
the illustrious warrior shall degenerate into a toying
swain? No, Major, follow the call of your higher
destiny.

Maj. T. Well! if the busy world has greater charms
for you, Minna, let us remain in the busy world! How
mean, how poor is this busy world; you now only know
its gilded surface. Yet certainly, Minna, you will . . . .
But let it be so! until then! Your charms shall not want
admirers, nor will my happiness lack enviers.

Min. No, Tellheim, I do not mean that! I send you
back into the busy world, on the road of honour, without
wishing to accompany you. Tellheim will there require
an irreproachable wife! A fugitive Saxon girl who has
thrown herself upon him——

Maj. T. (*starting up, and looking fiercely about him*).
Who dare say that! Ah! Minna, I feel afraid of myself,
when I imagine that any one but yourself could have
spoken so. My anger against him would know no
bounds.

Min. Exactly! That is just what I fear. You would
not endure one word of calumny against me, and yet you
would have to put up with the very bitterest every

day. In short, Tellheim, hear what I have firmly de·
termined, and from which nothing in the world shall turn
me——

Maj. T. Before you proceed, I implore you, Minna,
reflect for one moment, that you are about to pronounce
a sentence of life or death upon me!

Min. Without a moment's reflection! .... As certainly as I have given you back the ring with which you
formerly pledged your troth to me, as certainly as you
have taken back that same ring, so certainly shall the
unfortunate Minna never be the wife of the fortunate
Tellheim!

Maj. T. And herewith you pronounce my sentence.

Min. Equality is the only sure bond of love. The
happy Minna only wished to live for the happy Tellheim. Even Minna in misfortune would have allowed
herself to be persuaded either to increase or to assuage
the misfortune of her friend through herself. .... He
must have seen, before the arrival of that letter, which
has again destroyed all equality between us, that in
appearance only I refused.

Maj. T. Is that true? I thank you, Minna, that you
have not yet pronounced the sentence. You will only
marry Tellheim when unfortunate? You may have him.
(*Coolly.*) I perceive now that it would be indecorous in me
to accept this tardy justice; that it will be better if I do
not seek again that of which I have been deprived by
such shameful suspicion. Yes; I will suppose that I
have not received the letter. Behold my only answer to
it! (*About to tear it up.*)

Min. (*stopping him*). What are you going to do, Tellheim?

Maj. T. Obtain your hand.

Min. Stop!

Maj. T. Madam, it is torn without fail if you do not
quickly recall your words.—Then we will see what else
you may have to object to in me.

Min. What! In such a tone? Shall I, must I,
thus become contemptible in my own eyes? Never! She
is a worthless creature, who is not ashamed to owe her
whole happiness to the blind tenderness of a man!

MAJ. T. False! utterly false!

MIN. Can you venture to find fault with your own words when coming from my lips?

MAJ. T. Sophistry! Does the weaker sex dishonour itself by every action which does not become the stronger? Or can a man do everything which is proper in a woman? Which is appointed by nature to be the support of the other?

MIN. Be not alarmed, Tellheim! . . . . I shall not be quite unprotected, if I must decline the honour of your protection. I shall still have as much as is absolutely necessary. I have announced my arrival to our ambassador. I am to see him to-day. I hope he will assist me. Time is flying. Permit me, Major——

MAJ. T. I will accompany you, Madam.

MIN. No, Major; leave me.

MAJ. T. Sooner shall your shadow desert you! Come, Madam, where you will, to whom you will, everywhere, to friends and strangers, will I repeat in your presence— repeat a hundred times each day—what a bond binds you to me, and with what cruel caprice you wish to break it——

SCENE X.—JUST, *the rest as before.*

JUST. (*impetuously.*) Major! Major!

MAJ. T. Well!

JUST. Here quick! quick!

MAJ. T. Why? Come to me. Speak, what is the matter?

JUST. What do you think? (*Whispers to him.*)

MIN. (*aside to* FRANZISKA.) Do you notice anything, Franziska?

FRAN. Oh! you merciless creature! I have stood here on thorns?

MAJ. T. (*to* JUST.) What do you say? . . . . That is not possible! . . . . You? (*Looking fiercely at* MINNA.) Speak it out; tell it to her face. Listen, Madam.

JUST. The Landlord says, that Fräulein von Barnhelm has taken the ring which I pledged to him; she recognised it as her own, and would not return it.

MAJ. T. Is that true, Madam? No, that cannot be true!

MIN. (*smiling*). And why not, Tellheim? Why can it not be true?

MAJ. T. (*vehemently*). Then it is true! . . . . What terrible light suddenly breaks in upon me! . . . . Now I know you—false, faithless one!

MIN. (*alarmed*). Who, who is faithless?

MAJ. T. You, whom I will never more name!

MIN. Tellheim!

MAJ. T. Forget my name . . . . You came here with the intention of breaking with me . . . . It is evident! . . . . Oh, that chance should thus delight to assist the faithless! It brought your ring into your possession. Your craftiness contrived to get my own back into mine!

MIN. Tellheim, what visions are you conjuring up! Be calm, and listen to me.

FRAN. (*aside*). Now she will catch it!

SCENE XI.—WERNER (*with a purse full of gold*), *the rest as before.*

WER. Here I am already, Major!

MAJ. T. (*without looking at him*). Who wants you?

WER. I have brought more money! A thousand pistoles!

MAJ. T. I do not want them!

WER. And to-morrow, Major, you can have as many more.

MAJ. T. Keep your money!

WER. It is your money, Major. . . . . I do not think you see whom you are speaking to!

MAJ. T. Take it away! I say.

WER. What is the matter with you?—I am Werner.

MAJ. T. All goodness is dissimulation; all kindness, deceit.

WER. Is that meant for me?

MAJ. T. As you please!

WER. Why I have only obeyed your commands.

MAJ. T. Obey once more, and be off!

WER. Major! (*vexed*). I am a man——

MAJ. T. So much the better!

WER. Who can also be angry.

MAJ. T. Anger is the best thing we possess.

WER. I beg you, Major.

MAJ. T. How often must I tell you? I do not want your money!

WER. (*in a rage*). Then take it, who will! (*Throws the purse on the ground, and goes to the side*).

MIN. (*to* FRANZISKA). Ah! Franziska, I ought to have followed your advice. I have carried the jest too far.— Still, when he hears me . . . . (*going to him*).

FRAN. (*without answering* MINNA, *goes up to* WERNER). Mr. Sergeant——

WER. (*pettishly*). Go along!

FRAN. Ah! what men these are.

MIN. Tellheim! Tellheim! (TELLHEIM, *biting his fingers with rage, turns away his face, without listening*.) No, this is too bad. . . . . Only listen! . . . . You are mistaken! . . . . A mere misunderstanding. Tellheim, will you not hear your Minna? Can you have such a suspicion? . . . . I break my engagement with you? I came here for that purpose? . . . . Tellheim!

SCENE XII.—Two SERVANTS (*running into the room from different sides*), the rest as before.

FIRST SER. Your ladyship, his excellency the Count!

SECOND SER. He is coming, your ladyship!

FRAN. (*running to the window*). It is! it is he!

MIN. Is it? Now, Tellheim, quick!

MAJ. T. (*suddenly recovering himself*). Who, who comes? Your uncle, Madam! this cruel uncle! . . . . Let him come; just let him come! . . . . Fear not! . . . . He shall not hurt you even by a look. He shall have to deal with me. . . . . You do not indeed deserve it of me.

MIN. Quick, Tellheim! one embrace and forget all.

MAJ. T. Ah! did I but know that you could re-gret——

MIN. No, I can never regret having obtained a sight of your whole heart! .... Ah! what a man you are! .... Embrace your Minna, your happy Minna: and in nothing more happy than in the possession of you. (*Embracing.*) And now to meet him!

MAJ. T. To meet whom?

MIN. The best of your unknown friends.

MAJ. T. What!

MIN. The Count, my uncle; my father, your father..... My flight, his displeasure, my loss of property—do you not see that all is a fiction, credulous knight?

MAJ. T. Fiction! But the ring? the ring?

MIN. Where is the ring that I gave back to you?

MAJ. T. You will take it again? Ah! now I am happy. .... Here, Minna (*taking it from his pocket*).

MIN. Look at it first! Oh! how blind are those who will not see! .... What ring is that? the one you gave me? or the one I gave to you? Is it not the one which I did not like to leave in the landlord's possession?

MAJ. T. Heavens! what do I see! What do I hear!

MIN. Shall I take it again now? Shall I? Give it to me! give it! (*Takes it from him, and then puts it on his finger herself.*) There, now all is right!

MAJ. T. Where am I? (*Kissing her hand.*) Oh! malicious angel, to torture me so!

MIN. As a proof, my dear husband, that you shall never play me a trick without my playing you one in return. .... Do you suppose that you did not torture me also?

MAJ. T. Oh you actresses! But I ought to have known you.

FRAN. Not I, indeed; I am spoilt for acting. I trembled and shook, and was obliged to hold my lips together with my hand.

MIN. Nor was mine an easy part.—But come now——

MAJ. T. I have not recovered myself yet. How happy, yet how anxious, I feel. It is like awaking suddenly from a frightful dream.

MIN. We are losing time. .... I hear him coming now.

Scene XIII.—Count von Bruchsal (*accompanied by several servants and the* Landlord). *The rest as before.*

Count. (*entering*). She arrived in safety, I hope?

Min. (*running to meet him*). Ah! my father!

Count. Here I am, dear Minna (*embracing her*). But what, girl (*seeing Tellheim*), only four-and-twenty hours here, and friends—company already!

Min. Guess who it is?

Count. Not your Tellheim, surely!

Min. Who else!—Come, Tellheim (*introducing him*).

Count. Sir, we have never met; but at the first glance I fancied I recognised you. I wished it might be Major von Tellheim.—Your hand, sir; you have my highest esteem; I ask for your friendship. My niece, my daughter loves you.

Min. You know that, my father!—And was my love blind?

Count. No, Minna, your love was not blind; but your lover—is dumb.

Maj. T. (*throwing himself in the* Count's *arms*). Let me recover myself, my father!

Count. Right, my son. I see your heart can speak, though your lips cannot. I do not usually care for those who wear this uniform. But you are an honourable man, Tellheim; and one must love an honourable man, in whatever garb he may be.

Min. Ah! did you but know all!

Count. Why should I not hear all?—Which are my apartments, landlord?

Land. Will your Excellency have the goodness to walk this way?

Count. Come, Minna! Pray come, Major! (*Exit with the* Landlord *and servants.*)

Min. Come, Tellheim!

Maj. T. I will follow you in an instant, Minna. One word first with this man (*turning to* Werner.)

Min. And a good word, methinks, it should be. Should it not, Franziska? (*Exit.*)

Scene XIV.—Major von Tellheim, Werner, Just, Franziska.

Maj. T. (*pointing to the purse which* Werner *had thrown down*). Here, Just, pick up the purse, and carry it home. Go! (Just *takes it up and goes.*)

Wer. (*still standing, out of humour, in a corner, and absent till he hears the last words*). Well, what now?

Maj. T. (*in a friendly tone while going up to him*). Werner, when can I have the other two thousand pistoles?

Wer. (*in a good humour again instantly*). To-morrow, Major, to-morrow.

Maj. T. I do not need to become your debtor; but I will be your banker. All you good-natured people ought to have guardians. You are in a manner spendthrifts.—I irritated you just now, Werner.

Wer. Upon my life you did! But I ought not to have been such a dolt. Now I see it all clearly. I deserve a hundred lashes. You may give them to me, if you will, Major. Only no more ill will, dear Major!

Maj. T. Ill will! (*shaking him by the hand.*) Read in my eyes all that I cannot say to you—Ah! let me see the man with a better wife and a more trusty friend than I shall have.—Eh! Franziska? (*Exit.*)

Scene XV.—Werner, Franziska.

Fran. (*aside*). Yes, indeed, he is more than good!— Such a man will never fall in my way again.—It must come out. (*Approaching* Werner *bashfully.*) Mr. Sergeant!

Wer. (*wiping his eyes*). Well!

Fran. Mr. Sergeant——

Wer. What do you want, little woman?

Fran. Look at me, Mr. Sergeant.

Wer. I can't yet; there is something, I don't know what, in my eyes.

Fran. Now do look at me!

Wer. I am afraid I have looked at you too much already, little woman!—There, now I can see you. What then?

Fran. Mr. Sergeant—don't you want a Mrs. Sergeant?

WER. Do you really mean it, little woman?

FRAN. Really I do.

WER. And would you go with me to Persia even?

FRAN. Wherever you please.

WER. You will! Hullo, Major, no boasting! At any rate I have got as good a wife, and as trusty a friend, as you.—Give me your hand, my little woman! It's a match!—In ten years' time you shall be a general's wife, or a widow!

THE END.

LONDON: PRINTED BY WILLIAM CLOWES AND SONS, LIMITED, STAMFORD STREET AND CHARING CROSS.

BOHN'S LIBRARIES.

STANDARD LIBRARY.

336 Vols. at 3s. 6d. each, excepting those marked otherwise. (59*l.* 10*s.* 6*d.*)

ADDISON'S Works. Notes of Bishop Hurd. Short Memoir, Portrait, and 8 Plates of Medals. 6 vols.
This is the most complete edition of Addison's Works issued.

ALFIERI'S Tragedies. In English Verse. With Notes, Arguments, and Introduction, by E. A. Bowring, C.B. 2 vols.

AMERICAN POETRY. — *See Poetry of America.*

BACON'S Moral and Historical Works, including Essays, Apophthegms, Wisdom of the Ancients, New Atlantis, Henry VII., Henry VIII., Elizabeth, Henry Prince of Wales, History of Great Britain, Julius Cæsar, and Augustus Cæsar. With Critical and Biographical Introduction and Notes by J. Devey, M.A. Portrait.

—— *See also Philosophical Library.*

BALLADS AND SONGS of the Peasantry of England, from Oral Recitation, private MSS., Broadsides, &c. Edit. by R. Bell.

BEAUMONT AND FLETCHER. Selections. With Notes and Introduction by Leigh Hunt.

BECKMANN (J.) History of Inventions, Discoveries, and Origins. With Portraits of Beckmann and James Watt. 2 vols.

BELL (Robert).—*See Ballads, Chaucer, Green.*

BOSWELL'S Life of Johnson, with the TOUR in the HEBRIDES and JOHNSONIANA. New Edition, with Notes and Appendices, by the Rev. A. Napier, M.A., Trinity College, Cambridge, Vicar of Holkham, Editor of the Cambridge Edition of the 'Theological Works of Barrow.' With Frontispiece to each vol. 6 vols.

BREMER'S (Frederika) Works. Trans. by M. Howitt. Portrait. 4 vols.

BRINK (B. ten). Early English Literature (to Wiclif). By Bernhard ten Brink. Trans. by Prof. H. M. Kennedy.

BROWNE'S (Sir Thomas) Works. Edit. by S. Wilkin, with Dr. Johnson's Life of Browne. Portrait. 3 vols.

BURKE'S Works. 6 vols.

—— **Speeches on the Impeachment** of Warren Hastings ; and Letters. 2 vols.

—— **Life.** By Sir J. Prior. Portrait.

BURNS (Robert). Life of. By J. G. Lockhart, D.C.L. A new and enlarged edition. With Notes and Appendices by W. Scott Douglas. Portrait.

BUTLER'S (Bp.) Analogy of Religion, Natural and Revealed, to the Constitution and Course of Nature ; with Two Dissertations on Identity and Virtue, and Fifteen Sermons. With Introductions, Notes, and Memoir. Portrait.

CAMOËN'S Lusiad, or the Discovery of India. An Epic Poem. Trans. from the Portuguese, with Dissertation, Historical Sketch, and Life, by W. J. Mickle. 5th edition.

CARAFAS (The) of Maddaloni. Naples under Spanish Dominion. Trans. from the German of Alfred de Reumont. Portrait of Massaniello.

CARREL. The Counter-Revolution in England for the Re-establishment of Popery under Charles II. and James II., by Armand Carrel ; with Fox's History of James II. and Lord Lonsdale's Memoir of James II. Portrait of Carrel.

CARRUTHERS. — *See Pope, in Illustrated Library.*

CARY'S Dante. The Vision of Hell, Purgatory, and Paradise. Trans. by Rev. H. F. Cary, M.A. With Life, Chronological View of his Age, Notes, and Index of Proper Names. Portrait.
This is the authentic edition, containing Mr. Cary's last corrections, with additional notes.

CELLINI (Benvenuto). Memoirs of, by himself. With Notes of G. P. Carpani. Trans. by T. Roscoe. Portrait.

CERVANTES' Galatea. A Pastoral Romance. Trans. by G. W. J. Gyll.

—— **Exemplary Novels.** Trans. by W. K. Kelly.

—— **Don Quixote de la Mancha.** Motteux's Translation revised. With Lockhart's Life and Notes. 2 vols.

CHAUCER'S Poetical Works. With Poems formerly attributed to him. With a Memoir, Introduction, Notes, and a Glossary, by R. Bell. Improved edition, with Preliminary Essay by Rev. W. W. Skeat, M.A. Portrait. 4 vols.

CLASSIC TALES, containing Rasselas, Vicar of Wakefield, Gulliver's Travels, and The Sentimental Journey.

COLERIDGE'S (S. T.) Friend. A Series of Essays on Morals, Politics, and Religion. Portrait.

—— **Aids to Reflection. Confessions** of an Inquiring Spirit; and Essays on Faith and the Common Prayer-book. New Edition, revised.

—— **Table-Talk and Omniana.** By T. Ashe, B.A.

—— **Lectures on Shakespeare and** other Poets. Edit. by T. Ashe, B.A. Containing the lectures taken down in 1811-12 by J. P. Collier, and those delivered at Bristol in 1813.

—— **Biographia Literaria; or, Bio**graphical Sketches of my Literary Life and Opinions; with Two Lay Sermons.

—— **Miscellanies, Æsthetic and** Literary; to which is added, THE THEORY OF LIFE. Collected and arranged by T. Ashe, B.A.

COMMINES.—*See Philip.*

CONDÉ'S History of the Dominion of the Arabs in Spain. Trans. by Mrs. Foster. Portrait of Abderahmen ben Moavia. 3 vols.

COWPER'S Complete Works, Poems, Correspondence, and Translations. Edit. with Memoir by R. Southey. 45 Engravings. 8 vols.

COXE'S Memoirs of the Duke of Marlborough. With his original Correspondence, from family records at Blenheim. Revised edition. Portraits. 3 vols.
. An Atlas of the plans of Marlborough's campaigns, 4to. 10s. 6d.

COXE'S History of the House of Austria. From the Foundation of the Monarchy by Rhodolph of Hapsburgh to the Death of Leopold II., 1218-1792. By Archdn. Coxe. With Continuation from the Accession of Francis I. to the Revolution of 1848. 4 Portraits. 4 vols.

CUNNINGHAM'S Lives of the most Eminent British Painters. With Notes and 16 fresh Lives by Mrs. Heaton. 3 vols.

DEFOE'S Novels and Miscellaneous Works. With Prefaces and Notes, including those attributed to Sir W. Scott. Portrait. 7 vols.

DE LOLME'S Constitution of England, in which it is compared both with the Republican form of Government and the other Monarchies of Europe. Edit., with Life and Notes, by J. Macgregor.

DUNLOP'S History of Fiction. New Edition, revised. By Henry Wilson. 2 vols., 5s. each.

EDGEWORTH'S Stories for Children. With 8 Illustrations by L. Speed.

ELZE'S Shakespeare.—*See Shakespeare*

EMERSON'S Works. 3 vols.

Vol. I.—Essays, Lectures, and Poems.

Vol. II.—English Traits, Nature, and Conduct of Life.

Vol. III.—Society and Solitude—Letters and Social Aims—Miscellaneous Papers (hitherto uncollected)—May-Day, &c.

FOSTER'S (John) Life and Correspondence. Edit. by J. E. Ryland. Portrait. 2 vols.

—— **Lectures at Broadmead Chapel.** Edit. by J. E. Ryland. 2 vols.

—— **Critical Essays contributed to** the 'Eclectic Review.' Edit. by J. E. Ryland. 2 vols.

—— **Essays: On Decision of Charac**ter; on a Man's writing Memoirs of Himself; on the epithet Romantic; on the aversion of Men of Taste to Evangelical Religion.

—— **Essays on the Evils of Popular** Ignorance, and a Discourse on the Propagation of Christianity in India.

—— **Essay on the Improvemen of** Time, with Notes of Sermons and other Pieces.

—— **Fosteriana:** selected from periodical papers, edit. by H. G. Bohn.

FOX (Rt. Hon. C. J.)—*See Carrel.*

GIBBON'S Decline and Fall of the Roman Empire. Complete and unabridged, with variorum Notes; including those of Guizot, Wenck, Niebuhr, Hugo, Neander, and others. 7 vols. 2 Maps and Portrait.

GOETHE'S Works. Trans. into English by E. A. Bowring, C.B., Anna Swanwick, Sir Walter Scott, &c. &c. 14 vols.

Vols. I. and II.—Autobiography and Annals. Portrait.
Vol. III.—Faust. Complete.
Vol. IV.—Novels and Tales: containing Elective Affinities, Sorrows of Werther, The German Emigrants, The Good Women, and a Nouvelette.
Vol. V.—Wilhelm Meister's Apprenticeship.
Vol. VI.—Conversations with Eckerman and Soret.
Vol. VII.—Poems and Ballads in the original Metres, including Hermann and Dorothea.
Vol. VIII.—Götz von Berlichingen, Torquato Tasso, Egmont, Iphigenia, Clavigo, Wayward Lover, and Fellow Culprits.
Vol. IX. — Wilhelm Meister's Travels. Complete Edition.
Vol. X. — Tour in Italy. Two Parts. And Second Residence in Rome.
Vol. XI.—Miscellaneous Travels, Letters from Switzerland, Campaign in France, Siege of Mainz, and Rhine Tour.
Vol. XII.—Early and Miscellaneous Letters, including Letters to his Mother, with Biography and Notes.
Vol. XIII.—Correspondence with Zelter.
Vol. XIV.— Reineke Fox, West-Eastern Divan and Achilleid. Translated in original metres by A. Rogers.

—— **Correspondence with Schiller.** 2 vols.—*See Schiller.*

—— **Faust.**—*See Collegiate Series.*

GOLDSMITH'S Works. 5 vols.

Vol. I.—Life, Vicar of Wakefield, Essays, and Letters.
Vol. II.—Poems, Plays, Bee, Cock Lane Ghost.
Vol. III.—The Citizen of the World, Polite Learning in Europe.
Vol. IV.—Biographies, Criticisms, Later Essays.
Vol. V.—Prefaces, Natural History, Letters, Goody Two-Shoes, Index.

GREENE, MARLOWE, and BEN JONSON (Poems of). With Notes and Memoirs by R. Bell.

GREGORY'S (Dr.) The Evidences, Doctrines, and Duties of the Christian Religion.

GRIMM'S Household Tales. With the Original Notes. Trans. by Mrs. A. Hunt. Introduction by Andrew Lang, M.A. 2 vols.

GUIZOT'S History of Representative Government in Europe. Trans. by A. R. Scoble.

—— **English Revolution of 1640.** From the Accession of Charles I. to his Death. Trans. by W. Hazlitt. Portrait.

—— **History of Civilisation.** From the Roman Empire to the French Revolution. Trans. by W. Hazlitt. Portraits. 3 vols.

HALL'S (Rev. Robert) Works and Remains. Memoir by Dr. Gregory and Essay by J. Foster. Portrait.

HAUFF'S Tales. The Caravan—The Sheikh of Alexandria—The Inn in the Spessart. Translated by Prof. S. Mendel.

HAWTHORNE'S Tales. 3 vols.

Vol. I.—Twice-told Tales, and the Snow Image.
Vol. II.—Scarlet Letter, and the House with Seven Gables.
Vol. III. — Transformation, and Blithedale Romance.

HAZLITT'S (W.) Works. 7 vols.

—— **Table-Talk.**

—— **The Literature of the Age of** Elizabeth and Characters of Shakespeare's Plays.

—— **English Poets and English Comic** Writers.

—— **The Plain Speaker.** Opinions on Books, Men, and Things.

—— **Round Table.** Conversations of James Northcote, R.A.; Characteristics.

—— **Sketches and Essays,** and Winterslow.

—— **Spirit of the Age;** or, Contemporary Portraits. New Edition, by W. Carew Hazlitt.

HEINE'S Poems. Translated in the original Metres, with Life by E. A. Bowring, C.B.

—— **Travel-Pictures.** The Tour in the Harz, Norderney, and Book of Ideas, together with the Romantic School. Trans. by F. Storr. With Maps and Appendices.

HOFFMANN'S Works. The Serapion Brethren. Vol. I. Trans. by Lt.-Col. Ewing. [*Vol. II. in the press.*]

HOOPER'S (G.) Waterloo: The Downfall of the First Napoleon: a History of the Campaign of 1815. By George Hooper. With Maps and Plans. New Edition, revised.

HUGO'S (Victor) Dramatic Works. Hernani—RuyBlas—The King's Diversion. Translated by Mrs. Newton Crosland and F. L. Slous.

—— **Poems,** chiefly Lyrical. Collected by H. L. Williams.

HUNGARY: its History and Revolution, with Memoir of Kossuth. Portrait.

HUTCHINSON (Colonel). Memoirs of. By his Widow, with her Autobiography, and the Siege of Lathom House. Portrait.

IRVING'S (Washington) Complete Works. 15 vols.

—— **Life and Letters.** By his Nephew, Pierre E. Irving. With Index and a Portrait. 2 vols.

JAMES'S (G. P. R.) Life of Richard Cœur de Lion. Portraits of Richard and Philip Augustus. 2 vols.

—— **Louis XIV.** Portraits. 2 vols.

JAMESON (Mrs.) Shakespeare's Heroines. Characteristics of Women. By Mrs. Jameson.

JEAN PAUL.—*See Richter.*

JOHNSON'S Lives of the Poets. Edited, with Notes, by Mrs. Alexander Napier. And an Introduction by Professor J. W. Hales, M.A. 3 vols.

JONSON (Ben). Poems of.—*See Greene.*

JOSEPHUS (Flavius), The Works of. Whiston's Translation. Revised by Rev. A. R. Shilleto, M.A. With Topographical and Geographical Notes by Colonel Sir C. W. Wilson, K.C.B. 5 vols.

JUNIUS'S Letters. With Woodfall's Notes. An Essay on the Authorship. Facsimiles of Handwriting. 2 vols.

LA FONTAINE'S Fables. In English Verse, with Essay on the Fabulists. By Elizur Wright.

LAMARTINE'S The Girondists, or Personal Memoirs of the Patriots of the French Revolution. Trans. by H. T. Ryde. Portraits of Robespierre, Madame Roland, and Charlotte Corday. 3 vols.

—— **The Restoration of Monarchy in France (a Sequel to The Girondists).** 5 Portraits. 4 vols.

—— **The French Revolution of 1848.** Portraits.

LAMB'S (Charles) Elia and Eliana. Complete Edition. Portrait.

LAMB'S (Charles) Specimens of English Dramatic Poets of the time of Elizabeth. With Notes and the Extracts from the Garrick Plays.

—— **Talfourd's Letters of Charles Lamb.** New Edition, by W. Carew Hazlitt. 2 vols.

LANZI'S History of Painting in Italy, from the Period of the Revival of the Fine Arts to the End of the 18th Century. With Memoir and Portraits. Trans. by T. Roscoe. 3 vols.

LAPPENBERG'S England under the Anglo-Saxon Kings. Trans. by B. Thorpe, F.S.A. 2 vols.

LESSING'S Dramatic Works. Complete. By E. Bell, M.A. With Memoir by H. Zimmern. Portrait. 2 vols.

—— **Laokoon, Dramatic Notes, and** Representation of Death by the Ancients. Trans. by E. C. Beasley and Helen Zimmern. Frontispiece.

LOCKE'S Philosophical Works, containing Human Understanding, Controversy with Bishop of Worcester, Malebranche's Opinions, Natural Philosophy, Reading and Study. With Introduction, Analysis, and Notes, by J. A. St. John. Portrait. 2 vols.

—— **Life and Letters,** with Extracts from his Common-place Books. By Lord King.

LOCKHART (J. G.)—*See Burns.*

LUTHER'S Table-Talk. Trans. by W. Hazlitt. With Life by A. Chalmers, and LUTHER'S CATECHISM. Portrait after Cranach.

—— **Autobiography.**—*See Michelet.*

MACHIAVELLI'S History of Florence, THE PRINCE, Savonarola, Historical Tracts, and Memoir. Portrait.

MARLOWE. Poems of.—*See Greene.*

MARTINEAU'S (Harriet) History of England (including History of the Peace) from 1800-1846. 5 vols.

MENZEL'S History of Germany, from the Earliest Period to the Crimean War. Portraits. 3 vols.

MICHELET'S Autobiography of Luther. Trans. by W. Hazlitt. With Notes.

—— **The French Revolution to the** Flight of the King in 1791. Frontispiece.

MIGNET'S The French Revolution, from 1789 to 1814. Portrait of Napoleon.

MILTON'S Prose Works. With Preface, Preliminary Remarks by J. A. St. John, and Index. 5 vols. Portraits.

—— **Poetical Works.** With 120 Wood Engravings. 2 vols.

MITFORD'S (Miss) Our Village. Sketches of Rural Character and Scenery. 2 Engravings. 2 vols.

MOLIÈRE'S Dramatic Works. In English Prose, by C. H. Wall. With a Life and a Portrait. 3 vols.
  'It is not too much to say that we have here probably as good a translation of Molière as can be given.'—*Academy.*

MONTAGU. Letters and Works of Lady Mary Wortley Montagu. Lord Wharncliffe's Third Edition. Edited by W. Moy Thomas. New and revised edition. With steel plates. 2 vols. 5*s.* each.

MONTESQUIEU'S Spirit of Laws. Revised Edition, with D'Alembert's Analysis, Notes, and Memoir. 2 vols.

NEANDER (Dr. A.) History of the Christian Religion and Church. Trans. by J. Torrey. With Short Memoir. 10 vols.

—— **Life of Jesus Christ, in its Historical Connexion and Development.**

—— **The Planting and Training of** the Christian Church by the Apostles. With the Antignosticus, or Spirit of Tertullian. Trans. by J. E. Ryland. 2 vols.

—— **Lectures on the History of** Christian Dogmas. Trans. by J. E. Ryland. 2 vols.

—— **Memorials of Christian Life in** the Early and Middle Ages; including Light in Dark Places. Trans. by J. E. Ryland.

NORTH'S Lives of the Right Hon. Francis North, Baron Guildford, the Hon. Sir Dudley North, and the Hon. and Rev. Dr. John North. By the Hon. Roger North. Edited by A. Jessopp, D.D. With 3 Portraits. 3 vols. 3*s.* 6*d.* each.
  'Lovers of good literature will rejoice at the appearance of a new, handy, and complete edition of so justly famous a book, and will congratulate themselves that it has found so competent and skilful an editor as Dr. Jessopp.'—*Times.*

OCKLEY (S.) History of the Sara- cens and their Conquests in Syria, Persia, and Egypt. Comprising the Lives of Mohammed and his Successors to the Death of Abdalmelik, the Eleventh Caliph. By Simon Ockley, B.D., Portrait of Mohammed.

PASCAL'S Thoughts. Translated from the Text of M. Auguste Molinier by C. Kegan Paul. 3rd edition.

PERCY'S Reliques of Ancient English Poetry, consisting of Ballads, Songs, and other Pieces of our earlier Poets, with some few of later date. With Essay on Ancient Minstrels, and Glossary. 2 vols.

PHILIP DE COMMINES. Memoirs of. Containing the Histories of Louis XI. and Charles VIII., and Charles the Bold, Duke of Burgundy. With the History of Louis XI., by Jean de Troyes. Translated, with a Life and Notes, by A. R. Scoble. Portraits. 2 vols.

PLUTARCH'S LIVES. Translated, with Notes and Life, by A. Stewart, M.A., late Fellow of Trinity College, Cambridge, and G. Long, M.A. 4 vols.

POETRY OF AMERICA. Selections from One Hundred Poets, from 1776 to 1876. With Introductory Review, and Specimens of Negro Melody, by W. J. Linton. Portrait of W. Whitman.

RACINE'S (Jean) Dramatic Works. A metrical English version, with Biographical notice. By R. Bruce Boswell, M.A. Oxon. 2 vols.

RANKE (L.) History of the Popes, their Church and State, and their Conflicts with Protestantism in the 16th and 17th Centuries. Trans. by E. Foster. Portraits. 3 vols.

—— **History of Servia.** Trans. by Mrs. Kerr. To which is added, The Slave Provinces of Turkey, by Cyprien Robert.

—— **History of the Latin and Teu-** tonic Nations. 1494-1514. Trans. by P. A. Ashworth, translator of Dr. Gneist's 'History of the English Constitution.'

REUMONT (Alfred de). —*See Carafas.*

REYNOLDS' (Sir J.) Literary Works. With Memoir and Remarks by H. W. Beechy. 2 vols.

RICHTER (Jean Paul). Levana, a Treatise on Education; together with the Autobiography, and a short Memoir.

—— **Flower, Fruit, and Thorn Pieces,** or the Wedded Life, Death, and Marriage of Siebenkaes. Translated by Alex. Ewing. The only complete English translation.

ROSCOE'S (W.) Life of Leo X., with Notes, Historical Documents, and Dissertation on Lucretia Borgia. 3 Portraits. 2 vols.

—— **Lorenzo de' Medici,** called 'The Magnificent,' with Copyright Notes, Poems, Letters, &c. With Memoir of Roscoe and Portrait of Lorenzo.

RUSSIA, History of, from the earliest Period to the Crimean War. By W. K. Kelly. 3 Portraits. 2 vols.

SCHILLER'S Works. 7 vols.

Vol. I.—History of the Thirty Years' War. Rev. A. J. W. Morrison, M.A. Portrait.

Vol. II.—History of the Revolt in the Netherlands, the Trials of Counts Egmont and Horn, the Siege of Antwerp, and the Disturbance of France preceding the Reign of Henry IV. Translated by Rev. A. J. W. Morrison and L. Dora Schmitz.

Vol. III.—Don Carlos. R. D. Boylan —Mary Stuart. Mellish — Maid of Orleans. Anna Swanwick—Bride of Messina. A. Lodge, M.A. Together with the Use of the Chorus in Tragedy (a short Essay). Engravings.

These Dramas are all translated in metre.

Vol. IV.—Robbers—Fiesco—Love and Intrigue—Demetrius—Ghost Seer—Sport of Divinity.

The Dramas in this volume are in prose.

Vol. V.—Poems. E. A. Bowring, C.B.

Vol. VI.—Essays, Æsthetical and Philosophical, including the Dissertation on the Connexion between the Animal and Spiritual in Man.

Vol. VII. — Wallenstein's Camp. J. Churchill. — Piccolomini and Death of Wallenstein. S. T. Coleridge.—William Tell. Sir Theodore Martin, K.C.B., LL.D.

SCHILLER and GOETHE. Correspondence between, from A.D. 1794-1805. Trans. by L. Dora Schmitz. 2 vols.

SCHLEGEL (F.) Lectures on the Philosophy of Life and the Philosophy of Language. Trans. by A. J. W. Morrison.

—— **The History of Literature,** Ancient and Modern.

—— **The Philosophy of History.** With Memoir and Portrait. Trans. by J. B. Robertson.

—— **Modern History,** with the Lectures entitled Cæsar and Alexander, and The Beginning of our History. Translated by L. Purcell and R. H. Whitelock.

—— **Æsthetic and Miscellaneous** Works, containing Letters on Christian Art, Essay on Gothic Architecture, Remarks on the Romance Poetry of the Middle Ages, on Shakspeare, the Limits of the Beautiful, and on the Language and Wisdom of the Indians. By E. J. Millington.

SCHLEGEL (A. W.) Dramatic Art and Literature. By J. Black. With Memoir by Rev. A. J. W. Morrison. Portrait.

SCHUMANN (Robert), His Life and Works. By A. Reissmann. Trans. by A. L. Alger.

—— **Early Letters.** Translated by May Herbert. With Preface by Sir G. Grove.

SHAKESPEARE'S Dramatic Art. The History and Character of Shakspeare's Plays. By Dr. H. Ulrici. Trans. by L. Dora Schmitz. 2 vols.

SHAKESPEARE (William). A Literary Biography by Karl Elze, Ph.D., LL.D. Translated by L. Dora Schmitz. 5s.

SHERIDAN'S Dramatic Works. With Memoir. Portrait (after Reynolds).

SKEAT (Rev. W. W.)—*See Chaucer.*

SISMONDI'S History of the Litera-ture of the South of Europe. Trans. by T. Roscoe. Portraits. 2 vols.

SMITH'S (Adam) Theory of Moral Sentiments; with Essay on the First Formation of Languages, and Critical Memoir by Dugald Stewart.

—— *See Economic Library.*

SMYTH'S (Professor) Lectures on Modern History; from the Irruption of the Northern Nations to the close of the American Revolution. 2 vols.

—— **Lectures on the French Revolu-**tion. With Index. 2 vols.

SOUTHEY.—*See Cowper, Wesley, and (Illustrated Library) Nelson.*

STURM'S Morning Communings with God, or Devotional Meditations for Every Day. Trans. by W. Johnstone, M.A.

SULLY. Memoirs of the Duke of, Prime Minister to Henry the Great. With Notes and Historical Introduction. 4 Portraits. 4 vols.

TAYLOR'S (Bishop Jeremy) Holy Living and Dying, with Prayers, containing the Whole Duty of a Christian and the parts of Devotion fitted to all Occasions. Portrait.

TEN BRINK.—*See Brink.*

THIERRY'S Conquest of England by the Normans; its Causes, and its Consequences in England and the Continent. By W. Hazlitt. With short Memoir. 2 Portraits. 2 vols.

ULRICI (Dr.)—*See Shakespeare.*

VASARI. Lives of the most Eminent Painters, Sculptors, and Architects. By Mrs. J. Foster, with selected Notes. Portrait. 6 vols., Vol. VI. being an additional Volume of Notes by Dr. J. P. Richter.

WERNER'S Templars in Cyprus. Trans. by E. A. M. Lewis.

WESLEY, the Life of, and the Rise and Progress of Methodism. By Robert Southey. Portrait. 5s.

WHEATLEY. A Rational Illustra-tion of the Book of Common Prayer, being the Substance of everything Liturgical in all former Ritualist Commentators upon the subject. Frontispiece.

YOUNG (Arthur) Travels in France. Edited by Miss Betham Edwards. With a Portrait.

HISTORICAL LIBRARY.

22 Volumes at 5s. each.　(5l. 10s. per set.)

EVELYN'S Diary and Correspond-
dence, with the Private Correspondence of
Charles I and Sir Edward Nicholas, and
between Sir Edward Hyde (Earl of Claren-
don) and Sir Richard Browne. Edited from
the Original MSS. by W. Bray, F.A.S.
4 vols. 45 Engravings (after Vandyke,
Lely, Kneller, and Jamieson, &c.).

N.B.—This edition contains 130 letters
from Evelyn and his wife, printed by permission, and contained in no other edition.

PEPYS' Diary and Correspondence.
With Life and Notes, by Lord Braybrooke.
4 vols. With Appendix containing additional Letters, an Index, and 31 Engravings (after Vandyke, Sir P. Lely,
Holbein, Kneller, &c.).

N.B.—This is a reprint of Lord Braybrooke's fourth and last edition, containing
all his latest notes and corrections, the
copyright of the publishers.

JESSE'S Memoirs of the Court of
England under the Stuarts, including the
Protectorate. 3 vols. With Index and 42
Portraits (after Vandyke, Lely, &c.).

—— **Memoirs of the Pretenders and**
their Adherents. 6 Portraits.

NUGENT'S (Lord) Memorials of
Hampden, his Party and Times. With
Memoir. 12 Portraits (after Vandyke
and others).

STRICKLAND'S (Agnes) Lives of the
Queens of England from the Norman
Conquest. From authentic Documents,
public and private. 6 Portraits. 6 vols.

—— **Life of Mary Queen of Scots.**
2 Portraits. 2 vols.

—— **Lives of the Tudor and Stuart**
Princesses. With 2 Portraits.

PHILOSOPHICAL LIBRARY.

16 Vols. at 5s. each, excepting those marked otherwise.　(3l. 14s. per set.)

BACON'S Novum Organum and Ad-
vancement of Learning. With Notes by
J. Devey, M.A.

BAX. A Handbook of the History
of Philosophy, for the use of Students.
By E. Belfort Bax, Editor of Kant's
'Prolegomena.'

COMTE'S Philosophy of the Sciences.
An Exposition of the Principles of the
Cours de Philosophie Positive. By G. H.
Lewes, Author of 'The Life of Goethe.'

DRAPER (Dr. J. W.) A History of
the Intellectual Development of Europe.
2 vols.

HEGEL'S Philosophy of History. By
J. Sibree, M.A.

KANT'S Critique of Pure Reason.
By J. M. D. Meiklejohn.

—— **Prolegomena and Metaphysical**
Foundations of Natural Science, with Bio-
graphy and Memoir by E. Belfort Bax.
Portrait.

LOGIC, or the Science of Inference.
A Popular Manual. By J. Devey.

MILLER (Professor). History Philo-
sophically Illustrated, from the Fall of the
Roman Empire to the French Revolution.
With Memoir. 4 vols. 3s. 6d. each.

SCHOPENHAUER on the Fourfold
Root of the Principle of Sufficient Reason,
and on the Will in Nature. Trans. from
the German.

—— **Essays.** Selected and Translated by
E. Belfort Bax. [*In the press.*

SPINOZA'S Chief Works. Trans. with
Introduction by R. H. M. Elwes. 2 vols.

Vol. I.—Tractatus Theologico-Politicus
—Political Treatise.

Vol. II.— Improvement o the Understanding—Ethics—Letters.

THEOLOGICAL LIBRARY.

15 *Vols. at* 5s. *each (except Chillingworth,* 3s. 6d.). (3l. 13s. 6d. *per set.*)

BLEEK. Introduction to the Old Testament. By Friedrich Bleek. Trans. under the supervision of Rev. E. Venables, Residentiary Canon of Lincoln. 2 vols.

CHILLINGWORTH'S Religion of Protestants. 3s. 6d.

EUSEBIUS. Ecclesiastical History of Eusebius Pamphilius, Bishop of Cæsarea. Trans. by Rev. C. F. Cruse, M.A. With Notes, Life, and Chronological Tables.

EVAGRIUS. History of the Church. —*See Theodoret.*

HARDWICK. History of the Articles of Religion ; to which is added a Series of Documents from A.D. 1536 to A.D. 1615. Ed. by Rev. F. Proctor.

HENRY'S (Matthew) Exposition of the Book of Psalms. Numerous Woodcuts.

PEARSON (John, D.D.) Exposition of the Creed. Edit. by E. Walford, M.A. With Notes, Analysis, and Indexes.

PHILO-JUDÆUS, Works of. The Contemporary of Josephus. Trans. by C. D. Yonge. 4 vols.

PHILOSTORGIUS. Ecclesiastical History of.—*See Sozomen.*

SOCRATES' Ecclesiastical History. Comprising a History of the Church from Constantine, A.D. 305, to the 38th year of Theodosius II. With Short Account of the Author, and selected Notes.

SOZOMEN'S Ecclesiastical History. A.D. 324-440. With Notes, Prefatory Remarks by Valesius, and Short Memoir. Together with the ECCLESIASTICAL HISTORY OF PHILOSTORGIUS, as epitomised by Photius. Trans. by Rev. E. Walford, M.A. With Notes and brief Life.

THEODORET and EVAGRIUS. Histories of the Church from A.D. 332 to the Death of Theodore of Mopsuestia, A.D. 427 ; and from A.D. 431 to A.D. 544. With Memoirs.

WIESELER'S (Karl) Chronological Synopsis of the Four Gospels. Trans. by Rev. Canon Venables.

ANTIQUARIAN LIBRARY.

35 *Vols. at* 5s. *each.* (8l. 15s. *per set.*)

ANGLO-SAXON CHRONICLE. — *See Bede.*

ASSER'S Life of Alfred.—*See Six O. E. Chronicles.*

BEDE'S (Venerable) Ecclesiastical History of England. Together with the ANGLO-SAXON CHRONICLE. With Notes, Short Life, Analysis, and Map. Edit. by J. A. Giles, D.C.L.

BOETHIUS'S Consolation of Philo- sophy. King Alfred's Anglo-Saxon Version of. With an English Translation on opposite pages, Notes, Introduction, and Glossary, by Rev. S. Fox, M.A. To which is added the Anglo-Saxon Version of the METRES OF BOETHIUS, with a free Translation by Martin F. Tupper, D.C.L.

BRAND'S Popular Antiquities of England, Scotland, and Ireland. Illustrating the Origin of our Vulgar and Provincial Customs, Ceremonies, and Superstitions. By Sir Henry Ellis, K.H., F.R.S. Frontispiece. 3 vols.

CHRONICLES of the CRUSADES. Contemporary Narratives of Richard Cœur de Lion, by Richard of Devizes and Geoffrey de Vinsauf; and of the Crusade at Saint Louis, by Lord John de Joinville. With Short Notes. Illuminated Frontispiece from an old MS.

DYER'S (T. F. T.) British Popular Customs, Present and Past. An Account of the various Games and Customs associated with different Days of the Year in the British Isles, arranged according to the Calendar. By the Rev. T. F. Thiselton Dyer, M.A.

EARLY TRAVELS IN PALESTINE. Comprising the Narratives of Arculf, Willibald, Bernard, Sæwulf, Sigurd, Benjamin of Tudela, Sir John Maundeville, De la Brocquière, and Maundrell ; all unabridged. With Introduction and Notes by Thomas Wright. Map of Jerusalem.

ELLIS (G.) Specimens of Early En-
glish Metrical Romances, relating to
Arthur, Merlin, Guy of Warwick, Richard
Cœur de Lion, Charlemagne, Roland, &c.
&c. With Historical Introduction by J. O.
Halliwell, F.R.S. Illuminated Frontispiece from an old MS.

ETHELWERD. Chronicle of.—*See
Six O. E. Chronicles.*

FLORENCE OF WORCESTER'S
Chronicle, with the Two Continuations:
comprising Annals of English History
from the Departure of the Romans to the
Reign of Edward I. Trans., with Notes,
by Thomas Forester, M.A.

GEOFFREY OF MONMOUTH.
Chronicle of.—*See Six O. E. Chronicles.*

GESTA ROMANORUM, or Enter-
taining Moral Stories invented by the
Monks. Trans. with Notes by the Rev.
Charles Swan. Edit. by W. Hooper, M.A.

GILDAS. Chronicle of.—*See Six O. E.
Chronicles.*

GIRALDUS CAMBRENSIS' Histori-
cal Works. Containing Topography of
Ireland, and History of the Conquest of
Ireland, by Th. Forester, M.A. Itinerary
through Wales, and Description of Wales,
by Sir R. Colt Hoare.

HENRY OF HUNTINGDON'S His-
tory of the English, from the Roman In-
vasion to the Accession of Henry II.;
with the Acts of King Stephen, and the
Letter to Walter. By T. Forester, M.A.
Frontispiece from an old MS.

INGULPH'S Chronicles of the Abbey
of Croyland, with the CONTINUATION by
Peter of Blois and others. Trans. with
Notes by H. T. Riley, B.A.

KEIGHTLEY'S (Thomas) Fairy My-
thology, illustrative of the Romance and
Superstition of Various Countries. Frontispiece by Cruikshank.

LEPSIUS'S Letters from Egypt,
Ethiopia, and the Peninsula of Sinai; to
which are added, Extracts from his
Chronology of the Egyptians, with refer-
ence to the Exodus of the Israelites. By
L. and J. B. Horner. Maps and Coloured
View of Mount Barkal.

MALLET'S Northern Antiquities, or
an Historical Account of the Manners,
Customs, Religions, and Literature of the
Ancient Scandinavians. Trans. by Bishop
Percy. With Translation of the PROSE
EDDA, and Notes by J. A. Blackwell.
Also an Abstract of the 'Eyrbyggia Saga'
by Sir Walter Scott. With Glossary
and Coloured Frontispiece.

MARCO POLO'S Travels; with Notes
and Introduction. Edit. by T. Wright.

MATTHEW PARIS'S English His-
tory, from 1235 to 1273. By Rev. J. A.
Giles, D.C.L. With Frontispiece. 3 vols.—
See also Roger of Wendover.

MATTHEW OF WESTMINSTER'S
Flowers of History, especially such as relate to the affairs of Britain, from the beginning of the World to A.D. 1307. By
C. D. Yonge. 2 vols.

NENNIUS. Chronicle of.—*See Six
O. E. Chronicles.*

ORDERICUS VITALIS' Ecclesiastical
History of England and Normandy. With
Notes, Introduction of Guizot, and the
Critical Notice of M. Delille, by T.
Forester, M.A. To which is added the
CHRONICLE OF St. EVROULT. With Gene-
ral and Chronological Indexes. 4 vols.

PAULI'S (Dr. R.) Life of Alfred the
Great. To which is appended Alfred's
ANGLO-SAXON VERSION OF OROSIUS. With
literal Translation interpaged, Notes, and
an ANGLO-SAXON GRAMMAR and Glossary,
by B. Thorpe. Frontispiece.

RICHARD OF CIRENCESTER.
Chronicle of.—*See Six O. E. Chronicles.*

ROGER DE HOVEDEN'S Annals of
English History, comprising the History
of England and of other Countries of Europe from A.D. 732 to A.D. 1201. With
Notes by H. T. Riley, B.A. 2 vols.

ROGER OF WENDOVER'S Flowers
of History, comprising the History of
England from the Descent of the Saxons to
A.D. 1235, formerly ascribed to Matthew
Paris. With Notes and Index by J. A.
Giles, D.C.L. 2 vols.

SIX OLD ENGLISH CHRONICLES:
viz., Asser's Life of Alfred and the Chronicles of Ethelwerd, Gildas, Nennius, Geoffrey of Monmouth, and Richard of Cirencester. Edit., with Notes, by J. A. Giles,
D.C.L. Portrait of Alfred.

WILLIAM OF MALMESBURY'S
Chronicle of the Kings of England, from
the Earliest Period to King Stephen. By
Rev. J. Sharpe. With Notes by J. A.
Giles, D.C.L. Frontispiece.

YULE-TIDE STORIES. A Collection
of Scandinavian and North-German Popular Tales and Traditions, from the Swedish,
Danish, and German. Edit. by B. Thorpe.

ILLUSTRATED LIBRARY.

80 Vols. at 5s. each, excepting those marked otherwise. (19*l.* 17*s.* 6*d. per set.*)

ALLEN'S (Joseph, R.N.) Battles of the British Navy. Revised edition, with Indexes of Names and Events, and 57 Portraits and Plans. 2 vols.

ANDERSEN'S Danish Fairy Tales. By Caroline Peachey. With Short Life and 120 Wood Engravings.

ARIOSTO'S Orlando Furioso. In English Verse by W. S. Rose. With Notes and Short Memoir. Portrait after Titian, and 24 Steel Engravings. 2 vols.

BECHSTEIN'S Cage and Chamber Birds : their Natural History, Habits, &c. Together with SWEET'S BRITISH WARBLERS. 43 Coloured Plates and Woodcuts.

BONOMI'S Nineveh and its Palaces. The Discoveries of Botta and Layard applied to the Elucidation of Holy Writ. 7 Plates and 294 Woodcuts.

BUTLER'S Hudibras, with Variorum Notes and Biography. Portrait and 28 Illustrations.

CATTERMOLE'S Evenings at Haddon Hall. Romantic Tales of the Olden Times. With 24 Steel Engravings after Cattermole.

CHINA, Pictorial, Descriptive, and Historical, with some account of Ava and the Burmese, Siam, and Anam. Map, and nearly 100 Illustrations.

CRAIK'S (G. L.) Pursuit of Knowledge under Difficulties. Illustrated by Anecdotes and Memoirs. Numerous Woodcut Portraits.

CRUIKSHANK'S Three Courses and a Dessert ; comprising three Sets of Tales, West Country, Irish, and Legal ; and a Mélange. With 50 Illustrations by Cruikshank.

—— **Punch and Judy.** The Dialogue of the Puppet Show ; an Account of its Origin, &c. 24 Illustrations and Coloured Plates by Cruikshank.

DANTE, in English Verse, by I. C. Wright, M.A. With Introduction and Memoir. Portrait and 34 Steel Engravings after Flaxman.

DIDRON'S Christian Iconography ; a History of Christian Art in the Middle Ages. By the late A. N. Didron. Trans. by E. J. Millington, and completed, with Additions and Appendices, by Margaret Stokes. 2 vols. With numerous Illustrations.

Vol. I. The History of the Nimbus, the Aureole, and the Glory ; Representations of the Persons of the Trinity.

Vol. II. The Trinity ; Angels ; Devils The Soul ; The Christian Scheme. Appendices.

DYER (Dr. T. H.) Pompeii : its Buildings and Antiquities. An Account of the City, with full Description of the Remains and Recent Excavations, and an Itinerary for Visitors. By T. H. Dyer, LL.D. Nearly 300 Wood Engravings, Map, and Plan. 7*s.* 6*d.*

—— **Rome :** History of the City, with Introduction on recent Excavations. 8 Engravings, Frontispiece, and 2 Maps.

GIL BLAS. The Adventures of. From the French of Lesage by Smollett. 24 Engravings after Smirke, and 10 Etchings by Cruikshank. 612 pages. 6*s.*

GRIMM'S Gammer Grethel; or, German Fairy Tales and Popular Stories, containing 42 Fairy Tales. By Edgar Taylor. Numerous Woodcuts after Cruikshank and Ludwig Grimm. 3*s.* 6*d.*

HOLBEIN'S Dance of Death and Bible Cuts. Upwards of 150 Subjects, engraved in facsimile, with Introduction and Descriptions by the late Francis Douce and Dr. Dibdin.

INDIA, Pictorial, Descriptive, and Historical, from the Earliest Times. 100 Engravings on Wood and Map.

JESSE'S Anecdotes of Dogs. With 40 Woodcuts after Harvey, Bewick, and others ; and 34 Steel Engravings after Cooper and Landseer.

KING'S (C. W.) Natural History of Precious Stones and Metals. Illustrations. 6*s.*

KRUMMACHER'S Parables. 40 Illustrations.

LODGE'S Portraits of Illustrious Personages of Great Britain, with Biographical and Historical Memoirs. 240 Portraits engraved on Steel, with the respective Biographies unabridged. Complete in 8 vols.

LONGFELLOW'S Poetical Works, including his Translations and Notes. 24 full-page Woodcuts by Birket Foster and others, and a Portrait.

—— Without the Illustrations, 3*s.* 6*d.*

—— **Prose Works.** With 16 full-page Woodcuts by Birket Foster and others.

LOUDON'S (Mrs.) Entertaining Naturalist. Popular Descriptions, Tales, and Anecdotes, of more than 500 Animals. Numerous Woodcuts.

**MARRYAT'S (Capt., R.N.) Masterman Ready ; or, the Wreck of the *Pacific.* (Written for Young People.) With 93 Woodcuts. 3*s.* 6*d.*

—— **Mission ; or, Scenes in Africa.** (Written for Young People.) Illustrated by Gilbert and Dalziel. 3*s.* 6*d.*

—— **Pirate and Three Cutters.** (Written for Young People.) With a Memoir. 8 Steel Engravings after Clarkson Stanfield, R.A. 3*s.* 6*d.*

—— **Privateersman.** Adventures by Sea and Land One Hundred Years Ago. (Written for Young People.) 8 Steel Engravings. 3*s.* 6*d.*

—— **Settlers in Canada.** (Written for Young People.) 10 Engravings by Gilbert and Dalziel. 3*s.* 6*d.*

—— **Poor Jack.** (Written for Young People.) With 16 Illustrations after Clarkson Stanfield, R.A. 3*s.* 6*d.*

—— **Midshipman Easy.** With 8 full-page Illustrations. Small post 8vo. 3*s.* 6*d.*

—— **Peter Simple.** With 8 full-page Illustrations. Small post 8vo. 3*s.* 6*d.*

MAXWELL'S Victories of Wellington and the British Armies. Frontispiece and 4 Portraits.

MICHAEL ANGELO and RAPHAEL, Their Lives and Works. By Duppa and Quatremère de Quincy. Portraits and Engravings, including the Last Judgment, and Cartoons.

MILLER'S History of the Anglo-Saxons, from the Earliest Period to the Norman Conquest. Portrait of Alfred, Map of Saxon Britain, and 12 Steel Engravings.

MUDIE'S History of British Birds. Revised by W. C. L. Martin. 52 Figures of Birds and 7 coloured Plates of Eggs. 2 vols.

NAVAL and MILITARY HEROES of Great Britain ; a Record of British Valour on every Day in the year, from William the Conqueror to the Battle of Inkermann. By Major Johns, R.M., and Lieut. P. H. Nicolas, R.M. Indexes. 24 Portraits after Holbein, Reynolds, &c. 6*s.*

NICOLINI'S History of the Jesuits : their Origin, Progress, Doctrines, and Designs. 8 Portraits.

PETRARCH'S Sonnets, Triumphs, and other Poems, in English Verse. With Life by Thomas Campbell. Portrait and 15 Steel Engravings.

PICKERING'S History of the Races of Man, and their Geographical Distribution ; with AN ANALYTICAL SYNOPSIS OF THE NATURAL HISTORY OF MAN. By Dr. Hall. Map of the World and 12 coloured Plates.

PICTORIAL HANDBOOK OF Modern Geography on a Popular Plan. Compiled from the best Authorities, English and Foreign, by H. G. Bohn. 150 Woodcuts and 51 coloured Maps.

—— Without the Maps, 3*s.* 6*d.*

POPE'S Poetical Works, including Translations. Edit., with Notes, by R. Carruthers. 2 vols.

—— **Homer's Iliad,** with Introduction and Notes by Rev. J. S. Watson, M.A. With Flaxman's Designs.

—— **Homer's Odyssey,** with the BATTLE OF FROGS AND MICE, Hymns, &c., by other translators including Chapman. Introduction and Notes by J. S. Watson, M.A. With Flaxman's Designs.

—— **Life,** including many of his Letters. By R. Carruthers. Numerous Illustrations.

POTTERY AND PORCELAIN, and other objects of Vertu. Comprising an Illustrated Catalogue of the Bernal Collection, with the prices and names of the Possessors. Also an Introductory Lecture on Pottery and Porcelain, and an Engraved List of all Marks and Monograms. By H. G. Bohn. Numerous Woodcuts.

—— With coloured Illustrations, 10*s.* 6*d.*

PROUT'S (Father) Reliques. Edited by Rev. F. Mahony. Copyright edition, with the Author's last corrections and additions. 21 Etchings by D. Maclise, R.A. Nearly 600 pages.

RECREATIONS IN SHOOTING. With some Account of the Game found in the British Isles, and Directions for the Management of Dog and Gun. By 'Craven.' 62 Woodcuts and 9 Steel Engravings after A. Cooper, R.A.

RENNIE. Insect Architecture. Revised by Rev. J. G. Wood, M.A. 186 Woodcuts.

ROBINSON CRUSOE. With Memoir of Defoe, 12 Steel Engravings and 74 Woodcuts after Stothard and Harvey.

—— Without the Engravings, 3s. 6d.

ROME IN THE NINETEENTH CENtury. An Account in 1817 of the Ruins of the Ancient City, and Monuments of Modern Times. By C. A. Eaton. 34 Steel Engravings. 2 vols.

SHARPE (S.) The History of Egypt, from the Earliest Times till the Conquest by the Arabs, A.D. 640. 2 Maps and upwards of 400 Woodcuts. 2 vols.

SOUTHEY'S Life of Nelson. With Additional Notes, Facsimiles of Nelson's Writing, Portraits, Plans, and 50 Engravings, after Birket Foster, &c.

STARLING'S (Miss) Noble Deeds of Women; or, Examples of Female Courage, Fortitude, and Virtue. With 14 Steel Portraits.

STUART and REVETT'S Antiquities of Athens, and other Monuments of Greece; with Glossary of Terms used in Grecian Architecture. 71 Steel Plates and numerous Woodcuts.

SWEET'S British Warblers. 5s.—*See Bechstein.*

TALES OF THE GENII; or, the Delightful Lessons of Horam, the Son of Asmar. Trans. by Sir C. Morrell. Numerous Woodcuts.

TASSO'S Jerusalem Delivered. In English Spenserian Verse, with Life, by J. H. Wiffen. With 8 Engravings and 24 Woodcuts.

WALKER'S Manly Exercises; containing Skating, Riding, Driving, Hunting, Shooting, Sailing, Rowing, Swimming, &c. 44 Engravings and numerous Woodcuts.

WALTON'S Complete Angler; or the Contemplative Man's Recreation, by Izaak Walton and Charles Cotton. With Memoirs and Notes by E. Jesse. Also an Account of Fishing Stations, Tackle, &c., by H. G. Bohn. Portrait and 203 Woodcuts, and 26 Engravings on Steel.

—— **Lives of Donne, Wotton, Hooker,** &c., with Notes. A New Edition, revised by A. H. Bullen, with a Memoir of Izaak Walton by William Dowling. 6 Portraits, 6 Autograph Signatures, &c.

WELLINGTON, Life of. From the Materials of Maxwell. 18 Steel Engravings.

—— **Victories of.**—*See Maxwell.*

WESTROPP (H. M.) A Handbook of Archæology, Egyptian, Greek, Etruscan, Roman. By H. M. Westropp. Numerous Illustrations.

WHITE'S Natural History of Selborne, with Observations on various Parts of Nature, and the Naturalists' Calendar. Sir W. Jardine. Edit., with Notes and Memoir, by E. Jesse. 40 Portraits and coloured Plates.

CLASSICAL LIBRARY.

TRANSLATIONS FROM THE GREEK AND LATIN.

103 Vols. at 5s. each, excepting those marked otherwise. (25l. 4s. 6d. per set.)

ACHILLES TATIUS. — *See Greek Romances.*

ÆSCHYLUS, The Dramas of. In English Verse by Anna Swanwick. 4th edition.

—— **The Tragedies of.** In Prose, with Notes and Introduction, by T. A. Buckley, B.A. Portrait. 3s. 6d.

AMMIANUS MARCELLINUS. History of Rome during the Reigns of Constantius, Julian, Jovianus, Valentinian, and Valens, by C. D. Yonge, B.A. Double volume. 7s. 6d.

ANTONINUS (M. Aurelius), The Thoughts of. Translated, with Notes, Biographical Sketch, and Essay on the Philosophy, by George Long, M.A. 3s. 6d. Fine Paper edition on hand-made paper. 6s.

APOLLONIUS RHODIUS. 'The Argonautica.' Translated by E. P. Coleridge.

APULEIUS, The Works of. Comprising the Golden Ass, God of Socrates, Florida, and Discourse of Magic, &c. Frontispiece.

ARISTOPHANES' Comedies. Trans., with Notes and Extracts from Frere's and other Metrical Versions, by W. J. Hickie. Portrait. 2 vols.

ARISTOTLE'S Nicomachean Ethics. Trans., with Notes, Analytical Introduction, and Questions for Students, by Ven. Archdn. Browne.

— **Politics and Economics.** Trans., with Notes, Analyses, and Index, by E. Walford, M.A., and an Essay and Life by Dr. Gillies.

— **Metaphysics.** Trans., with Notes, Analysis, and Examination Questions, by Rev. John H. M'Mahon, M.A.

— **History of Animals.** In Ten Books. Trans., with Notes and Index, by R. Cresswell, M.A.

— **Organon;** or, Logical Treatises, and the Introduction of Porphyry. With Notes, Analysis, and Introduction, by Rev. O. F. Owen, M.A. 2 vols. 3s. 6d. each.

— **Rhetoric and Poetics.** Trans., with Hobbes' Analysis, Exam. Questions, and Notes, by T. Buckley, B.A. Portrait.

ATHENÆUS. The Deipnosophists. Trans. by C. D. Yonge, B.A. With an Appendix of Poetical Fragments. 3 vols.

ATLAS of Classical Geography. 22 large Coloured Maps. With a complete Index. Imp. 8vo. 7s. 6d.

BION.—See Theocritus.

CÆSAR. Commentaries on the Gallic and Civil Wars, with the Supplementary Books attributed to Hirtius, including the complete Alexandrian, African, and Spanish Wars. Portrait.

CATULLUS, Tibullus, and the Vigil of Venus. Trans. with Notes and Biographical Introduction. To which are added, Metrical Versions by Lamb, Grainger, and others. Frontispiece.

CICERO'S Orations. Trans. by C. D. Yonge, B.A. 4 vols.

— **On Oratory and Orators.** With Letters to Quintus and Brutus. Trans., with Notes, by Rev. J. S. Watson, M.A.

— **On the Nature of the Gods,** Divination, Fate, Laws, a Republic, Consulship. Trans. by C. D. Yonge, B.A.

— **Academics,** De Finibus, and Tusculan Questions. By C. D. Yonge, B.A. With Sketch of the Greek Philosophers mentioned by Cicero.

CICERO'S Works.—Continued.

— **Offices;** or, Moral Duties. Cato Major, an Essay on Old Age; Lælius, an Essay on Friendship; Scipio's Dream; Paradoxes; Letter to Quintus on Magistrates. Trans., with Notes, by C. R. Edmonds. Portrait. 3s. 6d.

DEMOSTHENES' Orations. Trans., with Notes, Arguments, a Chronological Abstract, and Appendices, by C. Rann Kennedy. 5 vols. (One, 3s. 6d ; four, 5s.)

DICTIONARY of LATIN and GREEK Quotations; including Proverbs, Maxims, Mottoes, Law Terms and Phrases. With the Quantities marked, and English Translations. With Index Verborum (622 pages).

— Index Verborum to the above, with the Quantities and Accents marked (56 pages), limp cloth. 1s.

DIOGENES LAERTIUS. Lives and Opinions of the Ancient Philosophers. Trans., with Notes, by C. D. Yonge, B.A.

EPICTETUS. The Discourses of. With the Encheiridion and Fragments. With Notes, Life, and View of his Philosophy, by George Long, M.A.

EURIPIDES. Trans. by T. A. Buckley, B.A. Portrait. 2 vols.

GREEK ANTHOLOGY. In English Prose by G. Burges, M.A. With Metrical Versions by Bland, Merivale, and others.

GREEK ROMANCES of Heliodorus, Longus, and Achilles Tatius; viz., The Adventures of Theagenes and Chariclea; Amours of Daphnis and Chloe; and Loves of Clitopho and Leucippe. Trans., with Notes, by Rev. R. Smith, M.A.

HELIODORUS.—See Greek Romances.

HERODOTUS. Literally trans. by Rev. Henry Cary, M.A. Portrait.

HESIOD, CALLIMACHUS, and Theognis. In Prose, with Notes and Biographical Notices by Rev. J. Banks, M.A. Together with the Metrical Versions of Hesiod, by Elton; Callimachus, by Tytler; and Theognis, by Frere.

HOMER'S Iliad. In English Prose, with Notes by T. A. Buckley, B.A. Portrait.

— **Odyssey,** Hymns, Epigrams, and Battle of the Frogs and Mice. In English Prose, with Notes and Memoir by T. A. Buckley, B.A.

HORACE. In Prose by Smart, with Notes selected by T. A. Buckley, B.A. Portrait. 3s. 6d.

JULIAN THE EMPEROR. Containing Gregory Nazianzen's Two Invectives and Libanus' Monody, with Julian's Theosophical Works. By the Rev. C. W. King, M.A.

JUSTIN, CORNELIUS NEPOS, and Eutropius. Trans., with Notes, by Rev. J. S. Watson, M.A.

JUVENAL, PERSIUS, SULPICIA, and Lucilius. In Prose, with Notes, Chronological Tables, Arguments, by L. Evans, M.A. To which is added the Metrical Version of Juvenal and Persius by Gifford. Frontispiece.

LIVY. The History of Rome. Trans. by Dr. Spillan and others. 4 vols. Portrait.

LONGUS. Daphnis and Chloe.—*See Greek Romances.*

LUCAN'S Pharsalia. In Prose, with Notes by H. T. Riley.

LUCIAN'S Dialogues of the Gods, of the Sea Gods, and of the Dead. Trans. by Howard Williams, M.A.

LUCRETIUS. In Prose, with Notes and Biographical Introduction by Rev. J. S. Watson, M.A. To which is added the Metrical Version by J. M. Good.

MARTIAL'S Epigrams, complete. In Prose, with Verse Translations selected from English Poets, and other sources. Dble. vol. (670 pages). 7s. 6d.

MOSCHUS.—*See Theocritus.*

OVID'S Works, complete. In Prose, with Notes and Introduction. 3 vols.

PAUSANIAS' Description of Greece. Trans., with Notes and Index, by Rev. A. R. Shilleto, M.A., sometime Scholar of Trinity College, Cambridge. 2 vols.

PHALARIS. Bentley's Dissertations upon the Epistles of Phalaris, Themistocles, Socrates, Euripides, and the Fables of Æsop. With Introduction and Notes by Prof. W. Wagner, Ph.D.

PINDAR. In Prose, with Introduction and Notes by Dawson W. Turner. Together with the Metrical Version by Abraham Moore. Portrait.

PLATO'S Works. Trans. by Rev. H. Cary, H. Davis, and G. Burges. 6 vols.

—— **Dialogues.** A Summary and Analysis of. With Analytical Index to the Greek text of modern editions and to the above translations, by A. Day, LL.D.

PLAUTUS'S Comedies. In Prose, with Notes by H. T. Riley, B.A. 2 vols.

PLINY'S Natural History. Trans., with Notes, by J. Bostock, M.D., F.R.S., and H. T. Riley, B.A. 6 vols.

PLINY. The Letters of Pliny the Younger. Melmoth's Translation, revised, with Notes and short Life, by Rev. F. C. T. Bosanquet, M.A.

PLUTARCH'S Morals. Theosophical Essays. Trans. by Rev. C. W. King, M.A.

—— **Ethical Essays.** Trans. by Rev. A. R. Shilleto, M.A.

—— **Lives.** *See page 7.*

PROPERTIUS, The Elegies of. With Notes, translated by Rev. P. J. F. Gantillon, M.A., with metrical versions of Select Elegies by Nott and Elton. 3s. 6d.

QUINTILIAN'S Institutes of Oratory. Trans., by Rev. J. S. Watson, M.A. 2 vols.

SALLUST, FLORUS, and VELLEIUS Paterculus. Trans., with Notes and Biographical Notices, by J. S. Watson, M.A.

SENECA DE BENEFICIIS. Translated by Aubrey Stewart, M.A. 3s. 6d.

SENECA'S Minor Essays. Translated by A. Stewart, M.A.

SOPHOCLES. The Tragedies of. In Prose, with Notes, Arguments, and Introduction. Portrait.

STRABO'S Geography. Trans., with Notes, by W. Falconer, M.A., and H. C. Hamilton. Copious Index, giving Ancient and Modern Names. 3 vols.

SUETONIUS' Lives of the Twelve Cæsars and Lives of the Grammarians. The Translation of Thomson, revised, with Notes, by T. Forester.

TACITUS. The Works of. Trans., with Notes. 2 vols.

TERENCE and PHÆDRUS. In English Prose, with Notes and Arguments, by H. T. Riley, B.A. To which is added Smart's Metrical Version of Phædrus. With Frontispiece.

THEOCRITUS, BION, MOSCHUS, and Tyrtæus. In Prose, with Notes and Arguments, by Rev. J. Banks, M.A. To which are appended the METRICAL VERSIONS of Chapman. Portrait of Theocritus.

THUCYDIDES. The Peloponnesian War. Trans., with Notes, by Rev. H. Dale. Portrait. 2 vols. 3s. 6d. each.

TYRTÆUS.—*See Theocritus.*

VIRGIL. The Works of. In Prose, with Notes by Davidson. Revised, with additional Notes and Biographical Notice, by T. A. Buckley, B.A. Portrait. 3s. 6d.

XENOPHON'S Works. Trans., with Notes, by J. S. Watson, M.A., and Rev. H. Dale. Portrait. In 3 vols.

COLLEGIATE SERIES.

10 *Vols. at* 5*s. each.*   (2*l.* 10*s. per set.*)

DANTE. The Inferno. Prose Trans., with the Text of the Original on the same page, and Explanatory Notes, by John A. Carlyle, M.D. Portrait.

—— **The Purgatorio.** Prose Trans., with the Original on the same page, and Explanatory Notes, by W. S. Dugdale.

DOBREE'S Adversaria. (Notes on the Greek and Latin Classics.) Edited by the late Prof. Wagner. 2 vols.

DONALDSON (Dr.) The Theatre of the Greeks. With Supplementary Treatise on the Language, Metres, and Prosody of the Greek Dramatists. Numerous Illustrations and 3 Plans. By J. W. Donaldson, D.D.

GOETHE'S Faust. Part I. German Text, with Hayward's Prose Translation and Notes. Revised, with Introduction and Bibliography, by Dr. C. A. Buchheim. [*In the Press.*

KEIGHTLEY'S (Thomas) Mythology of Ancient Greece and Italy. Revised by Dr. Leonhard Schmitz. 12 Plates.

HERODOTUS, Notes on. Original and Selected from the best Commentators. By D. W. Turner, M.A. Coloured Map.

—— **Analysis and Summary of,** with a Synchronistical Table of Events—Tables of Weights, Measures, Money, and Distances—an Outline of the History and Geography—and the Dates completed from Gaisford, Baehr, &c. By J. T. Wheeler.

NEW TESTAMENT (The) in Greek. Griesbach's Text, with the Readings of Mill and Scholz, and Parallel References. Also a Critical Introduction and Chronological Tables. Two Fac-similes of Greek Manuscripts. 650 pages. 3*s.* 6*d.*

—— or bound up with a Greek and English Lexicon to the New Testament (250 pages additional, making in all 900). 5*s.*

The Lexicon separately, 2*s.*

THUCYDIDES. An Analysis and Summary of. With Chronological Table of Events, &c., by J. T. Wheeler.

SCIENTIFIC LIBRARY.

50 *Vols. at* 5*s. each,* excepting those marked otherwise.   (13*l.* 6*s.* 0*d. per set.*)

AGASSIZ and GOULD. Outline of Comparative Physiology. Enlarged by Dr. Wright. With Index and 300 Illustrative Woodcuts.

BOLLEY'S Manual of Technical Analysis; a Guide for the Testing and Valuation of the various Natural and Artificial Substances employed in the Arts and Domestic Economy, founded on the work of Dr. Bolley. Edit. by Dr. Paul. 100 Woodcuts.

BRIDGEWATER TREATISES.

—— **Bell (Sir Charles) on the Hand;** its Mechanism and Vital Endowments, as evincing Design. Preceded by an Account of the Author's Discoveries in the Nervous System by A. Shaw. Numerous Woodcuts.

—— **Kirby on the History, Habits,** and Instincts of Animals. With Notes by T. Rymer Jones. 100 Woodcuts. 2 vols.

—— **Buckland's Geology and Miner-** alogy. With Additions by Prof. Owen, Prof. Phillips, and R. Brown. Memoir of Buckland. Portrait. 2 vols. 15*s.* Vol. I. Text. Vol. II. 90 large plates with letterpress.

BRIDGEWATER TREATISES. *Continued.*

—— **Chalmers on the Adaptation of** External Nature to the Moral and Intellectual Constitution of Man. With Memoir by Rev. Dr. Cumming. Portrait.

—— **Prout's Treatise on Chemistry,** Meteorology, and the Function of Digestion, with reference to Natural Theology. Edit. by Dr. J. W. Griffith. 2 Maps.

—— **Roget's Animal and Vegetable** Physiology. 463 Woodcuts. 2 vols. 6*s.* each.

—— **Kidd on the Adaptation of Ex-** ternal Nature to the Physical Condition of Man. 3*s.* 6*d.*

CARPENTER'S (Dr. W. B.) Zoology. A Systematic View of the Structure, Habits, Instincts, and Uses of the principal Families of the Animal Kingdom, and of the chief Forms of Fossil Remains. Revised by W. S. Dallas, F.L.S. Numerous Woodcuts. 2 vols. 6*s.* each.

—— **Mechanical Philosophy, Astro-** nomy, and Horology. A Popular Exposition. 181 Woodcuts.

CARPENTER'S Works.—*Continued.*

—— **Vegetable Physiology and Systematic Botany.** A complete Introduction to the Knowledge of Plants. Revised by E. Lankester, M.D., &c. Numerous Woodcuts. 6s.

—— **Animal Physiology.** Revised Edition. 300 Woodcuts. 6s.

CHEVREUL on Colour. Containing the Principles of Harmony and Contrast of Colours, and their Application to the Arts ; including Painting, Decoration, Tapestries, Carpets, Mosaics, Glazing, Staining, Calico Printing, Letterpress Printing, Map Colouring, Dress, Landscape and Flower Gardening, &c. Trans. by C. Martel. Several Plates.

—— With an additional series of 16 Plates in Colours, 7s. 6d.

ENNEMOSER'S History of Magic. Trans. by W. Howitt. With an Appendix of the most remarkable and best authenticated Stories of Apparitions, Dreams, Second Sight, Table-Turning, and Spirit-Rapping, &c. 2 vols.

HIND'S Introduction to Astronomy. With Vocabulary of the Terms in present use. Numerous Woodcuts. 3s. 6d.

HOGG'S (Jabez) Elements of Experimental and Natural Philosophy. Being an Easy Introduction to the Study of Mechanics, Pneumatics, Hydrostatics, Hydraulics, Acoustics, Optics, Caloric, Electricity, Voltaism, and Magnetism. 400 Woodcuts.

HUMBOLDT'S Cosmos ; or, Sketch of a Physical Description of the Universe. Trans. by E. C. Otté, B. H. Paul, and W. S. Dallas, F.L.S. Portrait. 5 vols. 3s. 6d. each, excepting vol. v., 5s.

—— **Personal Narrative of his Travels** in America during the years 1799-1804. Trans., with Notes, by T. Ross. 3 vols.

—— **Views of Nature ; or, Contemplations** of the Sublime Phenomena of Creation, with Scientific Illustrations. Trans. by E. C. Otté.

HUNT'S (Robert) Poetry of Science ; or, Studies of the Physical Phenomena of Nature. By Robert Hunt, Professor at the School of Mines.

JOYCE'S Scientific Dialogues. A Familiar Introduction to the Arts and Sciences. For Schools and Young People. Numerous Woodcuts.

JOYCE'S Introduction to the Arts and Sciences, for Schools and Young People. Divided into Lessons with Examination Questions. Woodcuts. 3s. 6d.

JUKES-BROWNE'S Student's Handbook of Physical Geology. By A. J. Jukes-Browne, of the Geological Survey of England. With numerous Diagrams and Illustrations, 6s.

—— **The Student's Handbook of** Historical Geology. By A. J. Jukes-Brown, B.A., F.G.S., of the Geological Survey of England and Wales. With numerous Diagrams and Illustrations. 6s.

—— **The Building of the British** Islands. A Study in Geographical Evolution. By A J. Jukes-Browne, F.G.S. 7s. 6d.

KNIGHT'S (Charles) Knowledge is Power. A Popular Manual of Political Economy.

LILLY. Introduction to Astrology. With a Grammar of Astrology and Tables for calculating Nativities, by Zadkiel.

MANTELL'S (Dr.) Geological Excursions through the Isle of Wight and along the Dorset Coast. Numerous Woodcuts and Geological Map.

—— **Petrifactions and their Teachings.** Handbook to the Organic Remains in the British Museum. Numerous Woodcuts. 6s.

—— **Wonders of Geology ; or, a** Familiar Exposition of Geological Phenomena. A coloured Geological Map of England, Plates, and 200 Woodcuts. 2 vols. 7s. 6d. each.

SCHOUW'S Earth, Plants, and Man. Popular Pictures of Nature. And Kobell's Sketches from the Mineral Kingdom. Trans. by A. Henfrey, F.R.S. Coloured Map of the Geography of Plants.

SMITH'S (Pye) Geology and Scripture ; or, the Relation between the Scriptures and Geological Science. With Memoir.

STANLEY'S Classified Synopsis of the Principal Painters of the Dutch and Flemish Schools, including an Account of some of the early German Masters. By George Stanley.

STAUNTON'S Chess Works. — *See page 21.*

STÖCKHARDT'S Experimental Chemistry. A Handbook for the Study of the Science by simple Experiments. Edit. by C. W. Heaton, F.C.S. Numerous Woodcuts.

URE'S (Dr. A.) Cotton Manufacture of Great Britain, systematically investigated ; with an Introductory View of its Comparative State in Foreign Countries. Revised by P. L. Simmonds. 150 Illustrations. 2 vols.

—— **Philosophy of Manufactures,** or an Exposition of the Scientific, Moral, and Commercial Economy of the Factory System of Great Britain. Revised by P. L. Simmonds. Numerous Figures. 800 pages. 7s. 6d.

ECONOMICS AND FINANCE.

GILBART'S History, Principles, and Practice of Banking. Revised to 1881 by A. S. Michie, of the Royal Bank of Scotland. Portrait of Gilbart. 2 vols. 10s.

RICARDO on the Principles of Political Economy and Taxation. Edited by E. C. K. Gonner, M.A., Lecturer, University College, Liverpool. *[In the Press.*

SMITH (Adam). The Wealth of Nations. An Inquiry into the Nature and Causes of. Edited by E. Belfort Bax. 2 vols. 7s.

REFERENCE LIBRARY.

32 Volumes at Various Prices. (8l. 18s. per set.)

BLAIR'S Chronological Tables. Comprehending the Chronology and History of the World, from the Earliest Times to the Russian Treaty of Peace, April 1856. By J. W. Rosse. 800 pages. 10s.

—— **Index of Dates.** Comprehending the principal Facts in the Chronology and History of the World, from the Earliest to the Present, alphabetically arranged; being a complete Index to the foregoing. By J. W. Rosse. 2 vols. 5s. each.

BOHN'S Dictionary of Quotations from the English Poets. 4th and cheaper Edition. 6s.

BOND'S Handy-book of Rules and Tables for Verifying Dates with the Christian Era. 4th Edition. 5s.

BUCHANAN'S Dictionary of Science and Technical Terms used in Philosophy, Literature, Professions, Commerce, Arts, and Trades. By W. H. Buchanan, with Supplement. Edited by Jas. A. Smith. 6s.

CHRONICLES OF THE TOMBS. A Select Collection of Epitaphs, with Essay on Epitaphs and Observations on Sepulchral Antiquities. By T. J. Pettigrew, F.R.S., F.S.A. 5s.

CLARK'S (Hugh) Introduction to Heraldry. Revised by J. R. Planché. 5s. 950 Illustrations.

—— *With the Illustrations coloured,* 15s.

COINS, Manual of.—*See Humphreys.*

COOPER'S Biographical Dictionary, Containing concise notices of upwards of 15,000 eminent persons of all ages and countries. 2 vols. 5s. each.

DATES, Index of.—*See Blair.*

DICTIONARY of Obsolete and Provincial English. Containing Words from English Writers previous to the 19th Century. By Thomas Wright, M.A., F.S.A., &c. 2 vols. 5s. each.

EPIGRAMMATISTS (The). A Selection from the Epigrammatic Literature of Ancient, Mediæval, and Modern Times. With Introduction, Notes, Observations, Illustrations, an Appendix on Works connected with Epigrammatic Literature, by Rev. H. Dodd, M.A. 6s.

GAMES, Handbook of. Edited by Henry G. Bohn. Numerous Diagrams. 5s. (*See also page* 21.)

HENFREY'S Guide to English Coins. Revised Edition, by C. F. Keary, M.A., F.S.A. With an Historical Introduction. 6s.

HUMPHREYS' Coin Collectors' Manual. An Historical Account of the Progress of Coinage from the Earliest Time, by H. N. Humphreys. 140 Illustrations. 2 vols. 5s. each.

LOWNDES' Bibliographer's Manual of English Literature. Containing an Account of Rare and Curious Books published in or relating to Great Britain and Ireland, from the Invention of Printing, with Biographical Notices and Prices, by W. T. Lowndes. Parts I.-X. (A to Z), 3s. 6d. each. Part XI. (Appendix Vol.), 5s. Or the 11 parts in 4 vols., half morocco, 2l. 2s. Also in 6 vols. cloth, 5s. each.

MEDICINE, Handbook of Domestic, Popularly Arranged. By Dr. H. Davies. 700 pages. 5s.

NOTED NAMES OF FICTION. Dictionary of. Including also Familiar Pseudonyms, Surnames bestowed on Eminent Men, &c. By W. A. Wheeler, M.A. 5s.

POLITICAL CYCLOPÆDIA. A Dictionary of Political, Constitutional, Statistical, and Forensic Knowledge forming a Work of Reference on subjects of Civil Administration, Political Economy, Finance, Commerce, Laws, and Social Relations. 4 vols. 3s. 6d. each.

PROVERBS, Handbook of. Containing an entire Republication of Ray's Collection, with Additions from Foreign Languages and Sayings, Sentences, Maxims, and Phrases. 5s.
—— **A Polyglot of Foreign.** Comprising French, Italian, German, Dutch, Spanish, Portuguese, and Danish. With English Translations. 5s.

SYNONYMS and ANTONYMS; or, Kindred Words and their Opposites, Collected and Contrasted by Ven. C. J. Smith, M.A. 5s.

WRIGHT (Th.)—*See Dictionary.*

NOVELISTS' LIBRARY.

13 Volumes at 3s. 6d. each, excepting those marked otherwise. (2l. 8s. 6d. per set.)

BJORNSON'S Arne and the Fisher Lassie. Translated from the Norse with an Introduction by W. H. Low, M.A.

BURNEY'S Evelina; or, a Young Lady's Entrance into the World. By F. Burney (Mme. D'Arblay). With Introduction and Notes by A. R. Ellis, Author of 'Sylvestra,' &c.
—— **Cecilia.** With Introduction and Notes by A. R. Ellis. 2 vols.

DE STAËL. Corinne or Italy. By Madame de Staël. Translated by Emily Baldwin and Paulina Driver.

EBERS' Egyptian Princess. Trans. by Emma Buchheim.

FIELDING'S Joseph Andrews and his Friend Mr. Abraham Adams. With Roscoe's Biography. *Cruikshank's Illustrations.*
—— **Amelia.** Roscoe's Edition, revised. *Cruikshank's Illustrations.* 5s.
—— **History of Tom Jones, a Found**ling. Roscoe's Edition. *Cruikshank's Illustrations.* 2 vols.

GROSSI'S Marco Visconti. Trans. by A. F. D.

MANZONI. The Betrothed : being a Translation of 'I Promessi Sposi.' Numerous Woodcuts. 1 vol. 5s.

STOWE (Mrs. H. B.) Uncle Tom's Cabin ; or, Life among the Lowly. 8 full-page Illustrations.

ARTISTS' LIBRARY.

9 Volumes at Various Prices. (2l. 8s. 6d. per set.)

BELL (Sir Charles). The Anatomy and Philosophy of Expression, as Connected with the Fine Arts. 5s. Illustrated.

DEMMIN. History of Arms and Armour from the Earliest Period. By Auguste Demmin. Trans. by C. C. Black, M.A., Assistant Keeper, S. K. Museum. 1900 Illustrations. 7s. 6d.

FAIRHOLT'S Costume in England. Third Edition. Enlarged and Revised by the Hon. H. A. Dillon, F.S.A. With more than 700 Engravings. 2 vols. 5s. each.
Vol. I. History. Vol. II. Glossary.

LAXMAN. Lectures on Sculpture. With three Addresses to the R.A. by Sir R. Westmacott, R.A., and Memoir of Flaxman. Portrait and 53 Plates. 6s.

HEATON'S Concise History of Painting. New Edition, revised by W. Cosmo Monkhouse. 5s.

LECTURES ON PAINTING by the Royal Academicians, Barry, Opie, Fuseli. With Introductory Essay and Notes by R. Wornum. Portrait of Fuseli. 5s.

LEONARDO DA VINCI'S Treatise on Painting. Trans. by J. F. Rigaud, R.A. With a Life and an Account of his Works by J. W. Brown. Numerous Plates. 5s.

PLANCHÉ'S History of British Costume, from the Earliest Time to the 10th Century. By J. R. Planché. 400 Illustrations. 5s.

LIBRARY OF SPORTS AND GAMES.

10 Volumes at 3s. 6d. and 5s. each. (2l. 6s. 0d. per set.)

BOHN'S Handbooks of Athletic
Sports. With numerous Illustrations. In
7 vols. 3s. 6d. each.

Vol. I.—Cricket, by Hon. and Rev. E.
Lyttelton ; Lawn Tennis, by H. W. W.
Wilberforce ; Tennis, Rackets, and Fives,
by Julian Marshall, Major Spens, and J. A.
Tait ; Golf, by W. T. Linskill ; Hockey,
by F. S. Creswell.

Vol. II.—Rowing and Sculling, by W.
B. Woodgate ; Sailing, by E. F. Knight ;
Swimming, by M. and J. R. Cobbett.

Vol. III.—Boxing, by R. G. Allanson-
Winn ; Single Stick and Sword Exercise,
by R. G. Allanson-Winn and C. Phillipps-
Wolley ; Wrestling, by Walter Armstrong ;
Fencing, by H. A. Colmore Dunn.

Vol. IV.—Skating, by Douglas Adams ;
Rugby Football. by Harry Vassall ; Asso-
ciation Football, by C. W. Alcock.
[*In the press.*

Vol. V. — Cycling and Athletics, by
H. H. Griffin ; Rounders. Field Ball, Base-
ball. Bowls, Quoits, Skittles, &c., by J. M.
Walker, M.A., Assistant Master Bedford
Grammar School. [*In the press.*

Vol. VI.—Gymnastics, by A. F. Jenkin ;
Clubs and Dumb-bells, by G. T. B. Cobbett
and A. F. Jenkin. [*In the press.*

Vol. VII —Riding, Driving, and Stable
Management. By W. A. Kerr, V.C., and
other writers. [*Preparing.*

BOHN'S Handbooks of Games. New
Edition, entirely rewritten. 2 volumes.
3s. 6d. each.

Vol. I. TABLE GAMES.

Contents :—Billiards, with Pool, Pyra-
mids, and Snooker, by Major-Gen. A. W.
Drayson, F.R.A.S., with a preface by
W. J. Peall—Bagatelle, by 'Berkeley'—
Chess, by R. F. Green—Draughts, Back-
gammon, Dominoes, Solitaire, Reversi,

Go Bang, Rouge et noir, Roulette, E.O.,
Hazard, Faro, by 'Berkeley.'

Vol. II. CARD GAMES.

Contents :—Whist, by Dr. William Pole,
F.R.S., Author of 'The Philosophy of
Whist, &c.'—Solo Whist, by R. F. Green ;
Piquet, Ecarté, Euchre, Bézique, and
Cribbage, by 'Berkeley ;' Poker, Loo,
Vingt-et-un, Napoleon, Newmarket, Rouge
et Noir, Pope Joan, Speculation. &c. &c.,
by Baxter-Wray.

CHESS CONGRESS of 1862. A
lection of the games played. Eoras.
J. Löwenthal. New edition, 5s.
ed

MORPHY'S Games of Chess, be
the Matches and best Games played by 5-
American Champion, with explanatory a
analytical Notes by J. Löwenthal. Wit
short Memoir and Portrait of Morphy. 5s.

STAUNTON'S Chess-Player's Hand-
book. A Popular and Scientific Introduction to the Game, with numerous Diagrams. 5s.

—— **Chess Praxis.** A Supplement to the
Chess-player's Handbook. Containin
most important modern Improvemen
the Openings ; Code of Chess Laws ;W;
a Selection of Morphy's Games. Annota
636 pages. Diagrams. 5s. 5;

—— **Chess-Player's Companic**
Comprising a Treatise on Odds, Collect
of Match Games, including the French
Match with M. St. Amant, and a Selection
of Original Problems. Diagrams and Coloured Frontispiece. 5s.

—— **Chess Tournament of 1851.**
A Collection of Games played at this celebrated assemblage. With Introduction
and Notes. Numerous Diagrams. 5s.

BOHN'S CHEAP SERIES.

Price 1s. *each.*

A Series of Complete Stories or Essays, mostly reprinted from Vol. in Bohn's Libraries, and neatly bound in stiff paper cover, with cut edges, suitable for Railway Reading.

ASCHAM (Roger). **Scholemaster.** By Professor Mayor.

CARPENTER (Dr. W. B.). **Physi-**ted from "Temperance and Total Abstinence. by W. H

SON. England and English relina-acteristics. Lectures on the Race, into lity, Manners, Truth, Character, D'Ar ealth, Religion. &c. &c. tes b

—— **Nature:** An Essay. To which are dded Orations, Lectures, and Addresses.

—— **Representative Men:** Seven Lectures on PLATO, SWEDENBORG, MONTAIGNE, SHAKESPEARE, NAPOLEON, and GOETHE.

—— **Twenty Essays on Various Sub-**jects.

—— **The Conduct of Life.**

FRANKLIN (Benjamin). **Autobio-**hy. Edited by J. Sparks.

VTHORNE (Nathaniel). **Twice-**l Tales. Two Vols. in One.

Snow Image, and Other Tales.

Scarlet Letter.

—— **House with the Seven Gables.**

—— **Transformation;** or the Marble Fawn. Two Parts.

HAZLITT (W.). **Table-talk:** Essays on Men and Manners. Three Parts.

—— **Plain Speaker:** Opinions on Books, Men, and Things. Three Parts.

—— **Lectures on the English Comic** Writers.

—— **Lectures on the English Poets.**

—— **Lectures on the Characters of** Shakespeare's Plays.

—— **Lectures on the Literature of** the Age of Elizabeth, chiefly Dramatic.

IRVING (Washington). **Liv** ol Successors of Mohammed.

—— **Life of Goldsmith.**

—— **Sketch-book.**

—— **Tales of a Traveller.**

—— **Tour on the Prairies.**

—— **Conquests of Granada** nd Spain. Two Parts.

—— **Life and Voyages of Colum**s. Two Parts.

—— **Companions of Columbus:** Voyages and Discoveries.

—— **Adventures of Captain Bon**ville in the Rocky Mountains and the West.

—— **Knickerbocker's History of N** York, from the beginning of the Worl the End of the Dutch Dynasty.

—— **Tales of the Alhambra.**

—— **Conquest of Florida under H** nando de Soto.

—— **Abbotsford & Newstead Abb**

—— **Salmagundi;** or, The Whim-Wha and Opinions of LAUNCELOT LANGSTA Esq.

—— **Bracebridge Hall;** or, The H mourists.

—— **Astoria;** or, Anecdotes of an Ente prise beyond the Rocky Mountains.

—— **Wolfert's Roost,** and other Tales.

LAMB (Charles). **Essays of Elia** With a Portrait.

—— **Last Essays of Elia.**

—— **Eliana.** With Biographical Sketch.

MARRYAT (Captain). **Pirate and** the Three Cutters. With a Memoir of the Author.

Bohn's Select Library of Standard Works.

Price 1s. in paper covers, and 1s. 6d. in cloth.

BOHN'S CHEAP SERIES.

Price 1s. each.

A Series of Complete Stories or Essays, mostly reprinted from Vols. in Bohn's Libraries, and neatly bound in stiff paper cover, with cut edges, suitable for Railway Reading.

ASCHAM (Roger). **Scholemaster.** By Professor Mayor.

RPENTER (Dr. W. B.). **Physi-**
- Temperance and Total Abstinence.

SON. England and English acteristics. Lectures on the Race, lity, Manners, Truth, Character, ealth, Religion. &c. &c.

— **Nature :** An Essay. To which are dded Orations, Lectures, and Addresses.

— **Representative Men :** Seven Lectures on PLATO, SWEDENBORG, MONTAIGNE, SHAKESPEARE, NAPOLEON, and GOETHE.

— **Twenty Essays on Various Subjects.**

— **The Conduct of Life.**

FRANKLIN (Benjamin). **Autobio-**
ahy. Edited by J. Sparks.

VTHORNE (Nathaniel). **Twice-**
l Tales. Two Vols. in One.

Snow Image, and Other Tales.

Scarlet Letter.

- **House with the Seven Gables.**

— **Transformation ;** or the Marble Fawn. Two Parts.

IAZLITT (W.). **Table-talk :** Essays on Men and Manners. Three Parts.

— **Plain Speaker :** Opinions on Books, Men, and Things. Three Parts.

— **Lectures on the English Comic Writers.**

— **Lectures on the English Poets.**

— **Lectures on the Characters of** Shakespeare's Plays.

— **Lectures on the Literature of** the Age of Elizabeth, chiefly Dramatic.

IRVING (Washington). **Lives of** Successors of Mohammed.

— **Life of Goldsmith.**

— **Sketch-book.**

— **Tales of a Traveller.**

— **Tour on the Prairies.**

— **Conquests of Granada and** Spain. Two Parts.

— **Life and Voyages of Columbus.** Two Parts.

— **Companions of Columbus :** Their Voyages and Discoveries.

— **Adventures of Captain Bonne-** ville in the Rocky Mountains and the Far West.

— **Knickerbocker's History of New** York, from the beginning of the World to the End of the Dutch Dynasty.

— **Tales of the Alhambra.**

— **Conquest of Florida under Her-** nando de Soto.

— **Abbotsford & Newstead Abbey.**

— **Salmagundi ;** or, The Whim-Whams and Opinions of LAUNCELOT LANGSTAFF, Esq.

— **Bracebridge Hall ;** or, The Humourists.

— **Astoria ;** or, Anecdotes of an Enterprise beyond the Rocky Mountains.

— **Wolfert's Roost,** and other Tales.

LAMB (Charles). **Essays of Elia.** With a Portrait.

— **Last Essays of Elia.**

— **Eliana.** With Biographical Sketch.

MARRYAT (Captain). **Pirate and** the Three Cutters. With a Memoir of the Author.

Bohn's Select Library of Standard Works.

Price 1s. in paper covers, and 1s. 6d. in cloth.

www.ingramcontent.com/pod-product-compliance
Lightning Source LLC
Chambersburg PA
CBHW031349290326
41932CB00044B/614